November 6–9, 2016
Denver, Colorado, USA

**Association for
Computing Machinery**

Advancing Computing as a Science & Profession

SIGUCCS'16

Proceedings of the 2016 ACM
SIGUCCS Annual Conference

Sponsored by:
ACM SIGUCCS

Supported by:
Easy Vista, Four Winds Interactive, Software2, TOPdesk, ComAround, TeamDynamix, WEPA, JourneyEd, LabStats, & Samanage

**Association for
Computing Machinery**

Advancing Computing as a Science & Profession

The Association for Computing Machinery
2 Penn Plaza, Suite 701
New York, New York 10121-0701

Notice to Past Authors of ACM-Published Articles
ACM intends to create a complete electronic archive of all articles and/or other material previously published by ACM. If you have written a work that has been previously published by ACM in any journal or conference proceedings prior to 1978, or any SIG Newsletter at any time, and you do NOT want this work to appear in the ACM Digital Library, please inform permissions@acm.org, stating the title of the work, the author(s), and where and when published.

ISBN: 978-1-4503-4095-3 (Digital)

ISBN: 978-1-4503-4711-2 (Print)

Additional copies may be ordered prepaid from:

ACM Order Department
PO Box 30777
New York, NY 10087-0777, USA

Phone: 1-800-342-6626 (USA and Canada)
+1-212-626-0500 (Global)
Fax: +1-212-944-1318
E-mail: acmhelp@acm.org
Hours of Operation: 8:30 am – 4:30 pm ET

Printed in the USA

ACM SIGUCCS Chair's Message

On behalf of the SIGUCCS Board, welcome to Denver, and the 44th annual SIGUCCS conference. Thank you for 'choosing your adventure' by being a part of the content of what is certain to be an amazing event.

If this is your first SIGUCCS conference, welcome. The SIGUCCS community is an incredible resource for professional development, whether it is through online discussions, a digital library with thousands of articles on best practices, or opportunities such as the conference that blends topics ranging from technical discussions to career advancement.

Please join me in thanking the 2016 Conference Committee, as this conference is the culmination of more than 18 months of volunteer efforts. They have pulled together an exceptional program, including guest speakers from higher education, and from industry. This is also the first year for our fully integrated annual conference format, which is the result of years of evaluation and planning based on feedback from conference attendees and multiple conference committees.

2016 marks SIGUCCS' 53rd year, and the Board is in the third of our three-year term. We have continued the Mentorship Program and webinars as part of our focus on professional development. We have expanded our participation in social media, and have made more content available to the community through our online newsletter and YouTube channel. We are piloting a Slack site to provide another way for our community to work together on topics. We have increased vendor contributions to the conferences to keep costs under control and to help enhance the conference experience. We have restructured the conference to reduce costs of attendance and allow for a greater focus on content. Most importantly, we are financially sound; since 2013 conferences have operated with a slight surplus, which allows us to invest in making SIGUCCS services even more useful for the community.

As we bring 2016 to a close, there is much to look forward to. Be sure to mark October 1-4 on your calendars for next year's conference in Seattle, Washington. Please volunteer; the SIGUCCS conference is the sum of attendee contributions and the year-round efforts of many volunteers. As the conference progresses look for people with ribbons and special badges that describe their role(s) in the organization. Please thank them for their contributions, and also ask them what they did. Chances are very good that you also can help future conferences in similar ways next year.

Mat Felthousen
Chair, SIGUCCS

Conference Chair Welcome

Welcome to SIGUCCS 2016 in beautiful Denver, Colorado.

The next three days are packed with engaging sessions, inspiring keynotes, and opportunities to network with peers from around the globe. The conference theme is *Choose Your Adventure*, and like the books I remember from my childhood, you have the choice of what happens next -- how will you get the most out of your SIGUCCS conference experience?

Thank you to the SIGUCCS 2016 Conference Core Committee, who started organizing the conference last summer. It has been a pleasure to work with each of you as we planned an outstanding event. I also want to thank the many that volunteered to help out in various ways throughout the planning stages; from the presenters, trek chairs and readers who have prepared an excellent program, to those that coordinate some unique part of the conference. Finally, I want to express my appreciation to my colleagues and friends on the SIGUCCS Board. Thank you for this amazing opportunity!

Enjoy your time in Denver (one of my favorite cities)! Learn new things; make new connections; have an adventure! The adventure doesn't stop when you leave Denver. Get involved with SIGUCCS, whether it be through social media and the email list, volunteering on a conference committee, or planning a presentation for SIGUCCS 2017.

Laurie Fox
SIGUCCS 2016 Conference Chair

Program Chairs Welcome

Dear SIGUCCS Attendees:

Welcome to SIGUCCS 2016 in the Mile High city of Denver, Colorado!

This year's theme, "Choose Your Adventure" hopes to inspire you to create your own learning path by "trekking" through this year's program. There's no perfect way to climb! You find the topics that peak your interest and you ascend to those.

We hope to elevate your ideas, heighten your strategies and set your career path on an incline! This year's program is meant to engage you technically, professionally and personally through engagement with the plenary speakers, peer dialogue, poster sessions, lessons learned and shared and opportunities to interact with exhibitors.

As you can expect, a great climb (conference) is marked by a dedicated group of climbers who plan, strategize, and commit to the success of the climb. Your program committee co-chairs, Chris King (NC State Univ.) and Shundra White (Univ. of Memphis), along with Melissa Bauer and Laurie Fox and other members of the core team, you can expect to find nuggets of valuable ideas, creative thoughts, and useful information to make this year's conference rewarding.

We hope you will enjoy the Mile High City and this year's conference program.

Here's to greater heights, a peak in your quality of work and to being at the pinnacle of your field!

Shundra White
SIGUCCS 2016 Program Co-Chair

Chris King
SIGUCCS 2016 Program Co-Chair

Table of Contents

Session: 11:00am

Session: 2:30pm – Poster Session

Session: 4:00pm

Session: 10:45am

Session: 1:15pm

Session: 2:30pm

Author Index

SIGUCCS 2016 Core Committee

Conference Chair:	Laurie Fox, SUNY Geneseo
Conference Treasurer:	Terry Ruger, Ithaca College
Program Chairs:	Chris King, NC State University
	Shundra White, University of Memphis
Conference Liaison:	Melissa Bauer, Baldwin Wallace University
Communications Awards:	Lisa Brown, University of Rochester
Exhibitor Chair:	Allan Chen, Muhlenberg College
First Timers Coordinator:	Alexa Spigelmyer, Penn State University
Graphics Designer:	Jean Tagliamonte, Vassar College
Local Arrangements Coordinator:	Nick Pistentis, Metropolitan State University of Denver
Mobile App Coordinator:	Shawn Plummer, SUNY Geneseo
Photography Coordinator:	Karl Owens, University of Oregon
Poster Session Coordinator:	Chris Wiesemann, University of Oregon
Pre-Conference Seminars:	Beth Rugg, UNC Charlotte
Publications Chair:	Jacquelynn Gaines, Oberlin College
Publicity Chair:	Kristen Dietiker, Menlo College
Registration Chair:	Shawn Plummer, SUNY Geneseo
Social Coordinator:	Robert Fricke, Whitman College
Social Media Coordinator:	Cate Lyon, Whitman College
Volunteer Coordinator:	Jason Vaughn, Texas A&M University
Webmaster:	Laurie Fox, SUNY Geneseo

SIGUCCS 2016 Exhibitors

The 2016 SIGUCCS Conference is made possible largely due to the generous support of our exhibitors. On behalf of the conference, we would like to extend our sincere thanks for your support and presence, both which enhance the entire conference experience.

Attendees face similar challenges and needs at their respective institutions. They come to SIGUCCS knowing there will be opportunity to engage with exhibitors in a significant dialogue. Many of our exhibitors already have relationships with participating institutions which provides an invaluable foundation for meeting new potential clients.

We hope you enjoy the experience, and we appreciate your support.

Best regards,
The 2016 SIGUCCS Conference Exhibitor Team

Platinum Exhibitors

EasyVista

Four Winds Interactive

Software2

TOPdesk

Gold Exhibitors

ComAround

TeamDynamix

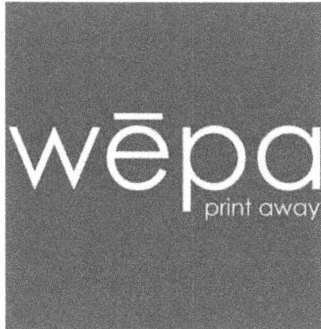

WEPA

Silver Exhibitors

JourneyEd

LabStats

Samanage

Longitudinal Relationship Management for Instructional Technologists

Amy Cheatle
Cornell University
126 Computing & Communications
Center, Ithaca, NY 14853
(607) 255-9760
Ac2288@cornell.edu

ABSTRACT

Instructional Designers who occupy a centralized position within the university structure face unique challenges when collaborating across discipline-specific communities of practice. In addition to wide diversity in subject matter-specific technological needs, different departments carry their own cultural values surrounding technology-enhanced instruction, as well as unique histories of successes and failures with technological systems used to support teaching and learning. In addition, schools and colleges within the same university, when decentralized, present challenges to interdisciplinary collaborations and communications across departments. Among teams of Instructional Designers specifically, the shifting nature of focus, working groups, vendors, versions, and interfaces, as well as changes in University leadership can compound issues of planning, organizing, implementing, and tracking technological work with faculty and departments longitudinally.

This paper offers a case study of the adoption and use of a cloud-based software tool used in pursuit of greater cohesiveness, support, collaboration, and partnering across a large campus infrastructure. It draws on organizational literature focusing on collaborative software in the workplace, as well as industry accepted best practices in customer relationship management.

CCS Concepts

Information systems ->Information storage systems -> Storage architectures -> cloud-based storage.

Keywords

Collaboration; Relationship Management; Instructional Design; Educational Technology.

SIGUCCS '16, November 06 - 09, 2016, Denver, CO, USA
Copyright is held by the owner/author(s). Publication rights licensed to ACM.
ACM 978-1-4503-4095-3/16/11...$15.00
DOI: http://dx.doi.org/10.1145/2974927.2974942

1. INTRODUCTION

1.1 Institutional Context

The Instructional Design Team within the Academic Technologies Department at Cornell University partners with the Cornell community to develop, deliver, and integrate high quality, innovative technologies for teaching and learning. In part, this means individual Instructional Designers must travel across a decentralized landscape comprised of 14 colleges on the main campus alone with over 100 unique departments that offer study to undergraduate, graduate and professional students. The Academic Technologies team currently consists of five groups: The Support Team, The Instructional Design Team, The Online Team, Labs and Classroom Technology, and the Student Technology Assistant Program (STAP) which is the walk-in student-staffed help center for teaching with technology. The University has over 1,600 faculty members and 21,000 students.

1.2 Institutional Complexities for Technologists

Each faculty member with whom we engage brings her own unique cultural values, experiences, funding sources (or lack thereof), and pedagogical leanings regarding the various technologies at hand. In addition, the University, as an overall structure, continuously evolves and reorganizes, to meet the needs of each new class of students and in order to stay in line with contemporary protocols, policies and cultural expectations. Such changes trickle down to affect staffing, budgets, team structures, and organizational systems, with implications for team changes and reassignments of responsibilities. When educational technology systems enter the mix, additional complexities, such as numerous vendors, competing systems, software versions, interface changes, and basic tool functionalities must be navigated. New technological developments consistently emerge as potential toolsets for faculty and campus. Departmental budgets must be evaluated and weighed against faculty needs, security, and accessibility considerations, as well as potentials for positive student learning outcomes.

1.3 Addressing Complexities with a Pilot Program

Given the above constraints, maintaining cohesive and exceptional levels of customer support presents unique challenges and opportunities for our larger Academic Technologies team. To help address these specific challenges and imagine ways to stay true to our mission, we slowly integrated a cloud-based Customer Relationship Management tool into our day-to-day practice. Presently, we are wrapping up a three-year informal trial meant to provide use case information. We questioned how such a tool might weave into our daily practices, what challenges to adoption and implementation might be, how effective this new data tool would be in our design to meet customer needs, and other unknown, but important, implications for future development, including deeper alignment with and support of our strategic mission.

Below, we explore our group's use cases, hoping that by doing so, we illustrate how instructors might best be supported while:

- teaching with technology;
- how practical work might be organized across multiple teams;
- how communities of practice might emerge and be nurtured across a decentralized campus;
- how changes in staffing might be softer transitions; and
- how important metrics can be gathered in support of short- and long-term planning and measurements of team efficacy.

2. PROJECT DESCRIPTION

In Summer of 2013, one branch of our team, the *Student Technology Assistant Program* (STAP), adopted the free version of *Insight.ly*, a cloud-based customer relationship management (CRM) tool, to assist staff with both customer and project tracking. An upgrade to the paid version was then initiated, allowing additional users and functionality. Over time and because of a change in staffing and budget, the Instructional Design Team joined using the "Opportunities" feature growing the "Contacts" list. Shortly after, the Online Team connected using an API with *Smartsheets* to collaborate on contacts, and currently the Labs and Classroom Team is being on-boarded. After three years of use, of over 600 faculty contacts representing 197 departments with 967 "projects" and "opportunities" were recorded into the software. Users in the larger Academic Technologies group were not directed to use Insight.ly. Although top-down software directives are often the norm in the department, CRM use was initiated by one team lead only – and participation was always optional on part of other managers and their teams. As the potential and potency of the tool began to be realized by other managers, use grew and budgets allowed for more licenses to be added to the contract.

2.1 What is a cloud-based CRM tool?

Customer Relationship Management (CRM) tools emerged out of the Information Technology development community during the mid-1990s as a way to enable tracking, managing, and improving customer relations (while converting customer leads into sales) [2]. Building customer relationships that are meaningful for both the customer and the organization is at the heart of CRM, as is the shaping of customers' perception about an organization [3]. Contemporary digital CRM platforms either live on the premises, or they are, increasingly, cloud-based technologies, accessible by any registered user from any computer at any time, synchronously and asynchronously, and they represent a holistic approach to managing customer relations. In our instance, the CRM tool we implemented was *Insight.ly*, a cloud-based software tool that was initially chosen because it was well-rated by other users, had a free version and a clean, enjoyable, and well-organized user interface. We also argued that if, at one point, we desired a license, it would cost us much less than larger, enterprise systems and at the time, than similar software on the market.

Insight.ly, like other CRMs, curates a database of customer information, enables analysis of data sets (such as contacts, projects, and other relevant information) and, as an added function, allows for the tracking of workflows and projects. Other features not used in our study include the linking of social profiles with customer cards, web-to-contact forms. Insight.ly utilizes LTI integrations to extend functionality, allowing it to connect to Google tools such as mail and calendar, Zapier, Mailchimp, and others.

2.2 Use cases

During the course of our work with the CRM tool, three main use cases emerged that are discussed below. We strove to merge the CRM with our strategic framework, as a functional implementation bringing us one step closer to achieving our department's mission.

2.2.1 Project management, workflows, tasks, and customer communications

The Student Technology Assistant Program (STAP), our student-powered help desk and digitization suite, initiated use of *Insight.ly*. STAP needed a project management tool that could also track customer communications. The team started with the free version, and each student in the lab used a shared Gmail account to login- a technique that helped to reduce cost, but also led to confusion as to who had entered what information into the "notes" field. Over the course of the study, students needed to be encouraged to follow protocol on entering data in a rule-based way. When entered formulaically, students would be able to access information regarding a project, such as:

- the current stage of the project's progress;
- the faculty member initiating the project, including their history of work with the team and their contact information and university department;
- which of their co-workers last worked on the project;
- any special problems they faced; and
- next steps for completion.

They could also access all communications with the faculty member to keep track of updates or changes. A flat screen in the STAP workspace shows a live Google Calendar feed, updated automatically from *Insight.ly*, providing a visual reference as to which projects are due on which day.

In some ways, the system was found to be beneficial to student-led collaborative work; e.g., it provided student training and support, resulting in proper data entry. The manager of the student space reported, *"Cost is a big concern – like other colleges and universities out there we need to be resource-smart on what products we invest in. The project management side of Insight.ly is okay - it doesn't seem to have been built specifically for that purpose so it feels like we're stretching the tool in some ways - but the calendar integration and nearly automatic correspondence tracking makes it useful. We also use pipelines that allow students to visually see what stage a project is at and easily determine what comes next. All that said, it's only as powerful as the data that's entered into it, so in some ways it becomes a training and supervision issue."*

2.2.2 Knowledge base, communities of practice and vital communications.

Other teams used the CRM to organize contacts into communities of practice for targeted outreach and preemptive care *(see Figure*

1). By entering data related to faculty consultations and course

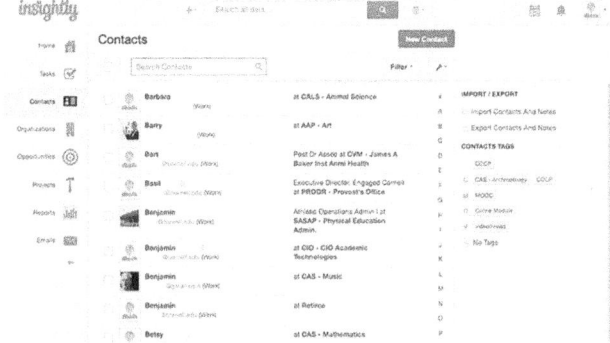

Fig. 1: Contacts with tags

types using the "tags" feature, a collection of faculty from across various disciplines with shared specific interests (e.g., interest in a particular piece of educational technology, such as teaching types, or those who manage exemplar use cases of a particular technology) could be collected for small batch communications, working groups, or pilots. Taxonomies in the CRM were agile and easy to add on-the-fly.

This group utilized the "*Opportunity*" feature as a way to organize consultations with faculty, and the "Notes" tab to add key links, findings or other referential or relevant information *(see figure 2)*.

This type of data entry, combined with the search feature of the CRM over time, led to an organically-produced, collaborative and informal knowledge base. To illustrate an example, one *Opportunity* record kept key information regarding a faculty

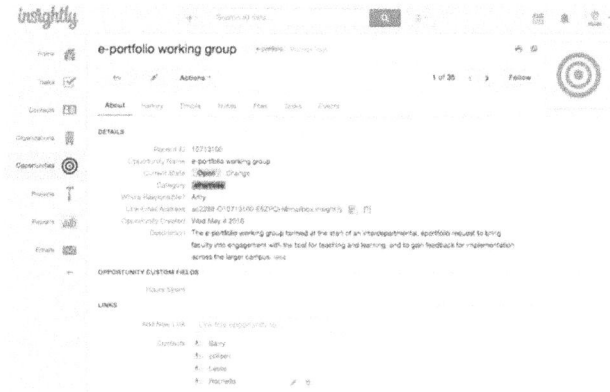

Fig. 2 Opportunity record.

member's use of a specific educational technology tool. In the note were communications from the vendor and vendor contact information, relevant links to send the faculty member, questions the faculty member had during the course of the project, the instructional designer's notes on successes and failures, components within the software to be aware of, links to other sites of support, screenshots of the tool built out with educational content, and key instructional touch points developed by the instructional designer and the faculty member over the course of the semester. Once generated, this collection could be mined using the CRM *search* for future use. In a workplace in which software tools are so prevalent, such a record acted as a refresher for the instructional designer, or her teammates.

Easy export of contacts into newsletter software also enabled the creation of a strong mailing list. In time, Instructional Designers could target and deliver content to teaching faculty, bridging the gap into communications technologies. With its sorting feature,

the CRM facilitated delivery of content where it was most applicable. "*I was sort of shocked that we had accumulated a collection of over 600 faculty members,*" said one Instructional Designer who used the CRM. "*All of the sudden we had a list of clients, faculty who were familiar with our group and our work, that we could reach out to with important communications; like specific new technologies or to see if they wanted to work on a pilot study. It was very cool and definitely something that we didn't have before. It actually allowed us to start a e-newsletter program that has had pretty high open and click rates.*" Lastly, the storing of communications between faculty and Instructional Designers (along with the above-mentioned notes) enabled collaborations and the handing off of faculty, when necessary, among staff across the team. During transitions in the workplace, such as one staff member joining another institution, this allowed those picking up projects to have access to organized and vital histories of communications and resources.

In addition, users of the tool could track faculty entry points to the larger team in order to gain an awareness of past work, or as a way to remember important details about a customer's history within the larger team. For instance, if a faculty member had a consultation regarding a Learning Management System's gradebook integration for a large class and returned a year later to work with an entirely different set of needs and with an entirely different set of staff, the CRM history would enable contemporary staff to inquire about the gradebook project, creating a consistent experience and setting a tone of familiarity and caring for the faculty member. However, as with the STAP use above, getting semi-detailed notes became key for historical inquiries.

2.2.3 Reporting, staff performance dialogues, tracking growth, and reach.

As the team moved to a paid subscription and slowly introduced over 20 team member, in addition to the student support team, individuals began running reports, gathering data on how many faculty and which departments and colleges they supported during a specific course of time (see Figure 3). Staff could run their own reports to see how many "tickets" they worked on during the quarter, and they could bring this with them during performance dialogue conversations with work and project managers. Every user can be given the permissions to look for trends in support cases, and mine the database for information on potential collaborators across the campus. Data could be used to track growth, to guide outreach, and to bring in larger numbers of faculty from strategically-targeted departments and colleges. In addition, management can use this data when reporting up the management chain.

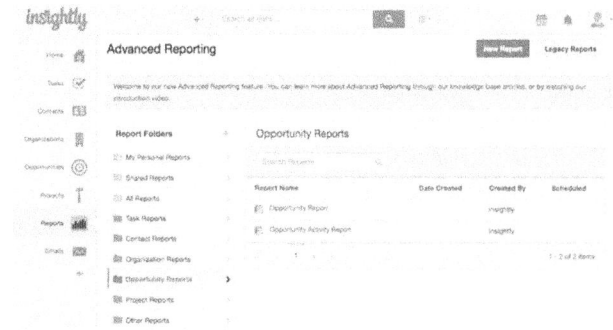

Fig. 3: Reporting and Metrics

2.3 LIMITATIONS / CHALLENGES TO ADOPTION

2.3.1 Bottom-up buy-in within technologically saturated workplaces

Implementing tools and new workflows into the daily practice of staff in a bottom-up, optional capacity presents an alternative method to the more traditional style of management requiring compliance from staff. However, with new methods of adoption come new challenges. The number of tools currently required in the daily practice of an educational technologist is "staggering" [1]. Team members may conclude that yet another tool in a technologically saturated workplace will increase their administrative responsibilities and may not deliver the value desired based on the time committed. The team already had several time and project-tracking software tools (in many of which, participation was mandatory) as well as collaborative cloud-based workspaces where notes and data could be stored. Adding another tool into the mix brought on anxiety in some team members who were already fatigued from too many tools – some of which seem too similar for sensible participation. *"We're asked to track our time, and track our time as we're tracking time. I'm not sure I can have another tracking tool!"* As such, our program was optional, with the hopes that benefits and affordances from use would trickle up and across to colleagues, potentially resulting in higher levels of participation once value could be measured against time investment.

Negotiating buy-in in bottom-up implementation systems may mean engaging in "selling" the tool to team members in both formal and informal ways. With CRM tools, success is found in full participation, so not having all team members involved means fewer connections happening within the software, and thus, incomplete data for analytics.

2.3.2 Finding a team member to act as data janitor, trainer, vendor communications, etc.

The role of data manager is not glamorous, but even small data needs to be cleaned, repaired, and cared for in order for it to function properly. Detailed how-to guides can help all users follow clean information entry procedures; but invariably, edits and monthly maintenance need to occur. The data is only as strong as what is entered into the software, and all software must have an administrator. CRM tools are no different.

2.3.3 Data, now what?

As our trial marked the beginning of its third year, we began questioning how we could query it in meaningful and thoughtful ways. Besides the opportunities presented above, using data with insight requires analytic mindsets and a feeling for what the 'right' types of questions are for the type of data at hand. Some of the questions we posed to the data were:

1. Where are we today?
2. How is that changing?
3. Why?
4. Where are we going, and where do we want to go?

3. CONSIDERATIONS AND FUTURE DIRECTIONS

Other groups interested in initiating use of a CRM tool would do well to investigate their current tool suites and other Enterprise solutions before implementing another product into the workflow. For CRM tools to be successful, as stated earlier, data entered must be important enough to make revisiting it useful and relevant to current work. Work practices that surround the building and sharing of information must be clearly defined, documented and maintained and supported by all users. CRM tools that can connect to central databases of campus community members can save crucial data entering time. As data coming out of various tools must be normalized for evaluating, the fewer translations and handwork done to clean the information the easier the tool use and the more accurate the data. Likewise, it is important to note that information is not always shared unproblematically across teams. Standards and workflows must support human endeavors to enter information.

Throughout the course of our study, we tried to keep in mind that data informs decisions, but that data, in and of itself, is not a driving force for change. It can help shed light on the stories you are trying to tell, but it cannot tell them for you. Data may help Instructional Design departments see the day-to-day from a perspective not usually in view, but insights are constructed and interpreted, not truths. Our questions may lead to new discoveries or reinforce "hunches", or they might just guide the next steps of a longer strategic procedure. CONCLUSIONS

In conclusion, our team continues to discover uses for the CRM tool. With more individual success stories, we hope to encourage all team members to participate in, and to help grow, the *Insight.ly* "database". By entering relevant information and encouraging the capture of communications between co-workers and customers, we hope to achieve a legacy tool with data relevant to moving forward into new spaces for Instructional Design, while improving our mission and our support of faculty. We hope our non-linear map of notes, links, and contacts will help future Instructional Designers and faculty support teams navigate the ever-evolving terrain of educational technology.

4. ACKNOWLEDGMENTS

Our thanks to readers of ACM SIGUCCS 2016 and our co-workers who were kind enough to follow along with our CRM adventures.

5. REFERENCES

[1] Garcia, Daniel D., and Luke Segars. "Technology That Educators of Computing Hail (TECH): Come, Share Your Favorites! (Abstract Only)." In *Proceedings of the 43rd ACM Technical Symposium on Computer Science Education*, 682–682. SIGCSE '12. New York, NY, USA: ACM, 2012. doi:10.1145/2157136.2157438.

[2] Payne, Adrian, and Pennie Frow. "A Strategic Framework for Customer Relationship Management." *Journal of Marketing* 69, no. 4 (2005): 167–76.

[3] Zinkhan, George M. "Relationship Marketing: Theory and Implementation." *Journal of Market - Focused Management* 5, no. 2 (June 2002): 83–89.

Internal Think Tanks for Innovation and Team-Building

Elizabeth Cornell
Fordham IT
Fordham University
718-817-0398
cornellgoldw@fordham.edu

ABSTRACT

Think tanks are usually associated with non-profit organizations and institutes that perform research and provide advice on subjects such as public policy, technology, culture, economics, and so on. But your IT organization can stretch that term to cover a group of staff members who convene to generate innovative ideas that can be acted upon to improve the overall functioning of their department and the institution that it serves. An internal think tank is also a way for staff to share ideas that may not otherwise have a proper place to be heard and discussed. It gives motivated staff a forum to change and improve the workplace status quo.

At Fordham University, our IT organization implemented the "Innovation Group," a collection of staff from IT and other university departments who met regularly to brainstorm, research, and carry out ideas to improve the workplace environment, build a stronger sense of community among IT staff and others in the university, and enhance the integration of technology within the university.

This paper gives an overview of the Innovation Group's goals and methods for organizing and carrying out ideas. It describes some of its successful initiatives and the benefits incurred. It also briefly reviews some of the challenges the group encountered and group's next phase, which will be based on lessons learned from the Innovation Group's first incarnation.

Keywords

Innovation, ideas, communication, collaboration, workplace environment, think tank, team work, mentoring, coaching, higher education

1. INTRODUCTION

Imagine a co-worker makes a suggestion for starting a mentoring program which pairs IT staff wishing to expand their technological, professional, or leadership skills with staff who have experience in that particular area.

SIGUCCS '16, November 06-09, 2016, Denver, CO, USA
© 2016 ACM. ISBN 978-1-4503-4095-3/16/11…$15.00
DOI: http://dx.doi.org/10.1145/2974927.2974932

Another colleague tells you and other lunchtime buddies that she wishes for more opportunities to connect with IT staff outside her immediate group, as well as with members of the larger University community.

Someone else in your IT department sees most people sitting at their desks and staring mutely into their screens. They move only to get snacks, eat lunch, and use the restroom. That person believes staff would benefit from some encouragement to get out of their office routine and into one that involves more physical activity.

Three good ideas, but the first two get aired to a small audience and no one hears the third one.

That's too bad, since those ideas might lead to improvements in employees' skills, their engagement with their job and coworkers, and overall attitude.

Surely everyone has come up with at least one terrific suggestion to improve some aspect of the IT workplace. But how do you prevent the scenario of a good idea getting broadcast to a random group of coworkers in the morning at the coffee machine, only to see it end up, by lunchtime, in the great big pile of great ideas that went nowhere? And even if coworkers are willing to help implement one or two ideas, how does one get those ideas out of the break room and into practice?

This paper is about Fordham IT's "Innovation Group," a think tank of staff from IT and a few others from departments elsewhere in the university, who met regularly to brainstorm, research, and carry out ideas to improve the workplace environment, build a stronger sense of community among IT staff and others in the university, and enhance the integration of technology within the university. This paper gives an overview of the Innovation Group's goals and methods for sharing, discussing, and implementing those ideas. It describes some of the successful initiatives and the benefits incurred. It also reviews challenges the group encountered and looks ahead at the group's next phase, which will be based on lessons learned from the Innovation Group's first incarnation.

2. BACKGROUND

Think tanks are often associated with non-profit organizations and institutes that perform research and provide advice on subjects such as public policy, technology, culture and economics. An IT organization may stretch that term to cover a group of staff members who convene to generate transformative ideas and discuss how to implement them. An internal think tank can be a valuable sounding board for staff with ideas that may not otherwise have a proper place to be heard and discussed. It gives motivated staff a forum to change and improve the workplace status quo.

2.1 Handpicking the Team

Roxana Callejo Garcia, Associate Vice President for Strategy and Innovation, who oversees the project management office, student technology services, and our help desk, implemented Fordham IT's Innovation Group in 2013. When Roxana was hired several years ago, Dr. Frank Sirianni, our CIO, asked her to create and lead the think tank to make Fordham IT a more effective, cohesive team. The Innovation Group was a strategy that seemed suitable for the organization, as Fordham IT is a diverse group of approximately 105 men and women serving an urban, Jesuit university with three main campuses and about 17,500 students, faculty, and staff.

To create the group, Roxana selected members based on their demonstrated ability to work together and think progressively. She also based her choices on the people she felt would move innovation forward at Fordham, especially in the area of technology. She handpicked about 25 staff, mostly from across the IT hierarchy. She also invited several people from the library and handful of administrators in other areas of the university. While this selection process may sound like an elitist approach in that it excludes some people, experts agree that selectivity is key to an effective innovation team. The most successful ones are built with "individuals of different backgrounds, talents, and training," who are eager "to come together and share ideas," and help implement them [8]. These staff excel at collaboration and can work independently. They generate new ideas and speak up when they have solutions to challenges. Team members also have a track record of following through. All that being said, if someone expressed a wish to participate in the group, he or she was invited to join. Motivated individuals are an essential feature of an innovation group committed to changing the workplace environment.

2.2 Meeting Spaces

To make it easy to share and discuss new ideas, the Innovation Group met face to face every other week. Many of our initial ideas for discussion came from a private online community that included not only members of the Innovation Group, but anyone on the Fordham IT staff who wished to join. For this, we used IdeaScale, an online application that helps institutions, corporations, and groups manage innovation [2].

Crowdsourcing lies at the heart of the IdeaScale platform: members contribute, vote on, and discuss ideas. IdeaScale identifies new ideas and the ones that are popular, or "hot," to use the application's lingo, because they have received a lot of votes. It keeps track of ideas in the process of being implemented and those that have been completed. When members of the IdeaScale group vote on ideas they like, the Innovation Group knows which ideas to discuss further in our face-to-face meetings. In a nutshell, IdeaScale fosters the sharing of ideas and provides a space for the early planning stages of collaborative efforts.

2.3 Taking Ideas to the Next Level... Or Burying Them

During those face-to-face meetings, the Innovation Group spent time analyzing, selecting, and planning the implementation of specific ideas [3]. A viable idea was then refined. We weighed benefits to staff against the cost of resources required to implement the idea, including money and time. We sought ideas that were simple to implement [6]. For example, an IdeaScale

contributor suggested we purchase a bocce ball set and play during lunch, a few times during the summer. For about $35 dollars, we found a way to get IT staff out of their cubicles and into the sunlight on the campus lawn. For that brief period, they took their minds off work, met some coworkers they didn't know well or who had recently been hired, and developed relationships with people they already knew. They returned to their desks feeling refreshed. Complicated ideas, on the other hand, rarely got off the ground.

In addition to planning, we often tested new products, such as Google Glass and Yammer. We spent a couple of meetings testing video conferencing and collaboration software. We also took turns researching a particular topic and sharing the information for discussion. One topic was on using Oculus and Google Cardboard to enhance the on-campus experience; another discussion topic covered digital citizenship.

2.4 Innovations that Worked and Some that Didn't

Overall, the Innovation Group implemented a number of effective ideas. Some of them are so well integrated into the fabric of our work lives that few can imagine the office without them. That fact is an indicator that those particular ideas were truly innovative: by definition, "innovation is the creation of something new that represents a communal adaptation or application used and embraced by" the community [4].

Here are descriptions of a handful of some of those ideas, most of which were first shared on IdeaScale.

2.4.1 Community Building

Rotating Lunch Groups: The poster of this suggestion wrote: "It would be great to meet with small groups of 2-6 people you don't normally interact with. Why not make it during lunch? This can break past silos and help IT staff get to know each other in a neutral setting." To implement this idea, we chose a moderator who created the lunch groups based on preferences for where and when to eat. Individual groups determined how often they should meet. At the end of four months, participants were reshuffled into new groups. Rotating lunches were discontinued after a year due to the organizer, who also initiated the idea, not having the time to organize the groups.

Meet and Greet Program: The poster of this idea wrote: "Meet with partners in other parts of the university for a breakfast or lunch meeting. This is to develop and/or improve relationships, get an understanding of how their particular area operates, gain feedback about IT, and provide information about your particular group." The idea inspired our business analytics group to promote their data analysis software. The staff from the help desk also visited specific departments and staffed information tables in public spaces around the campus. The Information Security office also staffs tables in public spaces several times a year. This idea has become common practice for groups who wish to promote their resources to staff and faculty. Department visitations and other outreach initiatives are now viewed as an important supplement to training, workshops, and online documentation.

IT Organizational Chart: The generator of this idea asked if "we could recreate our org chart to include photos of IT staff. We have a wonderful group, and I still wonder who some people are. I also think it would benefit new hires, as well as anyone outside of Fordham IT." We now have an extensive organization chart with photos, created using Visio and posted on our website [1]. One person is assigned to keep the chart updated. The org chart has been a huge help for identifying staff who work in a particular group. Moreover, departments outside of IT have much admired it and in some cases, sought to create a similar one for their group.

Digital Media Project: This was one idea we spent a lot of time discussing and researching. We considered offering a series of training programs to students and faculty throughout the year that included digital darkroom and graphic design tools, creating websites and blogs, making infographics, and video production. We thought about including a hack-a-thon and hosting contests for students to produce content to help us promote the use of technology at Fordham. Ultimately we decided that, though such a program was needed, it required too many resources (mostly human ones) from different areas of Fordham IT and elsewhere in the university. It also required people without much spare time to dedicate a lot of time planning and executing it.

Innovation Walks: To get staff out of the office and into a different setting, we hold monthly walking meetings during the spring, summer, and fall. Each walk has a theme, and is led by a different staff member. As the poster of this idea wrote: "The development of good ideas does not happen entirely in isolation. We need a change of scenery where we can hold sustained conversations about work-related challenges in a setting that doesn't involve chairs, computers, a lunch table, the hallway, or an elevator. That, along with some exercise, can do wonders for generating new ideas and refreshing your mind."

Two of Fordham University's main campuses are uniquely situated for incredible walks. Our Lincoln Center campus is a couple of blocks away from Central Park; the Bronx campus is across the street from the New York Botanical Garden. (Only a few IT staff are based on the third campus, in Westchester, NY).

When promoting the walks, we emphasize that they're not a lunch break, but rather an entirely different way of working that will give your body and your mind a chance to roam. When staff return to their desk, they report approaching their work with fresh energy. Terrific ideas have been generated during the Innovation Walk. They include a regular six-month step challenge, which we administer using the FitBit platform. In the summer of 2016 we started wellness lunches, where staff can learn meditation techniques, desk yoga, and gain healthy eating tips.

2.4.2 Professional Development

Mentoring Program: Fordham IT is committed to professional development for staff and enriching their expertise. The person who suggested the mentoring program idea wrote, "the mentee will prepare development goals for the coming year and we will match him or her with a mentor with experience in the areas identified by the goals." Our first round of mentoring has concluded and a second one has begun; each round lasts six months. Staff seek mentoring in a variety of areas, including vendor management and negotiation, performance management, leadership, budget administration, social media, public speaking, and writing.

Coaching Cafe: As part of its professional development support, Fordham IT initiated the Laureate Program, where eight individuals meet for 18 months to learn new management skills and models of engagement and collaboration. A graduate of the Laureate Program suggested we offer Coaching Cafe, a program to promote the Laureate Program to future applicants but also to introduce its concepts in a low-stakes way to any interested staff. Coaching Cafe takes place approximately every other month, lasts for 90 minutes, and has covered topics such as bullying, feedback, and bickering.

2.4.3 Communication

IT Newsletter: The poster of this idea wrote, "Because we are all so busy with our own jobs, it can be difficult to know what our colleagues are doing, as well as knowing how what each of us does fits into our collective goals. An internal newsletter that highlights events, milestones, new initiatives, and so on, would go a long way toward bringing the big picture into clearer focus." The Fordham IT Newsletter was born on Google Sites and is now in its third year. In 2014, it won the SIGUCCS award for the best electronic newsletter. We plan to migrate our newsletter to WordPress this summer. Many staff have contributed articles, and it's been a terrific way to document Fordham IT's internal events and activities. We also recycle some articles for our public facing blog, *Fordham IT News*.

Toastmasters: Many IT staff have to give presentations to small groups within IT, to external groups in the university, or at conferences. A coworker with previous Toastmasters experience made the suggestion. She wrote: "I used to freeze when confronted with a stage and a group of unknown people. I realized my public speaking skills were holding me back when I was asked to speak at a conference in Las Vegas. I refused. Then I joined Toastmasters, which helped me overcome my fear." Several IT staff worked very hard to implement this project. While several people expressed an interest, not enough people were ready to commit to it and meet Toastmaster's cost requirements to start a group. This idea, unfortunately, never got off the ground.

2.5 Innovation Group Challenges

Despite all the wonderful ideas we generated and implemented, the Innovation Group has been disbanded for now. There are several reasons for this. While 25 staff claimed membership, only 10-15 people, on average, showed up at any given meeting. Lack of time resources can be blamed on this. The group was an additional commitment to our regular workload; no one got time off from other duties in order to participate. Commitment did not just involve showing up to a meeting. If you showed up, you might be called upon to volunteer—whether it be to research a topic to present at the next meeting or to spearhead the implementation of a new idea.

Toward the end, the same three or four people seemed to always be tasked with planning and implementing the new ideas. Whether the projects are large and ongoing or small and finite, each requires planning, outreach, and follow-up. As in the case of the rotating lunches, many ideas require an ongoing effort of at least one or two people to keep them going. If those couple of people stop making the effort, for whatever the reason, the initiative stops.

In some sense, the Innovation Group was a victim of its own success. We implemented and continue to support many ideas, but no one has the bandwidth or time available to commit to doing more and expanding the program. For many ideas (like rotating lunches), there's no consequences to staff when the idea is quietly retired.

Roxana and our CIO recognize the positive benefits of this program and are exploring the idea of hiring someone whose role will include overseeing an innovation program. Ideally, the program would extend more deeply into the greater university community than this initial one.

3. CONCLUSION

Innovation is a bit like chemistry: You need the right mix of people, space, and the catalyst, which is a good idea. Perhaps our group would still exist if we'd started with some concrete guidelines for staff commitment, outcomes, and appropriate projects. However, we learned many things about the innovation process, and during that process, we gave our IT staff a place to be heard in ways that led to positive change. Though there are no plans to resume the Innovation Group anytime soon, our next incarnation will continue that work and draw from the successes and failures of the first group.

Here are some takeaways for fostering innovation with your group. These and other suggestions can be found in the article by John McAdam [5]:

- Less is more: look to extend what you do already, rather than introduce brand new ideas and inventions.

- Partner with other groups in your organization or university to carry out your idea; it reduces some of the workload and gains buy-in from more people.

- Establish dedicated spaces, on and offline, to generate ideas, to identify problems, and to pose solutions.

- Hold regular meetings to evaluate and select ideas.

- Select a diverse membership and prize diverse ideas, no matter how wacky (for example, we supported "World Cup Soccer Jersey Day," in which IT staff were allowed to wear their team's soccer jersey to work).

4. REFERENCES

[1] Fordham IT Organization Chart, http://www.fordham.edu/info/20614/about_fordham_it/1404/it_organization_chart

[2] IdeaScale. Innovation Management Software. 2016. http://ideascale.com/

[3] Llopis, Glenn. "5 Ways Leaders Enable Innovation in Their Teams." Forbes Leadership. April 7, 2014. http://www.forbes.com/sites/glennllopis/2014/04/07/5-ways-leaders-enable-innovation-in-their-teams/

[4] Marmol, Lorenzo del. "What is Innovation? A Short Guide." Creative Corporate Culture. February 23, 2014. http://www.creativecorporateculture.com/what-is-innovation/

[5] McAdam, John J. "How to Create an Innovative Workplace." Wharton Blog Network. Wharton Magazine. October 28, 2014. http://whartonmagazine.com/blogs/how-to-create-an-innovative-workplace/

[6] Patton, Patrick. "'Disruptive Innovation' in the Workplace—Can it be Applied?" Interactive Intelligence. November 7, 2013. http://blog.inin.com/disruptive-innovation-in-the-workplace-can-it-be-applied/

[7] Reed, Vanessa. "3 Ways to Sow Disruption in the Workplace." Mindjet MindManager Blog. April 22, 2014. http://blog.mindjet.com/2014/04/disruption-workplace/

Adventures in Starting a Service Desk

Kelly Wainwright
Lewis & Clark College
0615 SW Palatine Hill Road
Portland, Oregon 97219
(503) 768-7225
kelly@lclark.edu

Caitlin Power
Lewis & Clark College
0615 SW Palatine Hill Road
Portland, Oregon 97219
(503) 768-7225
cpower@lclark.edu

ABSTRACT

This paper will discuss the journey taken by one small school, Lewis & Clark College, to implement a Service Desk. There are many aspects that go into a Service Desk, or so we learned when we transitioned a year ago from multiple separate service points to a one-stop shopping model of service. This change was part of an overall IT reorganization and had the goal of streamlining the process of receiving technology assistance.

Some of the elements that helped this transition be successful include employing the correct staff and retraining existing staff, including student employees, implementing the correct tools (in our case for ticket tracking and equipment checkout) and creating an environment that would support and further our goal.

One hurdle that we faced was changing the technology support culture on campus. This required much marketing, communication and a Grand Opening event to introduce the entire campus to the change. Were we successful? To some degree yes, and in other areas we are still working or dealing with new challenges.

Keywords

Service Desk, Technology Support, Implementation, Student Staffing, Reorganization.

1. INTRODUCTION

Lewis & Clark College is a small, liberal arts college located approximately six miles outside of downtown Portland, Oregon. Our student body consists of close to 2000 undergraduates, 800 law students and nearly 1000 other graduate students, primarily in education and counseling.

2. REORGANIZATION

In 2013, Information Technology decided that we were past due to adjust our structure to the services and support we offered—the dreaded IT reorg. One focal point for this reorg was standardizing our service point. Over the years, our service points had multiplied until we had four different places that an individual could go for technology assistance: the student staffed help desk,

the Information Technology front office, the Instructional Media Services window for equipment checkout, and our high end computing lab, called the Resource Lab.

One result of having such numerous locations to get help was that individuals, especially those new to campus, didn't know where to go. Many individuals who had been on campus for any time had developed personalized support relationships with their favorite IT staff member. Phone calls often started with "You probably aren't the right person to ask this, but you helped me in the past so…"

Another consequence was that many of our services were unknown to the greater campus community. One alumnus told our board of trustees that Information Technology's Resource Lab which houses our high end computing equipment for image, video and audio manipulation and high end printing, was one of the best kept secrets at Lewis & Clark. Not to mention the plethora of audio visual equipment available for students to checkout for free. It was important to find a way to better inform individuals of what services Information Technology could offer.

The decision was made that we needed to simplify the process of getting help. We needed to have one point of contact for all assistance from Information Technology that could do basic intake and triage of calls, assign them to the appropriate group to fix them, and respond to further inquiries from the clients. We needed a face for IT. We needed a Service Desk.

3. STAFFING

One of the critical pieces in ensuring the success of the Service Desk was to get the correct staff in place and provide any required training. While most of the professional staff moved to specialized

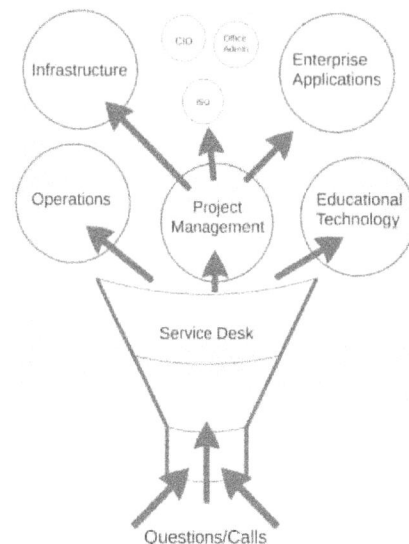

Figure 1. Reorganization Model,
©Lewis & Clark College

positions that played to their particular field or strengths, the Service Desk staff and student staff required significant cross-training in areas they had never worked before.

3.1 Professional Staffing

In our reorganization plans, there was one existing position that moved to the Service Desk and one position that was created new for the Service Desk.

The existing position was our Technology Support Coordinator. This position had been our primary front office point of contact for support. Their duties included triaging incoming issues and requests, management of our lab reservations, daily management of our training resources along with other office administration tasks. In moving them to the Service Desk, they would be gaining extra responsibilities in direct training of the students and managing the pool of checkout equipment.

The new position, which became the Service Desk Manager, was to be responsible for the day-to-day operations of the Service Desk and to be responsible for all aspects of our student staffing--hiring, scheduling, training and managing. We wanted to hire an individual who could also help us be visionary about promoting the Service Desk to the campus community and help us to create the desired Service Desk experience.

3.2 Student Staffing

Previous to our transition, we had separately managed student staffing for the Help Desk, Instructional Media Services (also known as IMS), and Resource Lab. Our original plans for the Service Desk involved the pooled student workforce to cross-train in all three of these areas, but post-reorganization it was much easier to fit most of the workforce into one of two categories: Service Desk (Help Desk and IMS) and Resource Lab. All students that were employed before the transition were re-offered a job in one of these two areas - although not all students chose to remain because of the change in job duties, most remained and underwent our first cross-training attempts.

The new Service Desk student worker position requires customer service skills both over the phone and in person, the ability to troubleshoot basic software issues, and competency in using our booking software to reserve, issue, and receive equipment. Students are expected to triage problems and enter work orders on a huge assortment of topics with the expectation that they can sort out which can be addressed by the student workforce and which must be escalated to staff.

The new Resource Lab position had much the same duties as were assigned before, with the added responsibility of competency in our standard ticketing/work order software so they could document and complete print requests.

With the Service Desk, we wanted to give the students clearly defined levels with a set path for moving from one level to the next. For each shift, we figured that we would need one student, at level one, with the most basic skills able to answer the phone, checkout equipment and enter work orders. We anticipated two students at level two able to handle some phone based troubleshooting as well as being able to work on routine problems on students' computers. Finally, we wanted two students at level three with more advanced skills and knowledge who could handle more complex issues and who we could potentially send out on house calls. With each level increase, we proposed a dollar raise. While our student levels haven't been fully implemented yet, we

have the structure and the training materials in place to begin implementation Fall semester of 2016.

4. SPACE

One of the most difficult parts of creating the Service Desk was determining the space. Bringing together three separate services required a significant amount of space, and potentially a sacrifice in visibility. The top two choices were 1) a space with high visibility (near the entryway of the building) but was currently occupied with offices and would have required a huge move process, and 2) the space that at the time housed the IMS and Resource Lab services and could easily accommodate the Help Desk, but had very low visibility (back of the building with little foot traffic). We chose the second option to ease the physical transition and pushed several marketing strategies to make the space attractive.

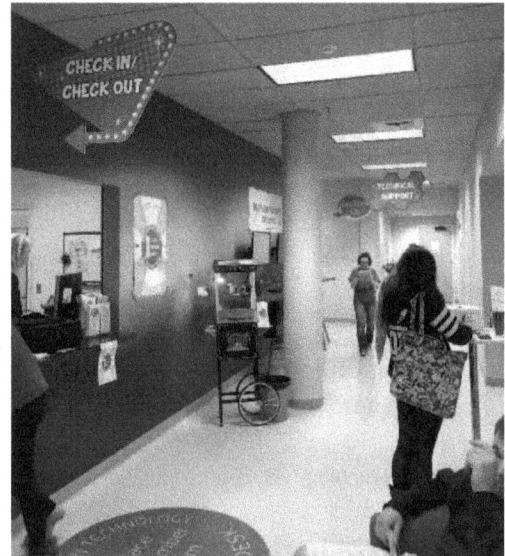

Figure 2. Service Desk Space Design
©Lewis & Clark College

One of our marketing strategies was to make the Service Desk easy to find, as well as making the space a destination. We marked the floor from the building entrance with blue vinyl dots inspired by our logo to lead users directly to the desk. As the dots were not permanent, we also added a blue stripe along key walls to guide users. We also enhanced the space with multiple incentives offered nowhere on campus – namely, a quick-charge station and a popcorn machine.

Our concept of the Service Desk was a unified space and service that served as the face of IT. All or most support calls, questions, and work requests would be directed towards it, and its staff would then direct all requests to the appropriate fixer groups. The goal was to have one place that our users went to when they needed help; one number they could call. This concept inspired our logo, and its motto of "one place, one number, one team." (Figure 3) Once we had established our concept for what the Service Desk would represent, we looked for inspiration of what it should look like. One such inspiration was the Apple Store and its Genius Bar. The Apple Store immediately brings to mind several things – it is an open space, with tables and chairs and easy entertainment. The space we were moving into mainly consisted of a checkout window that opened onto a hallway. Our first major addition to the space was a counter that ran along one wall next to the checkout window. It contained several monitors and hidden computers, and provided space for users to browse the internet or write a paper, while also giving us table-space to troubleshoot basic software problems or issues with mobile devices. We also added two chairs next to our charging station and a couch across from the counter to create a comfy atmosphere.

Figure 3. Service Desk Logo,

©Lewis & Clark College

5. TOOLS

Information Technology had historically used BMC's Track-It[1] to enter work orders for tech help related requests, whereas IMS and Resource Lab student workers had not worked with that tool before. IMS used Avante Reservation Manager[2] to log and maintain equipment checkout reservations, and dealt with classroom tech requests with written forms or notes. The Resource Lab used a combination of written notes and Google forms to process print requests. One of our first tool transitions was making Track-It a standard for entering requests (excluding, for the most part, equipment requests). As the Service Desk was organized to be the single point of contact for initial requests, the base expectation was set to open a work order for any and all work requested. The biggest transition was in the Resource Lab, where Track-It became the primary tool by which every transaction was recorded. The changes in organization and scope of work orders that were entered into Track-It resulted in many changes to the existing workflows within Track-It.

6. TRANSITION
6.1 Soft Launch

It was decided that we would begin with a soft launch of the Service Desk in October of 2014. We wanted to setting up the proposed Service Desk structure and seeing where there were holes or our well-laid plans didn't live up to expectations. This also gave our newly hired Service Desk Manager time to get up to speed as well as giving us time to begin acquainting the campus with the Service Desk concept and redirecting their calls and requests for assistance.

One of the largest hurdles during the transition was meshing the student staff previously from the various service points into one

team. This required an immense amount of cross-training which some of the students embraced and others were less than enthused.

In addition, the soft launch gave us the opportunity to test the flow of the space. We were able to learn where people like to hang out, where traffic jams occurred, and where people naturally went for assistance.

6.2 Grand Opening

To formally launch the Service Desk, we held a week of events geared toward introducing students, staff and faculty as to the location of the Service Desk and the services offered there. During the first week of February 2015, we hosted a reception for faculty and staff where we unveiled our newest marketing video, we hosted food events each day to draw students to the Service Desk, we had a "Rally your Residents" competition to see which residence hall could get the most residents to visit the Service Desk during the week, hosted a Star Wars movie marathon, and held daily drawings for prizes primarily donated by IT vendors. From the daily drawings, we can estimate that we had anywhere from 123 individuals (on Monday) up to 176 individuals (Friday) visit each day.

7. MOVING FORWARD

Shortly after we implemented our Service Desk model, we realized our current checkout software, Avante Reservation Manager was insufficient for handling the increase in reservations that came with increased exposure. It was also not adopted well by the student workers who migrated from the Help Desk to the new Service Desk, and reservations were prone to errors at multiple stages of the process. At the end of the first school year, we began researching new checkout tools to use. Our goal was to select software that supported users booking their own reservations to reduce lines at the checkout counter and speed up transactions. After researching several options, we selected a software called SiSo[3], an online booking tool that not only satisfied our original goals but also automated many processes that had previously required manual effort (such as reminder emails, late notices, and tracking late fees). In fall of 2015 we officially moved all reservations over to the new system and trained all returning Service Desk student workers in using the tool. Beginning spring of 2016, we announced the new checkout system and created a help-sheet and training video for new users to familiarize themselves with the tool. We are currently preparing to include the new online store in our new student orientation materials, and will begin tracking the rate of self-made reservations vs. walk-ups.

We also invested in new software to manage and schedule our collective pool of student workers. Past shift reporting had been done via Google Calendar, with shift trading reported using a separate online forum, which proved unsustainable for the number of employees. The Service Desk manager researched and implemented a tool called ShiftPlanning[4] to easily allow employees to report their availability for schedule planning and offer/accept shift trades in one unified space.

Our IT department as a whole also adopted a new repository for documentation, which previously had no unified location among the different divisions of IT. We used Atlassian's Confluence[5] wiki software to create single, organized space for IT documentation with the added goal of using its structure to eventually build a service portfolio for our department. The Service Desk took advantage of this move to gather our own documentation, combining two Google Sites (one used as a Knowledge Base for our Help Desk, the other outlining Resource Lab procedures) and several Google Drive documents (pertaining to equipment checkout procedures).

Our current project is to develop standardized training for student workers. Merging the different sections that became the Service Desk meant that much specialization was lost, as students were expected to perform a wider variety of tasks. Training became a larger time commitment on the staff's part, but most learning was done on-the-job with peer mentors. Unfortunately, misinformation spread easily this way unless quickly corrected by staff, as students would continue to repeat an erroneous answer to a question. The goal with our training program is to standardize the basic training and competency requirements for new hires, as well as incentivize students to voluntarily participate in specialized training to earn wage increases.

8. CONCLUSION

Since the Service Desk has opened, the campus community is taking advantage of having one location for addressing all their IT support needs. The number of request tickets that were worked on by the Service Desk in the seven months since it opened totaled 3196, or roughly 450 tickets per month. Additionally they handled roughly 200 incoming calls per month to the main Service Desk phone number. Even more impressive is the number of equipment checkouts. In the 2013-14 academic year Instructional Media Services had 1670 reservations for equipment. In the 2014-15 academic year, with the inception of the Service Desk, that number rose to 2815, an increase of 59%. These numbers indicate that the Service Desk is succeeding in making technology more accessible to individuals on campus.

After the Service Desk closes a work order, we invite clients to complete a customer satisfaction survey. We specifically ask them to rate their satisfaction in the following areas: overall service provided, convenience of use, friendliness of staff/students, willingness to help, understanding of the issue, level of communication and the resolution provided. The rating for the overall satisfaction for Spring 2016 had 66% of responses choosing extremely satisfied, and 96.43% choosing some level of satisfaction. This is up from a 95% customer satisfaction rating the previous semester. This has given us the understanding that, even as we continue to strive to make improvements, the campus is overall in favor of our move to a Service Desk model.

9. REFERENCES

[1] BMC TrackIt: http://www.trackit.com

[2] Avante Reservation Manager: http://www.avantesolutions.com/products/reservation-manager/

[3] SiSo: https://www.onlineresourcebooking.com

[4] ShiftPlanning: https://www.shiftplanning.com

[5] Atlassian Confluence: https://www.atlassian.com/software/confluence

Teaching, Learning, and Classroom Design

Miranda Carney-Morris
Lewis & Clark College
0615 S.W. Palatine Hill Road
Portland, OR 97219
1-503-768-7220

mccm@lclark.edu

Trevor M. Murphy
Williams College
56 Hopkins Hall Drive
Williamstown, MA 01267
1-413-597-2231

tmurphy@williams.edu

ABSTRACT

Our schools have a variety of classroom environments from the large lecture halls, to teaching labs with a computer for every student, to rooms with movable flat tables set in a circle. Many of our classrooms are equipped with data projection and podiums. Faculty often have favorite classrooms and try to book those rooms for their classes every year. Classrooms might be assigned by class size, but there are other factors about classrooms that either match or clash with teaching styles of our faculty.

In this paper we intend to explore how the classroom environment affects teaching and learning, and how classrooms can be designed to facilitate engagement and active learning at Williams College and Lewis and Clark College. We will also discuss the challenges in pursuing the creation of flexible learning spaces.

General Terms

Design, Human Factors, Standardization.

Keywords

Classroom Design, Learning Spaces, Education.

1. INTRODUCTION

1.1 Institutional Contexts

Williams College is a private, residential, liberal arts college located in the northwestern corner of Massachusetts in the town of Williamstown. The college has 2,000 students and 300 faculty members. The Office for Information Technology at Williams College consists of four groups including Networks and Systems, Desktop Systems, Administrative Information Systems, and Instructional Technology. The Instructional Technology group provides faculty with pedagogically informed technology support.

Lewis & Clark (L&C) College is a small liberal arts college located approximately six miles outside of downtown Portland, Oregon. Our student body consists of close to 2000 undergraduates, 550 law students, and nearly 600 other graduate students primarily in education and counseling. Serving these students, we have 400 full and part-time faculty. The Information Technology Department is organized in eight functional units including Service Desk, Educational Technology, Project Management, Institutional Operations, Academic Operations, Information Security, Systems

SIGUCCS '16, November 06 - 09, 2016, Denver, CO, USA
Copyright is held by the owner/author(s). Publication rights licensed to ACM.
ACM 978-1-4503-4095-3/16/11...$15.00
DOI: http://dx.doi.org/10.1145/2974927.2974945

Infrastructure, and Information Systems. Educational Technology provides faculty with pedagogically informed technology support.

1.2 Why Talk About Classroom Design?

Several reasons to rethink classroom design from the Journal of Learning Spaces include the growth of mobile computing that allow content creation and ubiquitous access to information, online based learning and online resources, the shift toward constructivist learning, and collaborative learning environments [4]. There is also growing evidence documenting the positive impact of active learning over traditional lecture on student performance, especially in STEM fields [6]. As schools look to create positive outcomes for students, there is growing interest in how we can revamp our learning spaces to be more student focused.

2. CURRENT ENVIRONMENT

2.1 Current Classroom Environments

2.1.1 Lewis & Clark College

Classrooms at each of the three schools at Lewis & Clark have been designed to suit teaching styles preferred by faculty.

2.1.1.1 Law School

Classrooms at the Law School are a mix of lecture style classrooms with tiered U-shaped layouts and smaller seminar rooms with a conference table. Tables in these rooms are fixed with flexible seating. This suits the preferred teaching style of most faculty which is lecture.

2.1.1.2 Graduate School of Education and Counseling

Most classrooms at the Graduate School have moveable tables and chairs. The default arrangement for classrooms is a hollowed square. There is a teaching computer lab with fixed tables for desktop workstations and movable chairs. Large classes and continuing education seminars are held in a room with movable circular tables and chairs. This suits the preferred teaching style of most faculty which focuses on discussion/group work.

2.1.1.3 College of Arts & Sciences (CAS)

The CAS, our undergraduate campus, has the greatest variety of classroom layouts from large auditoriums to smaller seminar rooms with chairs arranged around a central conference table. Teaching style differs depending on class size and discipline. Several professors also use multiple styles during each class.

Our largest lecture halls have auditorium style fixed seating with attached arm chair tablets. There are a handful of larger lecture style classrooms with U-shaped tiered fixed tables. Chairs in these rooms are movable.

Most classes are held in rooms designed to accommodate 20-40 students depending on table/chair configuration. Some of these rooms include movable tables and chairs, including four with trapezoid shaped tables. The majority of these rooms contain tablet armchairs which can be easily reconfigured and moved between rooms.

There are six computer teaching labs. Five have fixed tables with workstations and movable chairs. Three of these labs are arranged with rows facing forward. Two have workstations arranged on the outer wall with a conference table in the center. One classroom has a fixed laptop cart and contains movable rectangle tables and chairs.

Science labs are managed by the individual departments. Older labs have fixed tables and lab stools. Recently remodeled labs include a mix of fixed tables, stools and centrally located movable rectangle tables and chairs that can support group work or individual work with laptop workstations.

2.1.2 Williams College
Williams College has a variety of classroom types:

Socratic classrooms have almost horse shoe shaped seating that is sometimes tiered with several rows to facilitate discussion. Students can all see each other. The faculty member tends to be at the focal point of the classroom. There are five of these classrooms.

Seminar classrooms have seating around a central table. Some of the larger seminar classrooms have tables arranged in a circle with seating on the outside. There are 35 seminar classrooms at Williams.

Meeting rooms are essentially small seminar classrooms. There are three schedulable meeting rooms. They seat about 12 total.

There are 24 lecture halls with varied configurations. Some have fixed seating while others have movable furniture. Some of the fixed seating rooms look more like a movie theater. Many rooms in the sciences have chairs at heavy lab desks. One room has easy chairs with wheels on them that can be moved around. Movable furniture rooms have light chairs and light tables equipped with wheels for easy reconfiguration.

There are eight computer teaching labs. These rooms tend to have fixed tables to support the computers and monitors, but rolling chairs.

There are science labs that are managed by the science departments. If they have seating, it tends to be lab stools. The layout is dictated by the lab equipment. Other labs are conducted outdoors.

Tutorial classes are popular at Williams. Tutorials are classes where there is usually one professor and two students. They meet in faculty offices or in small rooms, such as a department conference room, that are not on the fixed classroom schedule. A chalkboard and a few chairs is a typical setup. Generally, these classes will have one student presenting an argument paper followed by an in depth critique by the other student. The following week, the students switch roles. There are 60 to 70 tutorial classes offered each year.

2.2 Classroom Equipment
Classroom equipment tends toward a standard and predictable setup allowing faculty who are familiar with the equipment to teach in any technology equipped classroom. However, exceptions exist to serve special requirements such as dual projection setups to support art history classes, for example.

2.2.1 Williams College
Classrooms are typically equipped with a PC desktop, a Mac desktop, laptop connections, a CD/DVD/VHS player, an audio system, and a data projector. Some classrooms have slide projectors or document cameras. Most have data projection for displaying output from computers and mobile devices. A few rooms have dual projectors with two projection screens. The classrooms are operated using an Extron System7 controller. Every teaching station has instructions for using the Extron System7 controller as well as a phone number to call for support.

An effort has been made to keep the classroom systems as identical as possible so that faculty can feel comfortable using a classroom they have never visited before. Exceptions are rare, but might include music classrooms where a phonograph record player is part of the audio system.

2.2.2 Lewis & Clark College
Classrooms are equipped with a standard equipment A/V rack controlled by a Crestron touch screen. Instructions for using equipment are provided. Classrooms include a phone with a number to call for support. Most racks include a Macintosh computer with a Windows virtual machine, laptop connection for projection, USB connectors, and a Blu-ray player or CD/DVD/VCR. Rooms have an audio system, data projector for use with computers and mobile devices and screen. Document cameras are part of the standard configuration on the Graduate Campus and on the Law Campus most classrooms are equipped with a lecture capture system. There are a few rooms with specialized equipment such as SmartBoards, slide projectors, an Apple TV, or dedicated video conferencing systems.

2.3 Classroom Assignment Process
2.3.1 Lewis & Clark College
At Lewis & Clark, classrooms are assigned by the Registrar for each school. Faculty are encouraged to inform the registrar early of any special needs such as a video conferencing system. Faculty who teach back-to-back classes are almost always scheduled in the same room. Faculty requests for specific rooms are honored on a first come, first served basis and registrar staff who schedule rooms work directly with faculty to accommodate these requests. In some cases, IT will suggest modifications to take advantage of specialized equipment such as video conferencing systems designed to support classes that enroll remote learners.

A challenge we face in promoting flexible learning spaces is that most faculty will accept a room that is available at a convenient time and location even if the layout is not well suited to their teaching style.

3. HOW CLASSROOM ENVIROMENTS AFFECT TEACHING AND LEARNING

There are numerous research studies on classroom seating arrangements [7] and comparing Active Learning Classrooms to traditional classrooms at large institutions [10]. While studies can inform or suggest broad goals and opportunities, they cannot not address circumstances unique to your institution. They are also often conducted at large public universities which may have an environment and focus quite different from your institution – this is definitely the case for small liberal arts colleges. Collecting feedback from your faculty and students is often necessary to develop an understanding of how your campus classroom environments are impacting teaching and learning practices typical of your students and faculty.

At Lewis & Clark, we learned this lesson the hard way when we failed to account for classroom environment factors such as furniture/space constraints, classroom assignment practices, and infrastructure during early efforts to promote technology associated with active learning. In response, we stepped up our internal data collection efforts and started to discuss reviving the CAS classroom committee which was disbanded at the conclusion of the last major building renovation on the CAS campus. In the summer of 2015, the committee was reconstituted by the Dean of the CAS and asked to provide oversight and review of the classrooms. The committee decided to expand membership to include those responsible for Graduate and Law School classrooms to allow for more coordinated data collection, sharing, planning and outreach.

Our charge for the 2015-2016 academic year was to research the following:

1. Do Lewis & Clark classrooms meet the needs of today's student? Are they configured, equipped and built to enhance the way students need to learn today vs. a decade ago? If not, what changes could be made? Aspects to consider included room configuration, environment, technology, impact on student learning outcomes and faculty interest in pedagogical approaches enhanced by reconfigured classrooms.

2. Review current task flows and renovations prioritizing to ensure that we are taking the best approach to maintaining our learning spaces.

The committee has spent much of the first year sharing and collecting data and discussing how to secure and make the best use of funds available for classroom renovations. To aid in this effort, the Associate Dean of CAS and Director of Administrative Services at the Graduate school sent the following email survey to their respective faculty:

1. Please describe strategies that would allow for greater faculty input in designing or improving teaching spaces.
2. What are your current obstacles in the classroom for group work?
3. How often do you reconfigure the classroom to match the lesson of the day, and how easy is it to do so?
4. Specific feedback on lecterns in Social Sciences building.
5. General comments
6. [Graduate School only] Please describe your teaching style. What classroom features, either present in our classrooms or not, would support you in your teaching style?

We received 33 individual responses. Much of what we had learned from feedback through other channels was confirmed, however, there were a few results that were surprising. Concerns raised included:

- Flexible chairs were seen as key. No one liked classrooms with fixed arm chair seating.
- Overcrowded classes/extra chairs. For example, smaller classrooms might be scheduled to only comfortably fit a lecture style tablet armchair layout. This is frustrating for faculty who prefer to arrange chairs in a circle or in small groups.
- Overcrowded rooms make it difficult or impossible for faculty to easily navigate the room to support group activity.
- Odd shaped rooms make it difficult to configure rooms in a discussion circle.
- Rooms with tables are favored by faculty teaching classes where students need table space for class materials.
- Rooms with trapezoid desks were universally disliked. The tables were described as heavy, hard to move and created a room difficult to safely navigate.
- Concerns about classroom projection screens which cover the whiteboard in the front of classrooms when in

use. Concerns varied from wanting to project and use the whiteboard at the same time to just wanting additional whiteboards.
- Reliable network/Internet connectivity for BYOD devices (faculty laptop, mobile device, etc.) was a concern for some.
- Inability to project wirelessly forces most faculty to teach from the front of the room when they want to use the projector.
- Reliable video conferencing connectivity for distance education students.
- Tablet armchairs are not big enough for today's student who may have a laptop, notebook and a water bottle.

One important environmental issue raised through another channel was poor soundproofing in some of our buildings. We learned of this issue during a faculty development event focused on active learning. Faculty who are flipping and looking to incorporate group work mentioned receiving noise complaints from neighboring classrooms.

4. HOW TO DESIGN CLASSROOMS THAT FOSTER ENGAGEMENT AND ACTIVE LEARNING

EDUCAUSE has assembled some materials on the topic of classroom design. Malcolm Brown provides seven principles for classroom design [1]. These principles include designing with the campus context in mind, having an inclusive planning and design process, insuring adequate support for operations, environmental quality, layout and furnishings, tools and technology, and innovation. In addition, there is a spreadsheet for rating a learning space on these categories. Each area has sub-topics that can be judged. The section on layout and furnishings, for example, has 14 items to look for in a learning space. These topics include the expected items like seating density, writable surfaces, and physical storage. There are also items relating to furniture configuration options, movable partitions, movement through space, and access to adjacent informal learning areas. [3]

FLEXspace.org provides access to images and comments about innovative learning spaces [5]. The FLEX in FLEXspace stands for Flexible Learning Environments Exchange. The learning spaces are sorted into categories for browsing. Some of the categories are: informal learning, demonstration, critique, and small group learning. The collection could use more contributions of photos to broaden the resource, but the idea of sharing images of learning spaces is a good one.

Inspiration can also be found from universities that are pioneering research in Active Learning Classrooms. The University of Minnesota Center for Educational Innovation has an extensive website that includes floor plans and best practices [2]. NC State University's SCALE-UP website [8] is geared more towards larger universities, but still has several examples, pictures and a directory of universities that have established active learning classrooms.

5. LESSONS LEARNED / CHALLENGES

- At Lewis & Clark, projects that incorporate only one of these design principles fall short of our goals. For example, early attempts to promote active learning focused primarily on researching state-of-the-art technology and tools such as interactive touch screens, BYOD projection and video conferencing technology.

This tech-focused outreach met with limited success as it failed to take in account multiple other factors (context, environmental, and cultural) which limited faculty interest or even ability to use these technologies. While we did come up with a few transformative uses for technology, the overall impact on teaching and learning at the College of Arts & Sciences was lower than hoped.

- A centralized classroom planning committee can be invaluable in creating the broad campus support often necessary to secure funding for experimental renovations when resources are limited.

- Collecting and sharing data about classroom experience and attitudes from faculty and students can be invaluable in directing classroom renovation efforts and faculty development programming/outreach.

- Creating flexible learning spaces can be costly both in terms of renovation and equipment costs, but also because of lower room capacity.

- Creating opportunities for faculty to get hands-on experiences with flexible classrooms in a low stakes environment can be key in promoting greater adoption. This is a challenge for campuses that do not have the space or funds to permanently establish experiential classroom spaces. At Lewis & Clark, our classroom committee is looking for classroom spaces where we can do small scale innovations and faculty development and outreach events where we can provide hands-on experiences with furniture and technology that supports active learning.

- While scheduling staff come to know over time what rooms specific faculty prefer, it would be better if information about teaching style preferences was routinely collected and considered when scheduling rooms.

- Collecting data that demonstrates the impact on student learning beyond the preferences of faculty and students may be beyond the expertise of Information Technology and other staff supporting classrooms.

6. CONCLUSIONS

Classroom design has a quiet and often hidden impact on teaching and learning at a liberal arts college. Faculty are adept at adapting teaching methods to the constraints of a given space and may not know how or when to advocate for change, especially when room assignments change semester to semester. At Lewis & Clark and at Williams College the reestablishment of a classroom committee has helped with data collection. In addition, it has made the most of limited resources by coordinating efforts to identify opportunities and funding sources for flexible classroom renovations and promotes spaces that currently exist.

7. ACKNOWLEDGMENTS

Thanks to Jonathan Morgan-Leamon, Director of Instructional Technology at Williams College, who supports the author's professional development.

8. REFERENCES

[1] Brown, Malcolm. 2015. Seven principles for classroom design: the learning space rating system. Educause Review. (Feb. 22, 2015), DOI= http://er.educause.edu/articles/2015/2/seven-principles-for-classroom-design-the-learning-space-rating-system.

[2] http://cei.umn.edu/support-services/tutorials/active-learning-classrooms

[3] http://www.educause.edu/eli/initiatives/learning-space-rating-system

[4] Felix, Elliot, and Brown, Malcolm. 2011. The Case for a Learning Space Performance Rating System. Journal of Learning Spaces, Vol. 1, No.1.

[5] Flexspace.org

[6] Freeman, S., Eddy, S. L., McDonough, M., Smith, M. K., Okoroafor, N., Jordt, H. and Wenderoth, M. P. 2014. Active learning increases student performance in science, engineering, and mathematics. Proc. Natl. Acad. Sci. U. S. A., 111, 23 (05/12 2014), 8410-8415. DOI=10.1073/pnas.1319030111.

[7] Harvey, E., Kenyon,M. 2013. Classroom Seating Considerations for 21st Century Students and Faculty. Journal of Learning Spaces, Vol. 2, No. 1.

[8] https://www.ncsu.edu/per/scaleup.html

[9] http://www.steelcase.com/eu-en/products/collaborative-chairs/node/

[10] Whiteside, A., Brooks, D. C. and Walker, J. 2010. Making the case for space: Three years of empirical research on learning environments. Educause Review. (Sept. 22, 2010), http://er.educause.edu/articles/2010/9/making-the-case-for-space-three-years-of-empirical-research-on-learning-environments

Toppling the Monolith: How SUNY Geneseo Ended the Use of Monolithic Images on Macs

Nikolas Emil Varrone
SUNY Geneseo
Newton Hall, Room 135; 1 College Circle
Geneseo, NY 14454 USA
+1 585-478-0161
varrone@geneseo.edu

ABSTRACT

Monolithic imaging for faculty, staff, and students access computer deployments is less than ideal. Image sizes are massive and are difficult and time consuming to build. Furthermore, images are often outdated immediately after building when essential packages, such as the flash player, receive updates. Package based deployments solve many of these issues. Individual packages within the deployment are updated one of the time, even automatically, while software repositories dictate which packages are required for each setup. Furthermore, solutions to handle these issues are often free and open source such as Munki, AutoPKG, and reposado. We will discuss how to create your own packaged based deployments using these tools.

CCS Concepts

• Social and professional topics→Professional topics→Management of computing and information systems

Keywords

AutoPKG; catalogs; deployment; desktop management; manifests; Munki; NetInstall; reliability; security; standardization.

1. ABOUT US

1.1 The Institution

SUNY Geneseo is located on 220 acres within the Finger Lakes region of New York, the county seat of Livingston County. There are approximately 5,600 full-time students enrolled, many of whom are residents. This campus is supported by fewer than 1000 faculty and staff members. Computing & Information Technology centralizes almost all support for the computing needs of the entire campus community. The Support Services group is responsible for the Help Desk and all Level 2 and 3 Desktop Support issues. Each Level 2 technician supports an average of 264 physical computers.

1.2 "Them Changes"

For a long time, campus computer labs held the only Macintosh computers (Macs) that were centrally managed. This was mostly accomplished using Apple Remote Desktop and NetRestores. Faculty and staff Macs, by contrast, were entirely unmanaged.

SIGUCCS '16, November 06-09, 2016, Denver, CO, USA
© 2016 ACM. ISBN 978-1-4503-4095-3/16/11...$15.00
DOI: http://dx.doi.org/10.1145/2974927.2974946

This resulted in a variety of issues. Ticket load was high for Level 2 tech support. "Which password should I use," was a common question issued by customers uncertain what resource was requiring authentication. Macs were built manually which took a great deal of time to do properly.

Eventually, Mac desktop management methods used in computer labs began to trickle into use for faculty and staff computers through a series of skunkworks projects meant to resolve repetitive issues. All computers began to be bound to Active Directory, connected to a Profile Manager, and could be connected to via Apple Remote Desktop.

1.3 NetRestore to NetInstall

As of Mac OS 10.7, NetRestores gave way to NetInstalls. NetInstalls are a package-based method of creating images that were smaller and easier to modify. Rather than build the perfect computer and then capture it, NetInstalls are given an OS installer from the AppStore, a set of packages, and then built. NetInstalls were much smaller than NetRestores but came with their own share of problems. Not everything could be installed in a NetInstall. This is **mainly** due to NetInstalls not being a fully built environment.

2. MUNKI

2.1 Enter the Munki

Eventually a product was needed that facilitated the update of software more consistently on faculty and staff Macs. Apple Remote Desktop was not powerful enough to perform the task of managing software updates and certainly wasn't robust enough to assist with deployments. A number of products existed that could perform the task but a trip to Penn State's Mac Admins conference made the initial choice of Munki a clear one. According to the description on the project's website, "Munki is a set of tools that, used together with a web server-based repository of packages and package metadata, can be used by OS X administrators to manage software installs (and in many cases removals) on OS X client machines." [4] Munki is free and open source which made it the perfect choice for the sort of skunkworks commonly engaged in by certain team members.

2.2 How Munki Works

Munki is mainly a series of Python scripts that run on a web server and a client computer to accomplish its work. Clients are assigned to manifests which are connected to software catalogs. Catalogs comprise various software packages that have corresponding package info files, typically in the form of a text based .plist file. Almost everything that Munki does exists in the form of a text file that can be edited either in Xcode or a full text editor such as TextWrangler.

The structure of a Munki repository's catalogs and manifests can take a variety of forms. Typically there is at least a testing and a production catalog. Newly imported items are usually placed in the testing catalog while the bugs of deployment are worked out and then graduated to the production catalog.

SUNY Geneseo has a testing, production, and beta tester catalog. Many large organizations have a manifest for each client which is then nested within other manifests. By contract, SUNY Geneseo has departmental and/or usage oriented manifests. Therefore, there are manifests for individual computer labs or entire departments. These departmental manifests are nested within other manifests that offer more generic software.

2.3 Working with Munki

Munki comes with some basic programs to manage it once the server is up and running. The Munkiimport configure option allows a client to add packages to a repository then allows you to import packages into your Munki repository. The main tool for the management of Munki Manifests and catalogs is a command line utility called manifestutil. The manifests and catalogs can be created and controlled from this interface and is all one needs for a basic setup.

Manifestutil commands are simple and straightforward such as add-catalog, copy-manifest, display-manifest, and the all-important help command. Thankfully tab completion is supported within the manifestutil interface. However, once manifests reach a certain size, a tool such as the server based munkiwebadmin or the OSX GUI MunkiAdmin makes them far easier to use. MunkiAdmin is a good start for the Desktop Manager to begin with because it doesn't require anything other than having the Munki client working on a computer. These programs allow for changes on a much larger scale.

3. AUTOPKG

3.1 What Is It?

It's nearly impossible to define, in as few words as possible, AutoPKG any better than what it says on the project page. It reads:

"AutoPKG is an automation framework for OS X software packaging and distribution, oriented towards the tasks one would normally perform manually to prepare third-party software for mass deployment." [1]

For us, this means that we can use AutoPKG to automatically download, package, and import into Munki applications that we use and rely upon. AutoPKG was a life saver that gave us a advantage in Mac deployments.

3.2 How It Works

AutoPKG follows a set of built in "recipes" that tell the program where to get and what do with requested software. Recipes are XML .plist files similar to those used by Munki. Recipes can be freely downloaded from a community of AutoPKG users worldwide and cover thousands of software solutions. If a particular recipe doesn't work exactly as what is desired, an override can be created that modifies the existing recipe download. A common example of this is the creation of an override to download Firefox ESR instead of the regular version of Firefox. It's a common AutoPKG can be run from the command line for each package, be given a list, or be pointed to a file that lists everything that AutoPKG should download.

3.3 Our Implementation

It was desirable to take this process a step further and automate the AutoPKG process through the use of cron jobs. For some time this was done in an individual's account, but a service account was eventually created to perform this process.

```
#    Update AutoPkg Repos
#
0   7   *   * 1  /usr/local/bin/autopkg repo-update all | mail -s "AutoPKG
Update" loremIpsum@geneseo.edu
#    Weekly AutoPkg Job
#
0   6   *   * 3  /usr/local/bin/autopkg run --recipe-list
/Users/Shared/AutoPkg/AutoPkgRecipes.txt | mail -s AutoPKGOutput
loremIpsum@geneseo.edu
#
#    Daily AutoPkg Job
#
0   5   *   *   *  /usr/local/bin/autopkg run --recipe-list
/Users/Shared/AutoPkg/DailyAutoPkgRecipes.txt | mail -s AutoPKGOutput
loremIpsum@geneseo.edu
#
#
#    Weekly Windows AutoPkg Job
#
0   6   *   * 2  /usr/local/bin/autopkg run --recipe-list
/Users/Shared/AutoPkg/AutoPkgWinRecipes.txt | mail -s "Windows
AutoPKGOutput" loremIpsum@geneseo.edu
```

Figure 1: Example crontab for automating AutoPKG actions

As shown in the included crontab, there are several process that run regularly. The first updates the AutoPKG repositories and emails the output to the desktop services group. The next three cron jobs use recipe lists to update application lists. The first list is one that runs weekly to update lower priority applications. Next is a list of applications that are not more critical that have security implications such as the Flash player or Java.

3.4 The AutoPKG approval process

When the AutoPKG process reports via email that there's an update available, a ticket is created in the ticket system (JIRA) and assigned to a student worker. The student worker then checks the installation of packages on a Mac that is configured to be a part of the testing manifest. The student checks to make certain that that package has been installed correctly by checking on the installed version of that software and making certain that it runs properly. Applications that are reported to be installed correctly are graduated from the "Testing" to the "Production" repository by the desktop support professional. These applications are then downloaded and installed by Munki clients as they check in with the Munki server.

4. BUILDING OUR NETINSTALL

NetInstalls, like their predecessors, are created with Apple's System Image Utility. In past versions of the Mac OS, this functioned almost exactly like Automator. It's currently more of a wizard style system that when the option is chosen to customize, it goes into Automator itself. The workflow (shown on the next page) is fairly straightforward.

An OS installer from the AppStore is chosen as the image source. Flat packages and Post-Install scripts are chosen that configure the client. Our set is relatively simple and includes: a package which creates a deployment account; the latest stable Munki client; and a package that sets some system options and configures Munki for deployments. This last item was initially tricky as the scripts that it delivers could not be run as a standard post-installation script in the more limited NetInstall environment. Instead, the package deploys the script to a location in the file system that is later run by a launchdaemon upon restart. This script, at the end, deletes both itself and the launchdaemon.

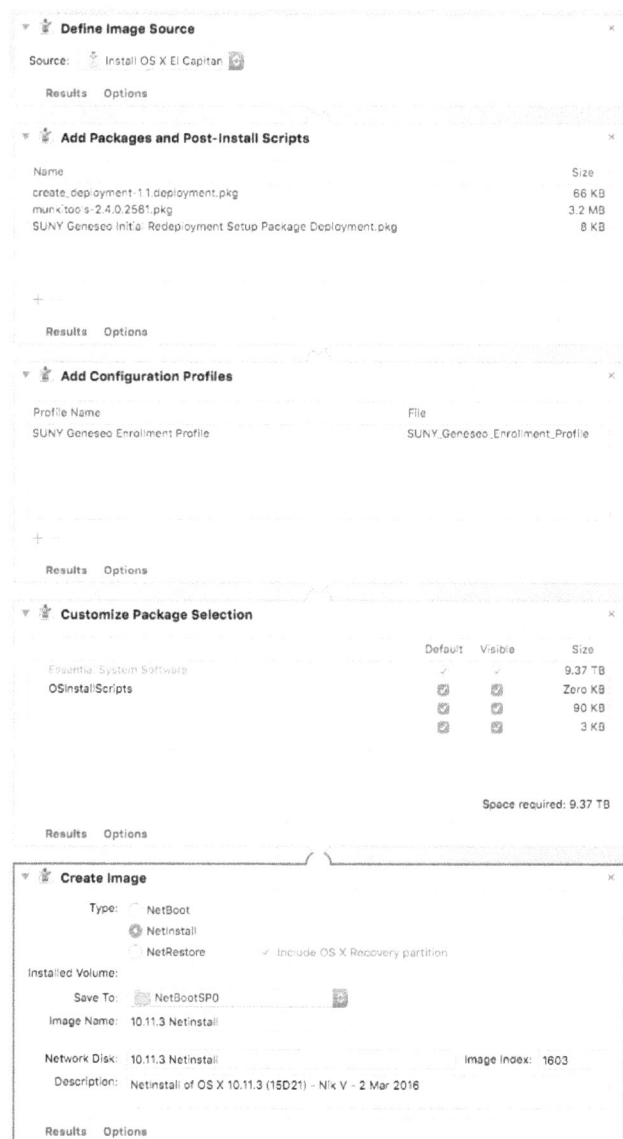

Figure 2: Example NetInstall Workflow

As of Mac OS 10.11, the optional Partition Disk step, which was so useful in 10.10, causes the NetInstall to freeze on startup. It's preferable to make this step optional and not automatic as it offers the ability to only reinstall the OS to troubleshoot certain issue. It's worth noting that we had several issues with 10.11 NetInstalls which were at their worst with 10.11.4 and still flakey with the 10.11.5 release. The NetInstall would rarely boot completely.

5. HOW STUDENTS PERFORM NETINSTALLS

5.1 First Steps

Student workers hold down the N key to boot to the default NetInstall option chosen to be the default by the sysadmin. Alternately, they can also hold down the "option" key to see a list of everything that's available to them. Ideally, they are prompted to partition the computer's hard drive. Past this point the process is like the installation of any other version of Mac OS. The student is prompted to pick a language to proceed in, is given the option of which volume to install on, and can choose amongst the default packages to install. Past this point the operating system is installed which takes around 20 minutes to perform. Once the operating system has been installed it restarts automatically and thanks to the startup script, should boot directly into the deployment account. It's at this point that Managed Software Center, the Munki front end that most end users interact with, is run and the first round of software is installed. Among this batch of software, a restart is typically required, the computer restarts and again automatically logs into the deployment account. Students are to check the managed software center until there are no more items left to run.

5.2 "Finalizing Issues"

Once all of the necessary software has been installed, the student worker needs to bind the computer to the domain and name it appropriately. Deployments also need to be connected to our Profile Manager to have the correct policies applied. This process used to cause a few problems. Student workers had no problem connecting clients to the Profile Manager but they used to have to wait for a professionals to put computers into the appropriate group to receive the proper policies. When there was a transition within the team, this caused an unnecessary bottleneck. Even bigger problems occurred with student workers being unable to completely name and bind computers to the domain. This was due to far too many confusing steps that students had to execute, mainly through the use of .command based bash scripts. Because of the technical nature of these command line based scripts, even the best student workers experienced issues with it. Far too often there were issues with finalizing deployments. Something had to change.

5.3 Fixing Finalization

Several scripts were merged them into one massive interactive script that deploys itself to the deployment account's desktop. Deploying directly to the desktop was difficult at first. Through a quirk in the application that is commonly used to build packages, we could not deploy directly to the deployment account desktop without corrupting the account's permissions. This was addressed by pointing the payload to the neutral location at /Users/Shared then moving the files into place on /Users/deployment/Desktop/ through a post installation script. Everything could be done properly through the script.

Deployment steps are done through a menu based system that implements error correction to prevent missteps. When operator entry is required, the system checks with the student worker to be certain that the step is being done properly. Most importantly, the script gives the students feedback on where they are at in a deployment through a display above the script's main menu. This script now displays, whether or not the computer is bound to the domain, the computer name if it's bound, the Munki repository, and whether or not profiles are installed. System status is queried every time the main menu function runs so that this information remains accurate. Students now only install the enrollment profile but they are directed to do this through the script. The script also takes care of the trickiest part of this process which is the removal of the deployment account, a tricky step made more difficult with encryption.

5.4 Final Check

Once the deployment account is removed, the student worker double checks to make certain that everything is working and runs the Managed Software Center one last time. If at any point in this process they ran across any issue, students are directed to escalate the deployment to a level 3 technician. These professionals are experts in the deployment process who are responsible for building deployments. If everything was fine or it didn't need to be attended to by the Desktop Services team, the Computer is handed back to level 2 techs who take one last look at the ticket before closing it. Deployments are expected to be finished in under 4 hours. In an ideal situation, from beginning to end, this whole process should take less than an hour. Most of the time the computer is unattended thus multiple deployments can run simultaneously.

5.5 In-place vs. Redeployment

In 2015 issues with App Store versions of software prompting users to update apps for which they had no password was generating far too many service requests. To resolve this issue, an "In-place" deployment process was created that skips the re-installation of the operating system and just installs this necessary packages To avoid pushing software that already exists on the client computer, the computer is placed in a slightly different manifest that lacks the iLife applications. This saves 20-30 minutes off a deployment.

This process was initially intensely manual and prone to operator error. The newest version of Mac OS and Server.app offers an option that will simply run scripts. A well trained student worker was able to build this script with the same packages that are used in an in-place deployment. At this stage, errors with a deployment are practically down to one a year.

6. JIRA AND DEPLOYMENTS
6.1 Opportunities within JIRA

When the department moved to JIRA Service desk, it offered exciting new possibilities for deployment workflows. In, Request Tracker, the prior ticketing system, all tickets were similar and there was no good way to distinguish certain steps that needed to be taken. JIRA is far more customizable and it made possible the ability to make a variety of improvements to the deployment process. By creating a deployment issue type, a new timer was created to track resolution times. Because deployments are both essential and mostly automated, it was decided to set the resolution time to only 4 hours. A custom workflow was also created to help streamline the process and improve the communication between student workers and the Technology Support Professionals waiting on the deployment.

6.2 The Deployment Workflow

When a computer is submitted for deployment it sits in the "to do" state. As a student worker works on the device it moves to "In Progress." If, for some reason, progress is halted the issue goes back to the "to do" state. If the student worker is able to complete the deployment without issue and then it goes to a state of "in review." When the issue goes to the "In Review", state ownership of the issue is passed from the student worker to the technology support professional. Technical Support Professionals then review the deployment to make certain everything performs to their standards and may resolve the issue if that is so. Deployments that are returned to the professional incomplete are returned back to the "To Do" state and expected to be handled by the student

workers. Occasionally, issues exist with the point that have to be handled by a Level 3 technician. That is the escalated state which causes the timer of the ticket while the issue is investigated. From the escalated state the student worker works with the Level 3 technician to finish the deployment to the satisfaction of the reporter.

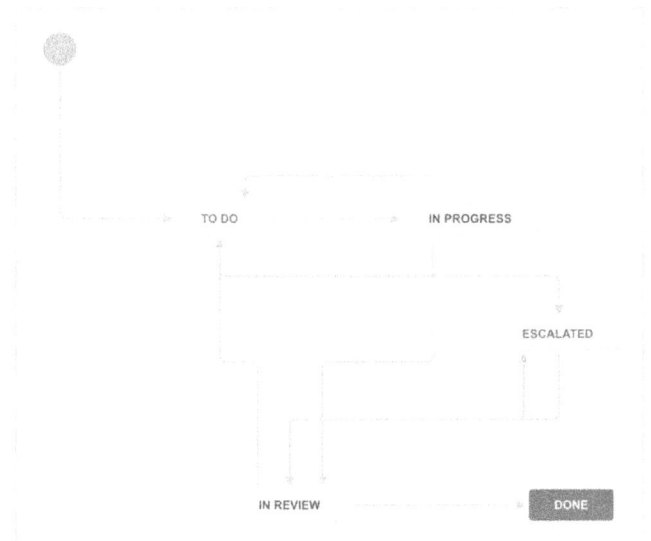

Figure 3: JIRA Deployment Workflow

7. PROBLEMS ALONG THE WAY
7.1 Growing Pains

The road to a good package based deployment is much more complicated than the traditional monolithic image. An in-depth knowledge of the operating system and how it functions is essential for building these sorts of NetInstalls. As such, the path to building a good deployment is fraught with difficulties. However, like solar panels, this is an upfront investment of time. If this time is not available to the primary person performing those deployments, then the method will suffer and not advance as quickly as it could if maintained by someone with enough time to do so. Skunkworks projects require the blessings of management to become official methodologies. While the occasional challenges are many, subsequent deployments are much smoother thanks to the work done when a lab is first constructed.

7.2 Bringing Along the Staff

Co-workers and direct reports can experience a variety of issues when moving to a more complicated deployment methodology. The reliance upon a more complicated deployment system makes troubleshooting issues more difficult for technicians not involved in the process. This can be extremely frustrating for workers who could get around issues more easily in the prior system. Between time constraints and experience levels, it can be difficult (if not impossible), and not cost effective to give Level 1 and Level 2 technicians an in-depth knowledge of this process. Furthermore, relying upon student workers creates its own realm of difficulties.

8. LOOKING FORWARD
8.1 New Systems

While Apple's System Image Utility and Server.app are excellent for getting started with creating and serving NetInstalls, other methods exist for doing so. More robust tools exist for the creation and deployment of NetInstalls. Tools such as

DeployStudio, Imagr, BSDpy, and AutoDMG are all very popular alternatives within the Mac Admin community. Switching to these methods should allow for further automation allowing for smoother deployments.

8.2 Resource Allocations

A recent modification to the team offered the opportunity to move a Level 2 technician to a Level 3 role. This technician will become the Level 3 Mac specialist and will offer a fresh balance to SUNY Geneseo's Level 3 Desktop support. These Level 3 technicians are currently expected to perform both Level 1 support, in the form of a helpdesk shift, and Level 2 support to a small group of users. Removing the burden of Level 2 support and a weekly helpdesk shift is something that needs to be investigated to allow Level 3 technicians to spend more time engineering solutions than they can at present.

9. REFERENCES

[1] AutoPKG Wiki. https://github.com/autopkg/autopkg/wiki

[2] Bruienne, P. Free Your NetBoot Server with BSDpy, Penn State MacAdmins Conference (Aug 2015). https://youtu.be/0WqKrC77eMw

[3] Helm, C. and Willmore, M. Thin OSX Deployment with Munki. Penn State MacAdmins Conference (June 2013). https://youtu.be/uABzxX2KrVw

[4] Munki: Managed Software Installation for OS X. https://www.munki.org/munki/

[5] Neagel, G., What's New with Munki, Penn State MacAdmins Conference (Aug 2015). https://youtu.be/kRmWO52i-4Q

[6] Neagle, G., You Oughta Check Out AutoPkg. Penn State MacAdmins Conference (July 2014). https://youtu.be/mqK-MAEZekI

[7] Trouton R. Managing FileVault2 with fdesetup on OS X Mountain Lion. Penn State MacAdmins Conference 2013. https://youtu.be/fsxtNHj_lY8

[8] Trouton R. and White V. Take Vacations Using this One Weird Trick - Documentation!, Penn State MacAdmins Conference (Aug 2015). https://youtu.be/jgsNxvlfWW8

[9] Walck, N. More Munki Tricks. Penn State MacAdmins Conference (June 2013). https://youtu.be/JbDDqwP7wf8

[10] Willmore, M. Practical Packaging. Penn State MacAdmins Conference (June 2013). https://youtu.be/MjiPNPYWzbI

AwardU: A Formal, Fair, Fun Program
to Honor IT Staff

Vicki Smith
West Virginia University
One Waterfront Place PO Box 6500
Morgantown, WV 26506 USA
+1 304-293-2286
Vicki.Smith@mail.wvu.edu

Steven Marra
West Virginia University
One Waterfront Place PO Box 6500
Morgantown, WV 26506 USA
+1 304-293-3137
Steven.Marra@mail.wvu.edu

ABSTRACT

In 2014, we began to create an employee recognition program for about 110 employees in the Office of Information Technology at West Virginia University. Immediately after initiating the project, the Chief Information Officer announced that our unit would be merging with several others, more than doubling in size under the new name, Information Technology Services. We needed a way to not only recognize good work and good deeds in a timely fashion, but also to create a stronger sense of unity among these newly merged IT organizations with different cultures and practices.

Over six months, a large, diverse committee built a scalable, transparent, accountable, peer-judged program aimed at improving employee morale and retention. With both positive and negative examples of past, unstructured, personality-dependent programs in mind, the AwardU Committee designed a system that is fair, unbiased and inclusive. With well thought-out definitions of recognizable excellence and three categories, we have awards that anyone in ITS can win, regardless of the nature of their duties.

Determining key ITS values and principles helped us design a meaningful, rule-driven program that staff would use, appreciate and support, all within the confines of financially restrictive state ethics laws regarding employee recognition. The RockIT Awards were designed BY employees FOR employees. The program today is formal, fair and fun, complete with an awards breakfast, unique prizes and hand-poured metal trophies that travel among winners like the Stanley Cup in the NHL.

"This program is bigger than any of us, required all of us and is made to continue without us," Chairman Steven Marra told the committee after our first year. Six quarters in, we have a charter, functional data, formative notes and anecdotes we believe could help others emulate this program even as it continues to evolve.

Keywords
Awards; Agile Management; Employee Recognition; Employee Retention; Management Morale.

SIGUCCS '16, November 06-09, 2016, Denver, CO, USA
© 2016 ACM. ISBN 978-1-4503-4095-3/16/11...$15.00
DOI: http://dx.doi.org/10.1145/2974927.2974947

1. INTRODUCTION

When several IT units merged to form Information Technology Services in 2014, many employees were anxious and uncertain about the future. Each unit had a different operational culture and leadership style, so our new entity lacked cohesion and shared purpose. With key positions vacant for months or years and four CIOs in five years, turnover was a continuing problem. When a talented young database administrator said she didn't know how much she was appreciated until she'd resigned, we began to recognize a problem and think about a solution.

An employee in the Project Management unit approached the Communications Director about creating an Employee Recognition Program (ERP) to improve morale and help retain employees by formally acknowledging outstanding performers. Both were new employees who had recently come from the private sector and had experience with robust, well managed, structured programs they believed we could emulate. They sought the blessing of the CIO to explore the concept and to identify the organizational values to reward. These values became the foundation of our categories: Role Model; Innovator; and Outreach. [1]

There were ERPs in some pre-merger units. There were also some perceptions of favoritism and a lack of employee buy-in. The first step was to determine if those connotations could be overcome. The Project Manager and Communications Director assembled a group representing an array of position and personality types in ITS. The first meeting of these volunteers, led by the project manager-turned-Chairman, involved no one from management. The discussions were a frank, honest exploration of past frustrations and shortcomings. Allowed to vent without fear of retribution, employees did so. By the end, the chairman wasn't sure the ERP would survive. But a week later, the group reconvened, energized by the cathartic discussion and determined to do an ERP right.

A Human Resources representative was enlisted to ensure compliance with state ethics, purchasing and other laws, and the committee had a small management presence by design. Great pains were taken to ensure it remained employee-focused and - driven. At every step, the committee tried to include the department at large in the process, even soliciting suggestions from staff then inviting them to vote on the name, the RockIT Awards. The committee determined that the umbrella program would be called AwardU, while the RockIT Awards would become our unique franchise of that program.

Eighteen months later, we have received 89 nominations and granted 11 RockIT awards. While our process relies on different judges each quarter, they consistently uphold the bar that has been set for the winners and the spirit of the program, declining to grant awards when nominations lack detail or examples. Awards are given thoughtfully, not automatically.

Table 1. Number of RockIT Award nominations by quarter

NUMBER OF NOMINATIONS (TOTAL PER QUARTER)

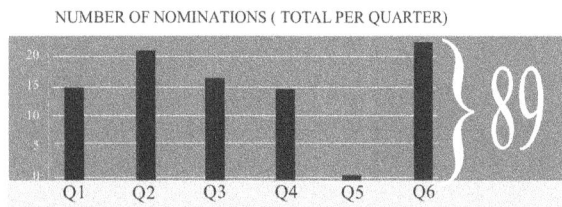

2. APPROACH

Democracy can be slow, but it is essential for buy-in. The AwardU Committee understood that to succeed, our work had to be inclusive. We voted on every decision, from the design of the iconography and the physical awards to the content of our website [2] and the functionality of the app to submit a nomination. Discussions on principles and processes were animated as we challenged each other's deeply held beliefs and built the charter piece by piece for nine months. Collectively, we had to create something that would become institutional and self-sustaining, without depending on a single personality or CIO to survive and thrive.

The groundwork was simple and structural at first but grew increasingly complex as we worked through endless details and scenarios: Who can/can't nominate? Who is/isn't eligible? Who will judge and how? What are the prizes? How do we make it fun? How do we eliminate favoritism? Is anonymous judging possible? What do we do when there's a tie? How do we recognize the winners? Should we provide an opt-out for people who don't like attention? What role, if any, should senior management have?

For credibility at all levels, we created a limited check-and-balance system to ensure that people were properly credited for work and that there was not a legal or HR reason to exclude a nominee. That led to both a small vetting role for our HR representative and for the ITS Senior Staff, who can challenge the judges' selections only within the narrowest confines using a checklist. After six quarters, a challenge has yet to occur.

For our colleagues to support what we created, they, too, needed a sense of ownership. But we faced numerous challenges, including how to make the recognition meaningful under a West Virginia law that limits expenditures on recognition gifts to $25 per employee per year. We also had a one-time start-up budget of just $3,000.

Ultimately, we settled on a prize package containing: a one-of-a-kind T-shirt and enamel pin with RockIT Award branding; a certificate we can print at nominal cost; virtual recognition on the AwardU website and in the University's cross-campus Climb Higher website [3]; and temporary possession of our unique RockIT Award trophies. It was important to the AwardU Committee that we have trophies designed by our group to reflect the unique nature of our program, our work and our people. We tried hard to use local businesses when able, and we were fortunate to have a committee member with a sculptor friend. Michael Loop created our three trophies within our budget, and even allowed our members to attend the metal pouring. It was a unifying experience for the committee that resulted in unique and impressive products.

By paying for them from our start-up budget and working with a WVU instructor and metal artist, we are able to give the program literal weight and remain in compliance with the ethics law limits on employee recognition awards.

We also needed a way to ensure fairness, forcing the judges to focus on the work, not the personality, of the nominees. That meant creating a process in which nominations are scrubbed of names and reviewed anonymously. Though even some committee members were skeptical that anonymous judging could work, it has. The identities of the nominees and the winners remain secret, known only to the Chairman, the Administrator, the HR representative and the Senior Staff until the day of the RockIT Awards ceremony.

More significant were the cultural challenges of the IT environment. Many people were not naturally communicative or comfortable with attention. Some had been reluctant to talk about their work, with some of those actively discouraged by former supervisors. Some had been subjected to a rigid, military-style chain of command and were not inclined to share information about themselves or others, even when positive. Some are simply introverted, horrified by the thought of standing in front of 200 people to accept an award. And some legitimately want to guard their own information intensely, leery of social engineering and concerned about privacy because of high levels of access they have to secure IT systems. For these reasons, we give our winners private notification and the ability to opt out of the public presentation. After six quarters, not one winner has opted out.

3. EXECUTION & BUY-IN

Once we had the broad strokes and enough detail to launch our program, we had to sell it. Because we had assembled a diverse group of IT staff with a wide range of talents, we were able to design and create an engaging, dynamic campaign for our product. Collectively, we built the AwardU website and the online application that accepts submissions. We designed visually compelling iconography and promotional collateral ranging from posters and calling cards to the colorful wall vinyls that not only brighten up a gray cube farm but bear the names of the winners in perpetuity.

We also recognized the need to respectfully retire old wall plaques from previous recognition programs, the last of which had not been updated in more than five years. We removed the plaques, attached the name plates to specially created cards, and delivered them to every past recipient, giving them the opportunity to display them in their workspace or at home with tiny easels. It was an important step toward uniting the once distinct units and guiding them to a shared path forward.

We created a visual presentation about the program and presented it to the ITS Leadership team, a group of about 40 directors, assistant directors and managers. Then we held open houses with Q&A sessions for all staff, complete with rocket-shaped cookies and coffee. We sought three volunteers to serve as our initial panel of judges, and we talked about the program in our respective units throughout ITS to get people interested.

For all our planning and preparation, the AwardU Committee still thought of our first quarter as a test launch. To our surprise, however, we received 15 nominations in the inaugural quarter, and the judges granted two awards – one for Outreach and one for Role Model.

On our first award day, we convened in the lobby of One Waterfront Place with a curious crowd. Outreach winner Ted Wiles of Desktop Management & Outbound Support was a well-known and outgoing employee, recognized for charitable work. Our first Role Model winner, Brian Gibson of Networking, was chosen for his quiet but unsurpassed dedication to the job – so quiet that the vast majority of ITS didn't know who he was. Even the judges were surprised when his name was announced. That was our first proof the program was solid: We had successfully focused on the work, not the personalities. Our "test" was a success, and the RockIT Awards were off and running.

Table 2. Award types and winners by quarter

RockIT Award judges have the power to choose winners and decide that no nomination merits an award. The Innovator award, arguably the toughest category to win because of its specific, high standards, has been issued only three times.

4. RESULTS & CHALLENGES

Our inaugural quarter was a resounding success. It was also the start of a continuing pattern: With each round of awards, we encounter new scenarios we hadn't anticipated, questions the AwardU Committee must answer and challenges we must solve. We consider this a sign of a healthy organization, and we remain eager to evolve and improve. Without feedback and change, we may not be meeting either our own goals or the needs of our department.

The first and most significant problems we encountered were a lack of understanding of the award categories and what kind of activity would qualify under each. Though we had shared our definitions, few people took time to read the charter, so we responded with the same information in digestible formats. We produced small, colorful cards that people could take and keep at their desks, and we placed those along with posters on all three floors of our building. We also offered the services of the ITS Administrator (Communications Director) to help choose a category in confidential conversations. The definitions include a vision, but by design, they are fluid enough for the nominator to find the appropriate fit. Outreach, for example, can be interpreted to mean within the WVU community and/or the scope of ITS work, or within our city, state or region. The current definitions of each award category follow.

ROLE MODEL:
The importance of having a role model can never be underestimated. Role models help inspire us and drive us. They can help us to focus, to define and achieve goals, and to constantly redefine and strive for success. A role model can be a coach/mentor, teacher, supervisor/manager, or colleague. The Role Model award honors people who embody qualities considered critical to the

success of ITS - positive attitude, collaboration, leadership, initiative and imagination.

INNOVATOR:
The innovation award is designed to showcase and recognize creative thinking in all areas of management and operations, whether you've come up with a clever solution to a problem or found a way to save ITS time, money, or both. At a time when everyone is exploring new options, it's a great source of both ideas and recognition for your achievements. The award is given for projects or initiatives that represent "innovation" in the true sense of the word; that is, the development of a new, more creative, more effective or more efficient approach to any aspect of management or operations.

OUTREACH:
The purpose of this award is to recognize outstanding individuals whose outreach embodies WVU's mission to enhance the well-being and quality of life of West Virginians. The outreach award honors significant contributions to the community, whether locally, regionally or nationally. Exceptional service to civic, and charitable groups may be considered, as well as other contributions that enrich a community's quality of life. This activity may but does not have to support the University's strategic goals for outreach, such as delivering lifelong educational opportunities and stimulating economic growth. Work being nominated also may: support WVU's research mission; empower faculty; support student success; facilitate access of under-represented populations; or improve the integration of specific groups of students, professionals or scholars.

The second major challenge we encountered is perhaps more pronounced in an IT environment, where people are often not comfortable with or confident in their use of the written word. Some nominators struggled not only with finding the right and relevant words to express their thoughts, but also the ability to provide specifics instead of generalities. The first nominations were extremely brief, with an average word count of 85. Those nominations often did not provide the judges enough substance on which to evaluate the nominee. The more concrete details and examples the nominator provides, the greater the likelihood of impressing the judges.

Again, we responded with an outreach initiative. To our Frequently Asked Questions [4] we added an item with **five tips** for creating a stronger nomination, then distributed them by email and posted them on our website. We also offered the services of the resident writer in ITS, the Administrator (Communications Director) in improving draft nominations. A handful of staff took advantage of this invitation.

By the second quarter, our average word count jumped to 132. We believe this indicated that people understood they needed to provide more detail. The nominations that won weren't and aren't always the longest, but they are the most detailed. By our sixth quarter, the average word county hit 279, with several nominations approaching 600 words. This metric indicates not only the understanding of what it takes to win, but growing comfort with the process and expressing thoughts in a convincing way.

Table 3. Average word count of nominations by quarter

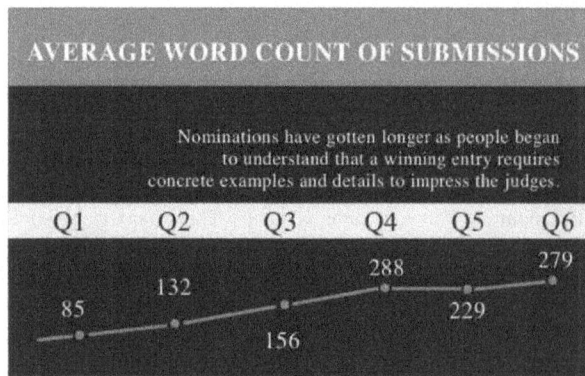

AVERAGE WORD COUNT OF SUBMISSIONS

Nominations have gotten longer as people began to understand that a winning entry requires concrete examples and details to impress the judges.

Q1	Q2	Q3	Q4	Q5	Q6
85	132	156	288	229	279

Recently, the committee decided to resubmit runners-up if/when they are designated by the judges. This actually grew from the word count issue. During our fifth quarter of the program, the three months ending Dec. 31, 2015, we experienced a sudden and alarming drop in participation. Only one nomination was submitted for the quarter. Again, the committee faced an unexpected scenario and had to create a process: We let the judges evaluate it, and when they decided it was not award-worthy, we resubmitted it with the Q1 nominations for 2016. The AwardU Committee engaged people about the drop in nominations, identifying a number of likely causes for the lack of interest:

- Multiple projects in ITS came to a close at the end of the calendar year, and people were exhausted. Some said they were too busy or too tired to nominate. We responded by reminding people that good work can't be celebrated if others don't know about it and by encouraging them to submit the same work during the subsequent quarter.
- Some people reported feeling demoralized after significant changes to the performance evaluation process in the late summer and fall of 2015, and this may have translated into both lack of self-confidence and enthusiasm for lifting up others. We reminded people that RockIT Award nominations and awards can be valuable tools in the self-evaluation process that precedes supervisory evaluations.
- We learned that people didn't understand some key rules for the program, including that there is no "statute of limitations" for submitting a nomination. Regardless of when the work was performed, it can be considered. We also learned that people didn't know they could submit three nominations per quarter instead of just one, or that they could resubmit nominations that didn't win. We responded by creating a five-question infographic in a Q&A format and distributing to staff twice during the first quarter of 2016.

The AwardU Committee convenes almost every Friday for one hour, committed to constant refinement and documentation of our processes, guidelines and other aspects of our charter to address these kinds of challenges.

We have changed the scoring system for our judges and begun resubmitting runners-up for the subsequent quarter. Both of these changes were recommended by our judges, who consistently provide excellent feedback and guidance for the program.

When we launched the program, we selected a member of the committee to serve as an informal facilitator, explaining the rules and process for picking winners to our first batch of judges. This position has proved so surprisingly valuable that we have formalized it and added it to the charter. The facilitator's interactions with the judges offer unique insight and always produce possible opportunities for improvement. We plan to train apprentice facilitators, ensuring continuity and consistency over time.

We created rules for filling vacancies on the AwardU Committee and on the judging panel when an award is withheld. We expanded the number of senior managers in ITS who are now ineligible for nomination, further focusing our efforts on recognition for the staff. And we created rules for ourselves for enacting these changes, ensuring we have an appropriate quorum for conducting business.

Throughout the first 18 months of the program, we have constantly sought feedback to address both the functional and human challenges of sustaining interest in the ERP. We have held several open houses and even invited staff to attend a committee meeting to watch us work. One encouraging sign is the interest we receive when we solicit volunteers for the judging process: Within an hour, we usually have a handful of people eager to participate, and we have had as many as seven. This suggests an interest in not only understanding the process but being part of it.

After our inaugural quarter and the tremendous turnout, we also realized we needed a different plan for the recognition ceremony itself. Our office building lacks a conference space large enough for even half our staff. At the CIO's urging, we forged an arrangement with a restaurant next door to host our event in the morning, before their lunch rush, and the event is now a combined CIO Quarterly Update for the staff and awards ceremony. Again, we are choosing to support a locally owned establishment that our employees often patronize. The change of scenery was enthusiastically received, and the event is also now an opportunity for the CIO to interact directly with staff. This change also has minimal cost at $400 per event, compared with $1,000-2,000 to rent a ballroom at the next closest location, a hotel ballroom.

5. EVOLUTION

To ensure the RockIT Awards continue to evolve and improve, the AwardU Committee will keep calling upon our judges, among others, for suggestions. A judge's insight is particularly valuable because it is different from that of the committee members, who are intimately familiar with the ethos of the program and the structural components that guide it. The judges also have a greater understanding of the mechanics and challenges of the program than the typical ITS staffer, who likely has only a general familiarity with and understanding of the rules.

In an April 2016 survey, a handful of prior judges suggested areas to contemplate going forward, including the need to:

- Identify a way to celebrate "small wins" in day-to-day work, such as compiling them into a single nomination that recognizes a body of work rather than "earth-shattering accomplishments;"
- Help judges determine whether nominees from units other than their own are just performing their job duties as formally described or are going above and beyond;
- Consider limiting the word counts of the nominations, which some judges now believe are too long;
- And consider whether Team nominations should be judged differently and/or separate from Individual nominations.

The AwardU Committee sees its charter as a living document that should evolve by consensus. We are not founders who laid down rules never meant to be broken. To the contrary, we collectively encourage, discuss and support change. After each award ceremony, the members solicit feedback from colleagues. The group then gathers to report back the impressions, some of which lead to alterations of the program.

This approach is what project management professionals call "agile management," or an iterative, incremental process for designing and executing software projects successfully. After each change in a small window of time, we look at the entire system from top to bottom with brutal honesty and transparency about both successes and failures. Agile management requires openness to consistent constructive criticism, as well as non-hierarchical forms of leadership.

"In an agile paradigm, every aspect of development — requirements, design, etc. — is continually revisited throughout the lifecycle. When a team stops and re-evaluates the direction of a project every two weeks, there's always time to steer it in another direction. ... Development using an agile methodology preserves a product's critical market relevance and ensures a team's work doesn't wind up on a shelf, never released." [5]

6. THE FUTURE

The AwardU program at West Virginia University was always intended to be scalable and adaptable. Theoretically, it could be expanded to include college, department or other technical staff who work independently of central IT. Non-IT units on campus could adapt it to meet their particular needs, too. The AwardU framework is there, and the RockIT Awards can be a template.

Through countless hours of volunteer effort, we developed a shared understanding of what constitutes individual value within our organization, and what traits we should collectively celebrate and emulate. The committee identified several factors we consider key to our own success and recommend they be considered by those trying to emulate this program.

- Committee members must, to some extent, be capable of selfless labor. For our inaugural quarter, we agreed all members would be exempt from nomination. The Chairman, too, waives the right to be nominated. We do not receive, nor do we expect any recognition for the work we do on the AwardU program. As a group, we are all driven by the satisfaction of creating something that works. We genuinely revel in seeing the hard work of others rewarded and publicly acknowledged.
- Titles and egos are left at the door in every meeting. All committee members must focus on the collective goal and the end results. All voices must be equal, all opinions must be handled respectfully, and all ideas should be debated fully. In the meeting room, there are no directors or subordinates. It is, in fact, so democratic that several AwardU members have described this group as the healthiest, most productive and must functional committee they've ever served on.
- Discussions, pending decisions and final actions must be reduced to writing and shared with all members so those who are unable to attend a meeting remain fully informed

and engaged. This ensures their continued participation, as well as their ability to speak knowledgeably to other ITS employees about the program.
- Vision and values must be shared. Although all ideas come in the door, some never go out. All members must remain prepared to adapt or even withdraw an idea, and we often persuade each other to embrace a different point of view. All conversation and, ultimately, action derive from the same objective: We do what is best for the program.
- The committee must be representative of the organization. It must have a balance of both newer and longer-term employees. It must reflect the array of positions and personalities within the organization, or at least include those able and willing to speak on behalf of that diversity to ensure all perspectives are considered. Its members must be high-energy but reasonable, thoughtful and articulate; unafraid to speak up and, above all, concerned about the well-being of the organization.

A few days after the Q1 2016 awards ceremony, the committee received the following message from Role Model winner, Ardell Moree of our Research IT team:

"Thank you for developing a program that motivates all of us to look for each other's positive contributions. It has made me see more -- the subtle efforts of some and the levels of dedication in others. I am grateful to be more aware of the positive energies that I would have otherwise taken for granted."

7. ACKNOWLEDGMENTS

We thank our current committee members for their diligence and sustained passion for this project: Terry Nebel; Jim Dunlevy; Brandi Shafer; Jamie Simmons; Lisa Bridges; Susan Walker; Kathy Fletcher; Brandon Foster; Rich Finnigan; and Stacey Kearns. We are also grateful to our former members: founder and first chairman Mike Rozycki; application developer Ashley Mulligan; website developer Josh Cook; and members Terri Sobel, Audrey Holsclaw, Jennifer Bennett; Barry Wilt; and Deborah Sartin. Finally, we must express our appreciation to Associate Provost & Chief Information Officer John P. Campbell for trusting us to work independently and providing the small start-up budget we needed, and for his continuing enthusiasm, including the personal presentation of the awards at our quarterly ceremony and CIO Update.

8. REFERENCES & LINKS

[1] http://rockit.awardu.wvu.edu/#about

[2] http://rockit.awardu.wvu.edu

[3] http://climbhigher.wvu.edu

[4] http://rockit.awardu.wvu.edu/#faqs

[5] http://agilemethodology.org

At Your Service: The NC State Experience Managing the Google Service Team

Sarah H. Noell
NC State University
PO Box 7109
Raleigh, NC 27695-7109
+1 919-515-5420
sarah@ncsu.edu

ABSTRACT

Formed in 2012 after NC State "went Google," the Google Service Team (GST), made up of staff from different units in the Office of Information Technology as well as representatives from across campus, has thrived and meets on a regular, most often weekly, basis. This service team model has been successful in running an enterprise-wide cloud service, in part because of a clear mission and solid representation from outside of the central IT organization. Additionally, service ownership has given a single point of contact and continuity in decision-making. The GST also helps streamline requests, issues, and escalations across teams as IT staff know where and how to funnel these items.

This paper and presentation will discuss NC State's Google Service Team (GST), including its mission and structure (including ties into governance) and the challenges and rewards of running and managing an enterprise-wide cloud service for both the team members and customer base.

CCS Concepts

• Social and professional topics ~ Project and people management
• Social and professional topics ~ Computing organizations

Keywords

Service Teams; Governance; Team Morale.

1. INTRODUCTION

In 2010 NC State University "went Google," and in 2012 the Google Service Team (GST) was officially organized and given a charter as a team. This team has a broad and diverse make-up and continues to thrive and meet on a weekly basis. The service team members were carefully selected to provide a team that was diverse in skills, cross-functional across units in Office of Information Technology (OIT) and across campus. The team provides the institution with a known service owner and single point-of-contact for this service. Moreover, it provides decision-making continuity and a repository of institutional memory.

As Google continues to enhance its services for higher education and expand their offering of available Consumer Apps, the GST

SIGUCCS '16, November 06-09, 2016, Denver, CO, USA
© 2016 ACM. ISBN 978-1-4503-4095-3/16/11...$15.00
DOI: http://dx.doi.org/10.1145/2974927.2974953.

continues to evolve its business processes and works closely with governance on campus to stay abreast of issues and policies. The GST also keeps campus informed of the changes and challenges in running a service that is in the cloud, enterprise-wide, and constantly changing.

2. DEFINITIONS OF SERVICES AND SERVICE TEAMS

The concept of services and service teams is not new, but it has gained more traction and awareness as more IT organizations look to incorporate the ITIL (Information Technology Infrastructure Library) framework into their business processes. ITIL defines a service as:

> *A means of delivering value to customers by facilitating outcomes customers want to achieve without the ownership of specific costs and risks.* [1]

The ability to make use of a service without having to account for other variables inherent in running a service, such as ongoing costs (e.g., infrastructure, personnel), support, training, and potential risks of running such a service.

Every IT organization is a service provider of multiple services usually involving both customer-facing services and backend infrastructure support services. The services offered are only as good as the organization that is running them; without strong management support for resources and awareness of customer needs, the services could be providing less value than they should. Service teams can help make sure that services are providing value both internally to the organization and to your customer base. A service team is typically responsible for a particular service offered by that organization, such as web services, data and voice networks, or email and calendaring services. Regardless of the service, it needs to be managed and be given the necessary resources so that it can continue to provide value to your customers as well as being as efficient and effective as it can be.

While there are different ways to define a service team, they tend to share common characteristics such as providing service-related information and input as well as recommendations to management. Service teams can be formal or informal and, depending on the service, the composition of the team should include IT staff from various units within the central IT organization, as well as having representation from customers and other stakeholders.

3. DRIVING FACTORS LEADING TO THE CREATION OF THE GST

NC State is a public, land-grant university that, while providing many IT services centrally, still has a fairly decentralized IT structure. All major colleges on campus have their own IT director; in larger colleges, there may also be IT managers and staff dedicated to individual departments. While coordination with central IT services has improved over the years, NC State remains fairly decentralized for some services.

In 2009, NC State hired its first Chief Information Officer (CIO) and prior to his arrival, the two central IT organizations were merged into one. Pre-merger, NC State was operating on the outdated model of "administrative" and "academic" computing organizations.

With two separate IT organizations, NC State was also running two separate email and calendaring systems: the academic side (faculty, students, and some staff who supported students) was using an open-source email system, Cyrus, and the administrative side used GroupWise (administrators, staff, and faculty that had administrative responsibilities). Previous attempts (about 4) to evaluate and agree on a single email and calendaring system had all failed and had left both our end users and IT staff burned out, frustrated, and with few resources to run either system well. In short, quite a sour mood existed on campus.

In an attempt to bring unity to the email situation, shortly before the CIO came on board, a decision was made to bring all staff and faculty on board to use GroupWise and students (plus some faculty/staff) would stay on Cyrus. But as these things usually turn out, having students and faculty on different systems is often an exercise in frustration.

When Marc Hoit, our new Chief Information Officer/Vice Chancellor for Information Technology (CIO/VCIT), arrived on campus, one of his first mandates was to fix email and calendar on campus by bringing everyone under one umbrella including students. A great concept that had failed before, but this time it *had to succeed*; we had one central IT organization and a desire to finally get it right! A large, diverse team was formed to:

- Evaluate options for students and involve students in this process
- Evaluate these same options for faculty and staff.

At the time of the evaluation two major products existed: Microsoft Live and Google Apps for Education (GAE). NC State selected Google Apps for Education as its email and calendaring platform. Students, faculty and staff on Cyrus would migrate first and the administrators and all other faculty and staff on GroupWise would follow.

The team that had worked on the evaluation of options morphed into the migration team for moving to Google. The *NexGen Implementation Team* was formed and it was the success of this highly diverse and experienced team that would provide the initial foundation for the GST.

However it wasn't just the email side of things that was changing. The VCIT, wanting to keep the momentum going for collaboration and partnership that his arrival was forging, needed to have ongoing efforts for partnerships and information sharing as well as beginning to lay the foundations for a strong IT governance infrastructure. The VCIT formed a new group composed of Campus IT Directors (CITD).

The CITD is the university-wide, top-level committee of campus IT personnel whose focus is on maintaining a broad technical awareness of the IT environment internally and externally, with an eye toward reducing duplication of effort, consolidating resources,

fostering innovation, and scaling solutions that have broad appeal or usefulness. [2]

The mission of the CITD fit well with how OIT was envisioning running a service such as Google and creating a service team to be responsible for the service.

4. THE GST: CHARTER AND COMPOSITION

NC State's migration from Cyrus was a relatively easy transition and was completed in 2010. The harder work was migrating faculty and staff from GroupWise and the impending changes to their business processes. After months of hard work, we finally had everything ready and on November 30, 2011, NC State *went Google*!

The next step was to pull together the service team and transition from a project to a service.

The initial scope of the team was straightforward:

The Google Apps, Email and Calendaring Service Team as a whole will be responsible for the coordination and delivery of email and calendaring for the campus. This will include items like the core Google Apps, mail relays, Majordomo2 list service, Postini message security/archiving/discovery, along with training and support for these services. Because Google Apps, email and calendaring interface with so many areas, the team will include members of or partner closely with other groups working on related services, such as unified communications, file services, mobile computing, security & compliance, learning management systems, identity management. [3]

It was a large scope for a team, but Google is a large service and is better suited to being managed by a service owner and service team for several reasons:

- Google is a cloud-based service and as such, OIT has limited control on how it is configured and administered;
- Google services and apps can change quickly; sometimes we can control the change and sometimes we cannot. It can also be difficult to gauge the impact of a change;
- Google is used by all faculty, staff, and students *on a daily basis*. Constant oversight and management is a must.

The makeup of the team that would manage Google would be crucial to its success as a solid, responsive service. As anyone who leads or participates on a team knows, successful, productive teams tend to share one major characteristic: the team members work well together. They respect each other, respect differences of opinion, and are willing to compromise for the better good of the service and end users.

Now in our 4th year as a team, there is a good, solid working relationship among team members. While some team members have changed due to turnover, no one has "quit" the GST. I believe this speaks to the value that the team is providing for campus as well as the value that the team members receive from being on a team that stays active, positive and healthy.

Good working teams also have active and engaged team members who take their role as stakeholders in the service offering seriously. With the GST, we've found this engagement to be crucial because of the breadth and depth of Google services that have become integrated into the campus DNA. As a team, we've found that sometimes what seems a simple tweak, in an environment like Google, may not be simple or may have broader ramifications and thus is anything but simple. It takes the whole team participating to stay on top of things.

4.1 Roles and Responsibilities

The service owner is responsible for:

- facilitating the meetings, keeping the discussions productive and forward moving;
- reporting back to management and Governance groups on a regular basis;
- providing a single point of contact for issues and requests;
- providing the voice and appropriate communications back out to stakeholders;
- representing the GST at various campus meetings and providing updates;
- providing overall structure and coordination of GST activities and priorities;
- submitting projects for approval and recommendations for service changes.

The team members are responsible for:
- being engaged stakeholders for their constituency and participating actively on the team;
- bringing their expertise to the discussions on Google services as well as sharing information and projects from their respective units on issues that may impact the GST;
- keeping their management informed of GST activities and priorities and how these fit in (or do not) with their overall job responsibilities;
- representing the GST at various campus meetings when their expertise is required.

As a working team, members will have action items and responsibilities assigned to them with the expectation they will take ownership of the item and reach back out to the team if there are issues or questions.

One potentially tricky aspect of managing a service team is that the service owner is not the manager of all the team members, and that is very much the case for this team. This is where the strong mandate and charter that this team has is important for keeping work and projects flowing. In addition, management has been very supportive of requests for staff time adjustments and project priority shuffling when necessary.

5. GOVERNANCE, MANAGEMENT AND THE GST

As noted earlier, our CIO implemented a stronger, more expansive IT governance structure [4] for information technology to help address the decentralization of IT on campus by improving coordination and collaboration, reducing inefficient use of resources, duplication of effort and conflicting policies.

This new IT governance structure offered a clear framework for overarching processes and structures regarding decisions pertaining to goals, policies, investment, infrastructure, and architectures. Guidance on resolving disputes, responsibility and accountability and methods for input and analysis of issues and options are also articulated.

From a *governance perspective*, the GST works closely with the Campus IT Directors (CITD) as well as the IT Strategic Advisory Committee (ITSAC) and several of their sub-committees (e.g., Client & Application Support sub-committee; Security and Compliance sub-committee).

From an *operational perspective*, the GST has a fair amount of independence to manage the infrastructure and perform system administration duties in our Google environment to keep our domain running smoothly as well as securely. The GST involves management when we are proposing changes that will have a large impact on our customer base, especially if it involves wholesale infrastructure changes.

For most operational changes the GST informs management that a change has been submitted to our change management system. The campus community is notified of changes either through a general email or via a larger, more comprehensive education campaign.

5.1 Real World Example: Phishing

Our policies and approach to phishing is a good example of how the University's governance structure and a strong service team work together to put into place better controls for a safer campus service. The steps required for compromised account holders to reactivate their account is a policy issue; the technical, back-end procedure and Help Desk assistance to get those accounts administratively disabled and then re-enabled is operational.

In 2014, the GST recommended strengthening our phishing policy so that penalties were clearly defined and the Help Desk and Security and Compliance had some "teeth" to handle repeat offenders. At the time, the GST believed a "three strikes" policy would be sufficient with the third incident resulting in students visiting Student Conduct and employees either visiting Human Resources or a discussion with their manager on potential impact of a compromised account. In addition, we encouraged the user to turn on 2-step. Graduated students, who typically can retain an account for life, would lose their account after three strikes.

In 2016, compromised accounts and phishing continue to increase at an unprecedented pace and the GST, in cooperation with the CITD and our CIO are recommending we move forward with a "one-phish / 2-step" policy (leveraging Google's 2 step verification). The GST reworked our compromised account policy and now phished account holders are put into an administratively managed group that enforces Google's 2-step verification. There are no exceptions to this policy.

The formalization of this process allowed the Google Administrators, the Help Desk, and Security and Compliance teams to perform their tasks, including developing tools for easier account clean up and reactivation with 2-step enabled.

Implementing a procedure such as this is not trivial and requires a great deal of time and effort from several team members on different fronts: tool development for Help Desk staff; cleanup processes for admins and security staff; and an education campaign for our campus community (faculty, staff, and students).

6. MANAGING THE BREADTH OF OPTIONS FROM GOOGLE

It's not just policies for security that we deal with; we get a lot of requests for various apps and add-ons that Google makes available. If you are a Google campus, you are aware of the vast array of Consumer and Marketplace Apps and Add-ons that you *could* enable for your campus. At NC State the GST, in conjunction with our software licensing unit, developed a working procedure for evaluating the risk that these types of products may present to our domain and end users.

Currently we have a broad range of Google features being used at NC State:

- Collaboration and sharing of information with Drive and associated apps (docs, sheets, etc.)
- Synchronous communication using hangouts and chat
- Email and Google Groups for communicating and sharing
- Calendar resources for individual, unit, and shared resources including appointment slots for faculty and students
- Sites for portfolio projects in classes
- Generic accounts for departmental resources that shouldn't be owned by an individual
- Consumer Apps that provide additional opportunities and resources for classes, staff, and faculty; a few are listed below
  - Google Maps
  - Google Analytics
  - YouTube
  - Google+
  - Chrome webstore
  - Google Books

Initially NC State turned on only the Core Apps; however, as more requests for Consumer and Marketplace Apps came in, a standard process was needed so that these apps could be evaluated for risk and an assessment of whether or not to deploy. This risk analysis and vetting of an app's impact (good and bad) is especially important since Google can be integrated into so many other business processes.

Click-wrap agreements [5] are an excellent example of delegated risk assessment. Our Google environment became a pilot project for delegated risk assessment from the Office of General Counsel. Risk assessments can be done by our software licensing manager if they fall below a certain monetary threshold ($5,000), which most of these requests meet. The procedure to review and accept terms of service that was developed for Google is now standard procedure on our campus.

Requests for apps come into the GST and are shared with our software licensing manager to review the Terms of Service. Together we review the app from both a security perspective as well as value-add to the campus and we attempt to answer the following:

On a scale of one to ten, if this app is enabled, what is the potential for something bad to occur and if that bad something does occur, what is the likely impact?

Items that the GST uses to help evaluate risk include:

- Cloudlock user trust ratings
- Permissions the app is asking for (contacts, email, docs/drive, location) and specifically, are the permissions required too broad given the functionality of the app?
- Overall impact to campus community if we enabled this app (i.e., does it appear for everyone, or only if they use it)

The concept of risk versus reward is somewhat tied to almost every decision for enabling / disabling anything in our Google domain. In addition, it is used when we are prioritizing workflow and projects. If we refer back to the phishing example, we have prioritized our first three projects for the next few months to focus on back-end infrastructure rather than customer facing requests. Fortunately, some of the back-end work that we are doing involves group automation and this will ultimately benefit things like Google Classroom since the work we are doing now will provide the framework for the tie-in to our LMS system.

Other projects in the pipeline that we will be focusing on over the next year include:

- Implementing One phish / 2-step policy changes
- Enabling Sender Policy Framework (SPF) and DomainKeys Identified Mail (DKIM)
- Annual renewals for graduated student and retirees accounts
- Enabling Google classroom
- Chrome Device management
- Celebrating 5 years of being a Google campus!

We have more projects and requests than time and we only recently hired our second Google Admin, whose primary responsibilities are to help manage the day-to-day activities that a domain of our size requires. In addition, this second admin helps manage the ".gov" domains we host at NC State and oversees many of our CloudLock policies and processes.

7. CONCLUSION

In summary, OIT's Google Service Team has a clearly defined service and service owner which allows for:

- **Consistency of Message.** All requests, questions, policies, anything to do with Google or email related services come to the GST for discussion. Replies are the voice of the team, regardless of who replies.
- **Single Point of Entry.** In line with the previous point, the GST allows everyone (governance groups, CITD, managers, the CIO, anyone) access to an operational body that they can submit a question to and it will arrive in the right group for discussion. No individual manager is tempted to answer it.
- **Institutional Perspective.** We truly have an OIT cross-functional team as well as diverse representation from campus allowing the team to make decisions with a broader eye to both the risks and rewards that come with changes to our enterprise environment.
- **Leadership Buy-in.** Strong support from management, CITD, and governance on campus. This service team is viewed as a team that listens, considers, and responds responsibly.

The care and feeding of Google requires an active and engaged team, monitoring of the service on a daily basis, keeping abreast of the constant changes, and keeping management and the campus informed of these changes and the impact on their business or academic endeavors and processes and procedures. Thus far, this team has been successful at meeting these responsibilities for the service and to the institution.

8. ACKNOWLEDGMENTS

I'd like to thank the Google Service Team for their hard work and diligence in providing our entire campus community with the tools and resources they need to continue to do their jobs and studies and to be able to investigate and use newer tools and applications in our Google environment. The Google Service Team members are: Tim Lowman, Jason Maners and William Setzer (Google Admins/SMTP relays); Neal McCorkle (Security & Compliance); Katie McInerney and Brian DeConinck (Training and Outreach); Chris King, Nik Davlantis and Noah Genzel (Help Desk); Lee Pipkin (Communication Technologies); David Tredwell & Jeff Webster (campus LMS partner: DELTA); and MeiMei Davis (Academic College partner). I'd also like to thank the management of OIT for their solid support and partnership with the GST.

9. REFERENCES & LINKS

[1] ITIL v3, Service Design

[2] *Campus Information Technology Directors (CITD)*: https://oit.ncsu.edu/governance-strategy/it-governance/committees/campus-it-directors/

[3] Google Service Team Charter; internal document

[4] *IT Governance at NC State*: https://oit.ncsu.edu/governance-strategy/

[5] *Click-wrap agreements at NC State*: https://software.ncsu.edu/clickwraps

Cyberinfrastructure as a Platform to Facilitate Effective Collaboration between Institutions and Support Collaboratories

Eric Coulter
Indiana University Pervasive Technology Institute
2709 E 10th Street
Bloomington, IN 47408
(812) 856-3250
jecoulte@iu.edu

Jeremy Fischer
IUPTI
2709 E 10th Street
Bloomington, IN 47408
(812) 856-0992
jeremy@iu.edu

Barbara Hallock
IUPTI
2709 E 10th Street
Bloomington, IN 47408
(812) 856-2364
bahalloc@iu.edu

Richard Knepper
IUPTI
2709 E 10th Street
Bloomington, IN 47408
(812) 855-9574
rknepper@iu.edu

Dave Lifka
Cornell University
512 Frank H. T. Rhodes Hall
Ithaca, NY 14853
(607) 254-8621
lifka@cornell.edu

JP Navarro
Argonne National Laboratory
Mathematics and Computer Science Division, TCS Building 240
Lemont, IL 60439
(630) 252-1233
navarro@mcs.anl.gov

Marlon Pierce
Science Gateways Research Center / IUPTI
2709 E 10th Street
Bloomington, IN 47408
(812) 856-1212
marpierc@iu.edu

Craig Stewart
IUPTI
2709 E 10th Street
Bloomington, IN 47408
(812) 855-4240
stewart@iu.edu

ABSTRACT

Researchers, scientists, engineers, granting agencies, and increasingly complex research problems have given rise to the scientific "collaboratory"—large organizations that span many institutions, with individual members working together to explore a particular phenomenon. These organizations require computational resources in order to support analyses and to provide platforms where the collaborators can interact. The XSEDE Community Infrastructure (XCI) group assists campuses in using their own resources and promotes the sharing of those resources in order to create collaboratories improving use of the nation's collective cyberinfrastructure. Currently XCI provides toolkits and training, and collaborates with organizations such as ACI-REF, XSEDE Campus Champions, and the Open Science Grid to identify tools and best practices that support the community. This paper discusses the progress in and barriers to developing a robust collaborative environment where computational resources can be shared.

SIGUCCS '16, November 06-09, 2016, Denver, CO, USA
ACM 978-1-4503-4095-3/16/11.
http://dx.doi.org/10.1145/2974927.2974962

Keywords

XCI; XSEDE; Collaboratories; ACI-REF; Open Science Grid; Computation Institute, Globus; Cluster Computing; Collaboration; Big Data; Jetstream; Science Gateways

1. INTRODUCTION

Collaboration is increasingly important to the way that academic work gets done. Nowhere is this more pronounced than in the sciences, where the complexity of certain instruments and the scarcity of funding necessitate that multiple organizations collaborate in order to make the most effective use of the resources available. Additionally, greater transparency in research is driving the need for increased access to the data on which scientific discoveries are predicated, and the amount and variety of such data are growing exponentially as computational capabilities and the complexity of the questions researchers seek to answer increase. Collaboration between institutions also fosters greater understanding, as organizations share insights.

Common tools such as email and file sharing meet many of the basic requirements for effective collaboration. Given the ubiquity of these technologies and their limited capabilities for advanced application, we instead focus this paper on the needs of scientists that go beyond what these technologies can provide. These needs are encompassed in the term cyberinfrastructure, a term popularized by the National Science Foundation (NSF) and now commonly defined in a fashion similar to the following [1]:

Cyberinfrastructure consists of computing systems, data storage systems, advanced instruments and data repositories, visualization environments, and people, all linked together by software and high performance networks to improve research productivity and enable breakthroughs not otherwise possible.

The NSF has prioritized the development of cyberinfrastructure to facilitate scientific collaboration among universities [2] and make collaboratories as effective and innovative as possible.

In this paper we briefly describe several major U,S, cyberinfrastructure projects that aim to aid the operation of collaboratories. We then discuss current efforts designed to improve the effectiveness of cyberinfrastructure services in the support of collaboration and the formation of collaboratories. We discuss the impact of these innovations on collaborative science as well as some of the needs for future development in order to support these activities more fully.

2. COLLABORATORIES

A collaboratory is a specific type of virtual organization—that is, a set of people with a common goal who are connected by a shared cyberinfrastructure need [3]—in which that specific need centers on the facilitation and completion of scientific experimentation. Scientific and technological advances in recent history have meant that scientific work is increasingly being done by groups of researchers in geographically disparate locations. Hence, some expansion on the traditional notion of the "laboratory" becomes necessary [4].

The collaboratory as a concept is a blending of "collaboration" and "laboratory"—"a center without walls, in which researchers can perform their research without regard to physical location-interacting with colleagues, accessing instrumentation, sharing data and computational resources, and accessing information in digital libraries" [3]. The benefits of the collaboratory are multiple and varied, depending on the goals and resources of the organizations participating. Most important, as scientific advances increasingly depend on large teams of experts with diverse backgrounds and expertise, supporting these scientific teams with collaboratories becomes increasingly important. This is not meant to imply that there no brilliant individual investigators are doing important and groundbreaking work; but most new insights today are the result of large collaborative teams.

A number of technologies have been key to the formation of collaboratories; perhaps the most fundamental ones are electronic mail and networking. Since these technologies are well established and unchanging, however, much of the body of the work presented here focuses instead on other resources that are being actively developed by the organizations described.

2.1 Examples of Collaboratories

Two of the largest cyberinfrastructure projects supporting collaboratories are the Open Science Grid and the eXtreme Science and Engineering Discovery Environment (XSEDE). These two cyberinfrastructure projects, and how they support the operation of collaboratories, are described below.

2.1.1 Large Hadron Collider and Open Science Grid

Perhaps the foremost example in modern science of collaborative work among multiple groups brought together by the need to share expensive instruments is the Large Hadron Collider (LHC). The world's largest machine, the LHC is a 27 km ring with four separate particle detectors situated at points around the circle: ATLAS, CMS, ALICE, and LHCb, each with its own set of tasks [5]. A notable result of this massive collaborative effort of over thirty years has been the detection of a particle consistent with the Higgs boson predicted by the Standard Model, which resulted in the joint award of the 2013 Nobel Prize in Physics to François Englert and Peter Higgs [6]. Because of the one-of-a-kind nature of the LHC and the importance of reproducibility in determining the viability of experimental results, the LHC also fits the "data" component of a collaboratory—with estimates in the range of 25 GB/s during run 2 [7]. The Open Science Grid (OSG) [8] is a computational, data analysis grid specifically designed to analyze the data created by the LHC. The OSG grew out of a set of other grid research projects related to physics experiments. It has proved particularly well suited for analyzing data from the LHC for several reasons. First and foremost the nature of the LHC data and the design of the OSG made it possible to ship data from centralized data repositories to distributed computational resources over long-haul networks in a way that well matched the amount of data shipped to a remote computing environment and the amount of computing to be done, managing a ratio of the two that was appropriate for long-haul networks of typical performance characteristics.

The OSG organizational model is based specifically on sharing resources. These resources include compute, core operational infrastructures, and networks of resource and user communities. OSG functions as a set of virtual organizations, or collaboratories, that tself-organize their support for collaborative activities. This philosophical approach has proven reliable, as the OSG has scaled to many institutions and user disciplines. The core OSG VO administers and supports smaller resource and user bases that do not have effort to maintain a full VO infrastructure. The number and activity of VOs working in other disciplines is now expanding as well, with a total of 89 VOs currently making active use of the OSG [9, 10].

2.1.2 The eXtreme Science and Engineering Discovery Environment (XSEDE)

XSEDE supports more than a dozen supercomputers and high-end visualization and data analysis resources across the country [11]. Funded by the National Science Foundation (NSF) as the successor to a previous project known as the TeraGrid, XSEDE could be considered a collaboratory in the business of supporting other collaboratories. Work on the bleeding edge of science has become increasingly computationally intensive as technology has improved; indeed, high-performance computing (HPC) is one of the few areas where supply seems to always increase demand, because the greater the capability and capacity of nationally accessible CI for research, the larger the data analyses that become possible and the more realistic become massive computer simulations of physical, astronomical, and biological phenomena.

XSEDE provides access to cyberinfrastructure in support of collaboratories, by integrating software and services that enable the infrastructure integration and that lower the bar for users to request access to and then use the integrated infrastructure. The ECSS (Extended Collaborative Support Services) unit of XSEDE brings together cyberinfrastructure experts with a wide variety of expertise to provide support for researchers, who can request ECSS services along with their allocation requests [12].

A particularly important aspect of XSEDE is the Campus Champions [13]. As their web page states, "The Campus Champions program supports campus representatives as a local source of knowledge about high-performance and high-throughput computing and other digital services, opportunities and resources. This knowledge and assistance empowers campus researchers, educators, and students to advance scientific discovery." Campus Champions provide essential human linkages connecting XSEDE as a resource provider and "community collaborator" and individuals on campuses across the United States.

Given the relatively high cost of acquiring and running the resources made available through and supported by XSEDE, one can easily understand the value of the collaborative approach and the value that XSEDE offers to collaboratories.

3. FACILITATING THE CREATION AND EFFICACY OF COLLABORATORIES

In 2011 a taskforce of the NSF Advisory Committee on Cyberinfrastructure concluded that "the current state of cyberinfrastructure software and current levels of expert support for use of cyberinfrastructure create barriers in use of the many and varied campus and national cyberinfrastructure facilities. These barriers prevent the US open science and engineering research community from using the existing, open US cyberinfrastructure as effectively and efficiently as possible" [1].

In retrospect, the chair of that committee—coauthor Craig A. Stewart—believes that this task force missed an important opportunity to communicate information about cyberinfrastructure and human resources available to enhance the efficacy of collaboratories.

Current social science understanding of technology adoption suggests adoption decisions are driven by the following [14]:

- Performance expectancy (perceived value)
- Effort expectancy (perceived ease of use)
- Social influence
- Facilitating conditions (including knowledge of a technology and the belief that end users will find it accessible)

Social influences and facilitating conditions largely involve informing people about what technology choices are available for adoption—an essential prerequisite to determining whether a particular bit of technology offers high value relative to any potential difficulties of adoption.

3.1 The Computation Institute and Globus

The Computation Institute (CI) (affiliated with the University of Chicago and Argonne National Laboratory) has developed over many years a set of tools designed to facilitate collaboration. The Globus suite of tools has evolved to be been of great use in facilitating collaboration between geographically disparate sites. Some of the most popular Globus tools supporting collaborators are the following:

Globus Transfer. Globus Transfer is an easy-to use, fast, secure client that allows users to move large amounts of data without having to attend to the entire process. Instead, Globus Transfer operates under a "set it and forget it" paradigm: the user simply starts the file transfer and waits for an email stating that the transfer has finished. The Globus Transfer software uses a

graphical user interface, rather than requiring users to learn to operate in a command line paradigm [15].

File sharing. Globus offers a file-sharing solution that allows users to configure shared endpoints in order to share large files with others securely and without having to move the data to a new location—something that can save significant time in the case of large datasets. Any storage system that is configured as a Globus endpoint can easily be configured to use the file-sharing capabilities. In addition to the cost savings and security advantages of being able to determine which files are and are not sharable, another advantage of the Globus model of file sharing is that it does not require collaborators from other institutions to have login access to the storage system in order to access files [16].

Data publication. Globus Data Publication allows organizations to publish datasets; metadata are stored in the cloud, while datasets are stored on campus, institutional, or group resources. Datasets may be curated into collections, and the Globus Data Publication platform enables access controls based on both user and group membership. The community that publishes the data can define their own workflows and licensing terms; published data is then searchable via the web interface. Once published, data may be transferred to a Globus endpoint for further processing [17].

3.2 XSEDE Community Infrastructure (XCI)

The XCI team grew out of the XSEDE organization and the 2011 report of the NSF ACCI Task Force on Campus Bridging [2]. During the first five years of XSEDE, what was then called the XSEDE Campus Bridging team focused primarily on "bridging" the gap between researchers and cyberinfrastructure. Created as a response to findings that even well-resourced researchers had difficulty completing the journey to results, the XCI team takes a number of approaches to making collaboration over a distance easier.

The XSEDE National Interoperability Toolkit is a software repository provided by the XCI group in order to facilitate a network of XSEDE-like collaboratories. Aimed at campuses or institutions that host their own computational resources, the XNIT offers the easy installation of a variety of scientific software in the same configuration as on the larger XSEDE Service Providers. This allows institutions with their own already-running computational resources to easily help researchers scale up to the resources available within XSEDE, to help researchers be certain they are using a tested version of their software, and to remove some of the burden on local system administrators. The XCI team works to foster communication among the communities using (or interested in) this resource, through the use of quarterly webinars, regular appearances at conferences, and communication via the XSEDE Campus Champions mailing list.

The XSEDE-Compatible Basic Cluster is a second toolkit championed by the XCI group, aimed at institutions that want their own computational resources but do not necessarily have the local expertise or time to build their own from scratch. The XCBC consists of the Rocks cluster management software (developed at the San Diego Supercomputer Center, for use on the large XSEDE resources hosted there), and an additional package of scientific software, similar to that found in the XNIT, that has been selected to work within the Rocks system. The XCBC has been found to be valuable particularly at resource-constrained institutions, where local system administrators may be unfamiliar with HPC, underfunded, and lacking in time for building a new resource without external help [18]. There is a small but steadily growing (at about 4 sites per year) community of XCBC-hosting institutions, and XCI is working to enable collaboration among them, by hosting conference sessions and fostering communication between site hosts. XCBC and XNIT provide a common technology basis that supports collaboration among institutions in conducting scientific research with the support of cyberinfrastructure.

XSEDE documents user infrastructure access and use requirements as formal use cases. These use case include most notably the ability for users to create and management use profiles information, link and use federated authentication identities to access infrastructure, login to distributed resources, move data between resources, execute remote jobs, and discover available infrastructure. XSEDE then identifies and evaluates community software/service components that can satisfy these use cases and integrates those components into the distributed infrastructure. Notable data capabilities integrated by XSEDE include the Globus reliable and high-performance data transfer service, the Globus data sharing service, and the Globus Connect data transfer endpoint, which facilitate data transfer and sharing between high-end HPC, visualization, storage systems, campus systems, and individual researcher personal systems.

3.3 Jetstream

Jetstream is the NSF's first production cloud for general-purpose science and engineering research and education. Jetstream, which began early operations in February 2016, is based on the OpenStack cloud environment software with a menu-driven interface to enable users to easily select a precomposed virtual machine (VM) to perform discipline-specific analysis. Jetstream uses the Atmosphere user interface developed as part of CyVerse (formerly iPlant), providing a low barrier to use by practicing scientists, engineers, educators, and students, and Globus services from the University of Chicago for seamless integration into the national cyberinfrastructure fabric. The team implementing Jetstream has as their primary mission extending the reach of the NSF's eXtreme Digital (XD) program to researchers, educators, and research students who have not previously used NSF XD program resources, including those in communities and institutions that traditionally lack significant cyberinfrastructure resources [19].

Jetstream was designed by using a formal architectural process based on definition of use cases and The Open Group Architecture Framework architectural processes. The design was based on a needs analysis of communities of researchers and research educators, taking into consideration NSF's goal of supporting the entire spectrum of NSF-funded communities. The strategy in defining the architecture, interface, and overall design of Jetstream was to identify communities that do not currently make extensive use of XD/XSEDE resources, document and understand their needs and work patterns, and architect a computing resource to meet those needs. One key aspect of this strategy was to collaborate directly with major research software projects, data resources, and groups with common needs, in order to create conditions that facilitate adoption of Jetstream and engage their community leaders as partners to leverage their community contacts and influence [20].

Jetstream specifically promotes collaboration by enabling researchers to share VM images that run on Jetstream or any other cloud system that runs on the open source OpenStack software.

Jetstream makes available to all users of Jetstream a library of what we call "featured" VMs. These provide commonly needed functionality, and we guarantee that they will work properly or we will fix them promptly. There is also a category of VMs that are contributed by one research team for use by others. An individual researcher can use any of these contributed VMs and then store versions of these VMs with, for example, data and scripts, in an individual researcher's private VM library. Jetstream thus provides a means by which researchers can distribute scientific software so that other researchers may discover and use it without downloading it to a local system. In addition, the team operating Jetstream offers researchers the opportunity to upload a VM image to Indiana University's digital repository (scholarworks.iu.edu) and associate a digital object identifier with that VM. In this way a researcher can make available a VM containing the entire lifecycle of their research—input data, scripts, all of the programs used to analyze the data, and output data—in a way that allows other researchers to discover that VM through citations in a paper. This provides an important mechanism for sharing code, sharing analyses, and supporting collaboratories. Furthermore, like the Open Science Grid, the Jetstream project relies explicitly on communities of practice, collaboratories, and virtual organizations to support the members of those virtual groups [19].

3.4 ACI-REF

The NSF-funded Advanced Cyberinfrastructure – Research and Educational Facilitation (ACI-REF) project [21] provides a community of cyberinfrastructure facilitators who can assist researchers in the "long tail" of scientific inquiry in order to increase the effectiveness of campus and national cyberinfrastructure in support of research. These campus facilitators work directly with researchers in order to assist in harnessing resources on their own campuses as well as in the national arena. The program provides training to help facilitators provide support and education to researchers at their institutions, including providing insight about the integral concerns of these researchers.

The members of ACI-REF's network of facilitators are able to leverage each other's skills and allow for specialization in domain areas. While many of the ACI-REF facilitators are skilled in the traditional cyberinfrastructure areas (HPC in support of high-energy physics, chemistry, astronomy, and materials science), facilitators also can provide support for research tools such as geographic information systems. Facilitators also provide an agnostic guide to resources available, whether they be XSEDE, Open Science Grid, or resources provided by campus or regional arrangements. In this way, the ACI-REF program is able to provide guidance to the overall cyberinfrastructure environment and engage deeply in the domain of research in order to identify the best ways to meet researchers' computational needs.

The ACI-REF environment is collaborative in that facilitators share technical information and tactics for working with researchers, It is a joint enterprise of research facilitators rather than being individual efforts focused on local campuses. This collaborative platform creates a template for researchers in their own work, sharing tools and techniques either through the facilitator network or via their own networks of contacts.

3.5 Science Gateways

Science gateways are software-based cyberinfrastructure that provide user-facing services, user interfaces, and APIs for virtual organizations [22] [23]. Gateways were originally considered to be browser-based Web portals for scientists to access remote computing resources through Grid middleware, but the software systems used to build gateways have matured to be considered first class cyberinfrastructure middleware in their own right. Projects such as Apache Airavata [24], HUBzero [25], CyVerse Agave [26], Galaxy [27], and others provide software and platform services for building gateways. Science gateways have also matured into production services for XSEDE, with the number of science gateway-based users surpassing traditional command-line users every quarterly reporting period since December 2013.

Despite notable successes, science gateways arguably have potential for much greater growth. Identifying the communities and organizations that would benefit from gateways implies two additional challenges: gateways must be easier to build and maintain technically, and communities operating gateways should plan for sustainability. Two organizations provide services to assist with these challenges. The XSEDE Extended Collaborative Support Services [28] effort's Science Gateway program provides gateway building experts distributed across XSEDE partner institutions who are available to provide supporting for building and integrating science gateways with XSEDE. The NSF-funded Science Gateway Institute, which began operations in August 2016, goes further, providing support for developers to use more diverse resources than just XSEDE, to provide "incubator" services that help gateway providers plan how to sustain their efforts, and a software collaborator that helps gateways find the software that they need.

Looking forward, there is a natural partnership between science gateways and the other components described in this section. Gateways are user support "force multipliers" that can help campus infrastructure providers using XCI tools to scalably support larger user communities than would be possible using one-on-one interactions.

4. CONCLUSIONS

Science has become largely a team undertaking, and the need for people and computational resources—in short, cyberinfrastructure—to support these teams is growing. In this paper we have discussed a number of organizations that are making efforts to bridge the gap between researchers and the tools they require in order to get work done. We also have discussed challenges of large-scale academic computation that such organizations aim to reduce or resolve. The tools and facilities described in this paper have already proved useful in supporting collaboratories and collaboration among institutions, and effort is ongoing to continue improving the computational landscape. We hope that by highlighting tools that are designed to aid collaboratories and collaboration between institutions, we will help members of SIGUCCS and the higher education community discover, evaluate, and adopt new cyberinfrastructure tools to aid collaboration in research and in education.

ACKNOWLEDGMENTS

This work was supported, in part, by awards from the National Science Foundation (Jetstream: ACI-1445604, XSEDE: OCI-1053575, OCI-0948142, OCI-1059812), and by the IU Pervasive Technology Institute. Any opinions, findings, and conclusions or recommendations expressed in this material are those of the authors and do not necessarily reflect the views of the National Science Foundation or Pervasive Technology Institute. This material was also based in part on work supported by the U.S. Department of Energy, Office of Science, under contract DE-AC02-06CH11357.

REFERENCES

[1] Stewart, C.A., Simms, S., Plale, B., Link, M., Hancock, D., and Fox, G. What Is Cyberinfrastructure? In: Proceedings of SIGUCCS 2010. (Norfolk, VA, 24-27 Oct, 2010). Available from: http://portal.acm.org/citation.cfm?doid=1878335.1878347.

[2] ACCI Task Force On Campus Bridging. National Science Foundation Advisory Committee for Cyberinfrastructure Task Force on Campus Bridging Final Report (2011).doi=http://hdl.handle.net/2022/13210.

[3] A. Mowshowitz. 1997. Virtual Organization. Commun. ACM 40, 9 (September 1997), 30-37. doi=http://dx.doi.org/10.1145/260750.260759.

[4] T. A. Finholt. Collaboratories. Annual Review of Information Science and Technology (ARIST), 36 (2002): 73-107.

[5] The Large Hadron Collider. http://home.cern/topics/large-hadron-collider.

[6] The Nobel Prize in Physics 2013. http://www.nobelprize.org/nobel_prizes/physics/laureates/2013/.

[7] Processing: What to Record? http://home.cern/about/computing/processing-what-record.

[8] Open Science Grid. http://opensciencegrid.org.

[9] Virtual Organization Summary. http://myosg.grid.iu.edu/vosummary?all_vos=on&active=on&active_value=1.

[10] Galison, P., Hevly, B. W. (1992). Big Science: The Growth of Large-Scale Research. Stanford University Press.

[11] What We Do. https://www.xsede.org/what-we-do.

[12] Extended Collaboration and Support Services. https://www.xsede.org/ecss.

[13] Campus Champions. https://www.xsede.org/campus-champions.

[14] Venkatesh, V., Morris, M. G., Davis, F. D., Davis, G. B. User Acceptance of Information Technology: Toward a Unified View. MIS Quarterly, 2003. 27(3): 425-478.

[15] How it Works. https://www.globus.org/how-it-works.

[16] Data Sharing. https://www.globus.org/data-sharing.

[17] Data Publication with Globus. https://www.globus.org/data-publication.

[18] Coulter, E., Fischer, J., Hallock, B., Knepper, R., Stewart, C. A. Implementation of Simple XSEDE-Like Clusters: Science Enabled and Lessons Learned. Proceedings of the XSEDE16 Conference on Diversity, Big Data, and Science at Scale. Article No. 10. Available from http://dl.acm.org/citation.cfm?id=2949570&CFID=837206729&CFTOKEN=83076021.

[19] Fischer, J., Tuecke, S., Foster, I., Stewart, C. A. Jetstream: A Distributed Cloud Infrastructure for Underresourced Higher Education Communities. In: Proceedings of the 1st Workshop on the Science of Cyberinfrastructure: Research,

Experience, Applications and Models (SCREAM '15). ACM, New York, NY, 2015, pp. 53-61. DOI=http://dx.doi.org/10.1145/2753524.2753530.

[20] Stewart, C. A., Cockerill, T. M., Foster, I., Hancock, D. Y., Merchant, N., Skidmore, E., Stanzione, D., Taylor, J., Tuecke, S., Turner, S., Vaughn, M., Gaffney, N. I. Jetstream: A Self-Provisioned, Scalable Science and Engineering Cloud Environment. In: Proceedings of the 2015 XSEDE Conference: Scientific Advancements Enabled by Enhanced Cyberinfrastructure, St. Louis, Missouri, July 26-30, 2015.

[21] Neeman, H., Bergstrom, A., Brunson, D., Ganote, C., Gray, Z., Guilfoos, B., Kalescky, R., Lemley, E., Moore, B. G., Ramadugu, S. K., Romanella, A., Rush, J., Sherman, A. H., Stengel, B., Voss, D. The Advanced Cyberinfrastructure Research and Education Facilitators Virtual Residency: Toward a National Cyberinfrastructure Workforce. Proceedings of the XSEDE16 Conference on Diversity, Big Data, and Science at Scale. Article No. 57. http://dl.acm.org/citation.cfm?id=2949584&CFID=8372067 29&CFTOKEN=83076021

[22] Wilkins-Diehr, Nancy, Dennis Gannon, Gerhard Klimeck, Scott Oster, and Sudhakar Pamidighantam. "TeraGrid science gateways and their impact on science." *Computer* 41, no. 11 (2008): 32-41.

[23] Lawrence, Katherine A., Michael Zentner, Nancy Wilkins-Diehr, Julie A. Wernert, Marlon Pierce, Suresh Marru, and Scott Michael. "Science gateways today and tomorrow: positive perspectives of nearly 5000 members of the research community." *Concurrency and Computation: Practice and Experience* 27, no. 16 (2015): 4252-4268.

[24] Pierce, Marlon E., Suresh Marru, Lahiru Gunathilake, Don Kushan Wijeratne, Raminder Singh, Chathuri Wimalasena, Shameera Ratnayaka, and Sudhakar Pamidighantam. "Apache Airavata: design and directions of a science gateway framework." *Concurrency and Computation: Practice and Experience* 27, no. 16 (2015): 4282-4291.

[25] McLennan, Michael, and Rick Kennell. "HUBzero: a platform for dissemination and collaboration in computational science and engineering."*Computing in Science & Engineering* 12, no. 2 (2010): 48-53.

[26] Dooley, Rion, Matthew Vaughn, Dan Stanzione, Steve Terry, and Edwin Skidmore. "Software-as-a-service: the iPlant foundation API." In *5th IEEE Workshop on Many-Task Computing on Grids and Supercomputers (MTAGS)*. 2012.

[27] Goecks, Jeremy, Anton Nekrutenko, and James Taylor. "Galaxy: a comprehensive approach for supporting accessible, reproducible, and transparent computational research in the life sciences." *Genome biology* 11, no. 8 (2010): 1.

[28] Wilkins-Diehr, Nancy, Sergiu Sanielevici, Jay Alameda, John Cazes, Lonnie Crosby, Marlon Pierce, and Ralph Roskies. "An Overview of the XSEDE Extended Collaborative Support Program." In *International Conference on Supercomputing*, pp. 3-13. Springer International Publishing, 2015.

Collaboration Made Easier - Working with Restricted Documents within Office 2013, OneDrive, and Office 365

William A. Bettermann
Lehigh University
8B East Packer Avenue
Bethlehem, PA
610.758.4619
wab3@lehigh.edu

Timothy Palumbo
Lehigh University
8B East Packer Avenue
Bethlehem, PA
610.758.3002
tip204@lehigh.edu

ABSTRACT

Lehigh University Athletics implemented restricted document editing in Microsoft (MS) Office 2013 and OneDrive for Business (ODB) to allow staff to work collaboratively on a single document for a bi-annual departmental report. This presentation will cover the steps to convert an old business process of sharing over e-mail, sometimes hundreds of times, to a single document with restricted editing housed in ODB. Restricted editing prevents staff from editing parts of the document for which they are not responsible. Storing the document in OneDrive allows for versioning and access from almost any internet-connected device.

This presentation will focus on why Office 2013/ODB, in combination with Office 365, was chosen as the best solution for the needs of Athletics and how this solution is applicable across a number of business units. Included will be a demonstration from start to finish of setting up a restricted document to show just how easy it is to do. Improving existing business processes is an often overlooked function of IT, making features such as restricted editing incredibly valuable in a myriad of situations.

CCS Concepts

• Document management & text processing→Document management → text editing, version control, document metadata.

• Collaborative and social computing → Collaborative and social computing systems and tools→Synchronous editors.

Keywords

Collaboration; cloud computing; Microsoft OneDrive for Business; Office 365; restricted editing.

1. INTRODUCTION

Lehigh University is a small university located in Bethlehem, PA, and is well known for engineering and business. The university's Athletics department is responsible for producing a bi-annual Internal Report for the Board of Trustees. The report includes information pertaining to all of the Athletics department's units, including varsity sports, club sports, fitness center, and intramurals. Until recently, the associate athletic director (AAD) stored the Microsoft Word file associated with the annual report on her computer's hard drive and emailed the file to her colleagues for

SIGUCCS '16, November 06-09, 2016, Denver, CO, USA
© 2016 ACM. ISBN 978-1-4503-4095-3/16/11 $15.00
DOI: http://dx.doi.org/10.1145/2974927.2974959

their input and revisions. Her colleagues returned the file with the necessary changes.

There are several inherent problems with such a method. First, the AAD had to compile data from dozens of returned attachments into her original document. If subsequent revisions needed to be made, the process could be repeated several times. Second, her colleagues did not always maintain the style of the original document. Font types, sizes, margins, and headers were frequently changed or missing. They may also inadvertently edit parts of the document that they were not supposed to. Finally, versioning issues with MS Word (2007, 2010, etc.) compounded the problems due to feature differences.

Athletics approached the technology support group to request a new solution that would enable the AAD to distribute the file for editing by the necessary personnel without compromising the original file formatting. Synchronous editing was also requested if possible. Ancillary provisions included secure cloud-based access, direct data links to Excel spreadsheets, and user access rights to sections of the file to be determined by the assistant athletic director.

2. PLATFORM SELECTION

2.1 Choosing the Right Platform

There are several options to facilitate access to the file by the department personnel who require it, including email, secure onsite server, and cloud-based options, such as Google Drive, Dropbox and Microsoft ODB / Office 365. Because the primary criterion for the new solution required maintaining the existing file formatting, email and secure server were immediately discarded. With those options eliminated, focus was given to a cloud-based solution that enabled synchronous and secure file access.

Google Drive and Microsoft OneDrive were both suitable alternatives for secure access. Both Google Drive and Microsoft OneDrive offer several benefits, including secure file access, real-time collaboration, and access from any internet-connected device.

2.2 Why We Chose Microsoft OneDrive for Business

Several features of Microsoft OneDrive for Business (ODB) provide critical benefits. The AAD mandated that the solution include maintaining the file integrity during the entirety of the collaborative editing process. The Microsoft solution maintains the integrity of the Microsoft Word file format, rather than the Google Drive provision that necessitates converting the document to Google's format. Microsoft enables the file creator to assign user access and edit rights to specific sections of the file or the entire file, as needed. Furthermore, font styles, sizes, and other formatting options can be enforced document-wide to maintain uniform file appearance. Also, because several Microsoft Excel spreadsheet files are embedded in the report, the integrity of those files and how they embed must be maintained. Microsoft ODB is a cloud solution that has the advantage of accessibility from the web or from a computer.

3. TESTING THE ENVIRONMENT

3.1 Small Scale Implementation

Technology support at Lehigh has historically taken a decentralized approach, with each college or administrative unit having separate teams of computing consultants to manage their hardware, software, and other needs. As a result of the decentralized support structure, this project required expertise from across support units, resulting in cross-team collaboration.

The consultant who supports Microsoft problems and training requests is not a member of the team that supports Athletics. The Microsoft support consultant and the consultant who supports Athletics planned for the testing and implementation of the MS ODB / Office 365 roll-out by first identifying a small group of Athletics personnel who were stakeholders in the file creation, distribution, and completion. Those stakeholders included the AAD, her assistant, and two other Athletics colleagues who are considered the department's technology liaisons. The test group was composed of the stakeholders and the two computing consultants.

Each stakeholder was upgraded to the latest version of Microsoft Office and provisioned with Lehigh-secure Microsoft ODB accounts. The two computing consultants were also granted Lehigh-secure ODB accounts. The Microsoft support consultant assumed ownership of the file, stored it in ODB, and provided edit rights to each of the members of the test group. Each of the test group members confirmed that he or she could edit the file, using both the Microsoft Word desktop application and the Microsoft OneDrive / Office 365 web interface.

The small scale testing was expanded to a small number of computing consultants on other college support teams, to ensure that access rights for the original stakeholders was not compromised by the addition of more editors. Also, minor changes were made to specific sections of the file. For example, a stakeholder was originally provided edit rights to the entire file and confirmed that she could access and edit the file in its entirety. Upon completion of that test, the same stakeholder's access rights were changed to specific paragraphs and sections of the file. She confirmed that her access was changed according to the changes made by the file owner.

3.2 Preparatory Training

With small-scale testing completed and verified, the stakeholder group confirmed the need to complete several steps before implementation for the department group. The department computing consultant was tasked with ensuring that every Athletics employee was upgraded to the latest version of Microsoft Office (2013 at the time) and that a Microsoft OneDrive / Office 365 account was provisioned and activated for each.

Because the method of file distribution (email) and editing (full file edit rights) was eliminated and replaced with a new method (restricted rights via the cloud), training was vital for the project's success. Each department member who was to be granted edit rights to the file was asked to attend a training session that detailed the genesis of the project, the product selection process, the small scale test, and the new file interface.

Training was provided by the technology consultants during two group sessions. Most of the Athletics department stakeholders were able to attend one of the sessions. Each of the sessions included a brief overview of the purpose of the report and the old method used to edit the report file. Emphasis was placed on the work required by the AAD to edit the file and repair its formatting for final distribution.

A brief Microsoft PowerPoint presentation was produced that included a graphical description of the old (email) method of file distribution and the problems that were inherent to that method. Because cloud computing is a new concept for many of the stakeholders, a brief description of cloud computing and its benefits, in terms of file distribution, sharing, and collaboration, as well as the benefit of accessibility from any internet-connected device, was offered. Because of the newness of cloud computing for most of the stakeholders, emphasis was given to the University's cloud computing policy security restrictions. Finally, a real-time demonstration on Microsoft OneDrive's capabilities, including file security, file sharing, real-time collaboration, and accessibility was given.

4. DEPLOYMENT

4.1 File Ownership & Sharing

The AAD maintained ownership of the file during the deployment phase of the project, as she was responsible for producing the end-product. However, the AAD and the technology consultants remained mindful of the need to change ownership at a future date, due to the AAD's impending retirement. The AAD provided edit rights to each of the collaborators in the Athletics department (Figure 1).

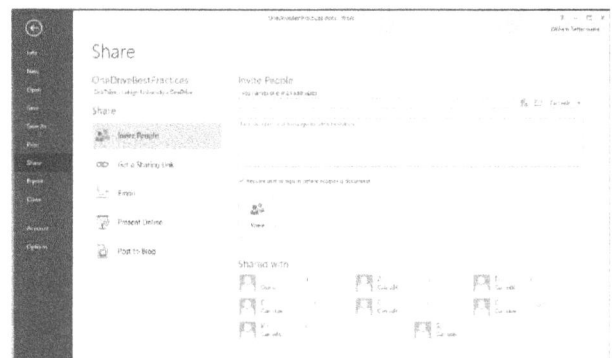

Figure 1. OneDrive File Share

4.2 Section Access

Microsoft OneDrive offers only edit and view rights, which are often sufficient for sharing and access purposes. In the case of the Athletics department report, the AAD wanted to employ access rights to paragraphs and topics sections of the report file, while excluding edit access to the remaining parts of the file by employing the Restrict Editing utility in MS Word.

This step required that the AAD determine which user(s) required access to specific sections of the report.

4.3 Cloud Access

Windows PCs and Macs are used throughout the Athletics department. Also, several Athletics personnel travel often, requiring the need for mobile computers, tablets, and smartphones. Microsoft OneDrive clients and apps are available for iOS and Android platforms, which enable the user to access the file remotely, as needed.

4.4 Synopsis

MS ODB accounts were created and implemented, including native MS Office upgrades and MS Office 365 account creation for all department collaborators. The transfer of the report document file to MS ODB and all requisite file access permissions were enabled in time to produce the report at the conclusion of the spring semester. No concerns or problems were reported during the editing and production of the report.

5. YEAR ONE IMPLEMENTATION REVIEW

5.1 File Ownership and Sharing

File ownership was transferred from the Assistant Athletic Director to the Associate Athletic Director during the course of the first year of ODB use. The addition of the Associate Athletic Director to the file author group within OneDrive was required. No problems were reported.

5.2 Section and Cloud Access

The Athletics department reported that many of the collaborators were unable to access the file as intended at the one-year mark. The most common problem cited was that the individuals could not remember their OneDrive password, thus rendering their OneDrive accounts and the file inaccessible via the cloud. Because Lehigh has not deployed Microsoft DirSync tool (see details, below), no

automated mechanism exists to reset passwords. As a result, due to a short timeframe for the completion of the report update, the email method was employed for those who could not access OneDrive.

5.3 Post-production Analysis

The university's network domain and directory services are structured and maintained using MS Active Directory. MS OneDrive for Business requires the implementation of MS Azure Active Directory Synchronization Tool (DirSync) to enable single sign-on (SSO) for all Active Directory accounts. However, the DirSync tool requires synchronization between the on-premises Active Directory server and the Microsoft Azure Active Directory tenant associated with an Office 365 subscription [1]. Because the university network support group does not allow access to the university's Active Directory from outside of its domain, DirSync and SSO cannot be deployed for ODB. The university's ODB account creation thus requires that the client create a password that is unique to Office 365 / ODB.

Mindful of many clients' propensity to perform work on an as-needed basis and within short timeframes, the university technology support team must investigate the best option to ensure that clients can make full use of the accessibility of Office 365 / ODB.

6. REFERENCES

[1] DirSync with Single Sign-On, https://msdn.microsoft.com/en-us/library/azure/dn441213.aspx

We Can Rebuild It, We Have The Technology: Modifying The Mac Mini For Use As A Classroom Instructor Station

Travis Freudenberg
Carleton College
One North College Street
Northfield, MN 55057
1-507-222-4074
tfreudenberg@carleton.edu

ABSTRACT

Apple's Mac Mini is a near perfect solution for use in the classroom; it has out of the box support for OSX and Windows, has a small form factor, and is relatively low cost. It does have its own unique challenges, one of which is a rear mounted power switch that requires a mechanical lever when securely rack mounted. At Carleton College, we were tasked with improving the performance and mechanical reliability of our Mac Minis by making them better than they were before. This means better hard drives, stronger power switches, and faster boot times. In this presentation, I'll discuss how we increased overall performance using a combination of new boot protocols, SSDs, auto parts, a soldering iron, and a drill press.

Keywords

Carleton College; Hardware repair; Mac Mini; classroom technology

1. CARLETON COLLEGE

Carleton College is a private undergraduate liberal arts college in Northfield, Minnesota. The college currently enrolls 1,991 students and employs 220 full time faculty, and has a professional IT staff of 40 with an additional 50 student staff at the helpdesk.

2. HISTORY OF CLASSROOM COMPUTING AT CARLETON COLLEGE

Previous to Apple's transition to Intel processors, Carleton ITS had several different plans for classroom computing, from separate Windows and Mac classrooms and labs, to classrooms with both Windows desktops and Apple desktops, to classrooms with a single Apple desktop that also ran Virtual PC. The eventual goal was to have both operating systems available in each classroom, ideally using the same hardware. The reasoning behind this was to simplify the scheduling of classes for the Registrar's office; if the instructional technology in each classroom is the same, then scheduling can be based on the size of the class, rather than what type of computer was in the classroom. The combination of Apple switching to using Intel processors and including support for Boot Camp in OSX Leopard allowed for using one dual boot Mac Pro in each classroom, which were first deployed in 2007. Using rEFIt as a boot loader, the end user could

SIGUCCS '16, November 06-09, 2016, Denver, CO, USA.
© 2016 ACM. ISBN 978-1-4503-4095-3/16/11 …$15.00.
DOI: http://dx.doi.org/10.1145/2974927.2974948

then log in to the OSX partition or the Windows partition. Upon logout, the OSX partition checks against the Radmind server to reverse any changes to the OS. For Windows, we utilized DeepFreeze for image integrity. As a cost savings measure, in 2011 the process of replacing the Mac Pros with Mac Minis began. Carleton ITS is currently deploying 73 Mac Mini 7,1 classroom instructor stations and 5 Mac Pro 5,1 classroom instructor stations.

3. MODIFYING THE MAC MINI

One of the first challenges we were faced with when deploying Mac Minis was the question of how to secure them. The previous Mac Pros in the classroom were secured into custom built podiums using brackets. Conveniently, MK1 Studio Products provides a solution for securely rack mounting a Mac Mini into a 1U rack space, including space for a SuperDrive (see Figure 1).

Figure 1. Rack mounted Mac Mini with SuperDrive

While the power button for the Mac Mini is located on the back of the unit, this rack mount utilizes a spring and lever to activate the power button while the device is secured in the rack. For classrooms that did not have instructor podiums with rack space, a different solution was needed. Sonnet's MacCuff mounting bracket was used to hold the Mac Mini securely in place. The issue with using the MacCuff in these locations was that the power button was inaccessible, and there was no access to a USB port for thumb drives. A solution was found by one of our staff members who, after researching a remote power switch for the Mac Mini, discovered a solution in use by automotive entertainment installers to easily connect the power adapter from a Mac Mini to a DC regulator for use in dashboard computer systems. The crucial component of this device, for our purposes, was a small power switch splitter that allowed us to connect the original power switch to an external SPST push button switch (see Figure 2).

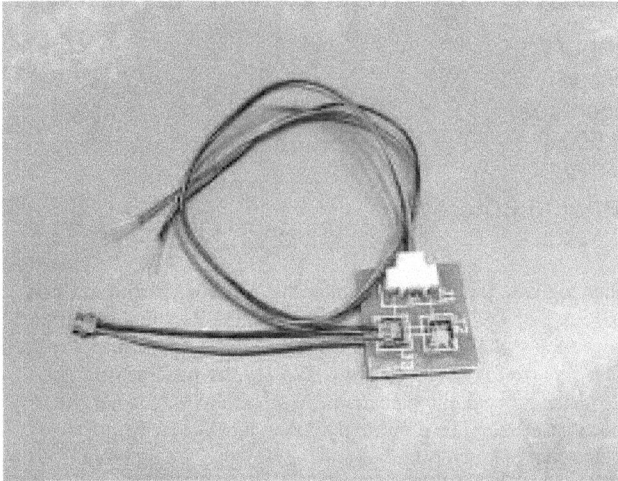

Figure 2. Power switch splitter

Attaching the power switch splitter to the logic board was a relatively simple and reversible process that involved removing the Bottom Cover and inserting it onto the logic board through use of a provided connector. In order to route the external switch wire to the outside of the Mac Mini, it was necessary to drill a 1/8 hole in the edge of the Mac Mini Bottom Cover, a removable (and replaceable) part. As such, it was possible to make modifications to the Mac Mini that were reversible, and by replacing the Bottom Cover, made no permanent alterations to the unit (see Figure 3).

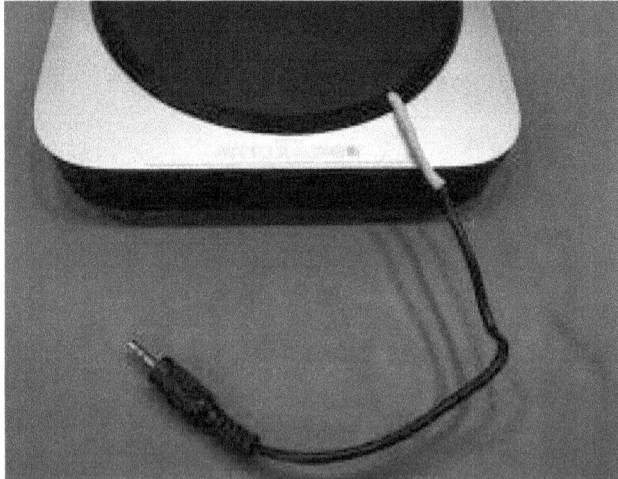

Figure 3 Quick disconnect cable

A quick disconnect cable was created by utilizing a headphone extension cable. By soldering the extension leads from the power switch splitter to the male connector portion of the headphone cable, and soldering the female connector wire to the external power switch, it was possible to remove the Mac Mini from the cuff for service quickly and easily. The power switch itself was attached to a custom made panel that was attached to the cuff, which had additional inputs for USB and Firewire (see Figure 4).

Figure 4. Custom plate for peripherals and power switch

4. IMPROVING SYSTEM PERFORMANCE AND BOOT TIME

In the spring of 2013, driven by the results of a MISO survey that showed Carleton ITS fared less favorably than our peer institutions in regards to classroom technology, faculty and ITS staff were involved in a series of meetings to discuss how to improve the end user experience while using instructor stations. Ultimately, a combination of changes to the login procedure and upgrading the internal Mac Mini hard drives to solid state drives was determined to be the best option to decrease the time necessary for staff to log in to the instructor stations. Previous to these changes, the ideal process for a faculty member logging in to a classroom instructor station was as follows:

1. Power on the machine.
2. Select the preferred OS from the rEFIt boot menu
3. Log in to the OS, and wait for the system to create your new account on the machine.

There were several different issues with this process. For example, if the previous user of the instructor station had been using the OSX partition and neglected to log out, and the next faculty member wanted to use Windows, they would need to log out of the OSX partition, allow for it to check in with the Radmind server and reverse any changes (approximately 2 minutes), choose the Windows partition, and log back in. This process took on average took 5 minutes, and there was frustration over the time this took out of the class period.

The login process was changed so that both OSX and Windows partitions logged in as generic users, and the logout procedure only refreshed user settings on the OSX partition, instead of fully checking for all software changes. And finally, all instructor station hard drives were replaced with Samsung 840 PRO 512GB solid state drives. The combination of these changes dramatically increased boot times; rebooting from the OSX partition changed from 3 minutes to 30 seconds.

The hard drives for all existing instructor stations were swapped during the annual summer maintenance window in 2013; as the Mac Minis were brought in to our imaging lab for reimaging, the hard drives were swapped with solid state drives. The process of swapping hard drives in the existing Mac Minis was straight forward, and with practice could be done in less than 15 minutes per machine. Due to the tiered approach in replacing the existing Mac Pros, roughly half of the Mac Minis were 4,1, and half were new 5,2 systems. The 4,1 Mac Minis required thermal sensors to be added to the solid state drives, while the 5,2 systems did not require these sensors.

5. APPLYING UPGRADES TO NEW SYSTEMS

In the summer of 2015, the 4,1 Mac Minis had reached the end of our four-year replacement cycle, and were due for replacement. In order to get all Mac Minis back on the same replacement cycle, we elected to replace the 5,2 Mac Minis one year early. This left ITS facing a curious dilemma; do we order new Mac Minis with pre-installed solid state drives, or do we order Mac Minis with standard hard drives and re-use the solid state drives in the soon to be retired Mac Minis? In the end, we made the decision to re-use the existing solid state hard drives. This process was once again straight forward; after removing the solid state drives from the retired Mac Minis, we simply swapped them for the standard hard drives in the new 7,1 Mac Minis.

The decision was also made to modify all new Mac Minis to include external power switches. The new 7,1 Mac Minis utilize a separate Bottom Cover and Antenna Plate, necessitating drilling a 1/8 inch hole separately in each piece (see Figure 5).

Figure 5. Splitter and modified antenna plate

The process of installing the power switch splitter was similar to installations in the older Mac Minis, and as we were already completely disassembling the Mac Minis, we simply installed the power switch splitter at the same time as we were replacing the hard drives with solid state drives. The most time consuming part of the process was production of the quick release cables in house, and preparing the existing rack mounts for mounting the external power switch. We utilized the SuperDrive mounting panels for this purpose; by drilling a ½ hole in this panel, we could prepare a number of panels in advance, and add them to rack mounts as they came in for replacement.

6. LESSONS LEARNED

Changing the login and refresh process of the instructor stations, combined with installing solid state drives, greatly increased the boot time and performance of our Mac Minis in a classroom setting. In addition, replacing the manual lever power switches on our rack mounted Mac Minis with external power switches tremendously improved power cycle reliability. In the future, as long as we are able to utilize external power switches (dependent, of course, on the design of future Apple desktops and the availability of third party parts), we will continue to do so. At our next replacement cycle, our existing solid state drives will be six years old; based on price trends it will most likely make more sense to purchase Apple Mac Minis with pre installed solid state drives as opposed to purchasing third party drives and installing them ourselves.

7. ACKNOWLEDGEMENTS

I'd like to thank Rebecca Barkmeier, Troy Barkmeier, Austin Robinson-Coolidge, and Jim Pierret for assisting me with the historical background of this paper. Additional acknowledgement goes to Russ Bauer and Jim Pierret from Carleton College and Dana Thompson from St. Olaf College for discovering the method to install an external power switch on the Mac Mini.

Creating a Motivated Student Worker

Mark Holm
The Evergreen State College
2700 Evergreen Parkway NW Olympia, Washington 98505
360 867-6627

holmm@evergreen.edu

ABSTRACT

I will give some tips in how to turn all student workers into motivated student workers. I have 13 years of working with student employees. My experience has taught me strategies that work to motivate students. Having students in a work area can be challenging and rewarding. With the proper tools we can remove many of the challenges. Certainly some student staff are productive but many others seem to languish in mediocracy. We will look at ways to avoid having a group of unmotivated workers and build productive employees. We will also touch on some de-motivators that should be avoided. I have found that giving proper time and training to learn the expected work is critical. For student success the work done needs to be monitored and corrected in a way that does not appear as being critical. I've discovered giving the student worker tangible results of the work accomplished can go a long way in creating productivity. Find the right job for the worker by playing to strength helps build confidence in tasks. Lastly, to have a motivated student they must feel appreciated therefore let them know they are appreciated for their work and how it helps you.

Author Keywords

Student worker; Employee Motivation; Student Success

SIGUCCS '16, November 06-09, 2016, Denver, CO, USA
© 2016 ACM. ISBN 978-1-4503-4095-3/16/11…$15.00
DOI: http://dx.doi.org/10.1145/2974927.2974933

INTRODUCTION

I have seen student workers on various college campuses throughout my career in higher education. There is a wide discrepancy in how they do their jobs. Some are fully engaged while others are entrenched in their cell phones. This presentation will provide some tips on how to turn all student workers into motivated student workers. I have 13 years of working with student employees and my experience has taught me strategies that work to motivate students. Having students in a work area can be both challenging and rewarding, but with the proper tools we can remove many of the challenges. Certainly some student staff are productive but many others seem to languish in mediocrity. This is even more noticeable when you have groups of students. We will look at ways to avoid having a group of unmotivated workers and build productive employees. We will also touch on some de-motivators that should be avoided. In addition, I will provide examples that have been successful for me. I have found that giving proper time and training to learn the expected work is critical. For student success the work done needs to be monitored and corrected in a way that does not come across as being critical. I've discovered giving the student worker tangible results of the work accomplished can go a long way in creating productivity. Find the right job for the worker by playing to their strengths helps build confidence in tasks. Lastly, to have a motivated student they must feel appreciated; therefore let them know they are appreciated for their work and how it helps you.

It seems obvious but training is essential. A common mistake is to assume telling your student worker what to do is the same as training. A student worker that is told what to do can perform some basic tasks and might be pretty good at them but they are essentially being used as a cog in a machine -- they are just spinning for process sake. Taking the time to properly train your student worker shows that you have interest in them and their ability. It also gives them confidence and understanding in their work. A student that knows what they are working on and why they are working are better at their jobs because they can be striving towards a goal. A student worker that is confident in what they are doing is going to be productive and motivated. At the Help Desk we train our students and have them shadow our more experienced students on calls before we have them perform any work on their own. We build the skills by repetition with the most common tasks before expanding the training into less frequent and unique tasks. At the Help Desk our work is broad based. The Help Desk Pro-staff are continually explaining how to do things and why they are done that way. Our students learn to use our wiki as a tool to support the training. The students are always learning new things until they graduate and leave us behind. Some things might seem obvious to professional staff, but for many student staff the job might be the first they have ever held. For example, the goal is not to close help desk tickets, but rather to resolve customer problems and we measure the work by closed tickets. Understanding the differences allows the student to be more successful in the job and properly directs their motivation.

The flip side of this is not giving the student worker enough time to learn the job, also known as throwing them to the wolves. Improper training can be a de-motivation. Speeding a student worker through training too quickly can lead to frustration, resentment and lack of productivity. I have noticed students that are not comfortable doing a particular job avoid doing that particular job. We once had a situation at the help desk where we had a large group of student workers graduate at the same time. The new student workers we hired were trained but the training was rushed. We noticed that there were more mistakes and far less confidence in those students. They were slow to pick up the phone and work through emails. We extended the training and did more teaming up. With time we were able to get them up to speed. We were fortunate we didn't have students lose motivation to the point of quitting.

Paying close attention to the work being done is important for the student worker to be successful. Monitor their work for mistakes and make corrections right away. Doing this early is part of the training process and can not only avoid bad habits but when done the right way gives the student confidence they are doing the job correctly. How the work or behavior is corrected is critical. By putting an encouraging spin on the correction or praising the work that is done well at the same time can have a positive impact on attitude and acceptance of the correction. Blunt corrections in many cases will cause the worker to become defensive and they are going to be more concerned with explaining themselves than correcting the addressed issue. Each person is different. How to address each individual will be slightly different as well. Some student workers do not handle subtlety well. A balance needs to be found between not being too tough in the correction nor being too soft. Too harsh and the worker might tune you out or hold resentment. Too soft and the student might not understand what is being corrected or outright dismiss it as no big deal. One example of dealing with a correction happened with a student that had a habit of getting flustered on the phone and telling the customer what they thought the customer wanted to hear instead of an accurate answer. These behaviors lead to the customers getting bad information. I called the worker into my office and started off complimenting how she has grown in her knowledge and let her know I noticed how WELL she did assisting customers that come to the Help Desk with account issues. I then talked to her about how difficult it can be dealing with customers that are worked up on the phone and gave her some tips on how she can take control of the phone call by asking questions and how that will also give her time to compose her thoughts on the subject. So at this point when I addressed the issue that needed corrective action she already had been given a tip on how to help deal with it.

To be properly motivated, people need to see accomplishments of their labor. To use a baking analogy; we could all agree it would be discouraging to pick out a cookie recipe, purchase ingredients, mix the ingredients and at the point the cookies are ready to go into the oven, you get kicked out of the kitchen and don't get to taste or even smell the results. In many process oriented work study positions the student worker is in just this situation. They work but never see the outcome, or never are recognized for their part in the accomplishment. Making their work feel more tangible can give them a sense of pride in their labor and be a strong motivator to do well. When I started at the Help Desk we had a big discrepancy between the amounts of issues handled by the students. We had a few motivated students and others that were marginally productive and were more than happy to sit on tickets and let others handle the workload. Our help desk ticket queue tended to be bloated with issues that would sit, many time for 2 to 3 days, before being addressed. One day one of our Help Desk Pro-staff and a manager were joking, debating if a dinner bell type ring or a DMV style counter would show our work better. I decided to combine the ideas and actually try it out. I wrote a program that was a full screen digital counter with the words "Customers Help" below it. Any time the spacebar was pressed a bell would ring and the counter would go up by one. We then instructed our students to ring the bell each time they closed a ticket. I ran the program on an old computer right in the middle of the help desk area in view of customers, pro-staff and students. What started as a joke turned into a motivator, and a recognition tool. Now anytime our help desk team closes a ticket instead of moving silently on to the next one they press the spacebar on the computer and a bell sound rings as the count increases. The pro-staff can, and does, immediately notes the accomplishment with a simple nod of the head or a woot as the count goes up. I was surprised how this simple tool was able to increase productivity and motivation. Pro-staff are now aware each time a worker resolves an issue and can praise the work. Additionally students and staff are aware of how many tickets have been closed for the week. It's apparent when the team has accomplished a lot and when things are slow. When we were really busy it has acted as an additional motivator. "Can we set a record for how many tickets we have closed in a week?" The counter gives immediate acknowledgement of a job completed where we didn't have one. Our workers have been consistent and motivated across the group since their work became visible.

Make sure you let your students know you appreciate the work they do and how it benefits you and the institution. Give them a reward for their help in accomplishing goals. If it's not your style you might have to go as far as scheduling it in your calendar as a recurring event to make sure you are thanking them consistently. I have un-official reviews where I bring each student in to my office and see how they are doing. I let them know how grateful I am to have good workers. I tell them because they are good at what they do it allows me to focus on other tasks. I ask them for their opinion on things like how Pro-Staff could improve training and where we could do things better. Asking a student's opinion shows you value and appreciate them. Don't ask them for opinions you don't want to hear or will not consider. This will appear as lip service and can act as a de-motivator. Some student ideas can be too grand to implement. In such situations I try to put a positive spin on the input before saying no. We have pizza parties and training a few times a year to show our students appreciation. The pizza parties not only work as a reward but allow the students to bond with each other. It pulls them out of work mode and they can be relaxed and social. Some of our workers have opposite shifts and though they may share emails and tickets they never have face to face conversations. When the more official pizza party is not feasible the occasional box of donuts is always appreciated in its place. It serves as a deserved pat on the back.

When possible, play to the students strengths. We work to have our students know every part of their job. However, it's beneficial to know where each worker thrives. Practicing what they are good at will add to their overall confidence and motivation. This can be a balancing act between improving a weak skill and letting them excel in what they are good at. Student jobs have their share of grunt work that needs to be done. They will not like everything they are asked to do. It's not feasible to have them avoid work they don't like but you can use their strengths to help build up where they are lacking. Our new hires always have a variety of strengths and weakness. For example, the ones with stronger phone skill and less technical skills I have cover the phones more frequently and schedule appointment as they build their other skills. I do make them learn and perform all areas of the job but by playing to their strengths early I build their confidence. We had a young man at our help desk that came into the job with very strong technical skills. His phone skills were very weak. He was too technical with customers and was not personable on the phone. If we had him on the phone as frequently as other students we would have been constantly correcting him. By sending him on more field calls working with equipment we lowered his average phone

conversations. We still had him answer phone. We coached him on almost every call as well. By playing to his strengths we were praising him for what he was good at frequently and correcting what he struggled with less. He improved over time and was always a solid contributor and was enthused in what he did. If this approach of playing to his strengths was not taken we could have easily ended up with a worker who avoided work due to lack of confidence or resentment.

Students can be great resource. You will get the most out of them when they are properly motivated to do the work. When the proper steps are taken it is possible to shape your student workers into valuable members of the team. The work put in to mold a student into a motivated worker is more than worth it in the results. It is much easier to manage a motivated student. They are happier, produce more work and make fewer mistakes. Using specific motivating techniques you can accomplish a lot with student workers. You must train your students, do not throw them into the job and expect high results. Be sure to monitor the work and be constructive and encouraging in your corrections. Make sure your students have a feeling of accomplishment in their work. Build confidence in your workers by having them be successful at what they are good at. Show your students you really do appreciate all the work they do. Make them feel involved and part of the process. When taking these steps you will discover your students are great resources that can accomplish a wide variety of tasks and be a great asset to your department.

Challenges of
Deploying PKI based Client Digital Certification

Satoshi Uda
Japan Advanced Institute of
Science and Technology
1-1 Asahidai, Nomi
Ishikawa 923-1292, Japan
zin@jaist.ac.jp

Mikifumi Shikida[*]
Kochi University of Technology
185 Miyanokuchi, Tosayamada, Kami
Kochi 782-8502, Japan
shikida.mikifumi@kochi-tech.ac.jp

ABSTRACT

We are confronted with the threat from the theft of user-id / password information caused by phishing attacks. Now authentication by using the user-id and password is no longer safe. We can use the PKI-based authentication as a safer authentication mechanism.

In our university, Japan Advanced Institute of Science and Technology (JAIST), we deployed On Demand Digital Certificate Issuing System for our users, and employ the PKI-based client certificates for log-on to web application, connecting to wireless network (including eduroam), using VPN service, and email sender signing. In addition, National Institute of Information (NII), which are providing common ICT infrastructure services for Japanese universities and institutes, started a service to issue client certificates in this year. So use of the electronic certificates will become more popular within a few years in Japan.

However, there are not so enough cases deploying the electronic certificate based authentication in University infrastructure, we still has many tips and issues on operating this. In this paper, we introduce the use case of the electronic certificate in JAIST, the challenges and issues, and consider the future prospects.

Keywords

Service Development & Management; User Authentication; Public Key Infrastructure (PKI); Digital Certification

1. INTRODUCTION

With the growth of the Internet, services in universities also become worldwide useable via the Internet. Now several services (e.g. VPN service, email service, etc.) need face the Internet even if these services are just for internal users.

[*]This work was done in his previous position in Japan Advanced Institute of Science and Technology.

It is important for its realization to correctly authenticate a requested user, authorize the user, and prevent abuse of services by evils.

Conventionally, authentication by the user-id and password are used widely. However, use and of simplistic password by the user, by the threat of password theft by phishing e-mails, etc., it has become vulnerable to abuse.

The authentication only with user-id and password is now become vulnerable to abuse because easy passwords will get caught out, and passwords will be stolen by phishing emails, etc. In actuality, we constantly face an incident in JAIST; our user has his/her password stolen, and the password is used for abusive email sending.

We can adopt PKI-based digital certificate for a safer authenticate mechanism. In following section, we introduce the use case of the digital certificate in JAIST, the challenges and issues, and consider the future prospects.

2. DEPLOYING DIGITAL CERTIFICATES

In JAIST, we had early concerning about the risks of fraud by email sender spoofing, and began the use of PKI-based digital certificate for email sender signing and authentication in 2004. Since then, we are servicing and utilizing the service while updating our on demand issuing system and expanding domain of applicability.

2.1 Public Key Infrastructure (PKI)

The Public Key Infrastructure (PKI)[1, 8] is infrastructure to enable secure communication on the Internet based on public key encryption technology. Users can use PKI-based digital certificate for authentication, digital signing, and cryptographic communication. In the Internet environment, the PKI is used for several purpose those are server certification (e.g. attestate web server owner), client certificate (e.g. attestate owner's affiliation and position), and code-signing certificate, etc. In this paper, we focus on the client certificates.

We can use a client certificate for following.

- Authentication to log-on on web service, connect to networks, etc.

- Digital signing and encrypting a message on email, etc.

The PKI-based digital certificate is issued by the Certificate Authority (CA) on demand from the Registration Authority (RA). The RA is a role for authenticate the request user, verifying or making certificate subject, and request to CA to issue it.

A CA can be public or private. A digital certificate signed by a public CA is believed by public. But a digital certificate signed by a private CA is believed in limited population such as company or organization members. The public CA service is provided by several companies with operating under strict rules, and typically for a fee to issue certificates. In the other hand, anyone can build and operate a private CA under their own rule, and issue certificates without any fee.

2.2 Design of our Service

At the starting of using digital certificate in JAIST, we assumed following as the main purpose of our service.

- Email signing

- Authentication on VPN service

- Authentication on Web service

This is because our prime concerns at the time were sender faking on email and prevent abuse of services from the Internet. Of course, we considered about extensibility for expansion of use case, now we are using not only for described above but also for authentication on connecting to wireless network.

And we decided we use public CA service for our service. In enterprise environment, many companies were using digital certificates issued by their own private CA for internal use. However, in university situation, our users have much cooperation with outside researchers, and usually communicate with them by emails. It was difficult for our users to select enable / disable signing an email message in adapting to receivers were inside or outside. While our users may use their own PC environments, we cannot manage all users' PC environment, and cannot install our private CA's certificate to all computers. We would find a dangerous warning message on email application if the system cannot verify signed email (despite the risk is not exactly higher than unsigned case), that was caused if there was no private CA certificate on the computer.

And we decided we issue users' certificate on demand from user's request. We provide user's certificate only for users need it. And any user who has entitlement to get certificate can request it anytime. This was also for economy reason, but not only for it. In JAIST, users can change their own email address anytime. The client certificate contain an owner's email address information. So users need to use the digital certificate matching to their current email addresses.

2.3 On Demand Digital Certificate Issuing System

The On Demand Digital Certificate Issuing System in JAIST is the system for providing client digital certificate for users on demand from users' request. This system is a web-based system, and assume the RA role in the PKI.

Our deployed On Demand Digital Certificate Issuing System in JAIST is 3rd generation now. The 1st generation system was deployed in 2004 at the start of using client digital certificate in JAIST. The 1st system is based on Verisign Managed PKI Service[7]. In 2008 we also deployed the 2nd generation system and replaced previous system with it. The 2nd system is based on Globalsign Managed PKI Service[4]

Table 1: Certificate's attributes on our G2 system

Subject: C=JP, O=Japan Advanced Institute of Science and Technology, title=[*User's position*], dnQualifier=[*User's ID number*], CN=[*User's full name*] / Email=[*User's email address*]
Validity Not Before: [*Issue requested time*]
Validity Not After: [*Issue requested time + 1year*]
SubjectAltName: email:[*User's email address*]
KeyUsage: TLS Web Client Authentication, E-mail Protection

as CA role, and NEC's PKI server / Carassuit[5] as RA role. And now we started using 3rd generation (current) system in 2016 based on NII's UPKI client certificate issuing service[6]. We introduce the 3rd system in detail in Section 3.2.

Every systems basically has same features. The followings are the key feature set of our On Demand Digital Certificate Issuing System.

Authenticate the requested user.

The system need to authenticate each user. In our environment, whole user information is centrally managed on a LDAP system. When user access to this system, the user need to log-on with his/her own user-id and password. This system decide the requested user has entitlement to get certificate or not by using our LDAP user database. The password-based authentication is not so safe, the system does not accept connection requests from outside of JAIST.

Generate certificate's attributes.

In our service, we don't allow specifying / editing any attributes on users' certificate to end-users. The system automatically generate certificate attributes information (e.g. certificate subject) by using users' infomation on user database. For example, Table 1 was snippet of our auto-generation rule on our 2nd generation system.

Request issuing a new certificate to CA.

After decided the user's certificate specification, the system request issuing a new certificate to CA. On every CA services usually has APIs for communicate with RAs, based on XML-RPC, SOAP, REST, or another proprietary protocols. The system would request by using these protocol, and users can get an issued certificate from CA.

Manage issued certificates.

The system also has a feature to manage users' certificate. System administrator can get a list of all issued certificates, a detailed infomation and status of each certificate, etc. End-users can request to revoke their own certificate, and administrators also can revoke any certificates. When each certificate get closer to the time of its expire, the system also send a reminder email to certificate owner to advise to renew it.

2.4 Use cases

We are using digital certificate for many purpose in JAIST. In this section, we introduce our major usage of digital certificate as use cases; Authentication on VPN service, Authentication on Web access, Email sender signing, and Authentication on Wi-Fi connection.

2.4.1 Authentication on VPN service

The VPN service is important service for our users. Users can use almost all network services in JAIST from everywhere on the Internet via the VPN service. The authentication on the VPN service is much important because the service also open to the whole Internet and authenticated users can use several services in JAIST.

In this service, we are using the SSLVPN as base platform, and authentication require two-factor authentication; that is a digital certificate and user-id / password. Users need prepare own digital certificate and install it on their web browser before going out and use the SSLVPN.

2.4.2 Email sender signing

Users can use digital certificate for email sender signing and making encrypted email messages by installing their certificate to Mail User Agent (MUA); e.g. Mozilla Thunderbird, Outlook, etc. Users can send signed email message just only with enable signing.

We also providing web mail user interface for users in our email services. We are using the Zimbra Collaboration Suite that support email signing, encrypting, and certificate verification with client side digital certificate on web mail. So our users also can use digital certificate via web mail.

However, sending encrypted email messages is require receiver's public certificate (this comes with his/her signed messages), so it is only too true that usability of encrypting purpose is limited due to email signing has not been in widespread use yet. In JAIST, several users are using digital certificate for signing, but encrypting is rarely used.

We are using public CA service to signing users' certificate. This is mean everybody on the Internet can verify our users' signed message. Users can keep enable message signing every time. And all receivers can believe our users' signed messages.

2.4.3 Authentication on Wi-Fi connection

This service was started in near years, but now this become a most popular service which using digital certificate in JAIST. We are using digital certificate for authentication on Wi-Fi connection. In our Wi-Fi infrastructure, we are using the WPA/WPA2 Enterprise authentication with EAP-TLS method. This authentication method require authentication server, we adopt the FreeRADIUS[3] server for it.

We are using this authentication system not only for authenticate on our private Wi-Fi infrastructure but also for authenticate on the eduroam[2] roaming access service. Our users also use digital certificate to connect to the eduroam enabled Wi-Fi infrastructure outside of JAIST.

In the eduroam scenario, anyone can try to authenticate to connect to eduroam enabled Wi-Fi, this mean the authentication is open to several people including evils. So we had hesitate to adopt user-id / password based authentication on the eduroam infrastructure, and try to use the EAP-TLS method.

3. ADOPT THE UPKI SERVICE

The UPKI service is the PKI services for Japanese universities and institutes provided by NII. In this service, NII start the service to provide client certificate in 2015.

Table 2: Issuing methods for client certificates on the UPKI

P12_single: Generate a private key on server side, and provide an issued certificate with the private key as P12 file. Each end-user download the file directly from the UPKI system.

P12_bulk: Generate a private key on server side, and provide an issued certificate with the private key as P12 file. Each site administrator download a file which containing multiple P12 files, and each end-user receive their own P12 file from a site administrator.

Browser_generate: Each end-user get an issuing web URL on the UPKI system, and get their certificate on the URL by themselves. Private key generation is just done on the end-user's browser, so the key will not share with any other system (incl. the UPKI system).

3.1 UPKI service for client certificate

The UPKI service is providing server certificates, client certificates, and code-signing certificates signed by a public CA for Japanese universities and institutes. The objective of this service is diffuse the PKI in academic network and increase security basis of the nationwide academic organizations. In this paper, we just focused to service for client certificates.

It was a big barrier for many organizations to deploying client certificates that the client certificate issued by public CA was much expensive. We could start using client certificate with paying a fee much early time, because we had only about 1,000 active account holders, and we could start with paying a fee. However, in big universities, they may have over 10,000 members, it is not realistic that they deploy the PKI with paying a cost. It was much innovative affair for Japanese universities and institutes to start deploying client certificates based service that NII start to provide client certificate with a little fee. Use of the client certificates will become more popular within a few years in Japan.

The UPKI service provide a CA role and the *UPKI support system for automatic issuing* which providing user interface to apply a request and support some RA roles for participating organizations. The user interface of the system is based on a Web interface, and this interface assume all operations are done by real human.

In case of applying issue request for client certificate, the system provide 3 kind of issuing / providing method; *P12_single*, *P12_bulk*, and *Browser_generate* (Table 2). For example, followings are the issuing and providing process in case of *Browser_generate* method. The UPKI service defined 2 roles for certificate administration in each participating organization; *Applocation Manager* and *Supervisor of each end-user*.

1. The *Unit Manager* of each end-user make a file for application; which contain end-user information (certificate attribute information) formatted in TSV.

2. The *Application Administrator* receive the TSV file, and review it.

3. The *Application Administrator* upload the TSV file to the UPKI system.

4. The UPKI system send a URL information to get a "Access PIN" to *Unit Manager* via email.

5. The *Unit Manager* access to the URL.

6. The *Unit Manager* download a "Access PIN" file.

7. The *Unit Manager* inform end-user the "Access PIN".

8. The PKI system send a URL information to issuing their certificate to the *end-user* via email.

9. The *end-user* access to the URL with the "Access PIN".

10. The *end-user* get an issued his/her certificate on the Web.

11. The *Application Administrator* receive an email which inform the *end-user* has finished getting their certificate.

3.2 J-UPKI: On Demand Digital Certificate Issuing system G3

We have adopt the UPKI service for our current On Demand Digital Certificate Issuing system. The UPKI service does not have any features which support automatic / on-demand operation. So we have implemented a front-end system named "J-UPKI" for the UPKI which provide our required feature (described in Section 2.3). The J-UPKI front-end system assumes roles of *Application Administrator* and *Unit Manager*, and automatically process requests from end-users by using back-end user information database, etc.

In adopting the UPKI service, we had considered in which issuing method on the UPKI is good for our situation. From the view of user interface, the *P12_bulk* is feasible because all certificate operations for end-users are completed in J-UPKI web interface. However from the view of security, the *Browser_generate* is better than others. It is important for client certificate based services to be guaranteed the owner of private key for each issued certificate is just a subject person described in the certificate. In adopting this issuing method, no systems other than end-users' need to handle yours private keys. So we have decided to adopt the *Browser_generate* method in J-UPKI.

In implementing the J-UPKI system, we faced some difficulty on communicate with the UPKI service. The UPKI service does not assume access from machine, the service has only human-friendly user interfaces. In our implementation, the system emulate accessing by web browser and parsing responses by using Web scraping technique, and the system also handle emails from the PKI system and parsing message bodies. We show the process of new certificate issuing on J-UPKI system in following.

1. The *end-user* log-on to the J-UPKI system (Figure 1).

2. The *end-user* request to issue new certificate (Figure 2).

3. The J-UPKI system generate user's certificate's attributes, and make a TSV file to request to the UPKI system.

4. The J-UPKI system upload the TSV file to the UPKI system.

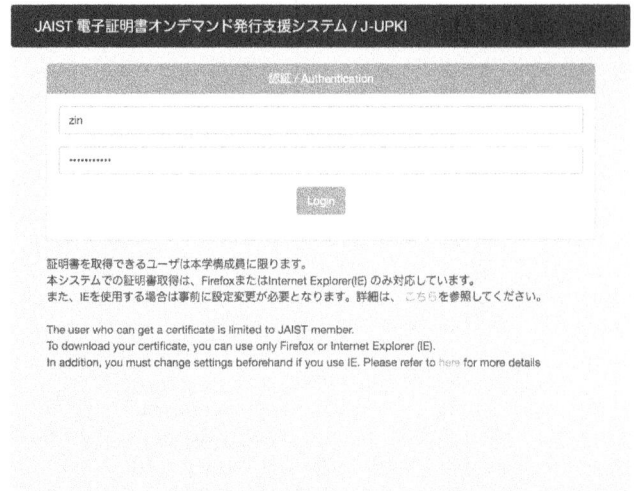

Figure 1: J-UPKI: Log-on to the system.

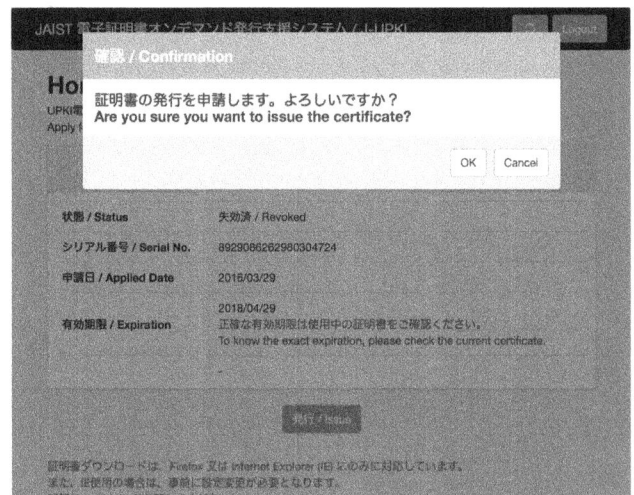

Figure 2: J-UPKI: Request a new certificate.

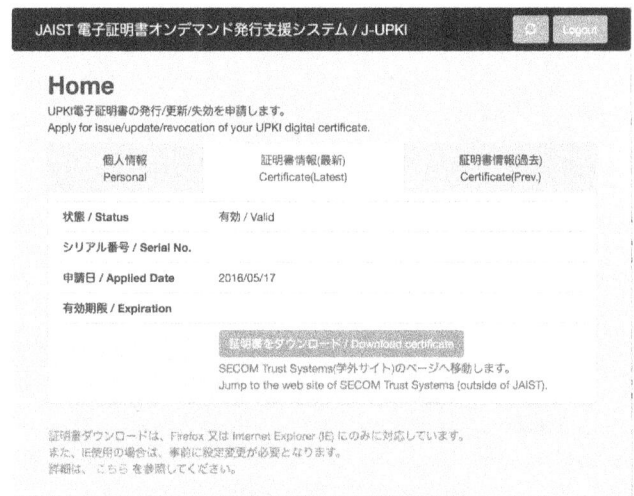

Figure 3: J-UPKI: Link to issuing new certificate.

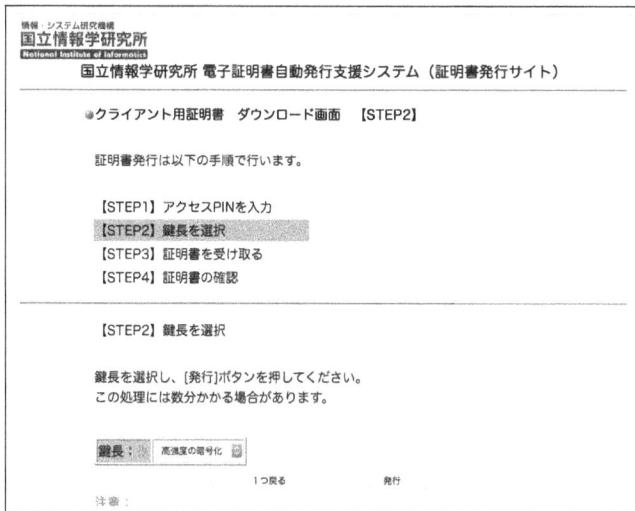

Figure 4: UPKI: Certificate Issuing Page.

5. The J-UPKI system receive emails from the UPKI system that contain issuing URL for the new certificate and Access PIN information (accurately the J-UPKI system collect all information by following the process described in Section 3.1).

6. The J-UPKI system show the *end-user* a link to issue new certificate on the UPKI system (Figure 3).

7. The *end-user* get a requested new certificate on the UPKI system (Figure 4[1]).

In this process, the end-user need to access to the UPKI system in last step. We are facing big issue on it that is the UPKI system's message only written in Japanese. We have many non-Japanese users, they cannot understand messages on the page. This issue is inescapable in our process, the only workaround now is providing translation document for users. We are also strongly requesting to add English messages on the page to NII.

4. CONSIDERATION

Now our client certificate infrastructure has been widely used in JAIST. Especially after adopting it for VPN service and Wi-Fi authentication, many users start using client certificates for them. But then using a client certificate on client PC require a bit more complex preparation, We need provide a more support to users who has a low ICT literacy or are not up on new technology.

And using digital certificate is not universally prevalent. So control user interface and process for digital certificates have not accomplished yet, end-users may get a situation like confusing or incomprehension. We show our knowledge, issues and workarounds in following.

4.1 Issues on Operating Systems

Controls interfaces on Operating Systems have not accomplished yet. Our concern of this reason is OS-vendors assume that digital certificates (esp. client certificates) are

used mainly by professional users with enough documents and generous support in corporate environment.

For example on MacOS environment, we may face a drop-down list which contain multiple same entry to select a certificate for using EAP-TLS authentication for Wi-Fi. This is CNs list of available certificates, and this may not has options displaying each certificate in detail. The CN is commonly used for user's full name, Users will confuse which one should be selected in case of there are multiple certificates which has same CN value.

And another example on Windows 10 environment, we face a bug of operating system that is users cannot statically set Username attribute on EAP-TLS authentication (CN's value is used in default). In eduroam environment, the Username attribute need has @[home_domain] postfix for roaming authentication routing. This is big problem for us, our users bumped into a problem that they could not use eduroam service when they had updated their PC to Windows 10.

As a workaround for these issues, we are taking in full name, issued time, and @jaist.ac.jp as postfix in CN value in JAIST. This workaround avoid these issues, however this workaround raise another issue that is the representation of certificate information is going to be clunky when a receiver of signed emails check the certificate in detail.

Smartphones become popular, and there are many users who connect the smartphones to Wi-Fi network also in JAIST. In our environment, these users need configure EAP-TLS setting on it (e.g. iOS or Android OS, etc.), however it is not so easy to install their client certification and configure wireless setting on the smartphones. Especially on the Android OS, some procedure and tips are depend on specific version, vendor, or network operator, because they can provide extend or limit configuration interface.

4.2 Issues on applications

We also have several issues on each application including web browsers. The first issue is about certificate holders. Now major operating systems has certificate holder, which is certificate manager on Windows and keychain on MacOS, and several applications are using digital certificates through operating systems' feature. On the other hand, some applications like Firefox have their own certificate holder which is independent from operating systems. Several users feel disorientated from this difference, and we'll receive several support requests.

And there is another issue on some browser. If once user rejected to present user's certificate in responding to request from a web page, the web browser never pop-up certificating selection dialog on the web page. We have no idea to clear this judgement cache other than restarting the web browser. Users may click "Cancel" button on certificating selection dialog in mistake, this behavior is not user-friendly.

In the case of using email service, we have introduced our users can use client certificates for signing, etc. on web-mail user interface. We are using the Zimbra Collaboration Suite for our email service. The certificate handling feature on the Zimbra's web-mail user interface is implemented in client-side Java program running on Java-plugin on browsers However we sometime face a problem on this feature after updating browser version, Java version, etc. When the problem occur, we'll not be able to read only signed emails. Some users hesitate to make signing on their sending emails to

---

[1]This page is written in Japanese only. It's problem in our service.

avoid the email will be un-readable on receiver's side during this kind of trouble. This issue is constricting to become the signing on email popular.

In many Japanese organizations including JAIST, each section has their email address (e.g. mailing list address), and member of the section use the address as *From* address especially in sending official emails. We think email signing is much helpful for this kind of official emails, but of course we don't want to recommend users to sharing private key for certificate. In our consideration, we should deploy server side support system for proxy-signing for this kind of requirement.

4.3 CA migration

We have certificate issuing systems migration experience twice, this migration involve the change of issuing CA.

The simplistic migration approach is that replacing all users' certificates at the same time. But this approach has hard impact to users. So we adopted another moderate approach; we configured to keep usable old and new certificate in migration period, and users can replace their certificate with new one independently.

We are using client certificates for authenticate on several systems, and the authentication on each system is independent with others in this time. So we need to configure to accept both (old and new) certificate in authentication on each system. Many systems were working fine by installing both CA chains to trust certificates configuration. However some appliance systems were not working file by this approach. We make two independent virtual service on these appliance as workaround, the one trust old certificates and the other trust new.

We are still discussing and considering for future systems. On the authentication element, we think we need to deploy unified authentication infrastructure and each service system should work in cooperation with the infrastructure. And the unified authentication system will support client certificates as one of authentication method.

5. CONCLUSIONS

In this paper, we show our challenges of deploying PKI-based client digital certification in JAIST. We also have several issues on using client digital certification, and yet at the same time we have several workarounds. The domain of applicability is consistently spreading.

In Japanese academic domain, using client certificate is meeting preconditions to become popular. The UPKI client certificate issuing service is encouraging it.

We are still discussing and challenging for spreading the domain of applicability of the PKI.

6. ACKNOWLEDGMENTS

We got special help from Prof. Motonori Nakamura and his staffs in National Institute of Informatics (NII) in adopting the UPKI client certificate issuing service and corresponding our latest On Demand Digital Certificate Issuing System to the UPKI system.

7. REFERENCES

[1] D. Cooper, S. Santesson, S. Farrell, S. Boeyen, R. Housley, and W. Polk. Internet X.509 Public Key Infrastructure Certificate and Certificate Revocation List (CRL) Profile. RFC 5280 (Proposed Standard), May 2008. Updated by RFC 6818.

[2] eduroam. eduroam. https://www.eduroam.org/.

[3] FreeRADIUS. Freeradius. http://freeradius.org/.

[4] GlobalSign. Managed pki platform. https://www.globalsign.com/en/managed-pki/.

[5] NEC. Pki server / carassuit. http://www.nec.co.jp/cced/pki/.

[6] N. I. of Informatics. The upki digital certificate issuing service. https://certs.nii.ac.jp/.

[7] Symantec. Managed pki service. https://www.symantec.com/products/information-protection/managed-pki-service.

[8] P. Yee. Updates to the Internet X.509 Public Key Infrastructure Certificate and Certificate Revocation List (CRL) Profile. RFC 6818 (Proposed Standard), Jan. 2013.

A PetaFLOPS Supercomputer as a Campus Resource: Innovation, Impact, and Models for Locally-Owned High Performance Computing at Research Colleges and Universities

Abhinav Thota
Pervasive Technology Institute
Indiana University
Bloomington, IN, USA
athota@iu.edu

Ben Fulton
Pervasive Technology Institute
Indiana University
Bloomington, IN, USA
befulton@iu.edu

Le Mai Weakley
Pervasive Technology Institute
Indiana University
Bloomington, IN, USA
llnguyen.edu

Robert Henschel
Pervasive Technology Institute
Indiana University
Bloomington, IN, USA
henschel@iu.edu

David Hancock
Pervasive Technology Institute
Indiana University
Bloomington, IN, USA
dyhancoc@iu.edu

Matt Allen
Pervasive Technology Institute
Indiana University
Bloomington, IN, USA
malallen@iu.edu

Jenett Tillotson
Pervasive Technology Institute
Indiana University
Bloomington, IN, USA
jtillots@iu.edu

Matt Link
Pervasive Technology Institute
Indiana University
Bloomington, IN, USA
mrlink@iu.edu

Craig A. Stewart
Pervasive Technology Institute
Indiana University
Bloomington, IN, USA
stewart@iu.edu

ABSTRACT

In 1997, Indiana University (IU) began a purposeful and steady drive to expand the use of supercomputers and what we now call cyberinfrastructure. In 2001, IU implemented the first 1 TFLOPS supercomputer owned by and operated for a single US University. In 2013, IU made an analogous investment and achievement at the 1 PFLOPS level: Big Red II, a Cray XE6/XK7, was the first supercomputer capable of 1 PFLOPS (theoretical) performance that was a dedicated university resource [2]. IU's high performance computing (HPC) resources have fostered innovation in disciplines from biology to chemistry to medicine. Currently, 185 disciplines and sub disciplines are represented on Big Red II with a wide variety of usage needs. Quantitative data suggest that investment in this supercomputer has been a good value to IU in terms of academic achievement and federal grant income. Here we will discuss how investment in Big Red II has benefited IU, and argue that locally-owned computational resources (scaled appropriately to needs and budgets) may be of benefit to many colleges and universities. We will also discuss software tools under development that will aid others in quantifying the benefit of investment in high performance computing to their campuses.

SIGUCCS '16, November 06-09, 2016, Denver, CO, USA

ⓒ 2016 ACM. ISBN 978-1-4503-4095-3/16/11. . . $15.00

DOI: http://dx.doi.org/10.1145/2974927.2974956

CCS Concepts

•**General and reference** → *General conference proceedings;* •**Social and professional topics** → *Professional topics; Management of computing and information systems; Computing education;* •**Applied computing** → *Physical sciences and engineering; Life and medical sciences; Arts and humanities;*

Keywords

supercomputing; HPC; university; innovation; petaflops, value, analytics, impact

1. INTRODUCTION

In 1997, Indiana University (IU) began a purposeful and steady drive to expand the use of supercomputers and what we now call cyberinfrastructure. This was one part of the IU Information technology organization response to a directive and challenge from then President Myles Brand for IU to be a "leader in absolute terms in the use and application of IT." In 2001, IU implemented the first 1 TFLOPS supercomputer owned by and operated for a single US University. In 2013, IU made a similar achievement at the 1 PFLOPS level: Big Red II, a Cray XE6/XK7, was the first supercomputer capable of 1 PFLOPS (theoretical) performance owned by a US university and funded exclusively with university funds. This means that IU was free to use this system entirely based on university priorities to best further the mission of IU. (There were of course prior to this other PFLOPS+ systems located at other universities – but these were funded in significant part with federal funds and were allocated in part as national resources, with federal guidance on how these systems were to be used and allocated). IU's strategy in high performance computing (HPC) has been to have locally funded resources available to the IU research community to enhance the research and creative activities of the IU community under what we refer to as a principle of abundance in which we make resources available to the research community as a whole, without application processes, with usage allocated on a fair share basis. To a first order approximation, the more people want to compute, the more they can compute.

We previously reported on the resources, support, and impact of HPC resources at IU [34–36]. Big Red II was purchased at a time of fiscal and political uncertainty. As a result, we felt particularly compelled to make strong commitments about the value IU would reap from the acquisition and use of this system. Thus, as part of our justification for funding of the system by the university, we made a commitment that the system would be used by and useful to researchers, clinicians, scholars, and artists representing at least 150 disciplines and sub-disciplines at IU. In this paper, we will describe Big Red II, the system and human resources that support and enable operation of Big Red II, the usage of Big Red II by the IU community, and some of the lessons we have learned in the implementation and use of Big Red II. Most importantly, we argue that regardless of the size of a local HPC resource, a HPC resource owned by and operated in keeping with the research priorities of a college or university can be an important asset to research, creativity, and scholarly accomplishment.

IU's implementation of advanced information technology services has been guided by faculty input since the very first days of the Research Computing Center at Indiana University. The first director of this center was noted astronomer Marshall C. Wrubel. More recently, the IU Chief Information Officer has been a faculty member and has received guidance from various faculty committees to develop strategic plans for IT for the entire university. Examples include the strategic architectural plan for IT, which was approved by the Trustees of Indiana University [11], and a 2005 report from a blue ribbon panel called the "Indiana University Cyberinfrastructure Research Taskforce" [9]. That report identified as a priority for IU that the central IT organization provide "education and training that is suitable to the particular needs of individuals in particular areas of research, clinical, engineering, and artistic pursuit". The implementation of Big Red II was one aspect of the central IT organization's specific responses to this taskforce report.

We will also discuss how, in our experience, it is beneficial for colleges and universities to have local advanced HPC resources or supercomputers with human resources to support the users. We will also discuss some tools that can be used by others to justify investments in cyberinfrastructure.

2. BIG RED II AND SUPPORTING SYSTEM AND HUMAN RESOURCES

By supercomputing we mean very large scale parallel computing systems with a low-latency internal network (and recognize that the old saw "if it costs more than $1M, its probably a supercomputer" has a lot of merit). By high performance computing (HPC) we mean any sort of integrated parallel computing system, including very small computer clusters that may have an internal network with modest performance characteristics.

2.1 System Resources

Big Red II [1] is a Cray XE6/XK7 supercomputer (Figure 1) with a total of 1020 compute nodes: 676 CPU/GPU compute nodes, each containing one CPU, one NVIDIA Tesla K20 GPU accelerator with a single Kepler GK110 GPU and 344 dual-CPU nodes. Having both CPUs and GPUs as part of the architecture allows researchers and students at IU to be able to choose the kind of compute resources that are best for their software to achieve the best performance, thus catering to both CPU and GPU computing users.

Big Red II is the flagship supercomputer of the university; but there are other HPC machines at IU. They are Karst (a high throughput and serial jobs cluster) and Mason (which is designed for high memory jobs). In addition, IU also runs Jetstream [31, 33] and Wrangler [17] that are part of the XSEDE [38] national cyberinfrastructure. These two systems are available to researchers across the country through an allocation system. In addition to the compute resources, we have storage systems that make it possible to use the supercomputers at scale. HPC users produce large amounts of data during their runs that require a huge number of I/O operations. The Data Capacitor II [6] filesystem is 6 PB parallel file system that can support this kind of usage. There is a home file system for more permanent storage for data that is used day to day and a 15 PB tape archive for archival needs.

Figure 1: Big Red II in the IU data center.

2.2 Organizational Structure

The central information technology services for IU are provided under the leadership of the Office of Vice President for Information Technology and Chief Information Officer. The areas that UITS supports include Enterprise Systems, Learning Technologies, Client Services, Networks, Clinical Affairs, and Research Technologies (RT). Research Technologies is also a core component of the Indiana University Pervasive Technology Institute (IUPTI) [15], a collaborative organization that encompasses leadership and staff from IU's School of Informatics, Maurer School of Law, and College of Arts and Sciences. Within IUPTI, we integrate the process of creating, hardening, delivering, and supporting new information technology and cyberinfrastructure services. IUPTI has received funding from various sources – primarily US federal science agencies. The fact that Research Technologies and IUPTI report administratively to the CIO (with strong collaboration with academic units at our university) means that advanced cyberinfrastructure support – including HPC systems – is well integrated with and leverages all of the core services of the central IT organization.

2.2.1 Pervasive Technology Institute

IUPTI has two types of affiliated centers: Research Centers, and Service and Cyberinfrastructure Centers. Research Technologies (RT) is a Service and Cyberinfrastructure (CI) Center. RT provides comprehensive HPC services for IU. As such, RT runs and manages the supercomputers and offers consulting and support services to users.

2.3 Human Resources

As stated previously, RT offers robust support services for HPC users at IU. There is an online resource called the IU Knowledge Base (KB) [12] that provides answers to hundreds of questions that a user of our HPC systems might have. This resource has been in place for decades, and when it has the answer to a user's question, is a more reliable way to deliver the proper command syntax than reading a command over the phone. More information about the value, cost- effectiveness, and utility of the Knowledge Base at IU is available [29]. While IU uses a system developed at IU (now in its 3rd generation), there are now many tools available and accessible for implementation of a KB at colleges and universities of all sizes. Examples include the hosted service offered by the University of Wisconsin- Madison [21] and the KB service built on Confluence [4] used by the University at Albany[20]. At IU, there are several teams of staff who support users, including:

- A team that does basic application support and also long term extended support for complex issues, including helping with performance tuning.

- A specialized team that does support for data statistical, data analytics, and mathematical applications.

- A visualization team that can assist with application of visual technologies and visualizing complex data.

- A team that focuses promoting and supporting use of supercomputers digital humanities team assists users with using supercomputers in humanities research

- A team that can help the computing center *and* users with automating workflows through convenient web-based workflow systems called science gateways [28].

As we will demonstrate with data in the following sections, and as we have described elsewhere, our experience is that a strong support infrastructure – people – is important to promote and enable effective local use of hardware resources [27]. And even for researchers who need hardware not available locally, expert support can help those researchers obtain allocations on federally funded CI systems like XSEDE or INCITE [10] for example. XSEDE has a Campus Champions [3] program which is a way to keep specific appropriate people at a university informed about the resources offered through XSEDE and the allocation policies that are being followed.

3. IMPLEMENTING BIG RED II AS A RESOURCE IMPORTANT TO MANY DISCIPLINES AT IU

3.1 Dedication and Early User Phase

In our experience, while events through out the academic year are important for bringing in new users and for keeping existing users updated, the time when a machine is first introduced is critical. We found that there need to be specific outreach efforts at probable users of the system and bringing them in during the early user phase. This way the system can go through its motions and the administrators can even out any issues before the production day. This period usually lasts anywhere from a few months to up to an year for experimental systems.

In addition to having an early user phase, we found that it was valuable to organize a dedication ceremony that can have an impact on the entire university audience. We made sure that the ceremony stressed the importance of the new system to the university community and made everyone notice it. This is a one time opportunity that does not come around again until the next new machine is purchased and dedicated to the university.

3.2 Usage

The operating system on Big Red II is the Cray Linux Environment [5] (based on SUSE Linux SLES 11). Users of Big Red II have access to their home directories with a 100 GB quota and a high speed scratch space that is for temporary storage of research data. Access to the system is through any SSH [16] client that users can run on their desktops or laptops. Users connect to one of two login nodes for Big Red II that they are directed to in a round-robin fashion. Login nodes are intended for light interactive tasks such as setting up the (shell) environment by exporting the right variables for use by various applications, compiling applications, or setting up input and output directories for the jobs that run on the compute nodes.

Given the shared nature of the login nodes, all of the computational work that users do happens on the compute nodes. There are 1020 compute nodes on Big Red II, but at any point in time, there is more demand than can be satisfied. These nodes are therefore allocated through a scheduling system. Big Red II uses the TORQUE resource manager [30] and the Moab Workload Manager [13] to manage and schedule jobs. Big Red II uses a fair share scheduling algorithm to set job priorities for users. Administrators set a usage goal for each user and when a user exceeds that goal, that user's jobs are given a lower scheduling priority [8]. There are multiple queues on Big Red II setup for different kinds of usage. There are separate queues for GPU and CPU applications and separate debug queues for people running quick jobs that are in testing phase. Users submit scripts using the "qsub" command and these scripts specify the job requirements like the amount of compute time needed, the number of compute nodes required and the type of compute nodes is specified through the queue type selected.

We strongly encourage and assist users in doing a benchmarking and scaling study of their code(s) to ensure that the applications are being run with the most efficient number of compute nodes. This is especially true for users running large numbers of jobs, as even a few percentage points improvement in performance can have a big impact over a few thousand jobs.

4. EDUCATION, OUTREACH AND SUPPORT

There are many very positive aspects of supporting students who are "digital natives" in terms of IT support in general. However, to the current generation of students who grow up using touchscreen devices that are highly intuitive, supercomputers are not what they expect. The vast majority of supercomputers run some version of Linux and are still almost always accessed through text terminals with a command line interface. Given this less than user-friendly computing environment, we found that it is important to have a strong education, outreach and support structure available for the users.

4.1 Outreach and Training

In this section we will describe all the activities that we think are important in making HPC accessible to the students and faculty on a university campus. If you consider a large public university, thousands of new students and tens of new faculty members come in every year. On top of this, computing hardware gets upgraded every three to five years and software changes happen even more frequently. To develop a new, larger user community and keep the existing HPC user community informed about the available resources, we host more than a dozen outreach events on campus every year. This includes presentations at departmental meetings, workshops for beginner and advanced users, data center tours, on site support for classes making use of HPC resource.

When Big Red II was first dedicated in 2013, we did a pre-launch workshop for the machine's launch that drew more than 100 people from the campus. We also did an introduction to Big Red II workshop after the machine went into production. Our goal was to get to 150 disciplines using the system, which is not possible with just the traditional HPC user departments like physics and chemistry. We also held information sessions for non-traditional user departments on campus. During the introduction to Big Red II workshops, we noticed that many attendees are not familiar with Linux. Many new comers to the HPC field do not usually have experience with command line terminals. IU started offering an introductory Linux class that is co-located with the introductory HPC workshop to address this problem. We also offer more focused workshops for specific research groups and departments. Since Big Red II was dedicated in the spring of 2013, we held 83 education, outreach, and training events at IU to promote its use. We reached over 2,000 faculty, staff, and students from across all the IU campuses. Coupled with over twenty news releases aimed at drawing attention to the capabilities of Big Red II, this outreach helped us immensely in achieving our goals. Even with these extensive outreach and training opportunities, there are more users who could benefit from our services.

4.2 Big Red II User Base

One of the critical challenges for us was to measure, track progress against, and then verify that we had achieved the goal of having researchers and students representing at least 150 disciplines using Big Red II. We began collecting these

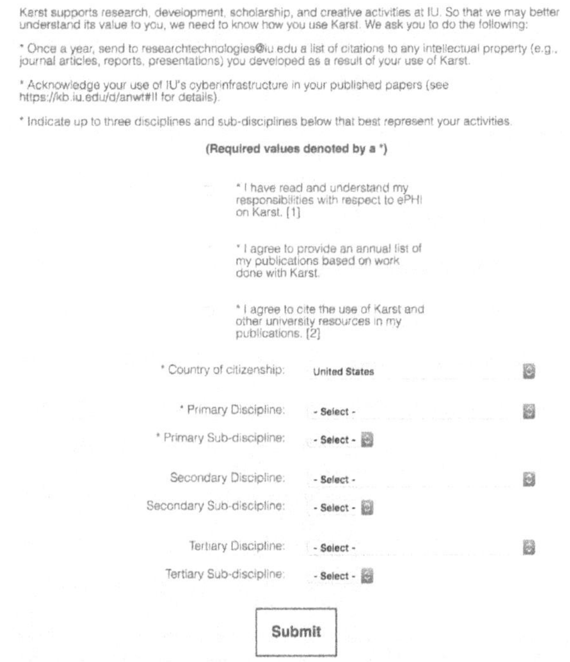

Figure 2: Users are asked indicate their discipline and sub-disciplines, if applicable, during the account creation process using this form. The form shown here is for Karst, but the Big Red II form is essentially identical.

data as we set up the signup system for people to get new accounts on Big Red II. As accounts were requested, users indicated the disciplines and sub-disciplines appropriate to describe their research. An image of the form people see to indicated disciplines is shown in Figure 2. A full listing of the disciplines and sub-disciplines is available online at [7].

4.3 Evaluation of the System

One of the primary means by which we evaluate all of the IT services at IU is through an annual survey of user satisfaction. The survey and methodology have been described previously [29]. In short, we contract with an independent survey organization within IU to do a stratified randomized survey sampling undergraduate students, graduate students, staff, and faculty. We measure usage (the percentage of the user community that indicate that they make use of Big Red II and other supercomputers), satisfaction scores (on a standard 5 point Likert scale), and what we refer to as a satisfaction percentage – the percentage of respondents who answer a score of 3 or higher where 5 is "extremely satisfied").

The survey asks about HPC systems generally, so the results include Big Red II plus our other high performance computing systems, but these results and user comments in the survey tend to focus on the flagship system at any given time – which has been Big Red II since it was put into service. We note that the percentage of people who indicate that they use Big Red II is actually higher than the percentage of people who have accounts and run jobs on the system. Our interpretation (which we have confirmed through interviews) is that this discrepancy comes from group leaders who "use" Big Red II in the sense of making use of it as a tool

Supercomputers and HPC	Average rating (out of 5)	Satisfaction	Usage
2016	4.09	95.32%	16.68%
2015	4.22	96.71%	13.64%

Table 1: The table shows the average user ratings of supercomputers and HPC at IU across all campuses for 2015 and 2016. The survey takers are considered to be satisfied if they give at at least a 3 rating to the services. The percentage of respondents who said they used the service is displayed under the Usage column.

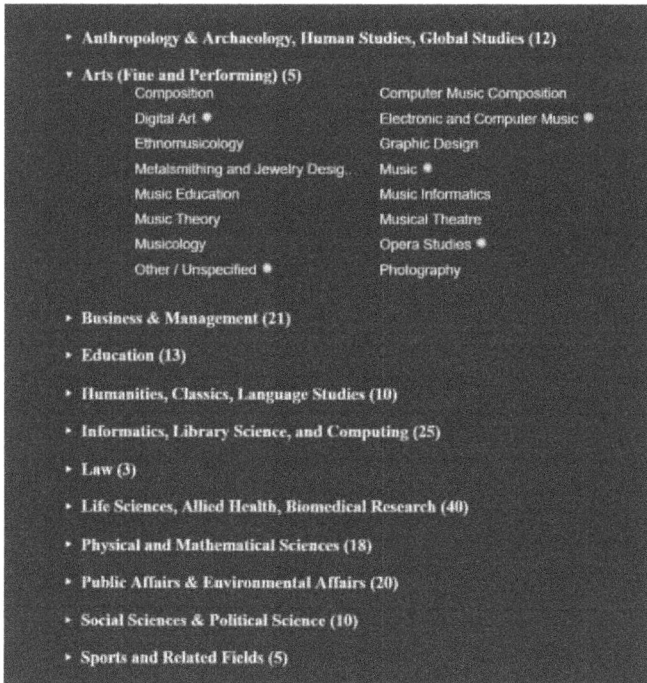

Figure 3: Disciplines available for user selection on Big Red II. The Arts (Fine and Performing) section is expanded to show the five sub-disciplines that are represented on Big Red II.

in their labs, but delegate the actual use of the computer and do not personally have accounts on the system. Data for usage and satisfaction of IU high performance computing systems and supercomputers for the last two years are displayed in Table 1. The community surveyed is what we traditionally think of as the research community – faculty, staff, and graduate students. Full details are available online at [19], and contains yearly survey information from the last 20+ years.

5. VALUE ASSESSMENT OF HPC INVESTMENTS AT IU

In 2005, the Indiana University Cyberinfrastructure Research Taskforce identified "Providing education and training that is suitable to the particular needs of individuals in particular areas of research, clinical, engineering, and artistic pursuit" [24] as a useful approach to accelerating the use of cyberinfrastructure. To further that goal, Indiana Uni-

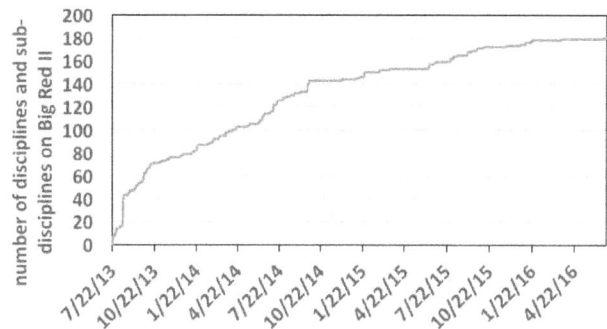

Figure 4: Number of distinct disciplines and sub-disciplines of users of Big Red II (self-reported) FY 2013-2016

versity promised at the time of dedication of Big Red II to "have such a breadth of impact that Big Red II would matter to at least 150 disciplines and sub-disciplines at IU", with a special focus on biological and biomedical disciplines, humanities, and the arts [32]. In order to fulfill this promise, administrators needed to to better understand what research was actually being performed on the machine. We thus asked users, at the time of account creation request, to self-select up to three disciplines from a total of 381 disciplines. Not restricted to the science disciplines typical of supercomputer users, the disciplines included the sub-disciplines of Fine Arts, Humanities, and Sport Science as well as life science, physics, and informatics (Fig. 3). By the end of FY 2014, IU researchers representing a total of 144 disciplines and sub-disciplines were using Big Red II, and by the end of FY 2016 the number had increased to 180 (Fig. 4).

Another way we have assessed the value of Big Red II (and other parts of IU's advanced cyberinfrastructure) is through interviews [14]. We contracted with an assessment group at another university to conduct interviews of faculty members who make extensive use of IU's supercomputers and HPC systems. This report is online and contains a number of anecdotes and analyses about the value of supercomputers such as Big Red II [14].

5.1 XDMoD Value Analytics

XDMoD (XD Metrics on Demand) [22] is an NSF-funded open source tool designed to audit and facilitate the utilization of the XSEDE cyberinfrastructure by providing a wide range of metrics on XSEDE resources, including resource utilization, resource performance, and impact on scholarship and research. We are developing novel modules to be added to the existing CI metrics tool to enable assessment of the value of investment in campus-based CI in scientific terms (number of publications) and in financial terms (grant income from researchers who use campus CI as compared to those who do not). IU has over the past several years been developing a set of tools that links financial information – such as grant awards to IU faculty members – with usage of our supercomputers and HPC systems. This allows quantification of financial income to the university in the form of grants and contracts with usage of our supercomputer and HPC systems. IU is now collaborating with The University at Buffalo to add these capabilities to Open XDMoD, a widely used software tool that enables analysis of usage of HPC systems and supercomputers.

XDMoD is already straightforward to install and operate. XDMoD_VA [23] will allow cyberinfrastructure centers and IT organizations to quantify the scientific and financial value of investments in HPC systems and supercomputers. XDMoD_VA is being developed so that it can be implemented with or without direct connections to a university or college's local financial systems. Where that is permitted by policy and practice XDMoD_VA will enable analysis of all sorts of grants and contracts received by a particular institution. If it is not possible for a college or university's IT organization to have direct read access from the institution's financial systems then XDMoD_VA will provide the capability to download NSF and NIH grant awards from the NIH and NSF grant data and perform an analysis against of data using these two federal funding agencies. We recognize that it may be relatively common that institutional policies restrict access to internal financial management systems, and this capability will enable institutions to work with data from the NIH and NSF which are in many cases the most significant sources of grant income for an academic institution.

5.2 Return on Investment

	All IU grants	IU College of Arts and Science grants
FY 2014	$11.7 million	$6.5 million
FY 2015	$24.5 million	$11.2 million
FY 2016	$39.8 million	$14.0 million

Table 2: The table shows the grant income to PIs/Co-PIs with accounts on Big Red II universitywide at IU and also specifically in the College of Arts and Science (COAS).

Existing studies of return on investment (ROI) in campus CI show that a steady and significant investment in high performance computing is very likely to lead to increases in publications and grant income [25, 26, 37]. Big Red II exemplifies this, having made its debut in 2013 on the Top 500 [18] most powerful computer systems list at #46. Table 2 shows the IU grant income for FY '14, '15 and '16 according to PI/Co-PI team use of Big Red II. The grant income is separated for the College of Arts and Science given that it is a much more relatable department that is present in many, if not most, institutions of higher education.

Big Red II, personnel, and support will have a total average cost, over the expected 5 year lifespan of the system, of something lower than $15 million dollars total. At roughly the halfway point of the life of Big Red II, grants to IU researchers that use this system total just under $40 M. A rough projection might be that over the lifespan of Big Red II the total grant awards brought to IU by PI/ Co-PI teams that use Big Red II will total $90 M. Of that, roughly one third might come to IU budgeted in grant awards as roughly $30M in facilities and administration funds. That's roughly $6M per year in facilities and administration monies to IU when IU's investment per year in Big Red II is $3M per year. In other words, the facilities and administration funds income to IU that comes along with grant awards to people who use Big Red II is twice what Big Red II costs to operate. Factor in the value of increased competitiveness for grant funds overall and impact on total grant income, and the scientific value of the research done with Big Red II, and all together one can make a qualitative but seemingly reasonable argument that Big Red II is a reasonable investment for the University. There are qualitative parts to this argument, and some of it depends implicitly on value judgments (such as "there is significant value to research done with supercomputers that could not be done without them"). But it's an argument reasonably supported by data and an argument that constitutes a reasonable start for facts-based discussions about investment priorities within a college or university. The ability to have the data that enable such discussions is overall the most important aspect of the data collection activities in which we have engaged and the capabilities that XDMoD_VA will put into the hands of many colleges and universities.

5.3 A Scalable Model for HPC Investment

Many institutions may be able to invest at some level in a local flagship HPC or supercomputer system, but perhaps not one with capacity and capability to meet all local computational needs. IU for example cannot meet all of the local demand for computer resources. Or, some institutions may not be able to invest in a central HPC flagship system at all. In these cases, investment in personnel to enable use of federally-funded HPC and supercomputer systems can be of great benefit to a university or college of most any size.

The basic components of HPC system are compute, a networked file system that is backed up and parallel scratch file system that is not backed up. The size of this system can be flexible and it can be configured to be built up to increase capacity later. The number of employees that are needed to effectively support this system depends on what kind of uptime and response time is expected. This is a difficult number to define as much depends on the usage model of hardware and the service expectations. From what we have observed in the HPC field in academia, about three full time employees could run the hardware described here, but more would be needed to do user support and outreach. This also does not address outages and issues that happen during non-business hours.

If this is not a possibility, having a few people on campus who are interested in HPC and are placed in a position within a department or organization that does IT support be XSEDE Campus Champions [3] is a great way to get inside information on the various HPC resources that are available as part of the national HPC infrastructure. Campus Champions get sample allocations on all the XSEDE resources, which makes it possible to quickly provide access to people on campus who are considering getting an account on one of those resources. Campus Champions can also be the de facto HPC user support person on the campus for both local and XSEDE resources.

For teaching colleges that do not have research as part of their organizational mission, having a small HPC system locally that can be used for teaching purposes or having a Campus Champion on campus that can get training accounts on XSEDE resources might make sense. Moreover, owning local supercomputing and HPC infrastructure does not preclude the institution from foregoing access to the national cyberinfrastructure that is available to researchers through XSEDE and other organizations. In fact, having an appropriate amount of local resources can act as a catalyst for local users to request and get more resources from national providers. And it is also true that while a university can hope to address 90% of the local needs by having local resources in place, it would not always be financially possible to address 100% of user needs. It might just make more financial sense to guide and support users with large requirements on national resources.

6. CONCLUSION

Our experience is that local investments in supercomputing and HPC resources and appropriate human resources foster and enhance innovation and academic achievement. Local resources reduce the hurdles that researchers and scholars needs to cross before getting access to HPC resources and this is having a transformative effect on departments. We are able to relate grants to Big Red II users at our university and this suggests that the benefits to the university in terms of grant income is a good value for the investment in supercomputing resources. Universities and colleges should consider investments in HPC at the appropriate scale for their campuses and they can use the XDMoD_VA tools in development to quantitatively evaluate the benefit of the investments to their campuses. We conclude this in the basis of interviews and on the basis of linkage of use of our HPC and supercomputing systems and grant success for IU researchers.

7. ACKNOWLEDGMENTS

This material is based, in part, upon work supported by the National Science Foundation under Grant No. 1053575 and 1566393 and also by the Indiana University Pervasive Technology Institute (founded with funding from Indiana University and the Lilly Endowment, Inc.). Any opinions, findings, and conclusions or recommendations expressed in this material are those of the authors and do not necessarily reflect the views of the National Science Foundation, Indiana University, or the Lilly Endowment. We would like to thank our vendor partners Cray and DDN for their collaboration in the implementation of Big Red II.

References

[1] Big Red II at Indiana University. https://kb.iu.edu/d/bcqt. Accessed: 2016-08-22.

[2] Big Red II Dedication. http://newsinfo.iu.edu/news/page/normal/24183.html. Accessed: 2016-09-08.

[3] Campus Champions - Overview. https://www.xsede.org/campus-champions. Accessed: 2016-08-22.

[4] Confluence - Team Collaboration Software. https://www.atlassian.com/software/confluence. Accessed: 2016-09-12.

[5] Cray Linux Environment (CLE) Software Release Overview. http://docs.cray.com/books/S-2425-52xx/. Accessed: 2016-08-22.

[6] Data Capacitor II. https://kb.iu.edu/d/avvh. Accessed: 2016-08-22.

[7] Discipline categories (for cyberinfrastructure) at Indiana University (PTI Technical Report PTI-TR13-008). http://hdl.handle.net/2022/20985. Accessed: 2016-09-09.

[8] Fairshare scheduling at IU. https://kb.iu.edu/d/avmu#fair. Accessed: 2016-08-22.

[9] Final Report of the Indiana University Cyberinfrastructure Research Taskforce. http://hdl.handle.net/2022/469. Accessed: 2016-08-30.

[10] INCITE Program. http://www.doeleadershipcomputing.org/. Accessed: 2016-08-22.

[11] Indiana University Information Technology Strategic Plan: Architecture for the 21st Century. http://hdl.handle.net/2022/471. Accessed: 2016-08-30.

[12] Indiana University Knowledge Base. https://kb.iu.edu/. Accessed: 2016-09-08.

[13] MOAB HPC Suite. http://www.adaptivecomputing.com/products/hpc-products/moab-hpc-basic-edition/. Accessed: 2016-08-22.

[14] Office of the Vice President for IT and CIO at Indiana University Cyberinfrastructure Value Assessment Report. https://scholarworks.iu.edu/dspace/handle/2022/20568. Accessed: 2016-09-12.

[15] Pervasive Technology Institute. https://pti.iu.edu/. Accessed: 2016-09-08.

[16] Secure Shell. https://en.wikipedia.org/wiki/Secure_Shell. Accessed: 2016-08-22.

[17] TACC Wrangler. https://portal.xsede.org/tacc-wrangler. Accessed: 2016-08-22.

[18] The TOP500 project. https://www.top500.org. Accessed: 2016-08-30.

[19] UITS User Satisfaction Survey. http://www.indiana.edu/~uitssur/. Accessed: 2016-09-08.

[20] University at Albany Information Technology Services askIT. https://wiki.albany.edu/display/askit. Accessed: 2016-09-12.

[21] University of Wisconsin-Madison Knowledge Base. https://kb.wisc.edu/page.php?id=3. Accessed: 2016-09-08.

[22] XDMoD (XD Metrics on Demand). http://xdmod.sourceforge.net/. Accessed: 2016-09-09.

[23] XDMoD (XD Metrics on Demand) Value Analytics Module. http://indiana.edu/~xdmodva/. Accessed: 2016-09-09.

[24] Final Report of the Indiana University Cyberinfrastructure Research Taskforce. 2005. Available at http://hdl.handle.net/2022/469.

[25] A. Apon, S. Ahalt, V. Dantuluri, C. Gurdgiev, M. Limayem, L. Ngo, and M. Stealey. High Performance Computing Instrumentation and Research Productivity in U.S. Universities. *Journal of Information Technology Impact*, 10(2):87–98, 2010.

[26] A. W. Apon, L. B. Ngo, M. E. Payne, and P. W. Wilson. Assessing the effect of high performance computing capabilities on academic research output. *Empirical Economics*, 48(1):283–312, 2015.

[27] L. Michael and B. Maas. Research computing facilitators: The missing human link in needs-based research cyberinfrastructure. *Research bulletin. Louisville, CO: ECAR, May*, 16, 2016.

[28] S. Pamidighantam, S. Nakandala, E. Abeysinghe, C. Wimalasena, S. R. Yodage, S. Marru, and M. Pierce. Community science exemplars in SEAGrid science gateway: Apache airavata based implementation of advanced infrastructure. *Procedia Computer Science*, 80:1927 – 1939, 2016. International Conference on Computational Science 2016, ICCS 2016, 6-8 June 2016, San Diego, California, USA.

[29] C. Peebles, C. Stewart, B. Voss, and S. Workman. Measuring quality, cost, and value of it services. In *EDUCAUSE Conference Proceedings, Indianapolis IN*, SIGUCCS '01, 2001.

[30] G. Staples. Torque resource manager. In *Proceedings of the 2006 ACM/IEEE Conference on Supercomputing*, SC '06, New York, NY, USA, 2006. ACM.

[31] C. Stewart, D. Hancock, M. Vaughn, J. Fischer, T. Cockerill, L. Liming, N. Merchant, T. Miller, J. Lowe, D. Stanzione, J. Taylor, and E. Skidmore. Jetstream - performance, early experiences, and early results. In *Proceedings of the 2016 XSEDE Conference: Scientific Advancements Enabled by Enhanced Cyberinfrastructure*, XSEDE '16, New York, NY, USA, 2016. ACM.

[32] C. A. Stewart. Doing science with big red ii as a campus resource. Presented at Cray Customer Briefing, a satellite meeting of XSEDE13 in San Diego, CA, 2013.

[33] C. A. Stewart, T. M. Cockerill, I. Foster, D. Hancock, N. Merchant, E. Skidmore, D. Stanzione, J. Taylor, S. Tuecke, G. Turner, M. Vaughn, and N. I. Gaffney. Jetstream: A self-provisioned, scalable science and engineering cloud environment. In *Proceedings of the 2015 XSEDE Conference: Scientific Advancements Enabled by Enhanced Cyberinfrastructure*, XSEDE '15, pages 29:1–29:8, New York, NY, USA, 2015. ACM.

[34] C. A. Stewart, D. Hart, A. Shankar, E. Wernert, R. Repasky, M. Papakhian, A. D. Arenson, and G. Bernbom. Advanced information technology support for life sciences research. In *Proceedings of the 31st Annual ACM SIGUCCS Fall Conference*, SIGUCCS '03, pages 7–9, New York, NY, USA, 2003. ACM.

[35] C. A. Stewart, M. Link, D. S. McCaulay, G. Rodgers, G. Turner, D. Hancock, P. Wang, F. Saied, M. Pierce, R. Aiken, M. S. Mueller, M. Jurenz, M. Lieber, J. Tillotson, and B. A. Plale. Implementation, performance, and science results from a 30.7 tflops ibm bladecenter cluster. *Concurrency and Computation: Practice and Experience*, 22(2):157–174, 2010.

[36] C. A. Stewart, C. S. Peebles, M. Papakhian, J. Samuel, D. Hart, and S. Simms. High performance computing: Delivering valuable and valued services at colleges and universities. In *Proceedings of the 29th Annual ACM SIGUCCS Conference on User Services*, SIGUCCS '01, pages 266–269, New York, NY, USA, 2001. ACM.

[37] C. A. Stewart, R. Roskies, R. Knepper, R. L. Moore, J. Whitt, and T. M. Cockerill. Xsede value added, cost avoidance, and return on investment. In *Proceedings of the 2015 XSEDE Conference: Scientific Advancements Enabled by Enhanced Cyberinfrastructure*, XSEDE '15, pages 23:1–23:8, New York, NY, USA, 2015. ACM.

[38] J. Towns, T. Cockerill, M. Dahan, I. Foster, K. Gaither, A. Grimshaw, V. Hazlewood, S. Lathrop, D. Lifka, G. D. Peterson, R. Roskies, J. R. Scott, and N. Wilkens-Diehr. Xsede: Accelerating scientific discovery. *Computing in Science and Engineering*, 16(5):62–74, 2014.

The Transition to Cloud-Based Student Printing

Melissa Bauer
Baldwin Wallace University 275
Eastland Rd. Berea, OH 44017
+1-440-826-6961
mbauer@bw.edu

Allan Chen
Muhlenberg College
2400 Chew St
Allentown, PA 18104
+1-484-664-3440
achen@muhlenberg.edu

ABSTRACT

At Baldwin Wallace University in Berea, OH and Muhlenberg College in Allentown, PA, student printing has traditionally used up a great deal of resources. This included hardware to maintain and replace, software to manage and deploy, and provision of supplies. Student printing also did not provide much in the way of convenience. While printing from a computer lab was easy enough, mobile printing was so painful at BWU that most students didn't use it, and Muhlenberg had not yet found a tenable solution. We did not provide for guest printing and color printing had to be sent to specific printers in specific locations. We had no campus card integration. In the Summer of 2015, BWU implemented wēpa, a cloud-based printing solution to reduce the use of these resources while not only minimizing the impact to students, but providing additional opportunities to the students. Muhlenberg College launched wēpa for the spring term, 2016. Come to this panel session to hear more about the challenges we faced, how we implemented wēpa, and our lessons learned.

Keywords

Printing; Cloud; Student Printing; wēpa

1. INTRODUCTION

Baldwin Wallace University and Muhlenberg College both implemented the wēpa cloud-based printing solution during the 2015 academic year. This paper will discuss the selection process, implementation, lessons learned and next steps.

2. Wēpa Background

Wēpa (http://www.wepanow.com) – which is short for "we print away" is a managed print services (MPS) provider based on print kiosk deployments. Rather than merely servicing and providing supplies for college-owned printers as most other MPS providers do, wēpa provides the hardware itself. A national company, wēpa utilizes local technicians to do field support.

This is a significant deviation from traditional print accounting and managed print services solutions. Most print accounting solutions utilize on-site hardware and servers. All data remains on campus, and quota management is entirely an internal affair. Most managed print services provide only supplies and hardware repair; wēpa is a hardware as well as a service solution.

Wēpa's cloud-based operation also means that there is significantly less hardware to maintain, fewer services to monitor, and much simpler connectivity requirements.

2.1 The Hardware

Wēpa utilizes Okidata laser printers – in both color and high-capacity black-and-white configurations – housed inside of kiosks. Designed to be the equivalent of a printing "vending machine," a small form-factor computer is located inside the kiosk as well. A touchscreen interface is mounted into the kiosk at the top. 2 USB ports are also available to users. Authentication to your campus system is via the card reader located on the front of the kiosk or via manual log-in via the touchscreen interface. The wēpa system connects to the campus system – such as LDAP or Active Directory - and does matching between card and account. For example, the LDAP system might include username, password, and student ID number. The card includes the ID number. Wēpa does the matching process that eventually connects to the print account.

Branding is available via replaceable inserts at the front and sides of the kiosk. The vinyl print surrounding the touchscreen can also be replaced if desired.

Figure 1 shows kiosk installations at Muhlenberg College and Baldwin Wallace University. Branding was foregone as it was deemed unnecessary to differentiate printing solutions from wēpa, and the signage was already sufficient. Baldwin Wallace chose to brand, including calling the service "Jacket Print." Muhlenberg did not differentiate between the color and black-and-white (B&W) printers, whereas Baldwin Wallace did. A B&W printer is in Figure 1 and indicated in the branding materials. Note the small handout holder along the right side of the kiosk. This holds a short instructional guide for users. Muhlenberg College Office of Information Technology added a stapler to the kiosk, bolted directly to the kiosk frame.

Figure 1. WEPA Kiosk Deployment at Muhlenberg College and Baldwin Wallace University

SIGUCCS '16, November 06-09, 2016, Denver, CO, USA
ACM 978-1-4503-4095-3/16/11.
http://dx.doi.org/10.1145/2974927.2974961

2.2 Cloud-Based Print Queue

Wēpa users print to a unified queue in the cloud. This queue is hosted on wēpa's servers rather than an on-campus print server. Regardless of print method, jobs are sent to this single queue, and it is this one listing of print jobs that is accessible from any kiosk. This has the significant benefit of "follow-me printing" and provides flexibility on the location of the printers themselves.

Because the queue is in the cloud, configuration of the kiosks is especially easy. The kiosks need only standard connectivity to the internet. Authentication, document retrieval, and queue access are all over standard connections.

In addition, there is no on-site print server to maintain, not special network configurations required, and no additional equipment to monitor or support. From a staff perspective the overhead is significantly decreased.

Print jobs are sent as black & white or color, single or double-sided. This cannot be reconfigured after it is sent to the queue.

2.3 Multi-Device/Channel Support

Wēpa supports a wide array of print channels. Along with printing from a computer, users can also print from mobile devices, via upload to the web, email to the print queue, and direct-attached USB flash drives. Cloud storage solutions such as Google Drive and Microsoft OneDrive can be accessed as well.

Because jobs are sent fully configured as black & white or color and single or double-sided, wēpa installs 4 separate printers on a user's computer.

- Black & White Single-Sided
- Black & White Double-Sided
- Color Single-Sided
- Color Double-Sided

Users must select to which printer a job is sent intentionally at the time of printing. Because each appears as a standard Windows or Macintosh printer, it is possible to make one of them the default options.

Both iOS and Android are supported for mobile devices. Printing is done via an app rather than the native device print solution (i.e. – AirPrint on iOS and CloudPrint on Android). A common process would be to share a document from one app to the wēpa app. The user then configures the document for black & white or color and single or double-sided before uploading to the queue. It is possible to directly open a document in the wēpa app as well.

2.4 User Authentication

Wēpa's system directly queries the institution's director service, such as Active Directory or LDAP. Wēpa searches the information on a user's ID card for a specific string (such as ID number) and matches that to the directory listing. It can then provide information such as print jobs and available funds.

2.5 Payment Options

Wēpa offers several options for payment. The first is the wēpa account, which is managed by the company. These can be either "virtual" dollars or actual funds deposited by the user via the http://www.wepanow.com website. Users are able to add funds to the account via the kiosk as well.

Integration with an institution's "OneCard" system is also available for select systems. An institution can create a set of funds (e.g. – "Print Bucks") that is tied to the institution's financial software. This can leverage internal management solutions as well as existing access and deposit options and processes.

Finally, wēpa also accepts direct payment by debit or credit with a surcharge.

A user's available funds is listed directly on the touchscreen display.

2.6 Supplies

All supplies are provided by wēpa. This includes paper and toner, as well as fusers and drums for more extensive maintenance of the printers. Traditional MPS programs include toner but usually not paper. The printers are accessed via the front panel of the kiosk, which is locked but keyed alike across campus. When a new toner is installed, notification is sent to wēpa and new supplies are sent to the school. Paper is sent on intervals based on usage, again monitored by the wēpa system.

2.7 Support

Wēpa provides a fully managed print solution. There is an expectation that the institution will make an effort to resolve basic problems before contacting wēpa. However, if needed, wēpa will send a local technician the next business day for more extensive repairs.

2.8 Metrics and Monitoring

Wēpa provides two web-based services to institutions. The first is a page indicating print statistics. This includes total print volume across all kiosks, as well as a breakdown between color and black & white prints. In addition, information about each individual kiosk is provided. This is an effective "snapshot" of usage around campus.

A second page with kiosk status is also provided. This indicates whether printers are out of paper or toner, as well as remaining life on the toner cartridges, drums and belts. Printers approaching low levels are indicated in yellow, and those out of paper, toner or other supplies are indicated in red.

2.9 Costs

The kiosks themselves are provided for free. Wēpa analyzes print usage across campus to determine how many kiosks are appropriate for that volume, and delivers and installs the units as per the school's preferences. Wēpa's revenue is based entirely on the per-page charge imposed upon the user or institution, depending on configuration. Table 1 shows wēpa's costs per page.

Table 1. Wēpa Costs Per Page

Black and White, Single Sided	$.09
Black and White, Double Sided	$.17
Color, Single Sided	$.35
Color, Double Sided	$.68

Users have funds provided as "virtual" dollars loaded by wēpa or loaded via the website or at a kiosk using a personal credit or debit card. In the case of virtual funds, the institution is then charged for prints.

2.10 PCI-DSS Compliance

Wēpa uses a secure VPN connection to their servers for all credit card transactions, meaning there are no PCI-DSS compliance issues for the institution.

2.11 Visitor and Guest Printing Support

An important feature of the wēpa system is that it allows for visitors and guests to print without intervention from IT or institutional staff. Wēpa is a standalone print account system unto itself. This means that guests and visitors can create an account at http://www.wepanow.com, add funds directly and login at any kiosk (including ones at other institutions) No intervention or support other than provision of information is required from the institution.

3. Baldwin Wallace University

Baldwin Wallace University (BW), founded in 1845, is a liberal arts institution located in Berea, OH. An enrollment of 4,000 students includes undergraduates, Conservatory of Music, MBA, several Health Sciences programs as well as other master's programs.

88% of our students reside on campus which is in an historic residential community just 20 minutes from the thriving business and cultural center of Cleveland, Ohio.

3.1 Printing Prior to wēpa

Student printing is managed by the Department of Information Technology. Prior to 2004, printing was free and unmetered. There was a lot of waste in addition to the high expense of printing without restriction. In 2004 we implemented the Pharos UniPrint system. Initially, printing was still free though we were able to meter student usage. After two years of analyzing data, we determined most students could meet printing requirements by implementing a print allowance and reduce the waste by students, faculty and staff who misappropriated the system. In the Fall Semester of 2015, IT managed 33 HP LaserJet printers and two Xerox color printers in 34 student computer labs and three residential complexes across campus using the Pharos UniPrint system. Each semester, full-time students received a $25 printing allotment and part-time students received a $15 printing allotment We used a networking tool provided by HP to notify the help desk of paper jams, low toner, paper outages and maintenance needs.

All but 4 of our laser printers were 10 years or older and requiring increased maintenance. Toner was becoming difficult to acquire for the oldest printers.

Maintaining the student printing environment was labor intensive due to the manual processes of printer installation, maintenance, and troubleshooting as well as supplies ordering and account reconciliation for faculty/staff printing and billing for student printing. Students were unable to use funds on their campus ID card to pay for printing in excess of their printing allotment.

Mobile and wireless printing using Pharos was tedious and cumbersome in our environment and there were no options for cloud or USB printing.

3.2 Decision Toward Managed Print Services

By the fall of 2015, Information Technology was making a concerted effort to move away from a device-centric/personal computing philosophy to align with the strategic goals of the IT Strategic Plan and the Campus Master Plan of an enterprise computing philosophy and an infrastructure-based operation. We decided to explore a vendor solution that would provide printers, supplies, and maintenance while allowing for ease of use, multiple billing options and more printing options such as mobile, wireless, USB and cloud printing. Students were unhappy with the existing offerings for mobile printing from their personal devices as well as the limited locations available for color printing.

3.3 wēpa Deployment

We chose wēpa out of Alabaster, Alabama as our print solution in mid-June of 2015. This solution provided print kiosks that could be skinned with university color schemes and logos. No local servers were necessary. The solution allowed for six print methods for students: Traditional print driver; web; email; several cloud storage options (including Dropbox, OneDrive, and Google Drive); mobile apps for phones and tablets; and a USB device. Consumables would be monitored by wēpa and shipped to meet anticipated demand. Secure document retrieval and public and guest printing were additional benefits. The system integrated with our campus card (Blackboard Transaction System) and vendor provided print cards and credit/debit cards could also be used for payment. Cloud technology allowed for document retrieval at any kiosk on the wēpa system. We decided to implement for the Fall Semester of 2015 which allowed us just six weeks for implementation after we signed the contract. This did not allow for a demo or test period. However, we were confident, based on our agreement with wēpa and conversations with other colleges and universities using the wēpa system that we would be able implement the solution in time for the start of classes.

We removed all BW-owned color and black & white printers and deployed 25 kiosks in key locations throughout campus. Eight high-capacity black & white printer kiosks were placed in high volume traffic areas and an accessible kiosk was placed in our library. We avoided placement in classroom environments to allow for unrestricted access to the kiosks for all students. To allow for copying, we provided a scanning station that sent the image directly to the print kiosk. Accounts were set up with Active Directory and our Admin team created a procedure to send a document every night with currently registered students. Faculty and Staff can only use a print card or a credit card to print at a student kiosk. BW provides over 60 campus-owned multi-function devices across campus for faculty/staff use. These are not tied to the wēpa system.

3.3.1 Print Costs

Baldwin Wallace does not have a technology fee and as such, the decision was made to phase in completely student-funded printing over three years. For 2015, full-time students received $20 in virtual credits and part time students received $10. In 2016, all registered students will receive $10 per semester and in 2017, students will pay for all printing. Table 1 indicates the per-page costs. Students will be able to use their campus card, apply a credit card to their wēpa account or buy a wēpa print card at the university bookstore or library.

3.3.2 Modifications and Adjustments Following Deployment

The software did not initially provide for single sign-on (SSO) and many of our students were confused by the need to login to wēpa from the lab computers when printing. Wēpa responded to our concerns and updated the program so students would only need to login to a workstation to send a traditional job to a printer from a lab computer. Students still need to authenticate at the kiosk to retrieve their jobs. They also customized the screen for our kiosk to use verbiage we thought our students would understand.

3.3.2.1 Marketing to students

Wēpa provided posters for the kiosk location with general instructions and kiosk location, as well as brochures to be distributed to students and available at kiosks. They also came to our campus and marketed to our students in our Student Union, dining hall and recreation center. They provided prizes and encouraged students to try the multiple methods of printing options available to them.

3.3.2.2 Overall Project Management
Working with wēpa was a positive experience, from evaluation to implementation. Their team was very responsive to our questions and requests. On-site installation went smoothly and was completed in just a few short hours. After a full year, we are still pleased with the service provided. Students have embraced this system because of all the printing options now available to them and the ease of use.

3.4 Usage
Usage statistics are in the following tables. Printing quantity stayed relatively stable from 2014 to 2015. Students used the all of the various methods available for printing. The early statistical printing information showed us that we would likely not realize any cost saving. And, in fact, this turned out to be true. Our supplies expenditures for the 2014 academic year was $19,219. Our expenditures for student printing at wēpa for the 2015 academic year were $56,729.04. Tables 1 through 4 indicate usage at Baldwin Wallace University across several parameters.

Table 2. Printing comparisons Fall 2014/2015

Total # of Sheets	
Fall 2014	392,178
Fall 2015	389,252
Spring 2014	374,110
Spring 2015	387,085

Table 3. Upload Print Method

Upload Method	
Print Driver	57%
USB	18%
Web Upload	13%
Email to Print	8%
Mobile Upload	2%
Google Drive	1%
Dropbox	< 1%
OneDrive	< 1%
Office365	< 1%
Box	< 1%

Table 4. User Information

User Information	
Total print jobs (10,182 anonymous)	180,603
Unique identified users	3,306
Users who printed more than one time	3,179

Table 5. Key Kiosk Location Usage – October 2015

Location	% total output
24/7 LAB/Comp Sci/Nursing (4)	16%
Library locations (3)	15%
Conservatory of Music (2)	10%
Student Union	7.30%
Rec Center	7%

3.5 Benefits
Students adapted to the wēpa solution quickly and the new functionality has been extremely popular. Staff time to administer printing has been greatly reduced. Students appreciate the various options to pay for printing (campus card, print card and credit card). Allowing university guests to have printing access is now easy and we no longer have to create guest accounts. The reports that are provided allow us to see what cloud storage solutions students are using (BW provides a OneDrive account to each student, listed in our upload methods as Office365), the volume at each kiosk, the volume by student type and black & white printing versus color printing. We were able to relocate kiosks to accommodate areas that had a higher printing volume than anticipated.

3.6 Challenges
Students initially had to sign in to their wēpa account to print which was problematic at the beginning of the fall semester. However, SSO was quickly implemented. The higher cost of printing shows unfavorably in our budget reports as we do not track the labor statistics of the reduced need for staff intervention to implement the student printing solution. We will be reducing the virtual dollars provided to students in the 2016-17 academic year and not providing funds at all in the 2017-18 academic year. The kiosk fans are noisy and this caused some angst among the faculty who had classrooms near the kiosks. We resolved this by moving the offending kiosks where possible. After the first year, there has been minimal maintenance required for the printers. The small amount that was needed was quickly handled by our technical staff.

3.7 Conclusions
The wēpa solution has been extremely successful at BW. The students use all the upload methods provided and appreciate the convenience of being able to print in the high-traffic areas that were not previously accessible. Printing quantity has stayed stable or, perhaps, has slightly decreased based on our increase in enrollment in the 2015-16 academic year. We continue to encourage faculty to accept electronic documents to reduce student printing. While the cost has increased, the time spent implementing printing has been greatly reduced.

4. Muhlenberg College
Muhlenberg College is a liberal arts institution located in Allentown, PA. With 2200 students in our undergraduate "day" program and another 150 in our adult program, Muhlenberg offers a wide array of classes with a diverse student body. Programs in the arts – especially theater and dance – are particularly strong, with growing enrollment in neuroscience and finance.

Roughly 2000 students live on campus across, with the remainder usually in close proximity. There are 9 major, traditional residences, a set of standalone-buildings known as the Village, and a number of single-family homes in the surrounding neighborhood that are part of the Muhlenberg Independent Living Experience (MILE) program. All academic classes take place on-campus.

4.1 Printing Prior to wēpa

Printing is managed by the Office of Information Technology (OIT). Until spring term 2016, the college provided traditional HP LaserJet printers deployed into labs throughout campus, including in each residence (or in a space dedicated to a group of residences, such as the Village). Printers were specific to that location – only users in the Ettinger 001 lab could use the printers in that lab. In some locations, printers were specific to a set of computers rather than an entire space; users in the library had to sit at one of eight workstations to utilize the high-capacity printer on the main floor.

27 printers were in public labs, including the library. Another five printers were in computer-equipped classrooms. Only 1 of these printers was capable of color output, and it was located in a specific lab with limited hours.

Printing was both free and unmetered printing was not tracked at all. The OIT Student Help Desk delivered paper and toner to labs throughout campus. Because the Help Desk rarely if ever received notification of paper or toner outages, resupply was done pro-actively but without any certainty of need or knowledge of when paper and/or toner actually ran out. At best, we received notification from our facilities and/or custodial staff of resupply needs. We did not know how long these printers had been offline.

Roughly half the printers were 10 years old, and the remainder were at least 5 years old. Investment in new printers was not a priority over the past decade, and the allocation for the 15-16 fiscal year would have only replaced a handful of units. Need for repairs was rising, and the work was becoming more and more involved as more parts broke down. Often students would attempt to repair the printers themselves and leave the machines in particular disrepair. Finally, we faced a number of challenges due to the age of the printers. Toner was becoming harder to acquire. Also, we had to use paper of low recycled-material content to avoid jams. This impacted institutional sustainability goals.

The college did not provide any print management services, nor print accounting. We did not support mobile or wireless printing. Students familiar with adding IP-based printers would manually add college printers to their personal computers, but this was not an official service. Officially, students had to use lab computers for printing. Guests and visitors were not a problem because there was no control over printing or computer usage at all – anyone, community member or not, could sit down at a computer and print.

4.2 Decision Toward Managed Print Services

In response to the current state of printers on campus, the decision was made to explore managed print services in early Fall 2016. The goal was to off-load repairs and supplies to a third party. However, this only addressed OIT's operational concerns. It did not improve the student experience in terms of printer access or mobile support.

Consequently, the decision was made to find a managed print solution that supported a greater number of devices, could give accurate metrics as to use, supported color printing, and provided the option of pay-for-print down the road.

4.3 wēpa Deployment

Wēpa was chosen as our print solution in late Fall 2016. It met all of our needs for a managed print solution while providing the added flexibility of locating printers around campus regardless of lab availability.

We had concerns about the cost-per-page from wēpa. While we had no hard numbers, we felt we were providing printing at less than wēpa would charge. However, our hypothesis was that switching to a release-based kiosk system would reduce the amount of abandoned print jobs and compensate for the increased per-page expense.

Due to the size of the kiosks, we did not replace the computer classroom printers. We did use this opportunity to standardize them all on the same model.

We initially deployed 20 standard color kiosks and 1 high-capacity black & white unit around campus. Noteworthy are the 4 units (including the high-capacity one) in the library, the unit located in Seegers Student Union, and the installation in the entrance area of Walson Hall, one of our academic buildings. The student union and Walson instances are the first installations outside of a formal lab and in a presumed high-traffic area, supporting wēpa's support of "drive-by" printing. Furthermore, the Student Union had no print services at all prior to the wēpa installation.

We communicated the pending changes to students primarily through email and blog posts. Timing eliminated other communication channels. Negotiating contract terms took us deep towards the end of the Fall term. The need for strong usage data meant we wanted to deploy for Spring term, which gave us little time in between for a formal marketing campaign. We did not feel this was a great loss as we were still providing printing in the same locations (and in a few new ones) as before. There was some confusion about whether printing would truly remain free (see 4.3.1 for details), and in hindsight a longer lead-up to deployment with more communication would have helped. We likely would have utilized outreach from additional offices such as the Office of Campus Sustainability.

By late March we had replaced 6 of the kiosks in the residences with high-capacity black & white units in response to demand and challenges in support. The lower-capacity printers would often run out of paper and/or toner overnight. We intend to install similar units in all residences over summer 2016.

Total time from receipt of test unit to deployment was less than 3 working weeks. Because of wēpa's cloud-based model, which does not require special ports on the firewall or other custom configuration, we were able to get up and running and into the testing phase with little trouble.

4.3.1 Print Costs

We made the decision to keep printing essentially free, as making a change in the middle of an academic year would be unwise and unpopular. We provided a $25 "virtual fund" credit to each student. With wēpa's help, this amount auto-reloaded when the balance fell below $5. No actual money was charged to the student, and the college bore the costs of however much printing actually occurred.

The $25 mark was chosen as it was enough to yield a significant amount of pages, but low enough to hopefully emphasize the need to be conscious of print volume. We did not want to provide an initial quota of $100 or more and remove any notion of "cost" from the mind of students.

4.3.2 Modifications and Adjustments Following Deployment

wēpa is especially attentive to customer comments, and we went through a number of changes and modifications to the software following deployment.

4.3.2.1 Out of Order Message

When a printer is offline either due to lack of paper or toner, the screensaver changes to one that indicates "out of order" with a map of other kiosks on campus. The previous setup did not inform a student the printer was out of service until after the card swipe, which was a bad experience.

Notably, wēpa decided to roll this out to other customers.

4.3.2.2 Change to Desktop Client

In our labs, we auto-logout users after each print job. We do not want someone to walk up after someone else and print on the previous user's account. However, we discovered a strange behavior: if the login client is already running but minimized and one is in an application (e.g. – Word) and a user hits "print," the client does not come to the front. You have to manually select it from the task bar to bring it forward. There is no way for a user to know he or she needs to login. When the client is closed (and recessed to the system tray) it does pop up.

After some testing, we recommended to wēpa the simply remove the "minimize" button from the client. A user could maximize it or close it. In either case it would work. We appreciated that wēpa not only listened but provided a nice simple fix.

4.3.2.3 Student Usage Portal

We are discussing with wēpa the notion of a portal for students on usage. wēpa currently offers one for administrators – it indicates usage per kiosk, across campus, per day, per month, etc.; but it also indicates revenue and a few other items that would not be of interest to students. We want students to understand their environmental impact, to know that others are in fact using mobile to print, etc.

wēpa and Muhlenberg have been going back and forth on mockups of what this page would look like. We are excited that wēpa has been willing to go this route.

4.3.2.4 Custom Loading of Funds

We discovered through discussions that science majors in their Cumulative Undergraduate Education course had a particularly heavy color-printing need. We were able to identify which students these were and asked wēpa to load a higher initial quota to these individuals. They accommodated this request for this small subset without problems.

4.3.2.5 Overall Project Management

In general, it has been a very collaborative experience working with wēpa. They continue to be very responsive to questions – both big and small - on their project management portal. As evidenced by the discussion on the portal, they continue to take our thoughts under serious consideration. When we've gone through our "growing pains" phases, they worked with us to either assure us supplies were on their way or bumped up the delivery day if needed.

4.4 Usage

Usage of the wēpa kiosks is provided in Table 6. We tracked usage closely following deployment. The amount of paper we went through in our labs fall 2015 is also included for reference.

Table 6. WEPA Kiosk Usage Data

Month	Pages	Sheets	B&W%	Duplex%
9/2015[1]	X	117,000	X	X
10/2015[1]	X	101,000	X	X
1/2016[2]	83,745	56,531	92%	65%
2/2016	180,799	121,088	89%	66%
3/2016	205,436	128,622	90%	65%
4/2016	272,183	171,923	89%	64%

[1]We have numbers of reams we supplied to labs. We do not have a specific number of pages printed.
[2]January 2016 term started 2.5 weeks into the month. We actually saw very high usage for only 1.5 weeks of the month.

It quickly became apparent that not only was usage extremely high, but also that we would not realize any savings through the release-based model. We are in fact seeing a slight increase in usage compared to the previous arrangement. Even as we moved later into the term, usage clearly remained very high.

On the positive side, we are seeing very strong use of double-sided printing and students are clearly consciously choosing black and white over color.

Table 7 indicates usage by kiosk location for April 2016. Note that the Student Union location is entirely new with the wēpa deployment, in a public thoroughfare away from any computers and is a small-capacity color unit. This means it runs out of paper more often than high-capacity units and therefore requires more frequent trips to restock. The Library location is in a dedicated lab space and is a high-capacity black & white unit. Despite these differences, the student union location consistently outstrips the library kiosk. We had also hoped that the locations throughout the academic buildings would encourage students to gather print jobs on their way to class. However, students are also clearly still printing in their residences. Also noteworthy is that several residence halls are high on the list. Interestingly, January and February saw the top 10 kiosks entirely in the residences, and this has shifted only recently.

Table 7. WEPA Kiosk Usage by Location

Location	% total output
Student Union	16%
Library Reference Location	12%
Science Building Lab	9%
Library Lab Location	8%
Academic Building	6%
Residence Hall	6%
Residence Hall	6%
24 Hour Computer Lab	5%

4.4.1 Conclusions from Usage

The high usage is perplexing in many ways. We had accurate data on how much we were *providing* in supplies and also knew from observation that many jobs were left on the printer, abandoned by users. In theory the release-based process should have led to a decrease in usage. While we did increase the number of locations at which a printer was available, we decreased the number of actual units as some labs previously had multiple printers.

Our conclusions are that 1) students did not in fact abandon nearly as many jobs at the printer as we suspected and were very conscientious about when they chose to print and 2) our metrics were grossly inaccurate. Printers may have been sitting empty, without paper for days on end and students simply found other ways to print. Perhaps they moved from location to location, or some students knew to only print at less-used labs.

4.5 Benefits

The metrics – despite indicating a discouraging pattern of high usage and costs – are very useful. We have valuable insight into how students are using printers. We also can now see how many print jobs are coming from computers vs. USB vs. mobile devices. Table 8 indicates the averages for each available printing option from January-April 2016. While use is dominantly from the computer (including lab computers), we have enough use from other options to be noteworthy. Web upload usage is higher than we had expected as it is a few more steps than the other options. Mobile has been lower than hoped but enough to indicate it was a needed solution.

It is especially interesting that cloud storage is being accessed. Muhlenberg does not currently provide cloud storage. The use of this option indicates that not only are students utilizing Google Drive or Dropbox on their own, but also that they are using them actively for school work. It is unlikely that they are using it merely as a way to get files to the wēpa kiosks. This suggests that they are using cloud storage for production and work.

Table 8. Print Upload Method by Percentage

Print Method	% by Method
Computer	68%
Web	18%
USB	6%
Mobile	3%
Cloud (Google Drive, OneDrive, Dropbox) [1]	4%
Email	1%

[1]Muhlenberg does not currently offer an institutional cloud storage solution. Students are using these services on their own.

The monitoring of supplies and status has been very useful. When we first rolled out the standard color printers with their lower capacity, we were running out to refill paper frequently. We have mitigated this through the installation of high-capacity units around campus, and we would not have known about this need without monitoring. The per kiosk reporting enables analyzing student use patterns. As we look towards summer 2016 we will be relocating kiosks to higher traffic areas, improving the student experience.

Finally, it has been useful to have wēpa as a managed print service as well. The printers have not presented many problems beyond the occasional jam that has been easily cleared. When we have had a problem, we have been able to call wēpa and have a technician out the next day. Our teams (including the library) always make an effort to resolve the issue ourselves, but the reality is that we cannot always have the right people with the needed troubleshooting skills available. Wēpa fills this gap.

4.6 Challenges

Along with finding a way to address the unexpectedly high usage, our biggest challenge is dealing with what is clearly a cultural tendency towards printing and working on paper. Part of this does lie with faculty – we are seeing a number of larger jobs that suggest students are assigned long readings for classes. Faculty have merely transitioned from printed course readers with 50 page excerpts to electronic versions of those same readings posted on the learning management system.

However, in discussions with students and based on informal surveys (soon to be formalized), there is a cultural emphasis on working with hardcopy. Students not only prefer to work with paper, but correlate academic success with the ability to take notes longhand on print-outs.

There are still a few faculty that forbid laptops and mobile devices from class, but not so many as to be a cited factor in the continued use of printed course materials, according to informal surveys of students.

4.7 Print Quotas

Starting in summer 2016, we will be instituting print quotas for students. These will be one-time contributions to the "virtual" dollars and will not be reloaded. Students will be responsible for printing costs above and beyond this quota. Our hope is to integrate with our OneCard system, based on Blackboard Transact. We have an online portal for that through which students (and their parents) could add funds to the quota. If we are unable to launch that service and integration in time, we will utilize wēpa's own virtual fund account. Students would add funds via the wēpa website.

We initially loaded $25 on every registered student in the spring. As those funds were depleted, these accounts were reloaded back to $25. Therefore, the amount of "virtual" dollars loaded over the course of the term roughly equated to dollars spent.[1]. There is some fuzziness to this data – a user that only printed 1 page still appears as $25 loaded to the account, leading to a baseline amount above $0. However, Figure 2 illustrates that only a small minority or users print substantially above a certain limit, with a single person printing above $550 (the equivalent of over 6500 black & white pages). Users, sorted by usage, are on the horizontal axis and dollars loaded is on the vertical. The very steep rise on the extreme right of the chart shows how the truly heavy users represent a minority of overall usage.

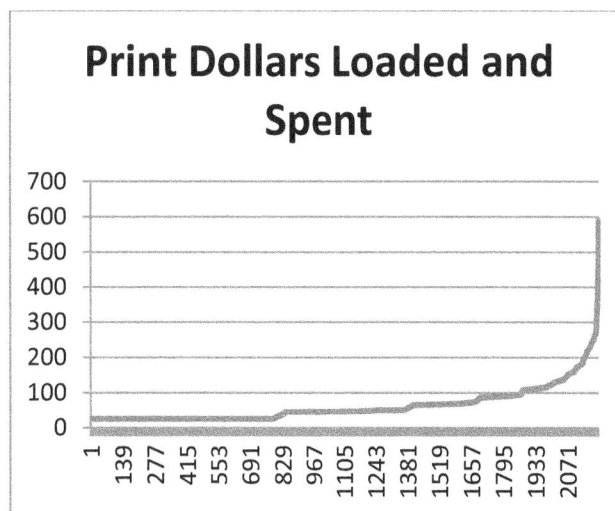

Figure 2. Print Dollars Loaded and Spent, Spring 2016

We found that the 70th percentile in dollars spent was $68.40. We have decided to allocate $70 per student, per semester. Because of the shorter summer term, $50 will be allocated during that time.

4.8 Conclusions

At the time of this paper's writing, we have not yet completed one academic term on the wēpa system. Even with that caveat, it is clear that we have a number of tough decisions ahead. Between continued high use and the increased per-page cost from wēpa compared to running our system in-house, our overall costs have gone up substantially. Even considering opportunity-cost savings from staff not having to go into the field for printer repairs, improved supplying of printers through the monitoring system and savings from not replacing aging printers; it is difficult to justify this continued expense.

However, we do feel there is an opportunity to shift away from the "culture of hardcopy" that exists currently at Muhlenberg. We will be working with the Provost and faculty as well as running digital note-taking workshops to help inform the student body on options. We are also hopeful that instituting a quota will have the impact on student printing that many other institutions have witnessed. Whether these changes will occur at all and fast enough for us to make an informed decision on the future of wēpa at Muhlenberg remains to be seen.

5. REFERENCES

[1] Kimmel-Smith, S., Sakasitz, S. 2010. It's Not Easy Being Green: Students and "the problem with printing:" In *SIGUCCS '10: Proceedings of the 38th Annual ACM SIGUCCS Fall Conference: Navigation and Discovery*, 223-228. DOI= http://doi.acm.org/10.1145/1878335.1878392.

Couch Learning Mode: Multiple-Video Lecture Playlist Selection out of a Lecture Video Archive for E-learning Students

Martin Malchow, Matthias Bauer, Christoph Meinel
Hasso Plattner Institute (HPI)
University of Potsdam
Prof.-Dr.-Helmert-Straße 2-3
Potsdam, Germany
{martin.malchow, matthias.bauer, christoph.meinel}@@hpi.de

ABSTRACT

During a video recorded university class students have to watch several hours of video content. This can easily add up to several days of video content during a semester. Naturally, not all 90 minutes of a typical lecture are relevant for the exam. When the semester ends with a final exam students have to study more intensively the important parts of all the lectures. To simplify the learning process and design it to be more efficient we have introduced the Couch Learning Mode in our lecture video archive. With this approach students can create custom playlists out of the video lecture archive with a time frame for every selected video. Finally, students can lean back and watch all relevant video parts consecutively for the exam without being interrupted. Additionally, the students can share their playlists with other students or they can use the video search to watch all relevant lecture videos about a topic. This approach uses playlists and HTML5 technologies to realize the consecutive video playback. Furthermore, the powerful Lecture Butler search engine is used to find worthwhile video parts for certain topics. Our approach shows that we have more satisfied students using the manual playlist creation to view reasonable parts for an exam. Finally, students are keen on watching the top search results showing reasonable parts of lectures for a topic of interest. The Couch Learning Mode supports and motivates students to learn with video lectures for an exam and daily life.

Categories and Subject Descriptors

K.3.1 [**Computer Uses in Education**]: Distance learning; H.5.2 [**User Interfaces**]: Training, help, and documentation

SIGUCCS '16, November 06 - 09, 2016, Denver, CO, USA

© 2016 Copyright held by the owner/author(s). Publication rights licensed to ACM. ISBN 978-1-4503-4095-3/16/11... $15.00

DOI: http://dx.doi.org/10.1145/2974927.2974937

Keywords

Teleteaching; Tele-Lecturing; Distance Learning; E-Learning; Self-Paced Learning; Video Lecture; Video Playlist; Lecture Video Archive

1. INTRODUCTION

During a semester several lectures are recorded for a course in a lecture video archive. Every lecture is about 90 minutes long. When you add up two lectures per week for a typical 12 weeks university course, the recordings sum up to 2160 minutes (36 hours) of video content. Students have to know parts of this video content for their final exams. Consequently, students have to watch several hours of lectures and have to search for important lecture parts during the learning process. The idea of the "Couch Learning Mode" is to create playlists with important parts from several lectures during the learning process in the ongoing semester. When students start learning for an exam they can play the created playlist, lean back on the "Couch", and start watching the exam relevant lecture parts for the whole semester automatically. Furthermore, students can share the best playlists with other students for learning purposes and to improve the playlist quality for fellow students.

While analyzing the tested lecture video archive tele-TASK[1] we investigated lecture recordings from different courses discussing similar or identical topics with various difficulty levels. This investigation encourages the development of the "Couch Learning Mode". Now playlists can be created for a specific topic which is discussed in several lectures of the lecture archive. This strategy is obviously aimed at students willing to upgrade their education and not for students learning for a final course exam. Nevertheless, it is a useful tool to enhance the learning experience for students willing to learn.

This paper is structured in five major sections. It starts with the current section "Introduction" to give an overview of the problem and ideas of the paper. The "Introduction" is followed by the sections "Related Work", "Approach", "Evaluation" and the final section "Results and Future Work". During the discussing of "Related Work" this paper gives an insight of further and close research in the e-learning context of video lecture archives. The following section "Approach" describes the actual research idea and realization of

---

[1]http://www.tele-task.de

the "Couch Learning Mode". In the section "Evaluation" we analyze the user acceptance of this approach. Sixty one students who are familiar with our lecture video archive evaluated the impact of this feature for their learning experience. Finally, the "Results and Future Work" section concludes the work of this paper. Additionally, an outlook shows further improvements and ideas in this research area.

2. RELATED WORK

An idea in the field of e-learning was proposed in a paper talking about the future of teleteaching [4]. This paper deals with the integration and interaction of classical video archives with upcoming MOOC platforms. One key point of this paper is the interaction between MOOC platforms and a video lecture archive platform and vice versa. Using this approach similar content can be connected between MOOCs and video lecture archive platforms. We think this is also interesting when you want to connect videos with similar or deeper content within a lecture video archive.

Another research goal in the area of lecture video archives is to find ways to identify difficult spots of a lecture [1]. The idea behind this topic is to find lecture parts which are hard to understand. Furthermore, the lecturer can use this information as feedback to improve the lecture in the following years by pointing out the problem in more detail. This will contribute to a better lecture and support students' learning experience. This paper's approach to use these difficult spots could be used in further versions of the "Couch Learning Mode" to create playlists automatically with the most difficult parts of the lecture. This will work out as a brain teaser for motivated students willing to learn more.

Another research area is semantic web. The semantic web represents a network with different topics which are connected to each other. By use of these connections similar topics can be found automatically [3]. These connections can be used to automatically create connections between videos and highlight relevant similar videos. One major problem of this approach occurs in the context of lecture video archives and keywords for a whole video. Since the videos are about 90 minutes per lecture videos are too long merge them together for a "Couch Learning Mode" session. As example, if only 5 connecting lectures were found which contain maybe 10 minutes of relevant content the student would have to watch 450 minutes of video with the couch learning mode. Therefore, an approach using time-relevant information of the lecture video like OCR [7] is an interesting idea for further research and automated creation of content for the "Couch Learning Mode". Lecture Butler research [5] will combine the OCR search results with the semantic network by using a powerful search which is able to find relevant parts of a lecture.

The native video support of HTML5 [2] enables browsers to play videos without an additional plug-in. Furthermore, no additional software has to be installed to run videos within the browser (e.g. Flash Media Player[2]) or for development of video players for a website (e.g. Adobe Flash Builder[3]). This evolution leads to faster and simpler HTML websites with custom video players. For example, a dual video player is possible which is able to play two video

streams in sync [6]. This is useful for lecture recording archives. Students have the possibility to watch the lecture slides and the lecturer in an appropriate and readable size. This approach is also going to be used for the "Couch Learning Mode" to show the videos and to be able to customize the player easily for the consecutive playback of several videos. This topic is going to be discussed in more detail in the following section.

3. APPROACH

This section describes the idea and implementation of the "Couch Learning Mode" in our prospective lecture video archive tele-TASK. This lecture video archive is based on the Python programming language using the Tornado web framework[4]. Tornado's strengths are handling thousands of text-based input/output-requests. Furthermore, several Tornado server instances can be started and handled with proxy balancing by a common web server such as nginx[5] which is already used to deliver static non-text content like images since Python with the Tornado web framework is not optimized and rather slow on non-textual data. The video content of our video lecture-archive is delivered with an Adobe Media Server[6] with the ability to stream RTMP and HTTP streams in the FLV and MP4 format. Due to historical reasons of the lecture archive portal we still offer a Flash-based player within the portal. Nevertheless, for new and old converted video content we recommend useing the standard HTML5-Player which is based on HTML5 video abilities.

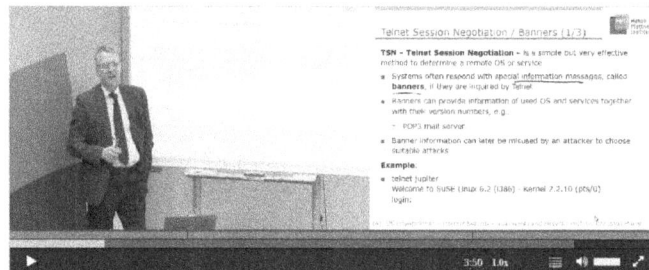

Figure 1: tele-TASK HTML5 Dual Video Player

The challenge for the video player is the synchronized playback of two video streams. Usually, the first stream shows the teacher and the second stream the slides. This dual stream video player is not officially supported by HTML5. Therefore, our player uses two video-tags which are synchronized by JavaScript and a custom user interface to jump within the video streams and to visualize the playback and buffering process. The player design is shown in Figure 1. The following subsections describe the adaptions of the tele-TASK video lecture archive to enable the couch mode within the HTML5Player.

3.1 Couch Learning Mode - Playlist

To realize the "Couch Learning Mode" by playing different video parts consecutively we need to define the video parts.

---

[2]www.adobe.com/products/flashplayer.html
[3]http://www.adobe.com/products/flash-builder-family.html
[4]http://www.tornadoweb.org
[5]http://nginx.org/
[6]http://www.adobe.com/de/products/adobe-media-server-family.html

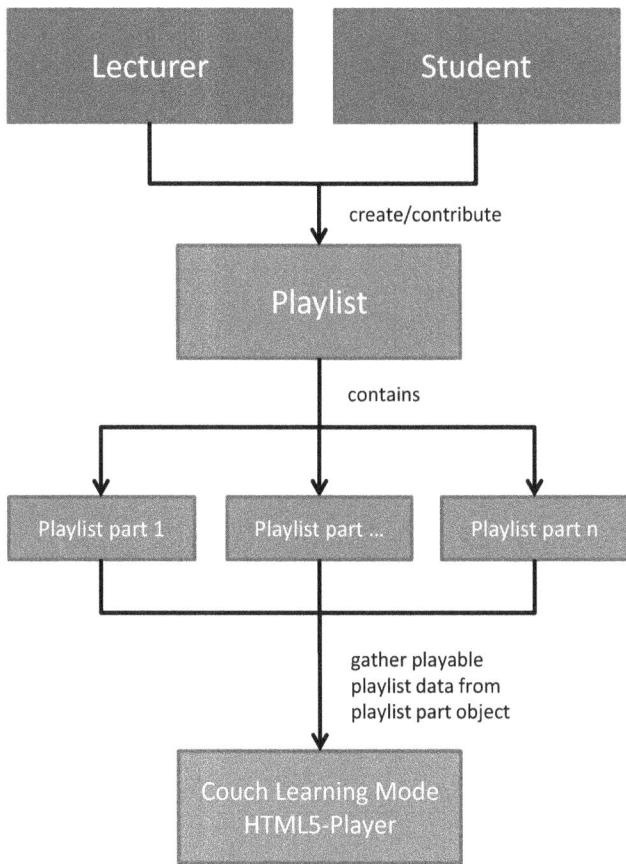

Figure 2: Couch Learning Mode Overview

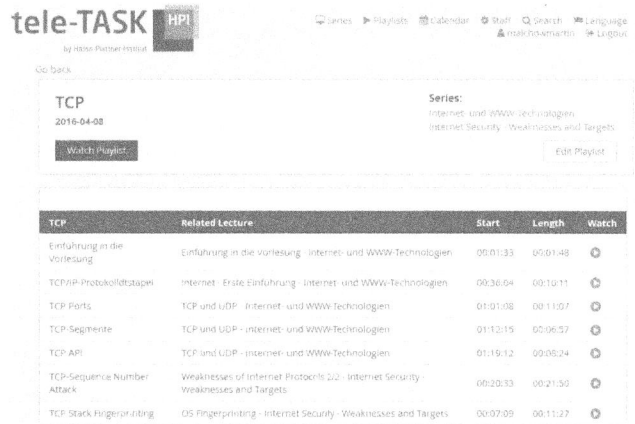

Figure 3: Playlist Overview for Students to Start Playlist

During the first implementation we decided for the playlist approach. The abstract overview of the playlist approach is visualized in Figure 2. On the top the students and lecturer (emphasized in brown) are highlighted as possible contributors of the "Couch Learning Mode" content. They have the ability to create playlists containing any number of playlist parts. A playlist part can be a mentioned video part of a lecture or a complete lecture. The data structure to store parts is a playlist in our approach and visualized in blue. Finally, the "Couch Learning Mode" HTML5-Player is emphasized in green as point of distribution for the playlist data as a video stream.

The implemented playlist overview in the video lecture archive is shown in Figure 3. When using a playlist a complete lecture, parts of a lecture, or a custom time frame of a lecture can be selected and added to the playlist. How this works in detail is described in Section 3.2. A playlist can contain from one to an arbitrary number of lectures or lecture parts. Furthermore, playlists can be limited to eligible users. These eligible users are selected by the playlist administrator. The playlist administrator can offer a playlist to the public that everyone is allowed to watch. Further details of access rights will be discussed in Section 3.3. Finally, the created playlist can be played in the HTML5-Player with added "Couch Learning Mode" which described in more detail in Section 6.

3.2 Couch Learning Mode - Playlist Management

A playlist can be created by any registered user on the lecture video archive. When creating a playlist the user is the administrator of the created playlist and has several options to manage the playlist. The user interface of the playlist management is shown in Figure 4. Basic manageable playlist settings are playlist image, playlist title, playlist description, playlist visibility (public/private), and playlist date. The most important parts are the playlist content overview and add lecture or lecture part to the playlist. When a user wants to add a lecture or a lecture part the user selects the appropriate series, which is a synonym for a course in a semester. After the user's series selection, an available group in this series and finally a lecture of this group within the series can be selected. When a lecture is selected all available lecture sections are shown. At this point the user can add the complete lecture to the playlist or can add parts of this lecture which are shown in the available lecture sections. After adding a lecture or lecture part the selection is added to the playlist, which is visualized in the playlist segments table. Due to hundreds of series and thousands of lectures the selection lists can also add a filter. Possible filters are "Series Type", "Organization" and "Lecturer". Filtering eases the process of finding lectures. We have applied the jQuery Chosen[7] plug-in, which enables a text search in HTML select fields.

Within the playlist segments table every segment (shown in every row) can be edited. The administrator of a playlist can change the playlist segment part name, the starting time within the full lecture and the duration of this segment showing in the playlist from the starting point. After a change is done the administrator user saves the changes and they are directly available for the invited users or when the playlist is publicy available for all users.

3.3 Couch Learning Mode - Playlist Access Permissions

The already mentioned access rights for the "Couch Learning Mode" is shown in Figure 5.

---

[7]https://harvesthq.github.io/chosen/

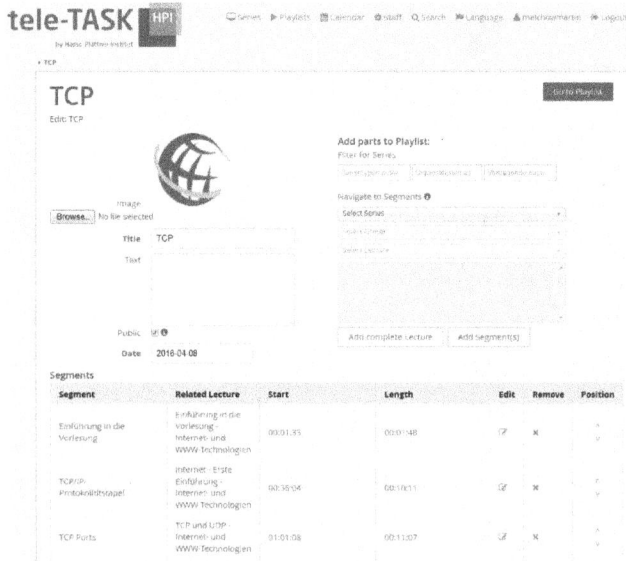

Figure 4: Playlist Management to Edit a Playlist

Figure 5: Access Permissions and Management for Private Playlists

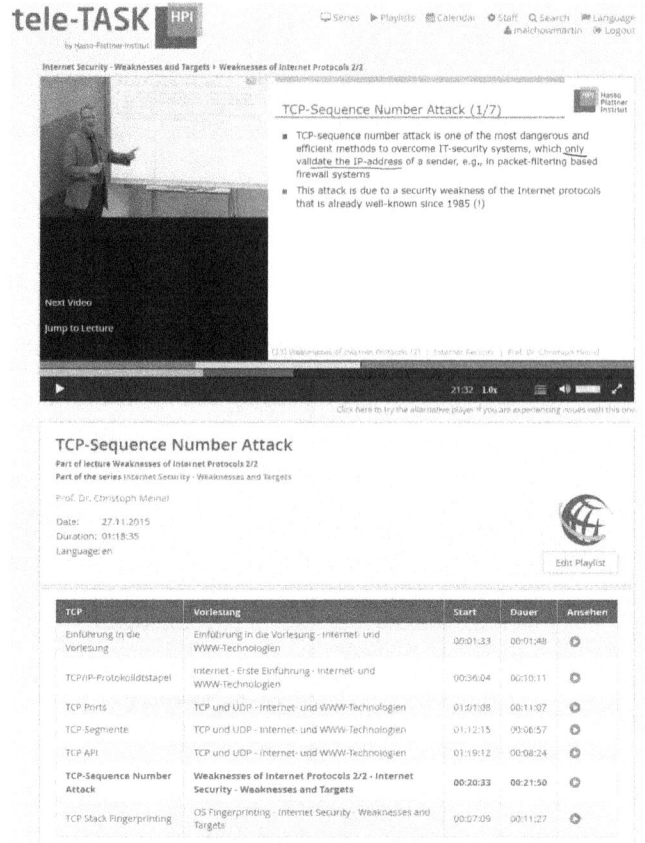

Figure 6: HTML5 Video Player During Couch Mode Playback

The access permissions can be set for private playlists. Additional users can be invited by email. We use the email identifier in this approach since users are recognized by email and user names are not used in the lecture video archive. The rights of added users can be increased to an administrator level. Administrator users can change the content of the playlist and invite other users to a playlist. Invited users with non-administrator privileges cannot modify a playlist or add users. When a playlist is public only an administrator of the playlist can edit the playlist and change the playlist visibility back to private.

3.4 Couch Learning Mode - HTML Video Player

The most important part for the "Couch Learning Mode" is the HTML5 player. It allows to play all videos of the playlist consecutively. For the realization the HTML5 player source code had to be modified to add the specific "Couch Learning Mode" functionality. The final player for this approach is shown in Figure 6.

When playing a playlist the player offers jumps within the available playlist part only. The available playable part is highlighted in the player with an orange bar (see Figure 6). The user can jump within the playlist video part. If the user wants to jump to a position before the playlist part the jump position will be the start of the current playlist part. When a user jumps behind the playlist part the start position is five seconds before the end of the current playlist video part. We

decided on a five seconds delay because the HTML5-Player in "Couch Learning Mode" shows the information, that the following playlist starts in five seconds. This countdown starts at five seconds and counts down to zero. When the countdown reaches zero the next video in the playlist will be started from the adjusted playlist position for the specified duration. In case the playlist reaches the last video the playback will stop after the last video part.

During playback of a playlist all following sections are visible below the player. In this playlist overview it is possible to jump to different parts of the playlist. Inside of the player jumping to the next playlist part and to the full lecture is also possible. When the student decides to go to the full lecture the "Couch Learning Mode" will end and a normal lecture video playback will start at the lecture time position the "Couch Learning Mode" was left.

In circumstances of a full screen playback the HTML5-Player just replaces the videos, playlist part information and start time. Normally, when a playlist part is over the next playlist part will be loaded and started with a redirect and reload of the page. Since this is not possible in full screen mode only parts of the player will be refreshed. When exiting the full screen a video change occurs the page will be loaded again and the player continues playback at the point in time where the full screen mode was ended.

4. EVALUATION

For the evaluation of the "Couch Learning Mode" we asked 61 students who are familiar with the video lecture archive to answer four questions about this approach. For the test case we created an playlist containing information about the topic TCP from several lectures and series. The students rated their experience with the "Couch Learning Mode". They answered questions about the overall experience, usage behavior and further improvement. The results are visualized in Figures 7 to 10.

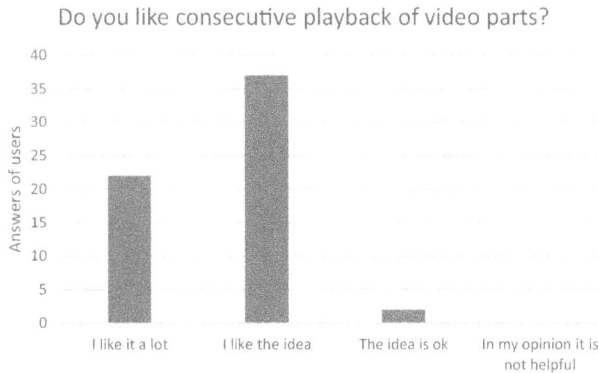

Figure 7: Evaluation Question 1: Do you Like Consecutive Playback of Video Parts?

The first survey question about the lecture butler was "Do you like consecutive playback of video parts?". The answers of the students are visible in Figure 7. Here it is obvious that students like the idea. Nearly 97% of the students say they "like it a lot" or they "like the idea". Only about 3% of the students said that the "idea was ok". Finally, 0% of the students think this idea is awful and useless in their opinion. This means the general acceptance of the approach is 100% and implementing this option in a lecture video archive is useful for the learning experience.

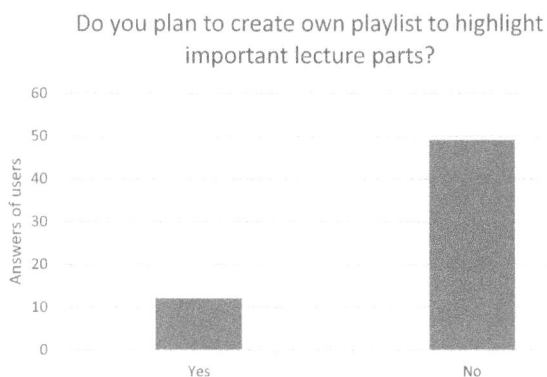

Figure 8: Evaluation Question 2: Do you Plan to Create own Playlists to Highlight Important Lecture Parts?

The following question two "Do you plan to create own playlists to highlight important lecture parts?" shown in Figure 8, is about user contribution to the lecture video archive by the use of the self-created playlist for the "Couch Learning Mode". Unsurprisingly, we found out that our students are more interested in being entertained and getting provided playlists they can use to learn. Only 12 students want to create own playlists to learn with them later for the exam and 49 students do not want to create playlists with valuable content for their fellow students or at least for their own exam preparation. This result shows that it is a good idea to offer students the possibility to create their own playlists. Nevertheless, most of the students will not use this learning possibility.

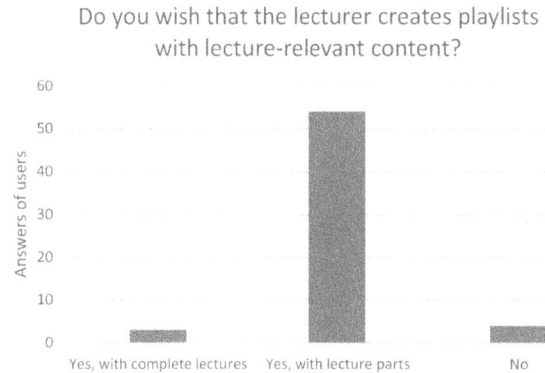

Figure 9: Evaluation Question 3: Do you Wish that the Lecturer Creates Playlists with Lecture-Relevant Content?

In question three "Do you wish that the lecturer creates playlists with lecture-relevant content?" plotted in Figure 9 we switch the perspective compared to question two. Now we want to know if students would like to get playlists for the "Couch Learning Mode" with relevant content for the homework and the exams. We expected this behavior, since the students want to have good exam results. Furthermore, it will reduce the the amount of content they have to learn if the lecturers will create playlists with exam-relevant content. This reduction of content is also highlighted, since 54 want to see only relevant lecture parts and only three students are fine with playlists containing the whole lectures. Only four students do not want to have playlist with relevant content created by the lecturer. It is a nice idea for the students to have lecturers creating playlists with major homework or exam topics. Nevertheless, the lecturers have to think about if they want to give so many exam hints and reduce the content students have to learn for the exam. Especially, when important parts for work life will not be learned by the students.

In the final question "Do you think it is useful to play video lecture archive search results consecutively?" shown in Figure 10 we asked students about further development of the "Couch Learning Mode" in the context of the video lecture archive search. About 70% of the students would like to have a "Couch Learning Mode" for the overall video lecture archive search. Thirty nine of the students want to have a consecutively playback for the most important lecture parts and only 4 students want to have a consecutive playback of full lectures. In contrast, nearly 30% of the students do not nead the "Couch Learning Mode" approach for the lecture search results. In conclusion of those questions it

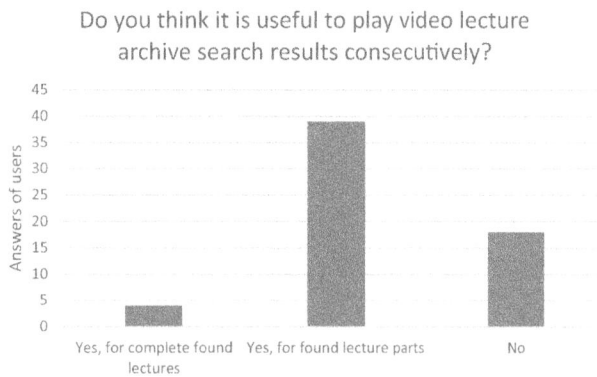

Figure 10: Evaluation Question 4: Do you Think it is Useful to Play Video Lecture Archive Search Results Consecutively?

seems to be useful to enable the "Couch Learning Mode" for the video lecture archive search in future since more than two-thirds of the students would like to have this functionality. In particular, students want "Couch Learning Mode" for the most relevant lecture parts of the search result.

5. RESULTS AND FUTURE WORK

In this paper we described "Couch Learning Mode" in a video lecture archive as a way to ease the learning process by watching reasonable lecture parts for a specific topic or relevant information for a semester course as homework or exam preparation. The functionality of "Couch Learning Mode" is currently very simple. First create a playlist based on lectures or lecture parts. Students can then use this playlist for their studies, invite friends to watch the playlist, or share it with the public. The overall results of the approach evaluation indicate that "Couch Learning Mode" supports the students during the learning process. A major problem for the success of the "Couch Learning Mode" could be the availability of playlists since most of the students are not interested in creating playlists. Actively contributing students have to share their playlists to make them more popular. Nevertheless, even if they decide to keep their created playlists private, they can still enhance their own learning and are also motivated to learn again and use their created content selection for the final exam. Another source for playlist creation could be the lecturer. The lecturers have to think about if they want to offer a complete list which is relevant for the exams and homework or if they just decided to create playlists for difficult topics. A full list of relevant exam content may lead to students learning behavior that other not so important topics are not learned at all. Even when the lecturers have to think about how they want to use the "Couch Learning Mode" in a course the implementation is valuable for students to support learning for a specific topic and motivate the students to decide to take time for learning. "Couch Learning Mode" can be particularly effective in helping students find all the important information on a specific topic.

Even when the "Couch Learning Mode" is useful for students we also have some additional ideas for future research. As already discussed in the evaluation in Section 4, search results should be playable in the "Couch Learning Mode". In addition earlier research of the "Lecture Butler" [5] should be considered. Another possibility of improvements could be a playlist containing internal and external video content to emphasize a thesis or deepen the knowledge about a special topic. Attention should be paid to the copyright when embedding external video content in the lecture video archive. Students who are not aware of copyright restrictions could violate copyright laws by embedding external videos. Further future work is an automated playlist creation to improve the available content for the "Couch Learning Mode" and motivate more students to watch specific lecture content. The automated creation can be done by an automated analysis of the most watched parts of a semester course which indicate difficult topics of a lecture [1]. Finally, we can improve the "Couch Learning Mode" with a video export. In this way we could support students that they have the possibility to watch the important parts offline on their computer or on the go with a mobile device.

6. REFERENCES

[1] M. Bauer and C. Meinel. A concept to analyze user navigation behavior inside a recorded lecture (to identify difficult spots). In *Information Technology Based Higher Education and Training (ITHET), 2014*, pages 1–4, Sept 2014.

[2] R. Berjon, S. Faulkner, T. Leithead, S. Pfeiffer, E. O'Connor, and E. D. Navara. Html5. Candidate recommendation, W3C, 7 2014. http://www.w3.org/TR/2014/CR-html5-20140731/.

[3] N. Englisch, A. Heller, and W. Hardt. Cross-system knowledge representation of learning content in systems for education. In *ICERI2015 Proceedings*, 8th International Conference of Education, Research and Innovation, pages 2269–2276. IATED, 18-20 November 2015.

[4] M. Malchow, M. Bauer, and C. Meinel. The future of teleteaching in mooc times. In *Computational Science and Engineering (CSE), 2014 IEEE 17th International Conference on*, pages 438–443, Dec 2014.

[5] M. Malchow, M. Bauer, and C. Meinel. Lecture butler: Teaching reasonable lectures from a lecture video archive. In *Proceedings of the 2015 ACM Annual Conference on SIGUCCS*, SIGUCCS '15, pages 3–9, New York, NY, USA, 2015. ACM.

[6] J. Renz, M. Bauer, M. Malchow, T. Staubitz, and C. Meinel. Optimizing the video experience in moocs. In *EDULEARN15 Proceedings*, 7th International Conference on Education and New Learning Technologies, pages 5150–5158. IATED, 6-8 July, 2015 2015.

[7] H. Yang and C. Meinel. Content based lecture video retrieval using speech and video text information. *Learning Technologies, IEEE Transactions on*, 7(2):142–154, April 2014.

Future of Computing Labs at Marriot Library

Harish Maringanti
University of Utah
295 S 1500 E
Salt Lake City, UT 84112-0860
801-581-8001
harish.maringanti@utah.edu

Matt Irsik
University of Utah
295 S 1500 E
Salt Lake City, UT 84112-0860
801-581-6575
matt.irsik@utah.edu

ABSTRACT

Citing recent ECAR[1] study [1], one may ask, when 91% of students own laptops, why continue with the physical computing labs on academic campuses? It is a fair question and one that we, at Marriott Library at University of Utah, constantly keep asking ourselves. Rising numbers in device ownership in student & general population have been predicted for sometime now (by various Educause[2] and Pew research center[3] studies). Some academics and technologists have looked at the implications of these rising numbers in device ownership. Their findings, though, have been mixed – while some argue that students prefer to use physical computers over their personal laptops for convenience & other factors, others have essentially proclaimed the death of these physical labs. An interesting quote from ECAR 2012 [2], suggests that, this question can be put to rest by "investigating this matter locally" as the local environment will dictate the shaping of successful strategy – for example, is IT support centralized, is it a commuter campus, does any department issue laptops for students as part of enrollment, etc.? While we plan to conduct student survey later this year, attempting to address this very question, we have taken a few steps that position us very well between the past and possible future.

Categories and Subject Descriptors

K.6.1 [**Management of Computing and Information Systems**]: Project and People Management – *Strategic information systems planning, staffing, systems development, training.*

General Terms

Management, Design, Economics, Experimentation, Human Factors.

Keywords

Computing labs, academic libraries, higher education, remote software delivery, 3D printing.

1. INTRODUCTION

1.1 Computing Labs at Marriott Library

Marriott Library offers technology assistance to students in the Library's 7 teaching labs, 2 outer computer labs (lab facilities located outside of the Library), classrooms, and Knowledge Commons with around 700 total systems (both PCs and macs combined). The Knowledge Commons is the largest student computing lab on campus, with over 250 systems, printers, hardware checkout, 3D printing, group study rooms, and is staffed by fulltime and part-time employees who offer a variety of technology services. Our users logged into these systems over 362,000 times last year, printed over 1.5 million pages, checked out over 51,000 technology items (laptops, chargers, etc) and registered over 75,000 interactions at the service desk. Students get help with technology related questions such as password assistance, wireless configuration, 3D modeling and printing; and they also get assistance on questions pertaining to access to information resources. The services we offer in Knowledge Commons supports "all aspects of student research from original resource discovery to creation of the final paper or other research product" [3]. We work with the University's Center for Disability Services (CDS), in providing technology infrastructure and assistance in the accessibility room located in the Library. The accessibility room provides a range of technology services for students with disabilities. Some of the highly used applications in this room include Dragon Naturally Speaking, Kurzweil 3000 (text to speech reader software), ZoomText, and JAWS (screen reader application).

Located in Salt Lake City, Utah, the University of Utah has more than 31,000 students, including over 7,500 graduate students enrolled in its various programs. The University is known for its outstanding medicine, business, and engineering schools, which feature one of the country's premiere Entertainment Arts & Engineering programs (EAE) and a recent Nobel Prize winner in Mario Capecchi[4]. Although primarily a commuter school, the 1535 acre campus features a large number of new and renovated buildings with state of the art facilities.

1.2 Changing Landscape

Though Pew Research Center studies have shown a slight decline in the device ownership of laptops and desktops in general population since 2012 [4], ECAR studies have consistently shown a steady rise in ownership of these devices in student population [1]. New Media Consortium's (NMC[5]) Horizon report lists Bring Your Own Device (BYOD) as one of the important developments in educational technology for higher education and states "as the link between the use of personal devices and learning has crystallized in recent years, the question is no longer whether to

SIGUCCS '16, November 06 - 09, 2016, Denver, CO, USA
Copyright is held by the owner/author(s). Publication rights licensed to ACM.
ACM 978-1-4503-4095-3/16/11...$15.00
DOI: http://dx.doi.org/10.1145/2974927.2974954

---

[1] Educause Center for Analysis and Research

[2] A nonprofit association whose mission is "to advance higher education through the use of information technology".

[3] A nonpartisan fact tank that informs the public about the issues, attitudes and trends shaping America and the World.

[4] An Italian-born American molecular geneticist and a co-winner of the 2007 Nobel Prize in Physiology or Medicine.

[5] A community of hundreds of leading universities, colleges, museums, and research centers.

allow them in the classroom, but how to most effectively integrate and support them" [5].

Given this general trend toward BYOD in learning environments, is there a role for physical computer labs on academic campuses anymore? University of Colorado – Boulder, in its report [7], outlined recommendations to repurpose some central computing labs into flexible-use spaces while increasing reliance on student-owned portable computers – these recommendations were made in response to the need to repurpose lab spaces and deliver lab services at lower costs. University of New Hampshire is tracking the use of its physical labs in the context of BYOD [8] and the general trend points toward shrinking of physical labs everywhere. On the contrary, a two-year study conducted at California State University San Marcos library analyzed student use of computers in the library, both the library's own desktop computers and laptops owned by students. The study found that, despite the increased ownership of mobile technology by students, they still clearly preferred to use desktop computers in the library [3]. Referenced in the same study is another study done at Australian University where the conclusion was "given a choice of central computer labs, residence hall computers, and the library's information commons, most students preferred the computers in the library over the other computer locations, with more than half using the library computers more than once a week. They rated the library most highly on its convenience and closeness to resources" [6]. Though more studies and research need to be done on this particular question, one can speculate that, computer labs located in the Libraries may follow a different trend than other computing labs, because of being co-located with other useful student services.

1.3 Strategy
How do we plan for technology development, student services, staffing and training in these challenging times when the future of student computing and learning environments is in flux? Our strategy and approach, at Marriott Library, has been to respond to students' needs by making incremental changes to our services and acting swiftly and pro-actively with the information we have at hand. What follows is a discussion of how we envisioned, initiated and expanded 3 specific technology services related to student computing in our learning spaces.

2. HARDWARE CHECKOUT PROGRAM
2.1 Overview
The Marriott Library runs a highly successful student hardware checkout program that saw over 51,000 items checked out in 2015 by students, including well over 10,000 laptops during that period. As computer labs continue to change, so do the technology needs of students outside of the usual software and desktop services that are generally provided by academic institutions. These technology needs encompass a wide variety of uses, from graphics tablets for Fine Arts assignments to laptops for class use and up to simply needing a charger for their mobile device for a study group after hours. Implementing, maintaining, and expanding this service provides constant challenges in an ever-changing technology landscape.

2.2 History
The Marriott Library computing labs have always provided basic computer and audio-visual hardware for student checkout. At first this consisted of headphones, external drives, mice, etc., but as the technology in systems, software, and the spread of mobile devices has expanded, so too did the requests of students to have more items offered. The basic hardware checkout inventory described

above quickly expanded to laptop chargers, cables for laptops to hook into AV systems, iPods, adapters, and more. Over the last five years, student hardware checkout needs have greatly accelerated to include graphics tablets, laptops, mobile hotspots, video cameras, 3D scanners, and a large assortment of cables, adapters, and chargers.

2.3 Funding
From its beginnings, the hardware checkout program used very little in the way of annual funding resources. As the needs of the students have expanded, so has the amount of funding set aside for this service each year. With the recent introduction of laptops for student checkout, the level of funding has struggled to keep pace, necessitating line items on the annual student computing funding proposals. Also, the large number of mobile devices that students bring into the Library, many of which do not use the same peripherals, has resulted in increased spending and additional inventory to meet these varied needs.

2.4 Staffing
While the basic hardware checkout service needs little in the way of staffing other than the usual staff who work at the service desks, the introduction of laptops has introduced a need for additional staffing. With the laptops being checked out so frequently, the need to update, re-image, and take care of problems that arise is more than the service desk staff is able to manage. This has necessitated the technical support groups having to assign staff to complement the work being done at the service desks. The technical groups maintain that laptops need approximately 1.25 times more maintenance than the standard desktop computer system. The heavy use coupled with multiple users each day has complicated the updating/re-imaging tasks as well as just providing general maintenance.

2.5 Training
The only additional training needed for this service revolves around getting the right hardware to the student for their particular needs, which could range from simply charging the device to needing an adapter to work with a particular set of AV equipment across campus.

2.6 Assessment
The best way to assess this service is by the usage statistics, which have continued to increase each year. Students are continually recommending new items that could be offered and the student staff members are essential in assisting full time Library staff in recognizing developing trends. The staff is very proactive and usually order extra hardware when new devices are first seen in the labs or through articles shared by the technical groups. There was a recent laptop checkout survey where students provided responses to a range of questions regarding the service. Most of the answers in response to the question related to the students' use of computers in the Library centered around their preference to not have to carry their own devices around campus, and software needs (this question was asked of students who owned laptops) – these results are pretty consistent with other published reports in the literature [3,8]. The most popular request was to increase the length of hardware checkout times (from 4 hours to at least a day). In the immediate future there are plans to run a survey for students about their hardware needs and how the Library could position itself to meet them.

2.7 Research/Curriculum Needs
The Marriott Library works with faculty to help determine the needs of students for their research and class assignments. The

expansion of graphic tablets, from two in 2014 to 24 in 2016 was the result of more classes being taught with those devices and students needing them outside of the classrooms for assignments. The mobile hotspot checkout program, which was a joint project with T-Mobile and University Information Technology (UIT), was the result from a request by Undergraduate Services to provide wireless access for under-privileged students. Library faculty, working as faculty liaisons to various academic departments on campus, convey class requirements to the Library's technical groups or put us in contact with faculty who will be teaching classes in the Library. This will often result in the Library adjusting the numbers of pieces of hardware items that are made available for checkout, to meet these needs each semester.

2.8 Sustainability

With the continual changes in device and software needs, it is essential for one or more lines of funding be developed to maintain this service at a reasonable level. Equipment can become outdated very quickly and the needs of faculty who assign students various projects, can change frequently. This service needs to be agile, always looking a few years out, and has available funding that allows it to quickly respond to student needs.

3. REMOTE SOFTWARE ACCESS

3.1 Overview

Although many students have a variety of mobile devices today, with most being laptops, the desktop systems in the student computing labs are still seeing heavy use. We speculate, based on anecdotal evidence, that the main reason for this is the inability of students to either being able to afford the more expensive software applications they need, or the issues with the installation and updating of these same applications. Other reasons that are often cited in studies include – the convenience of not having to remember to bring their laptop to school and "lug" it around [3], aging hardware, etc. The Marriott Library has been addressing this issue for the past few years, deploying a remote software access service based upon using Aqua Connect for Macs and Ulteo for PCs. After extensive testing and usage by students, Ulteo has been dropped in favor of Software2, a more robust and capable system. The Marriott Library is now preparing to make a major jump forward in this area by deploying these systems to a wider audience.

3.2 History

After attending Educause in 2010 and 2011, the Marriott Library student computing labs put forth a proposal to University of Utah Information Technology (UIT) for funding to pursue remote software access. At that time, the only two viable options were Citirx and various forms of VDI (Virtual Desktop Infrastructure), so a low cost alternative was sought that might be sustainable by the campus. The two systems chosen, Aqua Connect for Macs and Ulteo for PCs, initially showed great promise. The main issues encountered involved proper funding for a campus wide service and Ulteo had several development issues. While several classes and many individual students have used the service, the PC side of the equation needed a major overhaul, which has come to fruition this year with the purchase and deployment of Software2.

3.3 Funding

The initial funding of $30,000 was sufficient to purchase servers and licenses to begin work, which resulted in a service being deployed within six months of receiving the funding. In the following year additional funding was received to expand from 50 users per platform up to 100 users along with additional software licenses. In the last few years there has been minimum funding as the campus decides if the service should expand and there has been debate about how best to improve the service. The Marriott Library this year requested funding to continue Aqua Connect for the Mac side of the service and to continue with the deployment/expansion of Software2 for the PC side. Software2 can be purchased based upon a number of users that can access it or as a campus wide site license. If a campus wide site license was to be purchased there would need to be discussions about funding additional staff positions to offer technical support.

3.4 Staffing

No additional staffing was ever funded, so there has been a partnership between the technical groups who administer the service and Student Computing Services (SCS) who assist students with issues pertaining to the service. Once the service was set up the staff mainly do updates, administer the software licenses, and assist students with connection issues. With the introduction of Software2, the technical groups have spent a large amount of time learning the system, packaging applications, and testing. If the service would be approved to expand to all of campus there would need to be funding for dedicated staffing to administer the system, perform outreach with faculty, offer 24/7 student support, and more.

3.5 Training

The training plan for Software2 implementation has been quite extensive and has been ongoing for several months as the employees learn more about deployment, packaging, dependencies, and optimization. The Aqua Connect system took a few years to perfect for those wishing to use the Mac platform and with upcoming changes to this system the technical staff will need to invest more time to upgrading it. On the student support side, the full time and hourly student supervisors needed some training to learn how to access the system, assist students with their configuration, and how to troubleshoot common issues.

3.6 Assessment

Statistics over the last few years show that the service is being used, but not to capacity. Most of this has been due to the PC side of the service having multiple issues and the number of steps that have to be completed to fully use the service (user experience), plus some of the limitations in terms of what applications are offered, saving files, etc. In conjunction with a recent laptop survey along with discussions with students as well as faculty, being able to deploy large numbers of needed software applications is still needed on campus for those student with laptops so that they do not have to physically attend computing labs with specialized software packages.

3.7 Research/Curriculum Needs

When this service was being developed we were able to partner with several faculty who had specific needs for their class assignments that included applications such as Lightwright and Vectorworks. Students were often unable to get to the labs that had these applications during their open hours, so the ability to access these 24/7 was greeted enthusiastically. The Marriott Library has worked with several faculty members to make specialized applications available on this service as well as with student requests. For Software2 testing the Library will be partnering with Electronic Arts & Engineering (EAE) and the

Lassonde Studios[6] to provide Unreal Engine/Visual C++ and the PTC Creo suite available for certain classes.

3.8 Sustainability

Since its inception this service has been able to be sustained through minimal annual funding for equipment and licenses, but the service has been limited to 100 concurrent users (due to funding and support limitations) on each platform and has never been fully marketed to all of campus. With a possible change to where this service could be offered to all of campus there would need to be substantial funding applied for servers, software licenses, marketing, and support, at least for the initial year of expansion.

4. 3D PRINTING

4.1 Overview

3D printing has become one of the Marriott Library's most popular and talked about services since it's start almost three years ago. From a single printer that was used to train staff and begin a low cost, pay for print service for students to having a dozen printers with student usage climbing each day, this is a technology whose rapid evolving poses great challenges. Which printers to purchase, how to train staff and students, funding for equipment, which software to use, and more, are some of the obstacles that have come up during the creation of this service. With the rise of creative spaces, students learning new technologies, and faculty adding 3D printing to their curriculums, the need for both students and faculty to have access to this type of equipment is growing at a tremendous rate. The Marriott Library provides pay for print 3D printing services, publicly available 3D printers, and teaches various workshops for getting into this emerging technology.

4.2 History

3D printing at the Marriott Library began strangely enough with the purchase of a NextEngine 3D scanner. When students began looking for somewhere to print their scans and models, it was decided to look for funding to obtain a 3D printer, which we were able to do through central campus IT funding. The learning curve was quite substantial, especially with the first printer being one of the higher end (at that time) powder based 3D printers. Within 3 months there were several full and part time supervisors who were able to produce models with a very high success rate, which led to a low cost, pay for print service to be developed for students. The initial service cost, time to produce models, basic information, etc., has undergone several revisions due to student feedback and as more printers were introduced. After a year, two plastic printers were added to give students alternative and cheaper options to print their models.

With the pay for print program firmly in place and enjoying success, it was then time to expand out to introduce 3D printers for general use in the Knowledge Commons on Level 2 of the Marriott Library. After trying out several printers three Taz-4 plastic printers were purchased and deployed along with dedicated computer systems to create a 3D printing area. Training materials were created, a way to sell plastic by the foot was introduced, and the area was opened to students in January 2015. In July of 2015 a new department called Creativity and Innovation Services was formed to take over the 3D printing, 3D scanning, and creative spaces services that the Library had been developing. This has

resulted in numerous tours, outreach to K-12 programs, collaborations with faculty on various projects, improved service on the pay for print program, consultation services, and more.

4.3 Funding

The initial funding for the first powder based 3D printer came out of leftover funds from central campus IT during a funding cycle in 2013. With the success of the first few months of the new pay for print service it was quickly decided to allocate additional funds from the Library's student computing budget that were available due to savings in other areas. For the last few years any savings or leftover funds have been channeled into 3D printing and the revenue generated from the pay for print service has been used to purchase equipment, spare parts, and supplies to support the operation. 3D printing has become so popular that it is now a regular line item in the annual student computing funding request.

4.4 Staffing

When the pay for printing service first began there were no dedicated staff allocated to this service. Student Computing Services, who manage the Knowledge Commons and provide technology assistance to students, had several volunteers who quickly immersed themselves into learning 3D printing. Within the first six months there were two full time and six part time employees who had sufficient knowledge to assist students with almost any 3D printing question and/or problems. As more and more 3D printers came online along with numerous requests from faculty, a new department was created under the Fine Arts umbrella that would partner with Student Computing services to cover 3D printing operations. This added a dedicated full time staff member and two student workers who now handle most of the operational load, with backup provided by the full and part time staff from Student Computing Services.

4.5 Training

Using a 3D printer is not exceedingly difficult, but having successful prints requires experience in using the various 3D modeling programs as well as understanding how each printer operates with its features and the materials chosen. The Library's 3D training focused on how to get a sufficient number of staff members up and running on being able to process student jobs for the initial opening of the pay for print service. This training focused more on the operational issues of getting the student's job into the system, how to change the model to save on material cost and printing time, and doing basic consulting with the student to correct errors.

As this service has progressed and 3D printers were made publically available the emphasis has shifted towards dedicated staff members who can spend their time not only consulting and maintaining the printers, but teaching workshops and assisting with large scale printing projects. For the future there will be additional training guides and more emphasis placed on learning this technology for the student workers at the knowledge Commons as well as the full time staff.

4.6 Assessment

This has been a unique challenge in that it appears the only way to assess 3D printing in an academic environment is by seeing the amount of growth from semester to semester in terms of number of pay for print jobs, consultations, tour groups, and faculty who are including this into their curriculum. At this time all of the publically available printers are in use a majority of the Library's operating hours, there are an ever growing number of consultations being scheduled, and more equipment will be deployed in the near future.

---

[6] a building that will house more than 400 unique student residences and 20,000 feet of "garage" space where any student on campus can build a prototype, attend an event, or launch a company

4.7 Research & Curriculum Needs

Once there was a dedicated pay for print service available, there was extensive outreach with faculty and word of mouth by students who had successfully used the service. This led to several collaborations with the Utah Museum of Natural History, Fine Arts Museum of Utah, Huntsman Cancer Institute, and more, with several featured in local media. This in turn alerted campus faculty to our service and several classes began to have to print off assignments using this service. Once there were publically available printers more and more students began to use them, with faculty arranging for group workshops, tours, and consultations for how to use 3D printing in their curriculum.

4.8 Sustainability

As this service has continued to expand it has shown that a definite funding line needs to be available for new printers, parts, materials, and proper staffing. With the technology in this area continually changing, academic entities will need to experiment with various printers and materials to find the proper mix to either run a dedicated pay for print service or to allow free access by students. Operations can also only continue to be sustained by allocating well trained staffing resources as there need to be sufficient on call knowledge to both maintain the machines as well as assisting student to process printing jobs.

5. CONCLUSION

We have taken incremental steps in positioning the Library in between the old way of doing things and anticipated way of getting things done in the future first, by adding more laptops to our checkout program, we are able to increase the portability of our hardware resources and this is a good step in moving away from University-owned desktops toward the student-owned devices. Second, by investing in remote software delivery initiative, we are able to move beyond physical computing spaces toward virtual environments. Third, we are able to cater to new demands by shifting our learning environments to accommodate changing expectations from students as consumers to students as creators [9].

6. REFERENCES

[1] Eden Dahlstrom, with D. Christopher Brooks, Susan Grajek, and Jamie Reeves. ECAR Study of Students and Information Technology, 2015. Research report. Louisville, CO: ECAR, December 2015.

[2] Dahlstrom, Eden, with a foreword by Charles Dziuban and J.D.Walker. *ECAR Study of Undergraduate Students and Information Technology, 2012* (Research Repor). Louisville, CO: EDUCAUSE Center for Applied Research, September 2012, available from http://www.educause.edu/ecar

[3] Thompson, S. (2012). Student Use of Library Computers: Are Desktop Computers Still Relevant in Today's Libraries? *Information Technology and Libraries*, *31*(4).

[4] http://www.pewinternet.org/data-trend/mobile/device-ownership/

[5] Johnson, L., Adams Becker, S., Cummins, M., Estrada, V., Freeman, A., and Hall, C. (2016). NMC Horizon Report: 2016 Higher Education Edition. Austin, Texas: The New Media Consortium.

[6] Liz Burke et al., "Where and Why Students Choose to Use Computer Facilities: A Collaborative Study at an Australian and United Kingdom University," Australian Academic & Research Libraries 39, no. 3 (September 2008): 181–97.

[7] http://www.colorado.edu/oit/sites/default/files/LabsStudy-penultimate-10-07-11.pdf

[8] http://www.educause.edu/nercomp-annual-conference/2013/future-student-computer-labs

[9] Johnson, L., Adams Becker, S., Estrada, V., and Freeman, A. (2015). NMC Horizon Report: 2015 K-12 Edition. Austin, Texas: The New Media Consortium.

Developing Best Practices for Qualtrics Administration

Kathryn Fletcher
West Virginia University
Information Technology, PO Box 6500
Morgantown, WV 26506 USA
+1 304-293-8769
kathy.fletcher@mail.wvu.edu

ABSTRACT

In 2013 West Virginia University consolidated a few individually purchased college and individual licenses for Qualtrics survey software into a single campus-wide license that includes all of our colleges and regional campuses, to be implemented as a campus standard and enterprise solution for our campus. Due to some staff reorganizations over the past two years, I and the other Qualtrics brand administrators at WVU are all new to this administrative role. In this paper, I plan to share lessons that I learned while (1) participating in developing and documenting new business processes, (2) transitioning to serve as the main brand administrator, (3) cleaning up user accounts that had not been actively managed for years, and (4) working with the Qualtrics vendor, local group administrators, my IT colleagues, and campus users as we refine a set of best practices for product usage and administration. Although this paper discusses a campus-wide implementation of Qualtrics survey software, I feel that the lessons I learned during this process could be extrapolated to the development of best practices for other products or IT services.

Keywords

Application Administration; Best Practices; Survey Software.

1. INTRODUCTION

WVU uses Qualtrics survey software for online forms for administrative purposes in addition to researchers using it to conduct research and students using it to learn how to conduct surveys. In 2013 West Virginia University, through its Information Technology Software License Information Center (SLIC), consolidated multiple smaller licenses purchased by individual WVU colleges for Qualtrics into a single campus-wide license that would allow an unlimited number of accounts and an unlimited number of surveys.

For the next few years, WVU SLIC recovered part of this license cost by charging individuals, departments, and colleges a yearly fee to use the software. In Fall 2015, WVU SLIC modified its procedures as part of a project to deploy Qualtrics across campus as a true enterprise campus standard product for surveys that is centrally funded. As part of this project, a new team of application

SIGUCCS '16, November 06-09, 2016, Denver, CO, USA
© 2016 ACM. ISBN 978-1-4503-4095-3/16/11…$15.00
DOI: http://dx.doi.org/10.1145/2974927.2974952
.

administrators was assigned to work on refining support processes and to make it easier for units to comply with WVU guidelines for the appearance of online materials.

1.1 Disclaimer

This paper focuses on my experiences as a fledgling Qualtrics Brand Administrator and my quest to document our ITS best practices and procedures for managing WVU Qualtrics accounts and for providing local end-user support. This paper does not address West Virginia University's decision process to purchase a campus-wide license for Qualtrics nor should the paper be construed as a product endorsement. If you are interested in learning more about how a higher education institution decides to purchase Qualtrics as a campus-wide survey tool, you may want to refer to the article "Finding an Enterprise Solution for Distributed Research" by Eric Hawley at Utah State University [6].

1.2 About West Virginia University and ITS

West Virginia University (WVU) is the state's public land-grant institution with over 28,700 students on its main campus, classified as R1 Doctoral [1]. Information Technology Services (ITS) provides both systems and end-user support for all WVU campuses and statewide extension services. Some individual colleges and departments maintain their own information technology teams to provide front-line support or to supplement technology services provided by ITS.

1.3 History of Survey Software at WVU

Since WVU departments started providing content on the Internet in the mid-1990s, there has been a mixture of technical solutions implemented to collect information via online forms.

HTML form handling: the ability to create useful HTML forms to collect survey data was dependent on scripts or widgets that the web server administrator installed and allowed to be used. Survey form responses were emailed or saved in a database or both. This technique required HTML expertise on the part of the web page developer and cooperation from the web server administrator.

SimpleForms: an in-house tool was developed by WVU Web Services (now known as University Relations Digital Services) and made available for free to WVU employees and students in 2005. It was extremely easy to use. Individuals had to request access with written approval from a supervisor or from a faculty member on a research committee. Survey responses were saved on a University Relations file server and could optionally be emailed to a specified address. A simple built-in report was available but most users downloaded the responses to Excel for custom report building. The SimpleForms service was discontinued on June 30, 2013.

SurveyMonkey: some people on campus opted to purchase an individual license for SurveyMonkey, a cloud-based online form product. Some individuals who wanted to run small one-time surveys chose to use the free version of the software even though it meant their surveys would display a SurveyMonkey logo. During that time when we were charging recovery costs, it appears that the WVU SLIC may have set the price for one year individual Qualtrics license to be comparable to the cost of a one-year subscription to SurveyMonkey.

Wufoo: this cloud-based online form product was recommended by University Relations Digital Services to replace the discontinued SimpleForms product. The Digital Services group also created documentation and templates on how to use this product [4] and be compliant with WVU branding guidelines. Wufoo was acquired by SurveyMonkey in 2011 but both the Wufoo and SurveyMonkey products remain available separately. For cost savings reasons, I predict that units on campus will consider migrating from paid Wufoo subscriptions to using Qualtrics since WVU SLIC is no longer charging the individual units for access to Qualtrics.

Qualtrics Research Suite: before the discontinuation of SimpleForms was announced, some units on campus had purchased licenses for Qualtrics due to its features such as file upload, dynamic question branching, and maintaining panels of potential survey respondents which were not available in the free SimpleForms tool. I will not address the process for making the decision to obtain a WVU campus license for Qualtrics since I was not involved in that project. Note: in July 2016, Qualtrics Research Suite became known as the Qualtrics Insight Platform.

Other Tools: In addition to the web-based solutions listed above, some units and individuals at WVU have also used (and possibly continue to use) Adobe Acrobat PDF forms and Microsoft Word document forms hosted on their web pages to collect information. Google Forms and SharePoint data forms are also used on campus.

1.4 Terminology

I had to learn a new vocabulary for working with Qualtrics.

Brand – an instance of Qualtrics. At one time, WVU had five or more *brands* due to group licenses purchased by various colleges. When we, as new Brand Administrators, started work on our campus enterprise project, we kept getting *brand* confused with *theme* as we tried to create methods for our campus to adhere to WVU branding guidelines.

Brand Administrator – the highest level of Qualtrics account administrator in this hosted cloud-based solution. A Brand Administrator can create divisions, create themes, assign a user to a division, create/modify/delete accounts, view/reassign/delete surveys in any account within the brand, and can login as any user.

Contact List - a collection of email addresses that you wish to send links to surveys. Using a contact list allows for custom embedded data and sending reminders to those who have not responded. Formerly known as a panel.

Coupon Code – you can generate a special code number to serve as a coupon so an account holder can use it to upgrade their own account to join a division and be assigned to a certain user type without manual intervention from a Brand Administrator.

Division – a division is a smaller entity within your brand. You can create divisions with different account privileges to meet their members' needs. At WVU, we set up divisions based on our organization chart.

Division Administrator – this role has many of the same powers as a Brand Administrator but restricted to those user accounts assigned to that division. A division administrator cannot create brand administrators, cannot put a user into a division, and cannot delete user accounts. A division administrator can remove someone from their division, can create groups, and can manage groups that their users belong to.

Group – two or more accounts can be assigned to a group. Groups can share surveys based on group membership and can share templates by using a group library. You can also create a group that is open to all accounts assigned to a division.

Library – you can save survey templates, graphics, and other content in a personal library. If you are a member of a group, you can share content in a group library.

Project – surveys are now referred to as projects in the Qualtrics Insight Platform. At WVU, we have groups who use Qualtrics survey projects as long-term online forms for administrative purposes since we do not have a dedicated online form tool.

Template – a survey form that is saved as a template and can be used as the basis for a new survey project.

Theme – created by the vendor with assistance from an institution's Brand Administrator. Our license allows us to maintain five themes. Themes make it easy to apply a "look and feel" to a survey. The vendor also supplies a large number of themes. The Brand Administrator can control access to themes via the Division and User Type settings.

User Type – this is a way to define a set of permissions to make it easier to grant or modify privileges for a group of accounts at one time. At WVU, we decided to assign one main user type to both employees and students. In addition, we assign a default user type for new accounts that have limited privileges until assigned to a division by a brand administrator or using a coupon code.

2. DISCOVERY

When I would listen to my ITS co-workers talk about the *discovery* phase of a project, I naively thought that the time set aside for discovery had a start and end, and then the real project work gets to begin. However, I have learned during our Qualtrics rollout project that new and critical information can arise at any time and it is hard to search for what you do not know exists.

An early catalytic "discovery" event spurred our plan to offer Qualtrics to the campus community without charging them for individual or group licenses: a new WVU adjunct faculty member asked to import her Qualtrics surveys and retain the theme appearance from her previous institution. The Qualtrics vendor insists on obtaining permission from both brand administrators (from the current host and the would-be new host) when someone wants to move surveys from one Qualtrics brand to another. The contact from the vendor as part of this request spurred additional discussions and research, which contributed to our decision to offer access to Qualtrics as a centrally funded enterprise service to the entire campus community.

Once that decision was made, upper management requested an implementation plan to prepare for the management of numerous new account requests and to prepare for the increased support needs for those new account holders. As part of working on this plan, I decided to review our current collection of accounts once I had the administrative access I needed. During this research, I discovered that 21 individuals were listed as brand administrators and over 2,000 accounts had not been placed into a division. Since our plan was to demote most of the existing brand administrators to serve as division administrators, the unassigned accounts needed to be placed in the correct brand.

As part of providing end-user support, I discovered the existence of an older Qualtrics site for one of our colleges (we later learned that this was a "child brand") when a faculty member had problems trying to share her survey with a student in our main WVU brand. A few months after this incident during a phone call with the vendor's support line, we learned of at least two other child brands that were paid for by our license and of the existence of a Qualtrics Customer Success Manager who had been assigned to WVU as part of our contract.

I learned that during the years when individual colleges purchased their own brand license, their users created accounts with an email address as a login username and logged in at www.qualtrics.com or to a brand-specific URL. In some cases, these email addresses were not issued by WVU. Even though I could mark these accounts as disabled using my admin console, the account holders could still login at the old address until I eventually learned to modify the username and email address to prevent this. In one case, I thought a student had continued to use his old account for five years after he graduated; however, I eventually learned that his instructors knew its password and had continued to use it to run surveys.

3. DESIGN
3.1 Divisions and Accounts
I and the other new brand administrators met to make decisions on how to organize the accounts going forward. We decided to use the WVU employment hierarchy as inspiration for setting up the divisions at the vice president levels for administrative units and at the dean levels for academic units. To ease maintenance for the accounts in the Provost's Office and for improved support purposes, we created a separate division for Information Technology instead of leaving these accounts in the Provost's Division.

If a division didn't already have a Division Administrator assigned, we asked the IT Director with oversight over that college or unit to appoint an appropriate employee (or two) to serve in that role. Most colleges at WVU have at least one employee who formally or informally serves as an IT specialist. Any existing "power user" faculty member who had division administrator or brand administrator access before 2016 and who was willing to continue to informally help others in their units were retained as division administrators. These faculty members will be expected to adhere to the same guidelines and best practices as the IT employees.

For accounts, we decided to use the same account type for both students and employees. Although a lot of institutions create limited accounts for students, a single user type helps us avoid the issues of student employees using Qualtrics for their jobs and employees who take classes as students where using Qualtrics is part of the curriculum. This decision levels the playing field for all.

We use the email address to distinguish between students and full-time employees. If the email address ends in mix.wvu.edu, we use the student's enrolled college to determine the division; if the email address ends in mail.wvu.edu or hsc.wvu.edu, then we use the employee's home department. Accounts can easily be moved from division to division without interfering with live surveys or collected data—however, an account can only be assigned to a single division.

3.2 Themes and Templates
Lisa Bridges, a graphic designer on our ITS Communications Team, designed a new Qualtrics theme that she then used as a basis to create custom survey templates for each division. She made sure that the theme, the survey templates, and the division logos adhered to current WVU standards for colors, fonts, and logo usage.

4. IMPLEMENTATION
4.1 Sorting Accounts into Divisions
One of the first administrative tasks I took on was creating and renaming divisions to match our design plan. My second major task was to put user accounts into the correct divisions. When viewing the list of users, there was not a way to filter for a null value for division; if I modified an account on a second page of results, I would end up back on the first page after I saved the changes. To see a manageable list of users at one time, I would filter the list based on letters in the username. For each account that was not assigned to a division, I would look up the person in our online directory and then modify the account.

After I had finished, I found an easier way to view a list of unassigned accounts: download the account information from the Summary Information tab in the Qualtrics Admin console and use Excel to filter the file. However, I still would have had to look up information for each account holder and then look for each account individually to make a division assignment.

4.2 Additional House Cleaning
While I was looking up account holder information for division assignments, I discovered several accounts that belonged to former employees or to students who had graduated and were no longer enrolled. If the account did not contain any surveys or any surveys with responses, I deleted it. If there were surveys with responses, I disabled the account and put the account in a special division that I named "No Access" to deal with later.

In addition to examining accounts that had not been assigned to a division, I reviewed those accounts where the most recent login was before January 2014 and handled them the same way. I cleaned up duplicate accounts and worked with account holders to transfer ownership surveys from generic accounts to ones belonging to individuals, since we plan to have all access via single sign-on.

4.3 Themes and Templates
Originally all accounts had access to all five themes and the theme for Student Life was the default for all new surveys. I went into each division and gave its accounts access to the appropriate themes; however, if an account holder copies an old survey that used a theme available at that time, it would still be used for the new copied survey project. We created a new theme and will soon replace one of the themes with an updated generic WVU theme. We will also ask the vendor to rename the overall brand and the five themes to minimize confusion.

I distributed the newly created survey templates to the division administrators. The division administrators then placed the templates in their groups' libraries. I and the graphic designer have both retained copies of the survey templates since templates can be edited by the survey project owner and accidentally deleted by anyone who has access to the group library. I have created a knowledge base article for all Qualtrics users on campus on how they can use the division survey template to create new surveys.

4.4 Changing Login Authentication
In the summer of 2016, we plan to change the login authentication from Active Directory to CAS Shibboleth. At this time, we are also updating which account holders will have access. Neither newly admitted students who have not yet registered for classes nor retired employees will continue to have access to the product. In 2013

when we purchased a campus-wide license, this authentication technique was not an option.

4.5 Communications

I contacted IT directors across campus to determine division administrators. I also contacted those account holders whose usernames would no longer work once we changed the authentication method and helped them create new single sign-on accounts. When the Qualtrics Insight Platform was released in preview mode and prompted a switch upon login, our ITS Communications Team sent out reassuring messages to the campus community via email, Twitter, and Facebook on how to respond. Existing ITS Knowledge Base articles were updated to reflect the new campus licensing model and the Insight Platform interface change. Vicki Smith, the Director of ITS Communications, will announce the availability of Qualtrics to the campus community at a WVU Key Communicators meeting and via ITS announcements.

5. BEST PRACTICES

Tahlia Thomas, Director of IT Service Management, tasked me with creating a list of best practices to serve as guidelines for our Qualtrics Brand Administrators and Division Administrators.

5.1 Definition of "Best Practice"

I found multiple definitions of the term *best practice*. The one that seemed most applicable to my assignment was the one I found in the Glossary of Project Management at Visitask's web site:

"Best Practice is a superior method or innovative practice that contributes to the improved performance of an organization... It implies accumulating and applying knowledge about what is working and not working in different situations and contexts, including lessons learned and the continuing process of learning, feedback, reflection and analysis (what works, how and why)." [11]

5.2 Research

My background research for developing best practices went beyond the definition. When I started in my brand administrator role in January 2016, I could not find anything online directly relevant to serving as a good Qualtrics Brand Administrator. The Qualtrics web site provided excellent learning resources on how to perform administrative tasks which proved quite useful [10]; however, we were looking for guidance on how to make sound decisions and how to wisely wield our newfound magical powers. I also found several references on best practices for creating and managing surveys as a researcher that I will use in the future and some useful tips on application administration in general. I also talked to those who had more experience as a brand administrator and those who had a lot of experience using Qualtrics as a researcher.

5.2.1 Application Administration Best Practices

Qualtrics is a cloud-based hosted solution so the brand administrators are not true application administrators based on my understanding of those roles. During one of my online searches, I came across a collection of *IT Best Practices* for the University of Nebraska-Lincoln; I felt both inspired and validated by a subset of their best practices for application administration [7]:

- Maintain up-to-date versions of application documentation, both online and offline.
- Document configuration settings, especially changes from default settings.
- Properly source your administration accounts. Use LDAP for authentication where possible.

- Work at the right security/privilege level when diagnosing and resolving a problem.

5.2.2 ITIL

ITIL is a set of practices for IT Service Management [8]. Since some of my co-workers have achieved ITIL certification and since I knew some of my SIGUCCS colleagues have cited ITIL practices as part of their conference papers, I decided to search for any relevant advice on building a list of best practices in the ITIL documentation and ITIL training materials that I have access to such as the *ITIL 2011 Edition Foundation Syllabus* online courses [9] and the *ITIL Foundation Exam Study Guide* [5] that I had access as an ACM member via the ACM Learning Center [2]. Unfortunately, I did not have sufficient time to fully explore these resources and found myself overwhelmed and short on time.

I reviewed what Wikipedia had to say on ITIL. I decided that what I needed would be found under Service Operation: processes include event management, access management, request fulfillment, problem management, and incident management. My efforts to control Qualtrics account access aligns with the access management process; we will use the ITS Service Desk as a single point of contact for our users and to manage incidents and requests. Software Asset Management (SAM) "is the practice of integrating people, processes, and technology to allow software licenses and usage to be systematically tracked, evaluated, and managed." [8] One of our goals is to be more systematic in our management of Qualtrics accounts at WVU now that we are providing access as an enterprise service and to track its usage to justify central funding.

5.2.3 Assistance from Others

Lou Rovegno served as the main brand administrator before I was assigned that role; during that time, he would help me troubleshoot Qualtrics problems that were related to account and division settings. Carole Kiger, a division administrator in our College of Business and Economics, helped me gain a better understanding of the Qualtrics administrative tasks she performed most often.

Dr. Nicholas Bowman, a WVU faculty member and Qualtrics "power user", provided me with access to a Google Doc with usage tips on Qualtrics he maintains for his research colleagues. I plan to consult with him again when we prepare to publish our list of best practices for WVU researchers.

John Johnston at the University of Michigan shared what he and the other brand administrators at their institution had learned during a similar brand consolidation project and while managing a large campus license. His tips included create a users' group for brand and division administrators, use single sign-on, and to consider the use of coupons to assign divisions.

I also sought advice from Michelle Rodney, assistant director for application administration, who shared her experiences and a copy of one of the operations manuals that her team had created. In an informal discussion, she emphasized the need to determine access and roles, monitoring, backup and maintenance schedules, support escalation procedures, and the need to maintain the operations manual in a single location accessible to all who need it.

5.3 Best Practices as Implemented at WVU

Since we are still in our early days of actively managing our brand, I am unsure if I have created truly "best" practices; this list spells out our current practices that will be refined over time as needed. Other institutions might have different needs or priorities to consider when creating their own lists of best practices. Additional lists of best practices for WVU researchers, instructors, and students are being developed and will be documented in our ITS knowledge base.

5.3.1 Access

All login access to Qualtrics at WVU will be via wvu.qualtrics.com using current WVU login credentials and a "single sign on" solution.

Create and assign one user type for both employees and students.

5.3.2 Divisions and Division Administration

Create a division for each unit where there is a vice president or a dean in charge.

Assign at least one information technology staff person to serve as a division administrator in each division.

Provide guidelines and support to all division administrators and new brand administrators.

Have all brand and division administrators sign a statement of responsible conduct similar to the code of confidentiality used by our Blackboard administration team.

Brand administrators should review the division administrators on a monthly basis and update assignments as needed.

Before removing a division administrator, reassign the ownership of any templates to another division administrator in that division and make sure the templates are still accessible in the division's group library.

5.3.3 Accounts

Check the list of users at least twice per week for new users who have signed up for an account.

Assign a user account to a division as follows: assign employees to the division corresponding to their employer and students to the division where they are enrolled. If student employees need access to resources managed by a different division than the one they are enrolled in, a brand administrator will facilitate collaboration or temporarily move the account into a different division as needed. A user account can be assigned to only one division.

Do not create generic accounts.

Review accounts on a regular basis, at least twice per year. Check status of those individuals who have not logged in for over 12 months.

- If they are no longer a student, mark the account for deletion and move it to a special division.
- If they are no longer employed, check to see if any of their surveys need to be transferred to a new owner before marking the account for deletion.
- For these inactive accounts, deactivate any active surveys that have had no responses in the past year.

Before deleting an account, download any survey projects that did not get reassigned to a new owner. This step can be skipped if the survey did not collect any responses or if the surveys are classroom assignments.

Maintain downloaded survey backups in a secure location for one year beyond the account deletion date.

5.3.4 Coupon Codes for User Accounts

Create a coupon code for each division and share it with its division administrators. The coupon code allows a user to upgrade his/her own account to a specific account type and to be placed in the

correct division. This code would be especially useful for division administrators to share with instructors who plan to require their students to use Qualtrics as part of their coursework.

Keep track of which coupon code is assigned to each division as part of procedural documentation.

5.3.5 Groups

Create a group for each division where all members of that division are members to be able to store a template survey in the group's library.

Since all account holders are to log in with their own credentials, create groups upon request and provide details on how to share a survey project with an individual or a group. Brand administrators and division administrators must be willing to add and remove group members upon request.

Determine and document who is the leader of a group for making these requests, similar to the method we use to manage shared mailbox accounts for Office 365 and LISTSERV list ownership.

5.3.6 Themes and Templates

WVU is limited by its software license to five themes that we can maintain. Therefore, we will not be able to create a theme for each division. The themes will adhere to WVU branding guidelines as defined by WVU University Relations [3].

Create a template survey for each division that adheres to WVU branding guidelines and a custom logo for the division's name. Ownership of a template is assigned to one of the Division Administrators in that division and will be reassigned when the original owner leaves the division. A copy of the template will be copied into the group library for that division. Backup copies will be retained by two or more brand administrators.

5.3.7 Customer Support

We will update our ITS Knowledge Base and ITS Service Catalog to provide information to our IT support staff and to our campus community. Our campus users can use the ITS Service Catalog to request additional assistance or they can contact the ITS Service Desk via phone or email.

Members of the ITS Advanced Support Team will respond to questions about Qualtrics that are not resolved by the Service Desk. A Brand Administrator will contact the vendor as needed for advanced needs and specialized services. The Qualtrics account holders are allowed to contact the vendor directly if they so choose. Online training and documentation are freely available from the vendor's web site.

6. EVALUATION

6.1 Lessons Learned

Almost five months after we started our campus-wide implementation project, we discovered the existence of three additional Qualtrics *child brands* that had their own site addresses, brand administrators, and collections of accounts; these child brands were being paid for by the central license but we in ITS were unable to see nor manage these accounts since they were in a different brand. Advice: Find out about any subsidiary child brands at your institution early on when preparing to switch to a campus-wide license and insist on the migration of those accounts into the main brand at that time or as soon as possible and then completely deactivate the child brand(s) to improve account management and end-user support. If the software license is being centrally funded, it should be centrally managed.

We were astonished to discover 21 brand administrators in our system when we first started reviewing the Qualtrics account structure we inherited; several of these individuals were not ITS employees. Any of these brand administrators could have created divisions, created additional brand administrators, deleted accounts, or viewed research data for any account in our brand; we were lucky that these individuals did not execute any potentially harmful actions. Advice: If the Qualtrics software campus license is going to be managed by your information technology unit, brand administrators should be a limited number of IT staff members under your management.

When we experienced ITS staff turnover without an adequate transition plan, we lost critical account administrative skills and the history of and rationales for various administrative decisions. Our advice is make sure you have at least two fully trained Brand Administrators who maintain documentation of their actions.

Our efforts to roll the product out more widely to our campus community were hampered by a lack of documentation of the license agreement. Our new group of brand administrators did not learn about the existence of our assigned vendor representatives until months after we started our implementation project. Advice: Make sure software licensing details, contact information for vendor representatives, and your operating procedures are documented and that this documentation remains accessible, updated, and available for long-term access.

I discovered multiple accounts that had been created but had never been used. In some cases, the administrator who created these accounts had made an error in the username or email address; other times the account holder seemed to be unaware an account had been created for them. Advice: Have your users create their own accounts instead of division administrators manually creating them if you will be using university credentials for login.

I also spent a few hours manually assigning new accounts to the proper divisions when entire classes started using Qualtrics at the beginning of the semester. Advice: Distribute coupon codes for use by instructors for their students. Actively manage accounts as they are created so you are never faced with hundreds of division assignments to execute. Create, document, and regularly execute a procedure to deactivate old surveys and delete old accounts.

6.2 Future Plans

We will work with the brand administrators of the remaining child brands and the Qualtrics vendor to bring all WVU-owned accounts into the main campus brand. All WVU logins would authenticate via current WVU credentials at wvu.qualtrics.com instead of logging in at a child brand's web address.

We are considering communicating directly with the account holders soon after they create their accounts (and on a one-time basis for existing accounts) to make sure they are aware of WVU policies related to online surveys and online forms. We are also considering modifying our current practice on when to delete accounts and survey data, making sure that current account holders are aware of any policy change that we make.

We will update our login page to link to acceptable use guidelines instead of trying to display them at the bottom of the screen.

We will work with key communicators, front line professionals, and IT staff on campus to help them assist researchers and other account holders in their units in the use of the new WVU survey templates.

We will create an Administrators' Guide to share with all Brand Administrators and Division Administrators as part of their orientation and training for their role.

We will update our ITS Knowledge Base to include technical tips and best practices for researchers running surveys, for instructors and their students, and for division administrators.

We will refine our list of best practices based on our experiences after we make a formal announcement to the campus community.

7. ACKNOWLEDGMENTS

WVU colleagues: I would like to thank Tahlia Thomas, Director of IT Service Management, for her leadership and support for our implementation initiative. I would like to thank Ryan Campione, ITS Business Relationship Manager who has helped with advanced technical questions and the implementation planning process; Louis Rovegno, ITS Software Licensing Information Center; Lisa Bridges, ITS Graphic Designer; Michelle Rodney, ITS Assistant Director for Application Administration; Nicholas Bowman, Associate Professor of Communication Studies in the Eberly College of Arts and Sciences; and Carole Kiger, Instructional Designer and Qualtrics Division Administrator for the College of Business and Economics.

I would also like to thank John Johnston, Qualtrics Brand Administrator from the University of Michigan. I gratefully acknowledge the Qualtrics support staff who provided accurate responses in a timely fashion with much patience and kindness.

8. REFERENCES

[1] About WVU: WVU Facts. about.wvu.edu/wvu-facts

[2] ACM Learning Center. learning.acm.org

[3] Brand Center for West Virginia University. brand.wvu.edu

[4] Form Services, WVU University Relations Digital Services. universityrelations.wvu.edu/digital-services/form-services

[5] Gallacher, Liz and Morris, Helen. *ITIL Foundation Exam Study Guide*. Sybex. 2012.

[6] Hawley, Eric. Finding an Enterprise Solution for Distributed Research. *EDUCAUSE Review*. December 6, 2013. er.educause.edu/articles/2013/12/finding-an-enterprise-solution-for-distributed-research,

[7] IT Best Practices for Application Administration. University of Nebraska-Lincoln. its.unl.edu/bestpractices/application-administration

[8] ITIL (from Wikipedia). en.wikipedia.org/wiki/ITIL

[9] ITIL® 2011 Edition Foundation Syllabus. 9 courses. acm.skillport.com

[10] Qualtrics. www.qualtrics.com

[11] Visitask (online resource center for project management information). www.visitask.com/best-practice-g.asp

Making a Makerspace:
Designing User Services to Serve Designing Users

Owen G. McGrath
Educational Technology Services
University of California, Berkeley
omcgrath@berkeley.edu

ABSTRACT

As higher education institutions set up and run makerspaces, important choices and challenges arise in deciding how to approach the planning and design of both the spaces and the services to be offered [1,2]. This paper looks at the experience of growing maker-centric spaces and support in the context of transforming some traditional teaching and learning settings (e.g., library study areas, classrooms, and computer labs). The all-important planning phase for this transformation included a year-long service design initiative structured by user-centered design principles.

The resulting services, layouts of the spaces, and choice of technology and training offered are informed both by consideration of a new design oriented curriculum at the university and a general interest in creative do-it- yourself (DIY) creativity. The goals of this paper include: 1) explaining the service design process and key decisions made around what activities to support in the new settings; 2) describing issues and challenges for developing sustainable service models in these settings; and 3) talking about lessons learned in developing the staff expertise and capacity to manage and operate these new spaces and services.

CCS Concepts

• Social and professional topics~Project and people management

Keywords

Makerspace; Design Thinking; User-Centered Design

1. INTRODUCTION

Three UC Berkeley campus units, the University Library, Student Affairs IT, and Educational Technology Services, formed a partnership in 2014 with a general (if vague) aim of setting up and operating general access makerspace in the residence halls and the undergraduate library. Makerspaces are workshop settings where space, tools, equipment, and support are provided to support creative activities, especially modelling and prototyping. At Berkeley, makerspaces already existed across campus, but almost all were for exclusive use of specific courses, departments, or clubs. One goal of the new initiative was to create opportunity for all members of the UC Berkeley community to explore maker-

SIGUCCS '16, November 06-09, 2016, Denver, CO, USA
© 2016 ACM. ISBN 978-1-4503-4095-3/16/11…$15.00
DOI: http://dx.doi.org/10.1145/2974927.2974949

related activities, with the lowest possible barrier of entry, and to serve as a referral point to direct participants to locations for further exploration.

To explore better what that such an endeavor would entail, the partners embarked first on a planning phase consisting of research and design initiatives. The research benefited greatly from our participation in TechShop's Makerspace Academy, a week-long institute designed to guide educational organizations through the process of designing, equipping and operating safe and inspirational makerspaces based on the TechShop model [3]. The design initiative also drew upon Design Thinking for Educators, a human-centered design methodology developed in promulgated by IDEO, well known for decades of success in designing both products and services [4]. The IDEO methodology provided a framework for brainstorming, researching user needs, prototyping service components, and evaluating iteratively.

After many months of user researching, prototyping, and piloting, the partners finally opened the general access makerspace and accompanying services in 2016, with the dual mission of supporting students' makerspace needs related to the curriculum while also creating opportunity for all members of the UC Berkeley community to explore maker-related activities. The resulting makerspace is operated primarily by student staff and features a supporting partnership for student groups that have a focus on design technologies such as such as computer-aided design and computer-aided manufacturing (CAD/CAM), 3D printing, digital prototyping with digital electronics (e.g., Arduino, Raspberry Pi), robotics. The training programs are being developed to provide both online and in-person learning opportunities to help and guide students learning both the basics (e.g. safety and basic use of equipment, software applications) and more advanced tutorials for projects and guided learning activities for specific makerspace domains. In addition, the service also provides workshops and outreach via a "mobile makerspace" approach that travels around on a regular basis in the residence hall academic centers.

As we'll see, the design of the general access makerspace turns out to be about so much more than choosing equipment and staffing open hours. Crucial considerations in planning include actually understanding the potential users, defining ways to support their making activities, and developing customer services in order to deliver that support by building up the right sort of service culture.

2. BACKGROUND

Makerspaces have been sprouting up on college and university campuses over the past decade [5]. Initially, they were to be found mainly in engineering and architecture departments.

More recently, makerspaces have been included in new construction and building renovations in an effort to open up access to students in all disciplines. In many cases, campus libraries have taken the lead, seeing the opportunity to extend the traditional library mission of access, literacy, and training [6]. Successful early projects served as inspiration and also show the variety of approaches [7].

At least two different trends are at work in the movement towards makerspace on campus: 1) A discipline-focused trend driven by new curricular emphasis on the design process coming from engineering and product design industry with an emphasis on formal design process. 2) A more informal and person-oriented trend growing out of the Maker movement, which embraces an extremely broad range of do-it-yourself activities spanning from craft to science having in common an aim toward personal creativity [8].

For our makerspace, based on a partnership between educational computing, the library, and residential computing, it was very important to understand and address both trends. To do so well would require a structured process for thinking about how to design such spaces and services.

3. APPROACHING DESIGN

3.1 Design Process

Given our aim of setting up a general access makerspace on campus, there were many different ways to proceed. It would have been easy and comfortable to think simply in terms of filling a space with furniture and equipment—breaking the task into parts and assigning out different subtasks to different teams: space, equipment, software, training, etc. Here the makerspace might have been treated as merely an extension of the existing drop-in computing facility. An institutional perspective grounded in what has worked in the past makes it tempting, for instance, to view 3D printing as just another kind of printing. We know how to offer laser printing, so we fit 3D printing into that model. Among the potential pitfalls of this container-and-contents design approach is that the we-know-best outcome ends up not matching what users really want or need.

A different approach to creating a makerspace would be to borrow the sort of design thinking that makerspaces themselves are meant to encourage. The user-centered design methodologies being adopted in the curriculum and, in turn, creating part of the demand for makerspace can and should be used to design spaces and services, it turns out.

In our case, we undertook the makerspace design initiative as a group project in an online course provided by the design firm IDEO through Acumen NovoEd. The processes and structure of 'Design Kit: The Course for Human-Centered Design' helped to lead us iteratively through an inquiry into the potential users' perspective and an ideation phase that helped us consider service possibilities based on the users' needs and motivations. With its systematic approach to effective innovation, this is the same kind of repeatable and teachable design process that has made companies like IDEO consistently successful in the commercial world of designing products. Indeed, design thinking definitely has something to say about how to approach service design—even in a small scale, academic IT service setting. At the heart of the design methodology is the need to gain a deep understanding of the potential users by engaging them through interviews and observation. The insights into users' perspective as gained from these mini-ethnographies yield insights that can be gathered and then given some service definition. In the design process, creative brainstorming into possible service solutions then leads iteratively back to the potential users, who are presented with prototypes for further engaged observation and refinement of the ideas.

Synthesizing the insights we learned about users into a set of personas that represent different prototypical users' motivations, behaviors, and expectations helped us arrive at an initial service design for our pilot makerspace grounded in an understanding of local user needs on campus. Three distinct personas—Novice Explorer, Coursework Student, Student Club Member—emerged from our user research investigations.

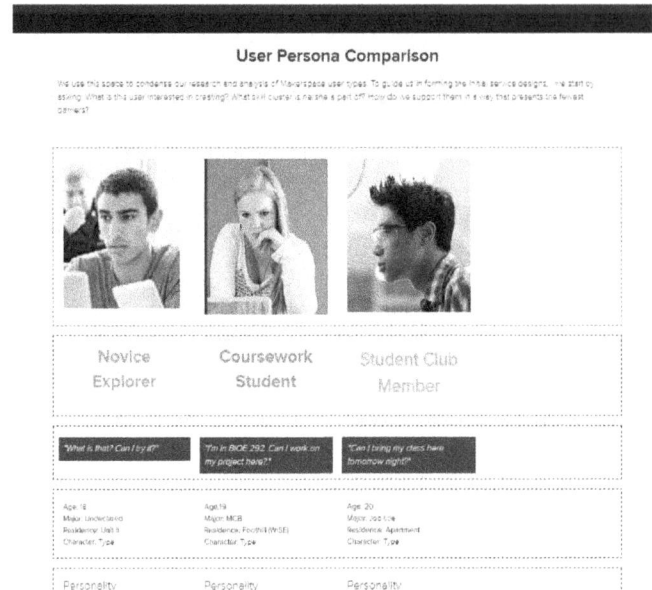

Figure 1. Persona Maps of Typified Users.

3.2 Designing Spaces and Services Together

For these personas, one can then develop unique journey maps for imagining how each persona would use and interact with the space services. These journey maps reveal different touchpoints and support needs. Where the Explorer Novice might require some enticement such as an orientation or workshop enrollment, a Coursework Student prefers fast lane access to the equipment in order to carry out a class assignment. Such insights can lead, in turn, to design considerations for the physical space and a service blueprint as well [9]. At the reception desk, for instance, front-line staff actions and physical traffic flow could be designed to accommodate both scenarios.

Imagining all the service and space issues is not possible. So service blueprinting can be validated best by prototyping, i.e., setting up pilots or experiments to test and refine blueprint concepts, answer questions, gather feedback. In our case, we were also able to compare notes with TechShop's extensive set of lessons learned. The week-long TechShop Makerspace provided an inside view into many aspects of the TechShop's approach to space design, customer service, staffing models, etc. Driven less by design theory and more by practical wisdom about what has worked for the company over the years, the Academy guidance aligns closely in many ways with the formal design thinking approach. The issue of accommodating both novice and experienced user, for instance, had also led to specific architectural and staff contact point designs replicated now in TechShops around the world.

Another development revealed by this the process was the need to fold presentation space into the service. The journey map for Student Club Member contained extensions that were not initially anticipated as service contact points. For members of student-run clubs and groups, being able to present their work or offer in-person presentations of a technique was a natural offshoot of their making processes. By adjusting our space and service design, we saw an opportunity to include access to a nearby classrooms that are available in the evenings when most of the group and club work happens.

3.3 Outfitting at Scale

In contrast to the user-oriented design factors, the selection of equipment turned out to be the easier challenge. For the initial scaling of the facility, the first year equipment offering plan includes additional 3D printers, vinyl cutters, and kits for experimenting with electronics and coding such as Arduino and Raspberry Pi, as well as tools for work in textiles, including wearable technology. Desktop and laptop computers connected to the new equipment for design creation are re-purposed from the adjacent computer. Consideration given to practical matters such work surfaces, tool racks, storage of material, and even table and stool height are shaped in large part by the persona-generated service blueprint and journey maps. To support a culture of curiosity and sharing, for instance, furniture placement and height can be optimized to allow for over-the-shoulder visibility while still allowing for safe focus on task [10].

Finally, the technology selection and space layout are one area in which the old informs the new. The Library and computer facilities share a strong tradition of providing access to patrons with disabilities. Assistive technology, adjustable furniture, and careful attention to paths of travel continue to be important in makerspaces. The additional need for accommodations around equipment and tools is a newer area of focus where the goals of independence and safety need balancing and are still being figured out [11,12].

3.4 Building a Staff Culture

Clearly, student engagement was crucial to the design process for understanding potential users. The appropriate role of student as future staff also surfaced early on. From the design thinking approach and the practical wisdom offered by TechShop, we saw convergence around the importance of building a staff with the right technical capabilities but also with a very special kind of customer service. In TechShop parlance, we needed to build a culture—one that could be attuned to novice and experienced users not simply working side by side safely but also encouraged to share, inquire, and try new things. Sharing expertise with others is a cornerstone of the maker movement [13]. Feeling free to try new things and fail in sight of others—the so-called "karaoke confidence"—is at the heart of recent maker-oriented changes to design curriculum in engineering and business fields [14].

Putting together a staff model—front-line and behind the scenes—to promote these creative and exploratory values becomes a high priority in the customer service oriented approach to building a makerspace. In our case, student staff are hired, trained, and evaluated not just on their technical aptitude but also

on their soft skills potential. The balance of front-line and behind-the-scene staff is also shaped by the considerations of student workers' overall skill set, with empathy and communication often being prioritized over technical and troubleshooting ability.

4. ITERATIVE EVALUATION

Design thinking methodologies don't stop with the roll-out of a product or service. Asking what quantitative and/or qualitative sustainability metrics the service will measure in operation is a question to pose early on in the design process. How will you understand the user's actual experience? How will you measure and report on these metrics during your project and upon completion of your project? Continuous service improvement in the design thinking points back to the journey maps and service blueprints as good starting points to compare with actual day to day operational experience. In our first year of roll-out, we are looking to compare frequently the service delivery plans with what is actually happening in order to see if the journey map and the actual observed journey match.

Differences and gaps identified allow for iterative improvement in both. In our case, traditional utilization metrics can also tell a story, especially when coupled with customer surveys that give easy opportunities to provide feedback. Use of specific equipment, use of the space, and attendance at events are some of the quantitative metrics that we are looking to track in order to get a sense of how the makerspace is being used. Of course, the student employees are also an avenue for informal assessment about use of the space, as well as needs for maintenance, instruction, or events. Our team seeks to evaluate the service and space regularly from the staff perspective during the semester and create reports with suggestions for future development.

5. CONCLUSION

This paper has been intended mainly as an overview of how our institution's efforts to set up makerspaces and associated services have benefited from many of the same design thinking principles and best practices that the spaces and services are meant to support. Even with these design thinking methodologies at hand, studying and comprehending usage activity and service metrics is a very time consuming challenge. So far, the combination of design thinking approaches and project management disciplines have enabled us to launch the space and service. The iterative nature of design thinking urge us not to halt the exploratory approaches to discovery and innovation anytime soon.

As this service matures, the next areas of activity be explored have already begun to surface from our continued engagement with users. Their creative making activities expand quite naturally to include more digital video use for documenting and representing their work in both tutorial and portfolio forms. Figuring out where to go with these interests will again mean re-initiating the design thinking cycle of brainstorming, researching user needs, prototyping. Singly or together these kinds of techniques can provide great benefits for assisting those in higher education who are responsible for implementing and deploying new types of technology-enabled teaching and learning spaces. For academic technology services in higher education to keep up with the increasing service demands that do-it-yourself creative activities bring, the design methodologies and processes we employ will need ever greater focus on users.

6. REFERENCES

[1] Cavalcanti, G. (2013). Is it a Hackerspace, Makerspace, TechShop, or FabLab. In Make, 22.

[2] Good, T. (2013). Three Makerspace Models That Work. American Libraries, 44(1-2), 45

[3] Wartzman, R. (2015). TechShop gives the Maker Movement a big boost. Retrieved May 25, 2016, from http://fortune.com/2015/06/11/techshop-makers-movement/.

[4] Rauth, I., Köppen, E., Jobst, B., & Meinel, C. (2010). Design thinking: an educational model towards creative confidence. In DS 66-2: Proceedings of the 1st International Conference on Design Creativity (ICDC 2010).

[5] Bacon, Jonathan, and Ben Ward. "The Horizon Report 2015 with Audience Participation Using Paper Clickers." (2015).

[6] Wong, T. (2013). Makerspaces Take Libraries by Storm. Library Media Connection, 31(6), 34-35.

[7] Sheridan, K. M., Halverson, E. R., Litts, B. K., Brahms, L., Jacobs-Priebe, L., & Owens, T. (2014). Learning in the Making: A Comparative Case Study of Three Makerspaces. Harvard Educational Review, 84(4), 505-531.

[8] Hlubinka, M., et al. "Makerspace playbook: School edition." Retrieved from Maker Media website: http://makerspace. com/wpcontent/uploads/2013/02/MakerspacePlaybook.

[9] Shostack, L. G. (1984). Design Services that Deliver. Harvard Business Review(84115), 133-139.

[10] Kemp, A. 2013. The Makerspace Workbench: Tools, Technologies, and Techniques for Making. Maker Media, Inc.

[11] Brady, Tara, et al. "MakeAbility: Creating accessible makerspace events in a public library." Public Library Quarterly 33.4 (2014): 330-347.

[12] Buehler, Erin, Shaun K. Kane, and Amy Hurst. "ABC and 3D: opportunities and obstacles to 3D printing in special education environments." Proceedings of the 16th international ACM SIGACCESS conference on Computers & accessibility. ACM, 2014.

[13] Hatch, M. (2014). The maker movement manifesto. New York: McGraw-Hill.

[14] Kelley, T., & Kelley, D. (2013). Creative confidence: Unleashing the creative potential within us all. Crown Business.

Brand New Designed
Virtual Computer Classroom in BYOD era

Kazuhiro Mishima
Information Media Center, Tokyo
University of Agriculture and
Technology
2-24-16 Naka-cho, Koganei-city
three@cc.tuat.ac.jp

Takeshi Sakurada
Information Media Center, Tokyo
University of Agriculture and
Technology
2-24-16 Naka-cho, Koganei-city
take-s@cc.tuat.ac.jp

Yoichi Hagiwara
Information Media Center, Tokyo
University of Agriculture and
Technology
2-24-16 Naka-cho, Koganei-city
hagi@cc.tuat.ac.jp

ABSTRACT

In Tokyo University of Agriculture and Technology, by the part of the information strategy, we promote to abolish the conventional computer room, and make the user to bring the user's own computer (BYOD: Bring Your Own Device). The trend of this BYOD is expanding progressively in other universities in Japan. The type of user's device is wide variety, its usability, is too. In this situation, it increases the cost of teacher due to the difference of the operation.

To reduce this cost, we propose our brand new designed computer environment, TUAT Virtual Computer Classroom (TUAT-VCCr). TUAT-VCCr is based on virtual desktop technology, and each user can use the TUAT-VCCr by accessing to the remote desktop, which can be accessed from everywhere in our campus. TUAT-VCCr can be used through an HTML5-compliant web browser (e.g. Google Chrome, Mozilla Firefox), instead of the dedicated client in a conventional VDI or remote desktop environment. This enables the use from a variety of access device that are independent of the device type of the user (e.g. Windows, Mac, Linux, or Chrome). As a result of this, convenience for the user is significantly improved.

We present the detail of the design and structure of TUAT-VCCr architecture. We also provide a TUAT-VCCr reservation system, which can adopt the class schedule in order to manage the number of the virtual desktops for class and self-study use efficiently. We also present the detail of this reservation system.

Keywords
BYOD, Computer Room, Virtual Desktop, Web Browser.

1. INTRODUCTION
Information Technology exercises education in Japanese Universities, are mainly classified into: 1) Foundation course: for

freshman, and 2) Specialized course: for more than second grade. Most of the classrooms which is used for these courses, called "Computer Room", has been equipped with a lot of the computer

terminal that has already been prepared, and, teachers and students just use these terminals. However, due to several factors: a) price reduction of information equipment, b) Increase of the computer room operation cost, and c) change of the environment of information-related education, there is a growing momentum of BYOD (Bring Your Own Device)[1],[2][3] in some Japanese Universities (e.g. Kyushu University, Kanazawa University, Tokyo Gakugei University). In Tokyo University of Agriculture and Technology (Our university), it was carried out BYOD. Thereby, we abolished the old-style computer room.

2. ACTUAL SITUATIONS IN JAPAN
We describe the actual situations of the Educational Computing System Environment at the Japanese university in below.

2.1 Traditional Computer Room
Educational computer system at the Japanese university, as previously described, there are many cases that are operated in a dedicated classroom, such as computer room, by installing multiple terminals of electronic computer (PCs). The number of installed terminals in one of the classrooms is about 20 to 100 units. Depending on the number of the installed terminals, impact of the instructor is increased. Therefore, in many cases approximately 50 units of terminal is installed. Furthermore, so that it can use in as many classes as possible depending on the size of the university, multiple computer rooms are operated. There are two types of the computer system, which is the form of the computer room. Each of the overview is shown in Fig.1.

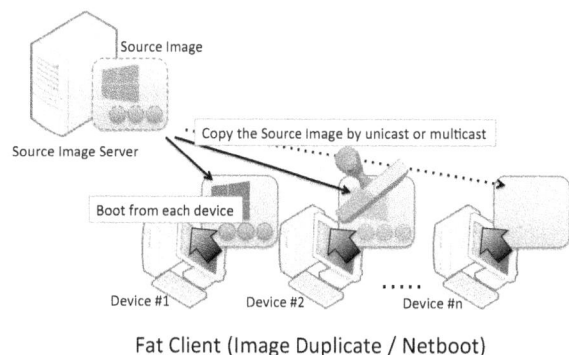

Fat Client (Image Duplicate / Netboot)

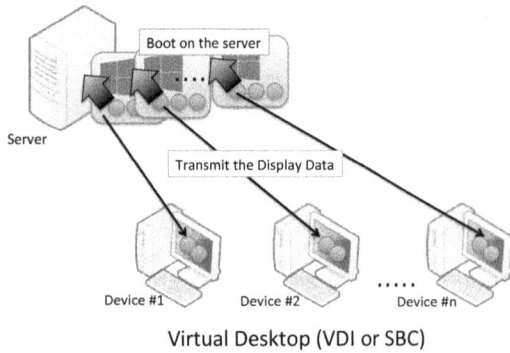

Figure 1. Terminal Styles of Traditional Computer Room.

2.1.1 Fat-client styled Computer

This is a method in which the OS is installed in each terminal. Fat-client, like a typical personal computer, OS and applications are installed in the storage device held by the terminal, and launch the terminal itself. It's also possible to manage each terminal individually. However, such as software installation and security updates must be carried out the number of installed terminal. For this reason, even a simple operation would become highly operational cost. To reduce this, there is a system for transferring a base image serving as a template to each terminal by constant operation. Each terminal is launch a terminal based on the image.

2.1.2 Screen-data transfer styled Computer

This is a method to aggregate multiple desktop environments on the terminal server. User can use each terminal by receiving only the screen data on the server via the network. This method is called "Virtual Desktop". By the method of holding the desktop environment on the server, there are three systems: 1) SBC (Server Base Computing) System[4][5][6], 2) VDI (Virtual Desktop Infrastructure) System[7][8], and 3) Server VDI System[7].

2.2 Bring Your Own Device (BYOD)

On the other hand, there are several advantages of BYOD. First of all, improvement of the utilization capacity of the information devices by handling their terminals is expected, rather than using the already prepared environment. Next, since it is the property of itself, by treating equipment more carefully, equipment failure rate is reduced. In addition, a reduction of the cost for own and management of a large number of the terminal by university is considered. In particular, the cost of maintaining a dedicated computer room is very high from the point of view of managing a large number of computers (e.g. managing the application software, system update, equipment failure, cleaning).

BYOD is, not only can reduce the cost for it to manage the terminal, can also enjoy the benefits which can be more convenient to use the computer for the user. A previous information exercise that needs to use the installed terminal is dependent on the location of the dedicated computer room. However, by using its own terminal, the exercises can be possible in any classroom, including general classroom. For this reason, if users are even under the campus network environment, there is no dependence on location.

As an issue of BYOD, there is a difference according to various terminals. This occurs because the user terminal models cannot be unique. The terminal models, which bring by the user, are such as Windows, MacOS, Linux and the others. This problem can be

avoided by the limiting the kind of bring equipment. However, in the university there are a lot of faculties and departments, limitation of the model is difficult. By this difference between the user is in the classroom, some troubled situations occur, e.g. OS is different, installed application is different, or the version of application is different. In the university preceded the BYOD, these cases have actually occurred. Finally, the absorption of the differences has to be accomplished by the teaching methods of each instructor. For example, teachers will have to check the applications that are installed on the each user's terminal, and must be made a class based on the difference between each terminal. This because the bear of the teachers will be very high, it is necessary to absorb the difference by should be in some kind of way.

3. IDEAL STYLE OF COMPUTER ROOM TOWARD THE BYOD SYSTEM

3.1 Virtual Desktop System for the purpose of difference absorption of terminal environment

While enjoying the benefits of BYOD as a technique to absorb the terminal differences, the combination of "BYOD" and aforementioned "Virtual Desktop System" can be considered. First of all, deploying common desktop environment for each user to use on the server. Furthermore, by transferring the screen data to the terminal held by each user, it is possible to utilize a common OS, screen and the application environment. When used together virtual desktop system, it is necessary to consider the "cost for providing the common environment". The system construction cost is of course necessary; in addition, it is necessary to consider the specific licensing costs in software (e.g. OS, application). Especially, when using the VDI system since the use of license in consideration of the number of user's terminal is required, a significant increase in licensing cost can be expected. On the other hand, it's possible to reduce the licensing cost by using the SBC system. However, the remote desktop system, which is most simple configuration in the SBC system, has some performance issues depending on user's terminal environment. Therefore, we investigated and verified the system that can be added acceleration feature for SBC system. Then, we decided to use the "Ericom AccessNow[9]" by Ericom Software. Ericom AccessNow is software to convert a remote desktop communication to the WebSocket[10] communication in HTML5[11]. By using own acceleration technique, Ericom AccessNow is unlikely to cause performance degradation even in WebSocket communication.

3.2 Virtual Computer Room (TUAT-VCCr)

Even when the combination of BYOD and virtual desktop system is carried out, actually, the class is carried out by the real-time synchronous learning style (in same place). The educational computing system for the class, are needed to have a mechanism that can collect multiple terminals, such as conventional computer room. Hence, we developed a completely brand-new mechanism, called "Virtual Computer Classroom". Virtual Computer Classroom can virtually group up multiple virtual desktop environments. Example overview of Virtual Computer Classroom is shown in Fig.2. In this example, some virtual classroom dedicating for each class is prepared at the virtual cloud infrastructure. It could be as if there is a classroom equipped multiple terminals in virtual space, like a conventional computer room. Thus, by using this Virtual Computer Classroom and

BYOD user terminal, general classroom (with no computer) will be transformed to the computer classroom. This system, set up the remote access software using HTML5-compliant Web Browser to the virtual desktop, user can remotely use the virtual desktop server in the remote data center on remote location. As a result, in a certain class, lecturer and students can utilize a unified desktop environment with all users, as if they received a class in one computer classroom. System (infrastructure) overview of our VCCr system is shown in Fig.3. Multiple servers, which are required for implementing the virtual computer classroom are set up by virtualization infrastructure at the remote data center.

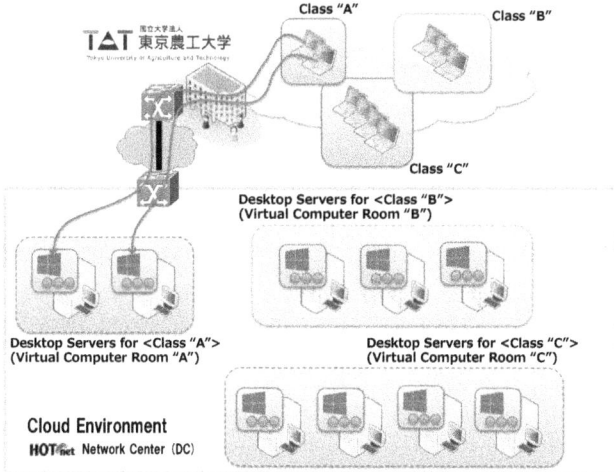

Figure 2. Virtual Computer Classroom (Grouping Virtual Desktops for Each Class)

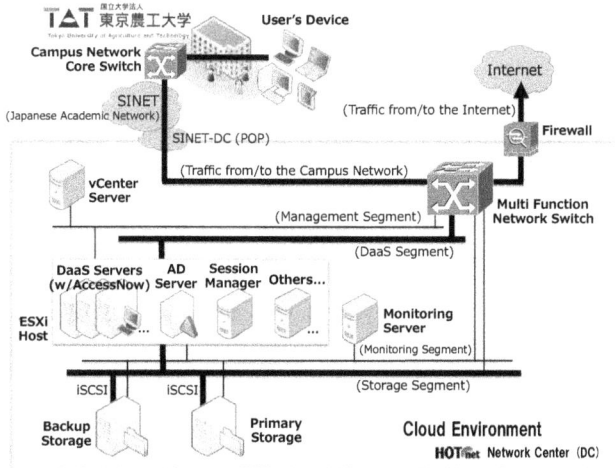

Figure 3. System Overview of TUAT VCCr.

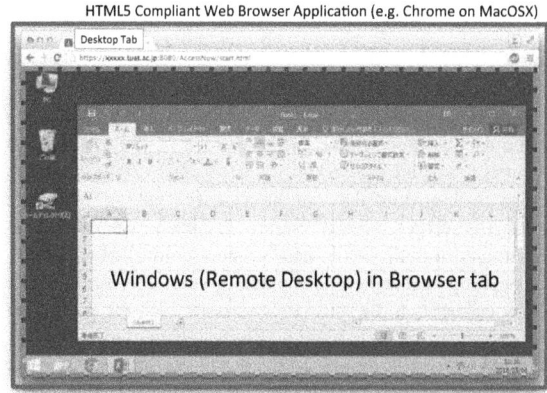

Figure 4. Virtual Desktop via Web Browser.

Ericom AccessNow's major feature is WebSocket communication capability. By using this, user can use Virtual Desktop Services only by the HTML5-compliant Web Browser (e.g. Mozilla Firefox, Google Chrome, Microsoft Edge, etc.). The situation of using virtual desktop service by web browser is shown in Fig.4. As shown, virtual desktop screen is displayed as one window of the Web Browser (one tab in this example). If user maximizes the browser windows, it can be used as just a Windows desktop. Because user can access the virtual desktop only with the Web Browser, the constraints of the terminal type, as it is WindowsOS, MacOS, or others, can be eliminated as much as possible.

3.2.1 Reservation of TUAT-VCCr

Usage of TUAT-VCCr for lecture purpose is required the advanced reservation. By this reservation, it is possible to make the virtual computer room for each class based on the information. User (e.g. lecturer) reserves the virtual classroom on the registration web interface, shown in Fig.5. The lecturer can assign a number of terminals required for class from a dedicated reservation page. Furthermore, by using the class schedule information, lecturer can easily reserve the terminal of virtual computer classroom. By registering the secret keyword in the reservation time, access of unrelated users on the class will be able to prevent. The terminal that remains without reservation will be automatically used as a terminal for the self-study user.

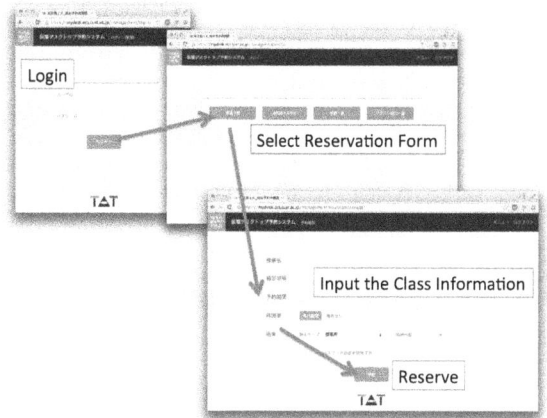

Figure 5. Reservation Interface for TUAT VCCr.

3.2.2 Use of TUAT-VCCr

User can use the TUAT-VCCr through the dedicated Web Portal. The example procedures of user's operation are shown in Fig.6. Once the user logged in the portal, the list of the virtual desktop environment (virtual classroom for each class). The list is shown only virtual classroom that can be accessed during that time. By selecting the target virtual classroom, each user can use the appropriate terminal. Dedicated session controller manages the virtual desktop server, which the user should use. Actually, when each user connects to the virtual classroom from the portal, virtual desktop server to be connected will be selected automatically, and the desktop screen is displayed on the user's browser window or tab. In addition, even if a user closes the browser without the sign out from Windows, the user can be connected to the same virtual desktop server again by accessing to the portal.

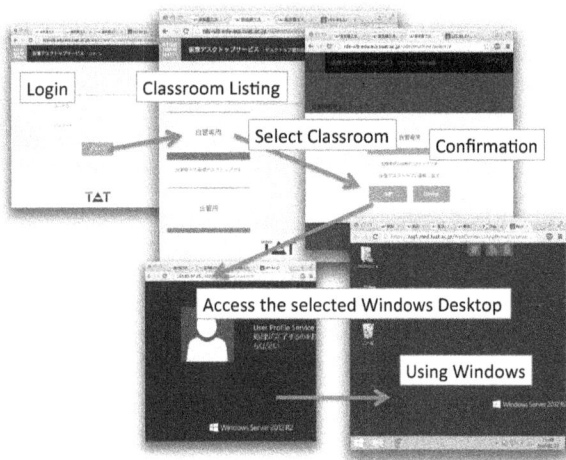

Figure 6. Web Portal for Using TUAT VCCr

4. CONCLUSION

In this presentation, we proposed brand-new computer classroom using virtual desktop system, called TUAT Virtual Computer Classroom (TUAT-VCCr). TUAT-VCCr has two functions: 1) Virtual Desktop System that can use by HTML5-compliant Web Browser, and 2) Virtual Desktop Session Management function. The system, set up the remote access software using HTML5-compliant Web Browser to the virtual desktop, user can remotely use the virtual desktop server in the remote data center on remote location. By introducing a mechanism to manage the session, it can gather multiple virtual desktops necessary for the class, and make up a virtual computer room. This virtual computer classroom, will redesign the way of electronic computer system for common university, fully utilize the cloud, and is an innovative service that an acceptable diversity of BYOD user terminal. In the future, we will have more various insights by promoting the virtual computer classroom in our university. Based on these insights, we plan to design a better virtual computer classroom style, eventually, want to issue the achievements for the ideal of computer classroom.

5. ACKNOWLEDGMENTS

Our thanks to Masato Kadowaki and Soshi Suzuki at Hokkaido Telecommunication Network Co., Inc. for designing and implementing the TUAT VCCr, and UNIADEX Ltd. for preparing this presentation.

6. REFERENCES

[1] Bradford Networks. 2013. *The Impact of BYOD in Education.* Bradford Networks White Paper.

[2] Rahat Afreen. 2014. *Bring Your Own Device (BYOD) in Higher Education: Opportunities and Challenges.* International Journal of Emerging Trends & Technology in Computer Science (IJETTCS). 3, 1(Jan.-Feb. 2014), 233-236.

[3] Cisco Systems, Inc. *BYOD Smart Solution.* URL:http://www.cisco.com/c/en/us/solutions/byod-smart-solution/overview.html [online] (Reference: May 2016)

[4] Microsoft. *Remote Desktop Services.* URL:https://technet.microsoft.com/en-us/library/cc770412.aspx [online] (Reference: May 2016)

[5] Microsoft. *[MS-RDPBCGR]: Remote Desktop Protocol: Basic Connectivity and Graphics Remoting.* Protocol Specification. URL:https://msdn.microsoft.com/en-us/library/cc240445.aspx?f=255&MSPPError=-2147217396 [online] (Reference: May 2016)

[6] Citrix. *XenApp.* URL:https://www.citrix.com/products/xenapp/overview.html [online] (Reference: May 2016)

[7] VMware. *Horizon6.* URL:http://www.vmware.com/products/horizon-view/ [online] (Reference: May 2016)

[8] Citrix. *XenDesktop.* URL:https://www.citrix.com/products/xendesktop/overview.html [online] (Reference: May 2016)

[9] Ericom Software. *EricomAccessNow.* URL:http://www.ericom.com/Ericom_AccessNow_Products.asp [online] (Reference: Oct 2015)

[10] I. Fette, A. Melnikov. 2011. *The WebSocket Protocol.* IETF RFC. RFC6455.

[11] W3C. *HTML5: A vocabulary and associated APIs for HTML and XHTML.* W3C Recommendation. URL:http://www.w3.org/TR/html5/ [online] (Reference: Oct 2015)

Constructing a Log Collecting System using Splunk and its Application for Service Support

Masaru Okumura
Fukuoka University
8-19-1, Nanakuma, Fukuoka
Fukuoka, Japan
okkun@fukuoka-u.ac.jp

Sho Fujimura
Fukuoka University
8-19-1, Nanakuma, Fukuoka
Fukuoka, Japan
fujimura@fukuoka-u.ac.jp

ABSTRACT

The operation of the education and research system, which includes network, server and client services, produces a variety of log output. The effective analysis of these logs makes it is possible to ascertain user trends, and often points to issues that require troubleshooting. However, due to the difference in the type and diversity of format of the log, it takes a considerable amount of effort to organize them in a cross-sectional manner in order to obtain useful information. To resolve this issue, we have constructed a log collecting system by using Splunk to centrally aggregate logs. Most logs are automatically stored on the Splunk database from each system. As a result, the administrator and service support staff can view these logs via a simple interface, and can check the usage of the users across multiple systems in near real time. In this paper, we introduce how to approach and construct a system in order to change the logs of the various systems to be able to obtain valuable information. We also show how you can utilize aggregated log for service support and security. Particularly based on the user ID and IP addresses, it is possible to gain a bird's-eye view of logs for analysis, making it a valid tool for understanding user behavior.

CCS Concepts

•Security and privacy → *Distributed systems security;*
•Human-centered computing → *Visualization systems and tools;*

Keywords

System log;Log collection;Splunk;Service support;User statistics;

1. INTRODUCTION

Fukuoka University uses the education and research system called FUTURE. The FUTURE education system connects the university network, 20 PC labs and 1500 PC and

offers 30 types of services to users including email. In order to gain an accurate overall view of the FUTURE system in operation, and obtain data necessary for its operation it is imperative that the system output logs be collected and be used for system operation and service for users. However, the type and status of the logs are wide and varied, and there are issues limiting the effective use of these logs. In the fifth generation system FUTURE5, which went online in September 2015, a log collection system based on Splunk[1] was constructed to solve existing issues, and commenced operation for the analysis of log data.

2. THE IMPORTANCE OF LOG COLLECTION AND EXISTING ISSUES

2.1 The Importance of Log Collection

The logs generated by each system provide all kinds of beneficial information. Time, user ID, IP address, specific actions, normal or abnormal function can be verified the log. Service errors due to hardware malfunction, security incidents, when such events occur they are recorded in the log data and is important in providing evidence for ascertaining what happened. Different systems incorporating NTP(Network Time Protcol) can maintain accurate time sequence between them, and it is indispensable in ascertaining what happened before and after an incident. In addition, by the collection of logs from a cross-section of systems instead of just a specific system log, it provides an accurate picture of users' activities and trends which is beneficial in providing support not only for everyday management, but for future system design, giving the collection of log information a special meaning.

2.2 Operation Methods without Using Log Aggregation Systems

As shown in Figure 1(A), Computers and systems have some form of log (raw log) output. Normally the log data is stored within the computer, and without a special installation, for the log operator to view logs of multiple systems, they must access each computer individually. In addition, to analyze active logs the person must be highly trained in the log format and its content. This means that the person attending to the logs must have previous experience in each individual system log format and its content. On top of that, when collecting log data for statistical analysis, it is necessary to collect data from each individual log in text and script language appropriate to each format. This is a required skill for gleaning useful data from logs. Also, for long-term log analysis storage volumes for each computer must be taken into consideration.

2.3 Issues in Realizing Log Aggregation

In order to effectively collect log data from the entire system for analysis the following issues must be resolved:

1. Unified aggregating the logs of multiple systems

2. Saving collected logs long term in an easy to search state

3. The ability to search logs without worrying about differences in log format

4. To be able to search, aggregate and analyze logs without having specialized skills

We aimed to resolve these issues in the implementation of the new FUTURE5 system.

3. IMPLEMENTATION OF NEW PROCEDURES

3.1 Viewpoint

In order to effectively view and search logs in the newly introduced FUTURE5 system, we needed create a structure that could handle a total of 440 host logs for aggregation and standardization. In addition, the logs needed to be not only collected and aggregated, but arranged in a searchable format and saved for long-term storage. We made a goal of creating a system that could standardize all the logs in the system for effective operator-friendly search, which could be used by any operator irrespective of skill level. To realize this goal we employed the Splunk log collection platform. Figure 1(B) shows our new log collection approach.

3.2 Log Collection Structure

The new log collection system consists of 1 server where operators can search logs by command through a web interface, 2 management servers for log data collection and indexing, and 1 storage unit for saving indexed logs as well as 1 backup storage unit, making a total of 5 units. We used a virtual machine for the log search server, and due to the large amount or input/output data we used an actual server for log management.

The 2 log management servers consolidate and index logs from approximately 440 hosts. The collection methods are via network syslog and Splunk forwarder as well as transferring the log files to the log management server. Furthermore, some logs are received manually if the size of the log is too big or it is necessary to acquire it in real time. An outline of log collection system using Splunk is shown in Table 1.

3.3 Why Splunk was chosen

There are a number of reasons why Splunk was chosen as the FUTURE5 log collection system. In the fourth generation FUTURE4 (2010-2015) a log collection system was introduced, but it was not the Splunk product. At first the FUTURE4 log collection system worked satisfactorily, and logs could be searched. However, in the latter part of the operation log search started to require a huge amount of time, which led to practically no use of the log search function. In order to use log stats the log files (text files) had to be collected manually and correlation needed much time and energy.

Against this background, FUTURE5 was designed so as logs could be searched at any time during its operation, and user statistics would be automated to a certain extend for easy access without the need for manpower. The log collection system could collect various logs, which could be used not only for user statistics, but also for big data analysis to analyze user trends and provide appropriate services based on their needs. In addition, audit of and verification of logs can also be conducted through this log collection system and detect any signs of unauthorized access. In order to realize these objectives, the Splunk log collection system was chosen.

4. OPERATION METHOD

4.1 Overall Merit

Splunk collects system logs from approximately 440 hosts in FUTURE5(Figure 1(B)). The collection from each host is, as a rule, automated, and when viewing collected logs there is no necessity to concentrate on the details of any individual system output log. Furthermore, all collected logs are indexed, therefore when specifying a timeframe for search the system can extract the necessary data from a cross-section of data. The Splunk internal log data format is linked, so conventional script and command data formatting to standardize data is not required. The environment allows operators to conduct a cross-sectional search over the entire system with search keys such as date, user ID, IP address etc.

These functions create data statistics for approximately 15 different services provided by FUTURE5. Splunk produces visualization of the search results in the form of simple graphs and charts, allowing for analysis and projection of expected user trends from the collected data. Also, Splunk is not just a single log search service, it provides cross sectional relative search results of multiple service logs. Statistics that may look unrelated can now provide valuable information. It can also be used in ascertaining facts relating to security incidents and finding solutions.

4.2 User Statistics for Each Service

Now that Splunk has been employed in the logs in various

Table 1: Log Collection Items

Service Category	Content	Log Type	Log input Frequency
Network	VPN	Login	Real Time
	DHCP(Wired)-LAN	Login	Real Time
	DHCP(Wi-Fi)-LAN	Login	Real Time
	Web Proxy	Access	Monthly
	Web Filter	Access	Monthly
PC	Windows	Login	Monthly
	Linux	Login	Monthly
	Mac	Login	Monthly
	Application on PC	Access	Monthly
	Application Server	Login	Monthly
	Printing	Printing	Monthly
Other	Moodle	Login	Monthly
	Web Publishing	Login	Real Time

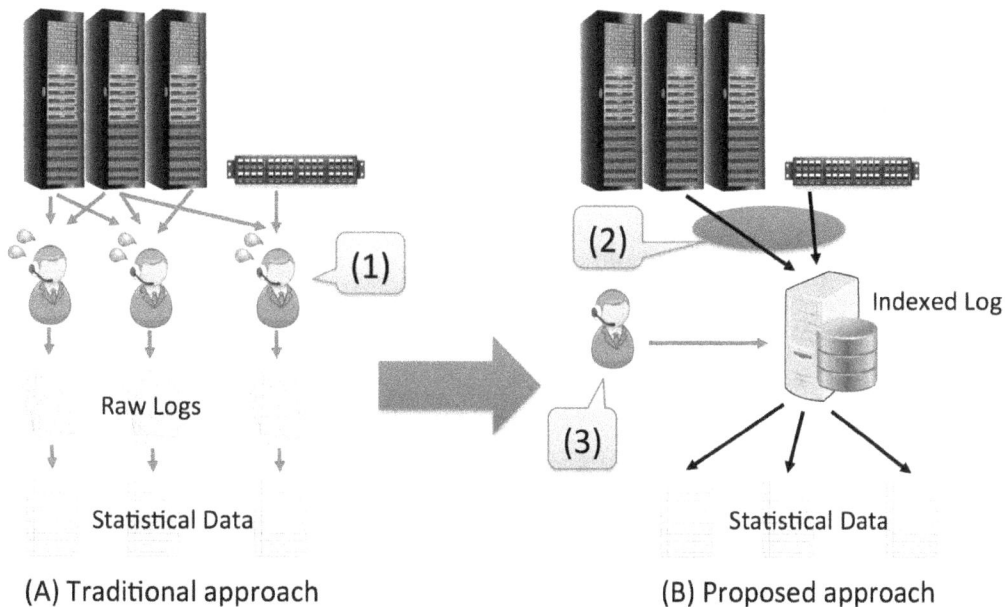

Figure 1: Traditional Approach and Proposed Approach.(1)Each system log scatterd so system operators must collect and analyze log data individually.(2)Aggregation and collection of server and network infrastructure logs.(3)Cross-sectional search of logs enables a single operator to analyze data, eliminating intermediate processing and saving time and effort.

FUTURE5 user services, it has become possible to extract statistical user data from PCs in the PC rooms, campus Wi-Fi usage etc. However, to be able to use search phrases to extract certain user statistics requires a certain amount of training. For these reasons we have created templates for statistical user data which are frequently used, allowing for simple operation for operators not accustomed to using Splunk. As shown in Figure 2, we have prepared 30 different report templates. Operaters are able to easily check the user statistics of FUTURE5 by using these report templates. Figure 3 shows a statistics of application usage in PC rooms.

4.3 Security Measures

Because Splunk incorporates log verification it was used to perform verification audit. Up until FUTURE4 there was no means to perform audit of verification, so only after a security incident arose was the log investigated. However, in FUTURE5 verification audit can be conducted in real time, if the threshold was exceeded (the number of failed verifications in a specific period of time) the Splunk alert function can be set to send an email alert to the administrator. However, this is only an alert email, and what measures are to be taken after the alert, and examining threshold tuning etc. and being able conduct practical audit remain pending issues.

5. ISSUES

Compared to the previous FUTURE4 log collection system, the range of collected data systems and search function have improved. However, this has given rise to new issues. Due to the new log collection system being fully integrated and covering the main systems, for example by searching a certain user ID it is possible to track all the user's on-campus

access/use details. This can be beneficial in resolving trouble or ascertaining the user's service usage. However, there is a possibility it may lead to a breach of privacy if the access record is used for unrelated purposes, therefore there is a need to strictly limit the scope of what information and who can view it. Furthermore, the collection of the entire system raw access logs creates a cross-sectional indexed log searchable. The search function has improved, but the search system storage repository has volume limitations, and it is difficult to maintain searchable logs over a long period of time. This has given rise to the issue of how long a timeframe search data should be maintained in operating the log collection system.

6. CONCLUSIONS

In order to resolve current log collection issues in FUTURE5 the Splunk log collection system architecture has been installed. This has resolved the issues of the collection of multiple system logs unified aggregation and multiple cross-sectional log search. Specialist knowledge is not required to analyze data and user statistics, resulting in many improvements. Another new use is the ability to overlook the total system for analysis and the ability to use it for security measures. In the future, we hope to effectively use the information garnered through the use of this log collection system to take on new initiatives.

7. REFERENCES

[1] S. Inc. Splunk. *http://www.splunk.com/*, 2015.

Figure 2: Prepaired Report Templates

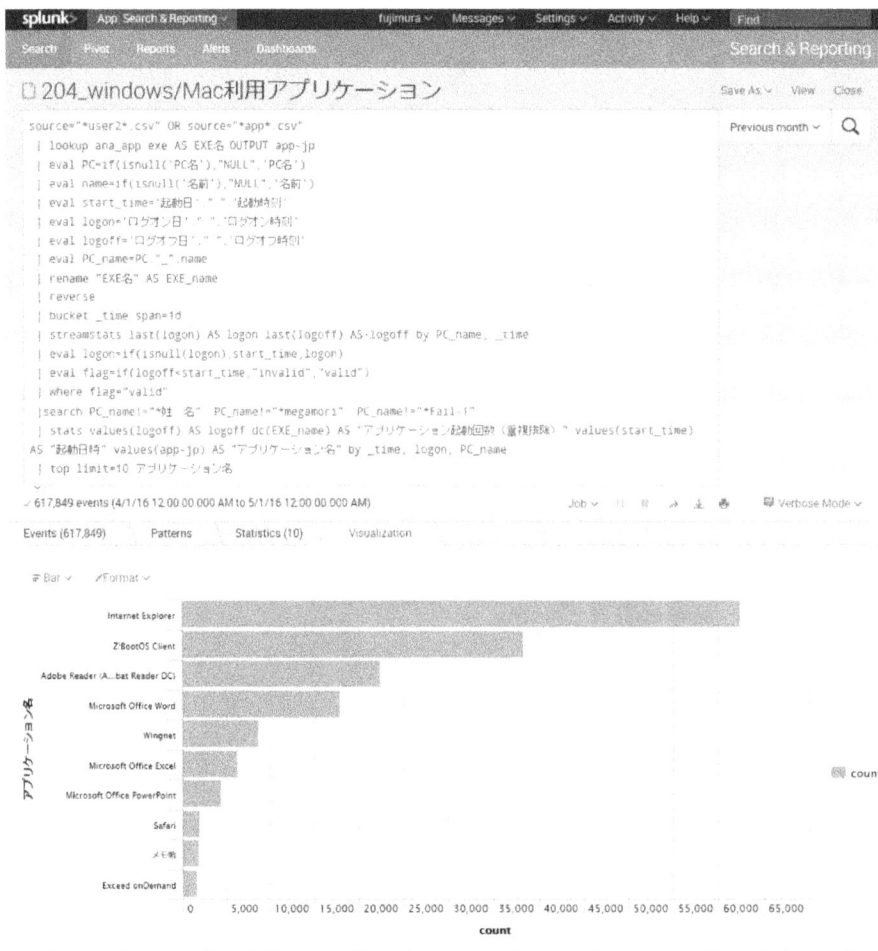

Figure 3: Application Usage Counts of PC Rooms(Template No.204)

Taking the S.T.A.I.R.S: A Philosophy in Managing Student Workers

Melissa Doernte
Stanford University
518 Memorial Way
Stanford, CA 94305
650-656-5158
mdoernte@stanford.edu

ABSTRACT

How would you develop, engage, mentor, train and assess a group of 30 part-time student workers at a non-conventional Tech Desk? As part of my interview to become the Service Desk Manager in the Vice Provost Office of Teaching and Learning at Stanford University, I was tasked with formulating an answer to this complex question. To accomplish this, I developed a philosophy entitled "Taking the S.T.A.I.R.S." It outlines the most important ideas and concepts to successfully manage a group of student workers. Specifically, these concepts include identifying Strengths in each individual student, being Transparent with them, emphasizing their Accountability and responsibility, seeking their Input and teaching them how to take initiative, emphasizing Respect toward each other and the university, and showing Support for them and their decisions. Now, roughly six months into my new position, I keep returning to this philosophy to evaluate its effectiveness.

Keywords

Students; Management; Service Desk; Evaluation

1. INTRODUCTION

Being a student worker is hard. They are simultaneously trying to get good grades, get job experience, make some extra spending money, and figure out what they are going to do with the rest of their lives. They have a lot on their plates and having a manager at work who doesn't understand them or their needs is a detriment to the student and the job. On the other side of the equation are the managers. Managing may look easy, but there are numerous elements that complicate the job: different personalities, time constraints, projects, sensitive information. Managers have many elements to consider, and they too, have a lot on their plates.

Now, consider managing 30 student workers at a Tech Desk. Daunting, right? It can be, but after six years of experience managing students, I have found a philosophy that helps to take the edge off of navigating the world of student management.

SIGUCCS '16, November 06-09, 2016, Denver, CO, USA
© 2016 ACM. ISBN 978-1-4503-4095-3/16/11…$15.00
DOI: http://dx.doi.org/10.1145/2974927.2974935

Taking the S.T.A.I.R.S. stands for Strengths, Transparency, Accountability, Input and initiative, Respect and Support. By understanding these six concepts and implementing them in the work environment, managers are able to cultivate and foster a healthy work experience for both their students and themselves.

2. STRENGTHS

There are many different elements and categories that a manager needs in order to engage and mentor their students. Most importantly, they first must identify the strengths of their employees. Specifically, they should engage the strengths of their students while also mentoring them past their weaknesses. Through observation, one-on-one meetings and casual conversation, managers can gauge a student's abilities. Additionally, there are tests, like the Myers Briggs personality test, that can aid a manager in determining these strengths and weaknesses. Eventually, the manager will be able to evaluate the tasks available and properly align student worker resources to those tasks. At the same time, managers can work to provide struggling students with any necessary additional assistance.

3. TRANSPARENCY

Above and beyond analyzing strengths and weaknesses, another important component of managing is communication. Specifically, a great manager provides transparent communication with student workers. The ability to articulate the expectations of the job is only half of the battle. It has become increasingly important to provide workers with the 'why' or 'rational' of projects. By being transparent and communicating the goals and objectives of tasks and projects, managers can stimulate a drive in students to complete the work and do it well. Much like any work environment, the key to success is to have open communication and provide transparency.

4. ACCOUNTABILITY

In addition to communicating the 'why' to student workers, it is equally important to emphasize to them that they are accountable for their actions and decisions. I have observed that many students, and some adults, tend to deflect accountability of their decisions or actions to others. As a manager, it is essential to emphasize the importance of accountability and responsibility for decisions made at work because of the effects this attitude has on the work environment. By empowering student workers, managers can solicit buy-in and show how students' actions affect the job, their coworkers, those they are serving and the greater community.

5. INITIATIVE

In order for students to be more engaged at work, it is essential for them to feel they can contribute to their job. Specifically, managers should stress the importance of taking initiative at work and should allow input on processes and procedures. When student workers feel like they have the ability to shape their jobs and make a change, their attitude and work ethic is drastically improved.

6. RESPECT AND SUPPORT

Finally, the last two concepts, respect and support, go hand in hand. It is critical in the workplace to have respect for one another, the job and the customers. A manager should stress respect for every aspect of the job because it will have an impact on all parts of the job. In addition, it is important for a manager to show support to their workers and the decisions they make in the workplace.

Managers need to reinforce their support of the actions and decisions of their subordinates in order to receive support themselves.

7. CONCLUSION

Overall, taking the S.T.A.I.R.S and adopting these principles into the process of managing students will significantly improve student workers' development and work ethic. These principles foster a supportive, responsible and transparent environment which will improve the service and support provided to the customers and community.

8. ACKNOWLEDGMENTS

Many thanks to my SIG friends who have made all of my greatness possible. Without them, my life would be a little bit duller and I would not have any amazing role models to aspire toward.

Choosing a Classroom Polling Vendor

Trevor M. Murphy
Williams College
56 Hopkins Hall Drive
Williamstown, MA 01267
1-413-597-2231
tmurphy@williams.edu

Randy Matusky
Lyndon College
1001 College Road
Lyndonville, VT 05851
1-802-626-6374
randolph.matusky@lyndonstate.edu

ABSTRACT

Classroom polling at Williams College is infrequent and sporadic occurring in classes only when they are most pedagogically appropriate for the content. Some courses use classroom polling once a semester. Other courses use classroom polling often, but the data is not used in grading or stored for future analysis. Flexibility and portability make classroom polling an easy tool to apply when the anonymous collection of class input serves a teaching purpose. Recently, classroom polling vendors have moved to a subscription model where classroom polling users have cloud accounts that require monthly fees. This new subscription model does not match with the use of classroom polling at Williams College. Students do not purchase accounts with monthly fees to participate in classroom polling that may or may not be used in classes. This paper follows Williams College as it creates and follows a new process for finding the right classroom polling vendor for its campus.

Keywords

Classroom Polling, Hardware Selection, Software Selection.

1. INTRODUCTION

1.1 Institutional Context

Williams College is a private, residential, liberal arts college located in the northwestern corner of Massachusetts in the town of Williamstown. The college has 2,000 students and 300 faculty members. The Office for Information Technology at Williams College consists of four groups including Networks and Systems, Desktop Systems, Administrative Information Systems, and Instructional Technology. The Instructional Technology group provides faculty with pedagogically informed technology support.

Lyndon State College is a public liberal arts college in northeastern Vermont. The college has 1,450 students and 57 faculty. The Office of Information Technology at Lyndon College consists of nine staff members including a Chief Technology Officer, a LAN/System Administrator, and a Coordinator of Instructional Technology.

SIGUCCS '16, November 06-09, 2016, Denver, CO, USA
© 2016 ACM. ISBN 978-1-4503-4095-3/16/11...$15.00
DOI: http://dx.doi.org/10.1145/2974927.2974944

1.2 Classroom Polling

1.2.1 Why Use It?

Classroom Polling is a system for requesting and receiving instantaneous and potentially anonymous feedback during a teaching session. Faculty often wonder if the class has understood a crucial component of a lecture or lesson. A faculty member could call out on a student and ask them a question, or pose a question to the whole class and ask for the class as a whole to raise hands if they agree or not. However, social factors interfere with this kind of data collection. Cold calling on a student can cause anxiety. Many students opt out of raising their hands altogether. Some wait to see how their peers vote and vote with them rather than vote based on their own thoughts.

Anonymous polling provides a high number of responses without the interfering social factors. Faculty can gauge if the pacing of the lesson is too fast or too slow. Faculty can change the course of the lesson to meet identified needs in real time.

Students need a break to analyze a lesson. A polling question allows time to assess and apply new knowledge. If a correct and incorrect answer had almost the same number of votes, faculty may ask the class to consult with a neighbor and tell them why their answer is correct. The question is then repolled. Peer instruction is a good way to make use of a learning break.

Polling can stimulate discussion in larger classes. Students can articulate a point if they know that a third of the class has the same idea.

1.2.2 History at Williams College

Classroom polling systems were initially tried at Williams College in 2005 [1]. In 2007 the college moved from Interwrite PRS software to Turning Technologies. The radio clickers from Turning Technologies continued to be used until 2016. Use of the clickers spread from the classroom to programming for athletics and even monthly faculty meetings where questions of college governance are decided.

Classroom polling has been used for a variety of purposes at Williams College.

- Ice breaker questions.
- Checking for understanding.
- Asking controversial questions about sensitive topics such as stances on abortion, or questions about politics, and religion. College athletes are asked about alcohol consumption, sleep habits, and drug use.
- Psychology research.
- Making classroom decisions such as when study sessions should be scheduled.
- Faculty governance votes.

Faculty would come up with interesting applications for the technology. Sometimes they wanted to reproduce the polling that colleagues or textbook publishers developed, but other times they would come up with novel uses. A philosophy professor uses classroom polling to find topics that divide the class on the issue so that a lively discussion can develop. If everyone is in agreement on a topic, he would skip discussion and move on.

1.2.3 A Moment to Reassess
Year after year the same hardware and software would be used for classroom polling. Advanced features became available, but the college did not update the hardware or software. The software did have regular updates, but the version of the software became the oldest software supported. The vendor removed the software from its website. The hardware we owned, 300 polling devices and 10 USB receivers were also depreciated. We called the vendor to find a path forward, but all paths required starting over with new hardware and software.

If our entire infrastructure for classroom polling was out of date and in need of replacement, it was a good time to survey the field and see if there were other offerings that would be suitable to our needs.

2. PROCESS AND PRODUCTS
2.1 Process
We queried a few listservs of peer institutions to see what other solutions were being used in higher education. One group is a google group called edu-place: http://p-lace.org/. The other list was from the Consortium of Liberal Arts Colleges: http://www.liberalarts.org/.

We contacted faculty and vendors to have a demo lunch to discuss options and try various possible classroom polling systems out.

2.2 Products
2.2.1 Plickers
Plickers: https://plickers.com/ make use of up to 63 unique images constructed of a 5 x 5 grid of black or white squares. The plickers app uses your device's camera to identify the patterns as unique and it also stores the orientation of the pattern. Students can choose their response to a question by changing the orientation of their pattern to one of four possible responses. The answers are displayed as a chart on a projected screen, or on your phone.

The app and the grids are free for download.

Our faculty did not respond well to plickers. There were obvious challenges in that larger classes that would benefit most from some form of interactivity would exceed the maximum number of plicker

2.2.2 iClicker
iClicker: https://www1.iclicker.com/ can be used with cell phones or with physical devices that can be passed out to the students. We did a demo with the physical devices. The faculty liked the hardware solution and found the software usable. The physical devices are large and the USB receivers were also large and required external power to run. To provide a class of 100 students with clickers would require several bins to store the physical clickers. The receiver would need to be set up and plugged into both a computer and a power source.

Although there is an option to use student owned cell phones as devices, the faculty preferred the physical clickers.

2.2.3 PollEverywhere
PollEverywhere: https://www.polleverywhere.com/ allows students to vote using their phones. During the demo, some faculty were distracted by their phones and started checking email. They became disengaged from the demo. The faculty are concerned about using phones in class. They see phones as being detrimental to teaching.

2.2.4 TurningTechnologies
TurningTechnologies: https://www.turningtechnologies.com/ is similar to iclicker in that students can use their phones or a physical clicker to participate in classroom polling. The new hardware and software were similar to the solution that had been in place at Williams College for 9 years.

The difference was that now faculty need to log in to use the software.

The model that Williams College uses with classroom polling is the kit model. Classroom polling is conducted using clickers and a receiver provided by the institution. Students do not purchase clickers at the bookstore or pay monthly fees for an app on their phone.

3. FACULTY FEEDBACK
Not all faculty were able to attend demos. Some faculty have independently tried out technologies on their own. Several faculty have polleverywhere accounts.

Faculty at the demos did not like cell phone polling. Some faculty from athletics and from the Psychology Department like the extra features that come from using student owned cell phones in classroom polling. The use of cell phones in the classroom divides faculty.

4. CONCLUSION
Classroom polling offers faculty a way to interact with large groups of students or to ask for anonymous feedback mid lecture. Controversial topics can be addressed in a way that does not embarrass individual students. While the teaching technique has proved its worth, there remain several options for hardware and software to implement classroom polling. Making a choice on a polling solution will involve many stakeholders.

5. ACKNOWLEDGMENTS
Thanks to Jonathan Morgan-Leamon, Director of Instructional Technology at Williams College, who supports the author's professional development.

6. REFERENCES
[1] Trevor Murphy. 2008. Success and failure of audience response systems in the classroom. InProceedings of the 36th annual ACM SIGUCCS fall conference: moving mountains, blazing trails(SIGUCCS '08). ACM, New York, NY, USA, 33-38.

Adventures in Mentoring:
Lessons Learned from a Peer Mentor

Kathryn Fletcher
West Virginia University
One Waterfront Place PO Box 6500
Morgantown, WV 26506 USA
011-304-293-8769
kathy.fletcher@mail.wvu.edu

Trevor Murphy
Williams College
Office of Information Technology
Williamstown, MA 01267 USA
011-413-597-2231
tmurphy@williams.edu

ABSTRACT

Often one thinks of mentoring being used to prepare a mentee for a new position, where the mentor has a job role similar to the goal position. However the ACM SIGUCCS Mentoring Program has always been open to other types of mentoring relationships, where the mentor is the "guide on the side" to help a mentee reach one or more goals during the 10 month mentoring period. In 2016, Trevor and Kathy applied for the mentoring program, requesting to be paired up. Trevor, who has past experience as a mentor (to someone else) is the mentee of the pair while Kathy, who has past experience as a mentee with a different mentor, is serving as a mentor for Trevor. Our goals for the year do not include seeking promotions or attaining a professional certification. Although one of us is ostensibly the mentor, we both plan to learn and grow from this relationship. We decided to keep track of any challenges and life lessons we encounter during this year and share our thoughts at the conference for the benefit of those considering applying for the program in the future.

CCS Concepts

• Social and professional topics ~ Project and people management • Social and professional topics ~ Employment issues

Keywords

employee development; goal setting; mentoring; personal growth

1. BACKGROUND

1.1 About the Authors

Trevor is an instructional technology specialist for the Office of Information Technology at Williams College and has worked there for over 15 years. He currently serves on the SIGUCCS Mentoring Advisory Board and has served as a mentor in the program in previous years. Williams College is a private liberal arts college in Williamstown, Massachusetts, with an undergraduate enrollment of about 2,000 students.

SIGUCCS '16, November 06-09, 2016, Denver, CO, USA
© 2016 ACM. ISBN 978-1-4503-4095-3/16/11…$15.00
DOI: http://dx.doi.org/10.1145/2974927.2974951

Kathy is a support specialist for Information Technology Services at West Virginia University and has held a variety of IT support roles at the university since 1982. She was a mentee in 2014 and is serving as Trevor's mentor in 2016. WVU is a public land-grant doctoral research institution with an enrollment of about 28,800 students on its main campus in Morgantown, West Virginia.

1.2 About the SIGUCCS Mentoring Program

The ACM SIGUCCS mentoring program was established in 2012, with the first cohort of mentors and mentees accepted for 2013. Potential mentors and mentees submit formal applications online and the SIGUCCS Mentoring Advisory Board makes the pairing decisions based on goals and skills [4]. Applications are due each year in December as each year's program runs from January until the Fall Conference in late October / early November.

A SIGUCCS Mentoring Advisory Board member is assigned to each pair and is available to both parties throughout the year as needed. Mentees set the goal(s) that they wish to work on during the year. Mentors meet with their mentees for a minimum of one hour per month. An orientation webinar is held in January plus optional monthly online meetings for all mentors and mentees to attend. Online resources are available for the mentoring pairs. [1]

1.3 One Definition of Peer Mentoring

According to the Best Practices: Mentoring guide published by the United States Office of Personnel Management, "peer mentoring is usually a relationship with an individual within the same grade, organization, and/or job series. The purpose of peer mentoring is to support colleagues in their professional development and growth, to facilitate mutual learning and to build a sense of community. Peer mentoring is not hierarchical, prescriptive, judgmental, or evaluative." [3]

2. TREVOR MURPHY'S REFLECTIONS

IT professionals make numerous decisions every day. Many decisions are made with little guidance. Some fraction of these decisions have oversight from a supervisor, or they are made in consultation with stakeholders. Other decisions are made in haste with little time for thought. The email inbox is full of items that require action. All of this activity somehow needs to be prioritized and accomplished. Strangely, IT professionals are left to develop their own protocols for handling most action items.

In addition to the day to day decision making, there are also career path choices, life work balance questions, training opportunities, and potential work efficiencies. The larger questions that have a longer time scale might require making big changes in work habits, or even thinking about a change in workplace. Working toward moving to a new position at a different institution might make human resources, supervisors, or colleagues less than ideal confidants.

Inevitably, mistakes are made and opportunities are missed. Inefficiencies come from prioritizing tasks incorrectly, or omitting important steps to make a project effective. These mistakes and miscues can take many forms. A colleague waited to be invited to apply for an internal position, but the invitation never came. A project testing innovative instructional technology was put into production without the necessary implementation plans in place to make it successful. Hopefully, some learning comes out of these missteps. In some cases, a supervisor can help. In other cases, it is communication with the supervisor that is the problem.

It would be advantageous if there were a place for the IT professional to turn to for advice on their workplace challenges. Better choices could be made if the IT professional could ask an experienced person they could call on who in their years had encountered situations that had lessons in them that were directly applicable to the challenges at hand. Add discretion and some distance from the professional's home institution and the mentee/mentor relationship provides instant utility and benefits.

Mentoring relationships can help connect IT professionals and provide a venue to formally discuss topics of mutual interest that can help guide a professional through difficult challenges. A trusted confidant at a separate institution can talk through topics of office politics or poor management discussions with an open mind and some distance from the situation. Years of experience and lessons learned can be used to help avoid creating new conflicts and challenges. A mentor can often recommend a course of action that doesn't occur to someone in the thick of a challenging situation.

Similarly, the mentor can share their experiences and build on their ability to mentor and communicate with professionals. Such skill development could help them stay in touch with the challenges of young professionals as they strive to improve their own skills.

3. KATHY FLETCHER'S REFLECTIONS

In the Summer 2016 issue of AWIS Magazine, Dr. Isabel Escobar from the University of Kentucky was asked to describe community using three words. She chose the words *collaboration*, *mentoring*, and *supportive*; as part of her interview quoted in the article, she goes on to say that "mentorship plays a pivotal role in what makes a community" and that "trust is essential" [2]. When I first decided to participate in the new formal mentoring program as a mentee and now as a mentor, I feel that I have strengthened my connection to the SIGUCCS community of IT practitioners.

When I was a mentee, I found myself making decisions to explore new learning or leadership opportunities at work, thinking to myself: "I can't wait to tell my mentor about this, she will be proud of me". I now feel that I no longer need so much external validation; my former mentor and I have eased into an ongoing friendship while she has moved on to mentor others.

During an early morning walk during the SIGUCCS 2015 Service and Support Conference, some of my walking buddies shared some of their experiences as mentors. Listening to these conversations led me to consider applying to serve as a mentor in the program as instead of reapplying as a mentee in search of a new mentor. Since I am no longer a manager, I was worried that perhaps I was not fit to mentor another person and almost did not apply. Luckily I had additional discussions with a few members of the SIGUCCS Mentoring Advisory Board and realized that I

could mentor someone new in the field of IT support due to my 30+ years of experience as an IT professional or someone new to IT training since I had many years of experience in that area. I also remembered a conversation during the mentoring celebration dinner where one of the mentors at my table reminded me that there is a difference between *management* and *leadership*, that one can exhibit leadership at work without serving as a supervisor or manager.

After a long conversation during a conference event, Trevor and I decided that we would apply to serve as peer mentors with each other. Peer mentoring works well for our situation since neither of us have aspirations for new jobs at this time and our personal growth goals mesh well. I applied to serve as the mentor since I wanted to learn more about mentoring from the other side of the table and Trevor had some important goals that he wished to address during 2016.

While serving as a mentor these past few months, I have noticed that my attention will light on tips and resources that I want to share with Trevor instead of always thinking of my own goals and needs. I also have found myself informally mentoring co-workers (whether they realize it or not).

4. LESSONS LEARNED SO FAR
4.1 Trevor

When you are close to a problem, it may seem that there is only one untenable solution. This is almost always false. It takes years of experience to see the multitude of possible paths and approaches to problems. I pose a problem to my mentor and they reply with why don't you split the difference and have a hybrid approach. There is a moment of doubt about this new advice. It cannot work that way, can it? Upon reflection, it seems the idea might have some merit. If nothing else, some of the stress about being stuck with a poor path forward is reduced. Maybe there is another way? Strangely, when the stress dissipates, logic and reason come back to the forefront and you find yet another solution that is a good and supportable path to follow.

Communication styles differ between people. Words that people might choose might lead a person to jump to the wrong conclusion. I have used poor words myself and I'm always grateful when someone asks me for clarification. Yet sometimes when I hear someone using words I find disagreeable, I fail to ask for clarification. A mentor who has worked with a multitude of different colleagues and managers can provide a contrary perspective on what someone might have meant in using possibly a poor choice of words. Encouraged, I ask for clarification later and find myself better understanding the goals and intentions of a colleague.

Sometimes when I'm asked what I want to do in life, I answer with simplistic and trivial things that are not so close to the heart. Sometimes I treat it as an invitation for a humorous answer. I might say I want to win second place in a beauty contest. It isn't true, but it deflects a real evaluation of the differences between what I'm doing and what I want to do. I've learned that sometimes what you think you want would actually be rather unpleasant, but other times being in touch with what you want is the key to reducing stress and finding new ways to grow as a person and as a professional. When a mentor asks and really wants to understand your answer, then the joke reply doesn't work. A real discussion of these sensitive topics can lead to good changes that might replace bad habits with better choices. I've been encouraged personally to put more creativity in my weekly schedule through drawing, writing, and music. These activities have reduced stress and helped me make better choices as a person and as a professional.

4.2 Kathy

One lesson that I have learned so far as a fledgling mentor is that the mentee is the one who has to do the actual work required to reach the goals. My job as a mentor (according to the expectations we set up for each other) is to serve as a brainstorm partner, an accountability buddy, a place to safely vent—yet sometimes, I would find myself wanting to fix things where a solution had not been requested or wanting to understand something that was beyond my abilities and truly unnecessary for the task at hand.

Since Trevor and I already knew each other from working on SIGUCCS conference papers together over the past ten years and hanging out together at conferences, we were able to hit the ground running in January and didn't have to take much time for that "getting to know you stage" and we are not trying to impress each other. However, our existing friendly relationship could be a disadvantage from an accountability point of view. I think sometimes we give each other a little too much slack—although perhaps it is okay that we are kind and very patient with each other.

4.3 Time Challenges

Our biggest mutual challenge so far has been to find enough time for our monthly mentoring meetings and engaging in additional email communications. We have both been crazy busy at work and both of us served as trek chairs for the 2016 conference while writing our own conference papers.

5. FUTURE PLANS

Trevor and Kathy definitely plan to finish out the year as a mentoring pair and will share our insights and experiences at the poster session during the conference. We may continue as peer mentors for an indeterminate period of time past the formal end date in November. One or both of us might choose to apply to serve as a mentor or mentee to another SIGUCCS member next year.

6. ACKNOWLEDGMENTS

We would like to thank Beth Rugg, Gail Rankin, and other past and current members of the ACM SIGUCCS Mentoring Advisory Board for their contributions to the creation and maintenance of the mentoring program.

7. REFERENCES

[1] ACM SIGUCCS Mentoring Program. http://www.siguccs.org/mentoring.shtml

[2] Lorentzen, Laura. Association for Women in Science. 2016. From the cover: Isabel C. Escobar PhD. *AWIS Magazine.* Summer 2016. 48(2): 3

[3] United States Office of Personnel Management. *Best Practices: Mentoring.* 2008. https://www.opm.gov/policy-data-oversight/training-and-development/career-development/bestpractices-mentoring.pdf

[4] Rugg, Elizabeth; McRitchie, Karen; Herrick, Dan; Allen, Brian; Zocher, Mark; Vucinich, Christine. 2013. Elevating your career and making a difference: the SIGUCCS mentoring program. *Proceedings of the 41st Annual ACM SIGUCCS Conference on User Services* (SIGUCCS '13). ACM, New York, NY, USA, 13-18. DOI=http://dx.doi.org/10.1145/2504776.2504785

VDI: Third Times a Charm when Comes to Digital Signage.

Chris Wiesemann
University of Oregon
1208 University of Oregon
Eugene, OR 97403
541 346 1000
chris@uoregon.edu

ABSTRACT

Starting in 2010 and culminating in 2015, the College of Business at the University of Oregon implemented Digital Signage. This process began in 2010, with Virtual Desktops and ended in 2015 with Virtual Desktops. However, during the middle three years, Digital Signage ran on Mac Minis. This poster will show you how we display digital signage today. In person you will see a current sign, working remotely, via a Virtual Desktop. The paper that accompanies this poster will outline our three step process, why we made the mistakes we did, and where we sit today.

Keywords

digital signage, public displays, VMware, virtual desktop infrastructure, VDI, virtual desktop, thin client, PCOIP

1. INTRODUCTION

In 2010, college leadership concluded that Digital Signage would improve our institution-to-student communication. When tasked with deploying Digital Signage, our IT team decided this would be an ideal use case for VDI. Over the next four years both communication and technology teams developed a love/hate relationship with VDI. The saga begins with VDI and ends with VDI, but has a really expensive Band-Aid in the middle. Today, our environment runs completely virtual, is nearly stress free, and problems are be addressed at the click of a mouse.

In 2011, the University of Oregon was just beginning to embark on an Emergency Management roadmap. Digital Signage would come up as one of the hurdles along the way. The College of Business elected to take the lead in acquiring and implementing Digital Signage for our university.

2. Phase One

The University signed a contract with Four Winds Interactive, a vendor identified as a leader in signage and electronic communication. Three months into my new role, as a server admin, I was tasked with creating a VMware environment to

support Virtual Desktops. If you find yourself asking if this is relevant, consider it foreshadowing.

This environment would support and provide the back end to facilitate our deployment of Digital Signage. Since we used VMware for our server infrastructure, it was logical to use them as a vendor and bolt this service onto our existing infrastructure. We purchased VMware View and then built VDI in our dev/test environment. Armed with a new piece of virtualization, zero understanding of VDI, zero understanding of Digital Signage, off I went. The college acquired a batch of Dell FX100 (tera1) thin clients. One month later, I had a Windows XP image, replicated as thick clones, in VDI. The entire environment was built, tested, and designed in dev/test.

While IT was off creating production virtual sign players, a test machine was made for the Communications department. The communications folks would be responsible for all of the content within Four Winds. IT would be responsible for installation, maintenance, and support of the infrastructure behind the software. This was roughly modeled on the concept/relationship evolved out of managing our website. This model worked well for that environment and we assumed it would for Digital Signage as well. The Communications department was building content on their test sign, which was a 5-year-old Windows workstation. At the same time, facilities was installing and mounting TV's around our complex. Power, network, and televisions were in place. VDI had been built. The Dell FX100 clients were individually configured and installed at each location.

One of the physical locations we built was a TV in the Communications department. This would enable them to have an identical clone and test environment in their office. After we deployed the thin client to their location, they commented that it was not working as expected. The video was jarring and not smooth. Specifically, the Communications department identified two problems: playing YouTube videos at 1080p within a frame was skipping frames and the stock ticker at the bottom of the screen, playing our Twitter feed, was choppy and not scrolling smoothly. In the dev/test environment, it was clear that YouTube videos were playing poorly. In the dev/test environment, you could watch the stock ticker scroll blank space, but skip the width of each letter. The comparison workstation, a 5-year-old Dell desktop, had 90% less jitter as content scrolled the screen. The comparison workstation was able to play the YouTube video about twice as well as the test environment. IT assured Communications that moving from the dev/test VMware cluster to the production cluster would resolve the choppy issues. Logically, the 5-year-old dev/test environment would be significantly outperformed by the 1-year-old production VMware cluster.

A month later, we migrated from the dev/test VMware cluster to the production VMware cluster. IT evaluated the performance of the two identified problems. The YouTube videos were playing reasonably, but still skipping frames. It was watchable, but not smooth. The stock ticker was skipping once per word, instead of once per letter. All in all, things were smoother. IT worked with VMware and learned of the Teradici PCOIP console as well as PCOIP group policies. These allowed control of multiple thin clients at once and granular control of the performance of VMs. Prior to tuning PCOIP, our thin clients output 16fps. After tuning PCOIP, they output 21fps. Performance, from an IT perspective, was bearable. Performance, from a Communications perspective, was unusable.

IT and Communications managers had multiple meetings with an Associate Dean. The Communications manager insisted upon performance congruent with a physical PC. The IT manager was unable to promise that performance from the Virtual Desktops. To appease the Communications manager, the decision was made to replace all of the thin clients with Mac Mini computers. Two days later, IT installed a Mac Mini at each location running Boot Camp, and Four Winds software.

During its first phase, VDI was a complete failure for our use case.

3. Phase Two

Phase two of Digital Signage was Mac Minis. The Mac Minis were acquired to solve two problems: YouTube video performance and stock ticker performance. The Mac Mini was able to provide 28 fps when playing YouTube videos. It was able to provide a stock ticker that skipped once every three or four words. I specify these details to demonstrate that even brand new, multi-core Mac Minis were unable to completely remove the video failures. As an IT person, it was difficult to accept a work-around as a solution to a problem.

At this point, we began working with Four Winds. The software vendor and our communications staff went back and forth for several months and several versions of the product. As functionality and behavior improved, the vendor admitted that they were having issues with the performance of the ticker. With each new version of their software, performance would creep forward.

Several issues developed on the Mac Minis.

Mini's do not have Wake-On-LAN. So, the first time we had a campus power outage, all the signs went out and required physical manipulation to be powered on. The Apple Remote Desktop software package provides this functionality, but our IT department did not own it nor have the resources to support it.

One of our locations was inside of an enclosed case. This case was built without fans, ventilation holes, or easy access to its internals. Mac Minis are warm objects. Keeping one in a poorly ventilated space results in it occasionally turning off (over heating?) and being non-functional.

Our Mac Mini image was built with Windows 7 and Boot Camp 1.2. They were manually imaged one at a time with a static image. This meant that if the image failed, it took hours of Windows update to maintain and restore. Due to a glitch in the Four Winds software, it is possible for a player to get out of sync from the master. Our experience was that a complete re-image was the only solution to this. This was untenable. In addition, Boot Camp 1.2 was replaced by 2.0 and 3.0. We were never able

to successfully create a working Windows Bootcamp image for these Minis within an automated imaging platform. Our Communications department learned that the best way to display video was by using locally stored WMV files. It turns out that down-scaling YouTube videos from 1080p to 90% of the size of 1080p, to fit into a frame, actually causes frame loss. A year after initial launch of digital signage, the stock ticker was dropped during a "branding overhaul". The two issues that were roadblocks to VDI had been removed.

During the three years in which VDI was not used for Signage, IT continued pushing Virtual Desktops. Staff was trained in VDI. Infrastructure was acquired and built specifically for Virtual Desktops. A proper understanding of Virtual Desktops, their delivery, and their management was acquired.

During the three years in which Digital Signage was run on Mac Minis, Communications continued to simplify, standardize, and consolidate their management of Digital Signage content. Daily utilization, implementation, management, and battling of the Four Winds system helped them feel confident in the product and its limitations.

4. Phase Three

During 2015, phase three of Digital Signage was implemented. LG thin clients (Tera2) were acquired to replace the Mac Minis. A pool was built, using linked clones, in the new production VDI environment. During an academic break, all the Macs were replaced with thin clients.

Today, our Four Winds Interactive digital signage is entirely virtual. Our content managers, sign player machines, and test machines are all running as virtual machines. When a machine breaks, a recompose replaces it in less than 10 minutes. When a player has broken cache, a recompose replaces it in less than 10 minutes. A recompose is the process of recreating a virtual machine.

In this process, the entire existing virtual machine is deleted, a new one is created in its stead. The new one is then individualized, added to the domain, and powered on. In the case of recomposing signage, we also must go and tell four winds to re-deploy current content after a re-compose as it is not quick to recognize the change. When the power goes out, the thin clients are set to power back on and reconnect to a session. For the IT department, a win has been secured. For the Communications department, they no longer sacrifice performance and have a system that is as responsive as their needs require.

5. Conclusion

There is one significant lesson that can be learned from this experience; I'm just not certain what it is. What stands out in hindsight are the following: Do not let a customer-facing system be implemented without proper testing. Do not deploy software platforms without understanding their limitations. When implementing large, expensive projects that cross multiple divisions be sure to have a pre-planned failure condition and a budget to accommodate any changes. If you want to implement VDI, do not do so in a VMware environment designed for servers. (I/O requirements are drastically different).

Enhancing Campus Cyber Security through a Class with Combination of Computer Ethics Videos and Logical Thinking

Takashi Yamanoue

Fukuyama University
Fukuyama, Hiroshima
729-0292, Japan
+81-84-936-2111
yamanoue@fuip.fukuyama-u.ac.jp

Noboru Nakamichi

Fukuyama University
Fukuyama, Hiroshima
729-0292, Japan
+81-84-936-2111
nakamiti@fuip.fukuyama-u.ac.jp

Kunihiko Kaneko

Fukuyama University
Fukuyama, Hiroshima
729-0292, Japan
+81-84-936-2111
kaneko@fuip.fukuyama-u.ac.jp

ABSTRACT

Further trials in a class for enhancing campus cyber security are discussed. The class uses computer ethics video clips and logical thinking teaching material. Rubrics (evaluation criteria) are shown to students and their activity in the class is evaluated by the rubrics. The video clips are designed for promoting discussion, and the logical thinking teaching material shows ways of discussion in a group. They should raise the retention rate of the class according to the "Learning Pyramid".

CCS Concepts

• **Security and privacy~Human and societal aspects of security and privacy**

• **Social and professional topics~Computing literacy**

Keywords

Cyber security; Education; Video clips; Logical thinking; Rubrics

1. INTRODUCTION

Campus cyber security is one of the most important and one of the toughest subjects for ICT managers in universities and colleges today. It is relatively easy to control the security of technical aspect of a campus using technologies such like firewalls, IDSs, IPSs and so on. However, it is hard to control behavior of people in a university or a college. Their cooperation is essential for keeping the cyber security of a university or a college. In order to have their cooperation, ICT managers are having various ways of education for them.

According to the "Learning Pyramid" [1] by Edgar Dale, the learning retention rate of audio-visual material is 20%. It is much better than the rate of a lecture, which is 5%. So a group in Japan, including one of the authors of this paper, have made "Computer ethics video clips" **Error! Reference source not found.** and updated them for enhancing the human

SIGUCCS '16, November 06-09, 2016, Denver, CO, USA
© 2016 ACM. ISBN 978-1-4503-4095-3/16/11...$15.00
DOI: http://dx.doi.org/10.1145/2974927.2974939

aspect of campus cyber security for more than ten years **Error! Reference source not found.**. These video clips became one of the indispensable teaching materials for many universities in Japan.

In order to have a good discussion in a computer ethics class, we have designed a new course with "Logical thinking" **Error! Reference source not found.** or "Critical thinking" teaching material. We use the teaching material of critical thinking **Error! Reference source not found.**, which is available from the Information-technology Promotion Agency (IPA), Japan. It is based on the "Learning Pyramid," and discussions in a group are encouraged in the material.

We are having the class now. This paper shows the outline of the class in section two, an example of one day's class and students' feedback in section three, related work in section four, and the conclusion in section five

2. OUTLINE OF THE CLASS

2.1 Syllabus

In order to enhance cyber security in a campus, every member of the campus should take a class for cyber security. As an intermediate step to realize this, we have planned to have an introductory information processing class (IP1 class) with cyber security and computer ethics for freshmen of computer science. For other members in our university, brochures for keeping campus cyber security were made and distributed to everyone in our university. In addition to this, the video clips in this paper can be viewed by all members in our university at specific PCs on our campus.

The class in this paper was the place for learning a part of office software by freshmen of computer science. Many of the students are used to using office software now. So we have changed the main theme of this class from learning office software to learning cyber security and computer ethics.

There are 41 students in this class. They were divided into ten groups to have group discussions. One group consists of three to five students.

We have made the syllabus of the IP1 class as follows.

- Outline of the class: Teaching knowledge and techniques of basic cyber security, computer ethics, and using a presentation software (PowerPoint). Training the attitude toward them. Having group practices of them using IT tools. Such knowledge, techniques and attitude will be useful in all of learning, the graduation project in our university, getting jobs, and working after graduation.

- Objectives of the class: Learn the knowledge, techniques of the above and attitude toward them.

- Course Schedule: Shown in Table 1.

- Grading Procedure: Grading every practice of each day of class.

Table 1. Course Schedule

Day	Contents
1	Outline of this class. Turn on/Turn off the PC. Login/Logout. ID/Password. Basic operation of Windows OS. Basic operation of a Web browser. How to use the university's student management system. Initial settings of the student management system.
2	How to use PowerPoint software. Making groups.
3	Outline of "Logical Thinking."
4	"Why tree" of logical thinking and drawing the "why tree" using SmartArt graphic feature in PowerPoint.
5	"How tree" of logical thinking and drawing the "how tree" using SmartArt graphic feature in PowerPoint.
6	Importance of a password.
7	Know-how for preparing for losing private information, Losing private information by using a reward card.
8	Privacy and GPS. Where is the data?
9	Flooding of complaints because of phishing. Using Internet services safely.
10	Responsibility and privacy of seminar activity. A community in which it is difficult to refuse to participate.
11	Taking pictures and uploading them to a Web site without permission. It is difficultto withdraw the statement on the Internet.
12	It is No Good to copy an item from the Web and paste it to your paper. It is dangerous to cheat to write a paper.
13	Is it possible to introduce a mail in a blog? Is it possible to use a smartphone while doing something else?
14	A smart phone knows everything.
15	Concluding the class.

In day one, students learn the basic features to use PCs and Web sites of our university. In day two, they learn the use of PowerPoint software. However almost all of them said they have used the software. From day three to day five, students learn the basic features of logical thinking. From day six to day 14, they learn cyber security and computer ethics using the computer ethics video clips, logical thinking, PowerPoint software and LMS

(Learning Management System) of our university. In order to enhance students' activity in each class, rubrics (evaluation criteria) are shown to students and students are evaluated by the rubrics.

2.2 Preparation

Day one through day five of the class are preparation for the rest of the class. Students learn tools for understanding and giving solutions of problems, which are related to cyber security and computer ethics, during this term. Their main tools are logical thinking. The SmartArt graphic feature of PowerPoint software is used for assisting the logical thinking.

Logical thinking includes the following elements.

- Ways of thinking
  1) Induction and deduction
  2) MECE (mutually exclusive and collectively exhaustive)
  3) Zero base thinking
  4) Hypothetical thinking
- Tools
  1) Logic tree
  2) Pyramid structure
  3) Matrix
- Ways of proceeding
  1) Card brain storming
  2) Facilitation

2.3 Main Classes

Main classes, which teach cyber security and computer ethics, start from day six and continue until day 14. Each of the main classes proceeds as follows

1) The MC (master of ceremonies) and the secretary are selected in each group of students. We have asked students to change the MC every day of the class in order to let every member in our class have the experience of becoming MC.

2) Students see the episode (problem) part of a video clip.

3) Rubrics are shown to all students.

4) Each group of students starts discussion about why the problem happened and how to cope with the problem. They use elements of the logical thinking.

5) Each group writes the why tree to analyze the problem and writes the how tree to cope with the problem using the SmartArt function of PowerPoint software.

6) They submit the two trees to the LMS as the result of the discussion.

7) Students see the explanation part of the video clip.

8) Students evaluate their activity by themselves using the rubrics. The quiz function of the LMS is used for this evaluation.

2.4 Rubrics

Students are expected to acquire not only knowledge of cyber security and computer ethics but also the ability to co-operate with others and to think more deeply using various tools. In order to realize this and evaluate this, we use the following rubrics.

- Your contribution to the group

MC	5 points
Secretary	4 points
Support the MC	3 points

- Your contribution to the group work to make the why tree.

More than or equal to three ideas (cards)	5 points
Two ideas (cards)	4 points
One idea (card)	3 points

- Number of layers of the why tree of your group

More than or equal to four	5 points
Three	4 points
Two	3 points

- Number of items of the why tree of your group

More than or equal to 20	5 points
Between 10 to 19	4 points
Between 5 to 9	3 points

- Your contribution to the group work to make the how tree.

More than or equal to three ideas (cards)	5 points
Two ideas (cards)	4 points
One idea (card)	3 points

- Number of layers of the how tree of your group

More than or equal to four	5 points
Three	4 points
Two	3 points

- Number of items of the how tree of your group

More than or equal to 20	5 points
Between 10 to 19	4 points
Between 5 to 9	3 points

3. A TYPICAL DAY OF THE CLASS

We show day six of the class as an example of the class. The day of the class proceeded as follows.

1) The MC (master of ceremonies) and the secretary were selected in each group of students.

2) Students saw the episode (problem) part of a video clip. We have used the video of "More than Ever! The Importance of Passwords." The duration of the episode part of this video is 5min. 59sec. Figure 1 shows a scene from the video.

The following is the outline of the episode part of this video clip.

"Kento (a male student) saw the news of leaking the ID and the password. This news upset him because he was using the ID for various services. However, he did not have trouble because he had changed the password of the ID at the official Web site of the ID. Masami (a female student) used the same password for various services. She changed the password of the leaked site and felt at ease. But she has not changed the password of other services because she thought that they are different services from the leaked site. Her ID of one of these sites has been used by some others and her money was used for music downloading."

Ten years ago, there was a common sense that passwords should be memorized and should not be noted on a piece of paper. However, ten years later, any short password can be uncovered easily by recent computing power. So passwords should be long enough to endure such computing power. It is hard to memorize such long passwords precisely in the brain of most people. In order to cope with this problem, the explanation part of the clip of "More than Ever! The Importance of Passwords" suggests a way to note long passwords on a piece of paper

Hookups of services on the Internet were not so common ten years ago. On the other hand, hookups of services are common today. Any of the services of a hookup can be used by entering only one pair of ID and password today. When the password of a hookup of services on the Internet is leaked, all services of the hookup can be intruded upon by other people. On-line payment is also common today.

Figure 1. A scene of the video of "More than Ever! The Importance of Passwords"

Figure 2. Students seeing the video in class

119

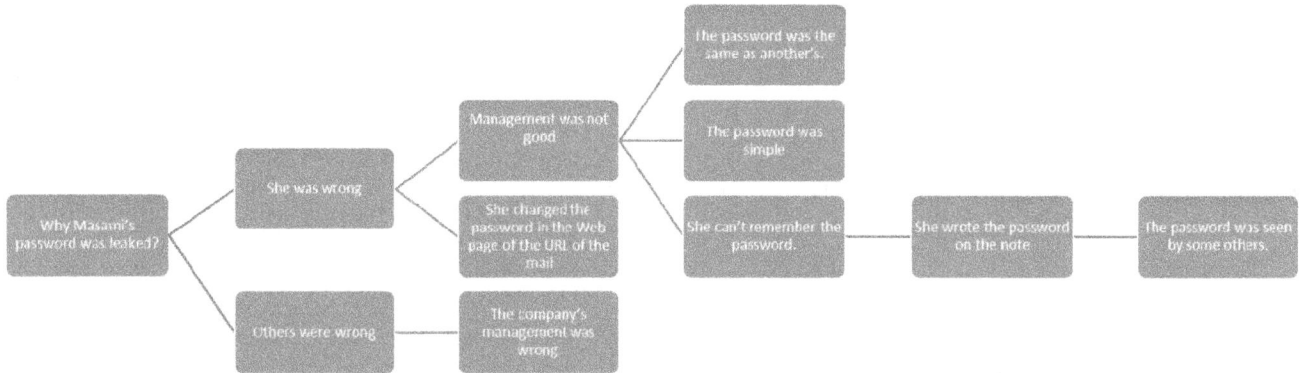

Figure 3. Why tree of a group in the class.

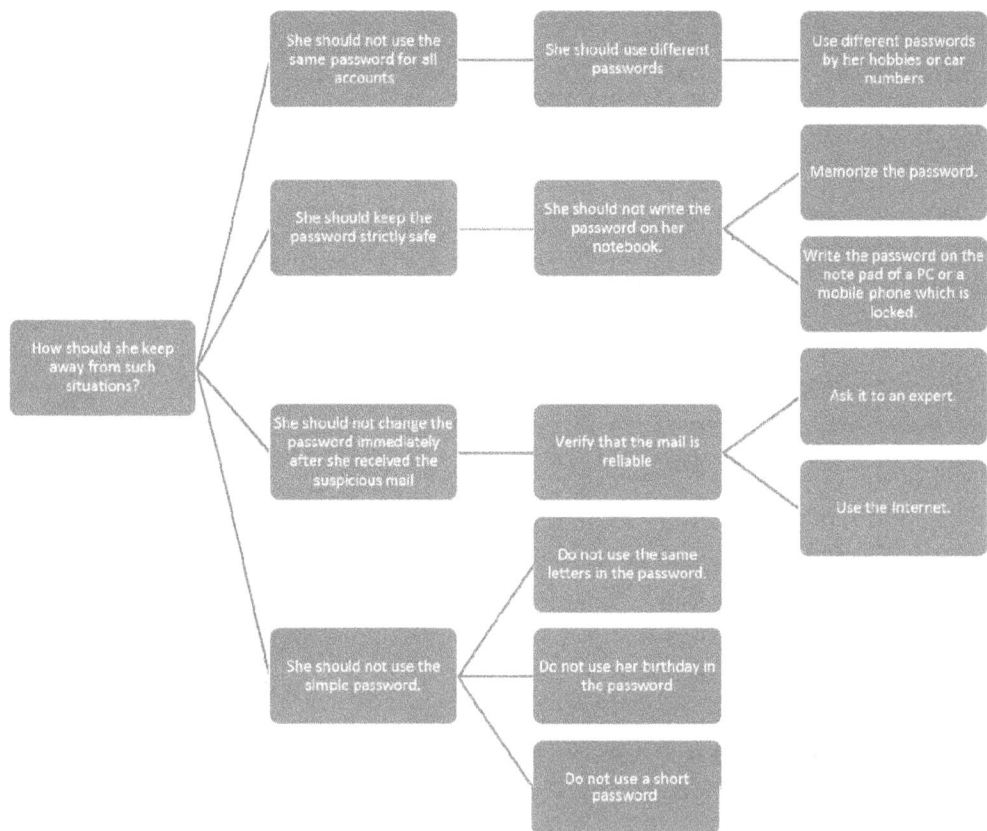

Figure 4. How tree of a group in the class.

If a user was using the same password for a service with on-line payment and a service without on-line payment, and if the password of the service without on-line payment was leaked, the password of the service with on-line payment can also be leaked and malicious people may steal money of the user. The clip of "More than Ever! The Importance of Passwords" also includes topics of such situations. We expected that some groups of students would deduce such ideas.

3) After viewing the episode part of the video clip, rubrics were shown to students.

4) Then, students had group discussions for making the why tree and the how tree.

The root node of the why tree was "Why Masami's password was leaked?" The root node of the how tree was "How should she keep away from such situations?"

One group of two students was using the SmartArt graphic feature of PowerPoint directly. Other groups were using cards before writing the trees.

Figure 5. Group discussion

5) After the discussion term, each group wrote the why tree and the how tree.

6) Each group has submitted the why tree and the how tree to the LMS. Figure 3 is an example of a why tree and the Figure 4 is a how tree of a group in this class. Figure 5 shows pictures of the discussion.

The node "The password was the same as another's" in the why tree, shows the reason of the password leak in the video. Almost all groups have reached this reason because the episode part gives viewers the suggestion. Students of the group show possible reasonable reasons--not only the reason in the video but also others--in the why tree. Students of other groups also show many reasonable reasons.

The node "Write the password on the note pad of a PC or a mobile phone which can be locked" in the how tree, is a reasonable solution which solves the conflicting conditions

of "a password should be long enough" and "she should not write the password on the note."

Unfortunately, there were many nodes of "She was off guard" or similar words, in a leaf node of why trees in other groups. These were not wrong, but we expected that students would think more deeply and show the reason of "why she was off guard."

7) Students evaluated their activity by themselves using the rubrics. The quiz function of the LMS is used for this evaluation. Table 2 shows the quantification of the discussion for making the why tree which was acquired by evaluation using the rubrics. Table 3 shows the quantification of the discussion for making the how tree which was acquired by evaluation using the rubrics.

These rubrics were also useful to make the class active. Many groups tried to get a high score, so students tried to give many ideas in the group discussion. Many ideas may contain many good ideas.

8) Students saw the explanation part of the video clip.

Table 2. Quantification of the discussion for making the why tree and its result.

Number of all cards of the card brain storming in the group discussion for making the why tree in the class.	150
Average number of cards of one student in the group discussion	4
Total number of nodes of the why tree in this class	123
Average number of nodes of one why tree	12.3
Smallest number of nodes of the why tree	8
Largest number of nodes of the why tree	20
Average height of the why tree	4.5
Least height of the why tree	3
Greatest height of the why tree	6

Table 3. Quantification of the discussion for making the how tree and its result.

Number of all cards of the card brain storming in the group discussion for making the how tree in the class.	153
Average number of cards of one student in the group discussion	4.6
Total number of nodes of the how tree in this class	134
Average number of nodes of one how tree	13.4
Smallest number of nodes of the how tree	9
Largest number of nodes of the how tree	20
Average height of the how tree	4
Least height of the how tree	3
Greatest height of the how tree	5

We obtained the numbers in Table 2 and Table 3 from the self-evaluation of the rubrics in the LMS of our university. This way realizes the visualization and quantification of activity of group work. It also realizes the visualization and quantification of how the group thinks deeply. These visualizations and quantifications can be useful to improve this class. Figure 6 shows a screenshot of a part of the self-evaluation of the rubrics in the LMS.

The following statements are examples of students' feedback of this class. From the feedback, our aim of enhancing cyber-security of our campus by enhancing users' consciousness of cyber-security seems to be achieved.

- "I was thinking, the discussion is boring before. However, the discussion was very fun after the start."

- "At the first, the group discussion was awkward. However, on the way of the discussion, co-operation in the group has been developed."

- "This class was very useful".

- "I was re-using the same password for many accounts. I would like to change them."

4. RELATED WORK
There is the following related work. However, we could not find out a cyber security class which combines video clips, logical thinking, and rubrics.

4.1 Thinking in Computer Ethics Education
Jones said, "… it is part of the task of computer ethics to define, develop, and modify existing moral theory when existing theory is insufficient or inadequate in light of new demands generated by new practices involving technology." [2] He said, in order to cope with such changes, thinking is important in computer ethics education. We have shown a way for thinking through group discussion.

4.2 Logical Thinking in Computer Science Classes
References [6], [7], [8], and [9] are cases for using logical thinking for computer science education, not for cyber security.

.

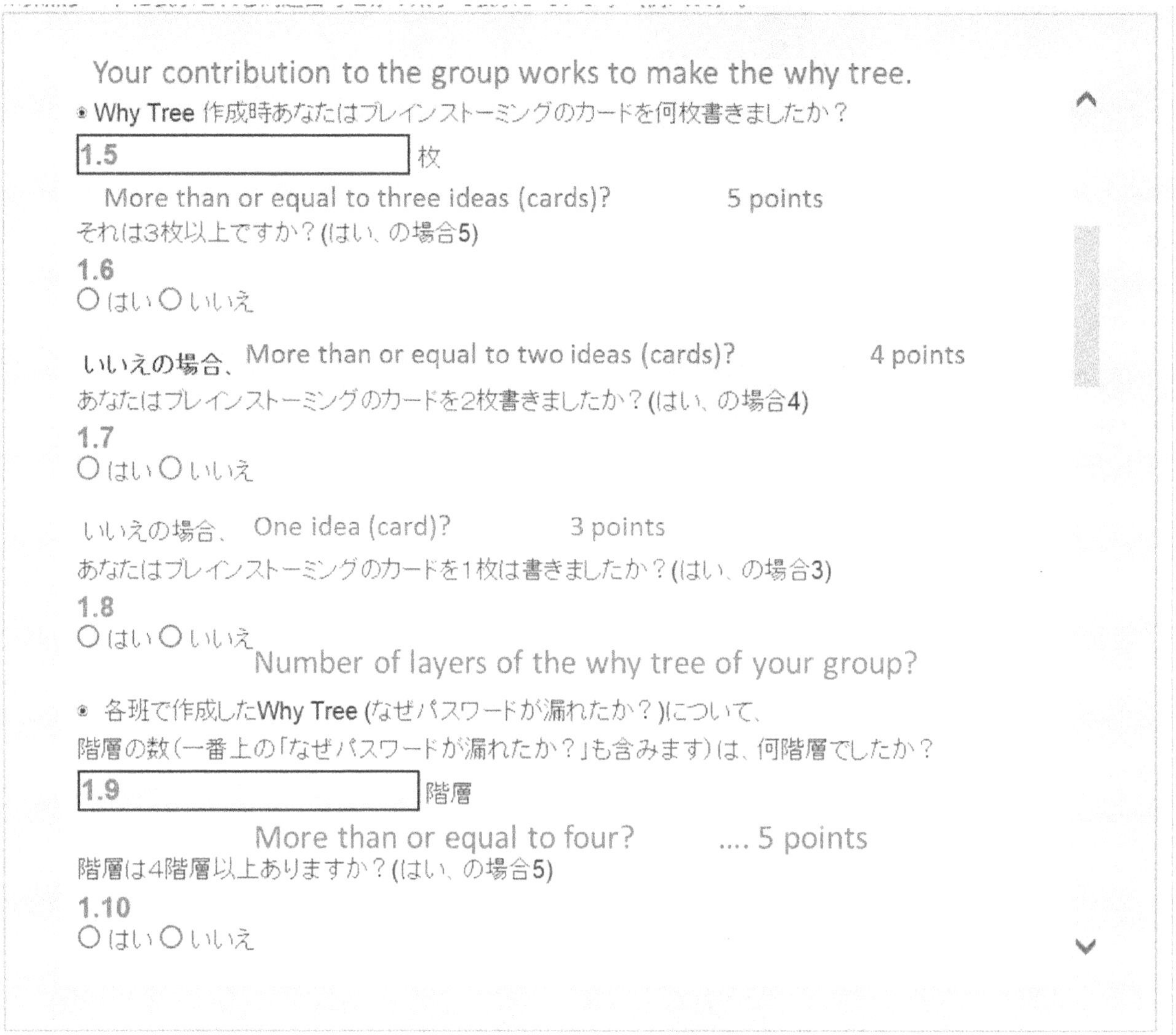

Your contribution to the group works to make the why tree.
- Why Tree 作成時あなたはブレインストーミングのカードを何枚書きましたか？

1.5　　　　　　　　　　　枚
　　　More than or equal to three ideas (cards)?　　　5 points
それは3枚以上ですか？(はい、の場合5)
1.6
○ はい ○ いいえ

　　いいえの場合、More than or equal to two ideas (cards)?　　　4 points
あなたはブレインストーミングのカードを2枚書きましたか？(はい、の場合4)
1.7
○ はい ○ いいえ

　　いいえの場合、One idea (card)?　　　3 points
あなたはブレインストーミングのカードを1枚は書きましたか？(はい、の場合3)
1.8
○ はい ○ いいえ
　　　　Number of layers of the why tree of your group?

- 各班で作成したWhy Tree (なぜパスワードが漏れたか？)について、
階層の数(一番上の「なぜパスワードが漏れたか？」も含みます)は、何階層でしたか？
1.9　　　　　　　　　　　階層
　　　More than or equal to four?　　　…. 5 points
階層は4階層以上ありますか？(はい、の場合5)
1.10
○ はい ○ いいえ

Figure 6. Screenshot of a part of the self-evaluation of the rubrics in the LMS of our university

4.3 Rubrics and Computer Ethics

The reference [10] shows grading essays of a computer ethics class using rubrics. Rubrics were useful for decreasing ambiguity of grading essays in the reference. Our rubrics also help decrease ambiguity of grading group discussion and grading why trees and how trees.

5. CONCLUSION

The purpose of the class in this paper is enhancing the human aspect of the campus cyber security. We expect that students of this class understand the importance of cybersecurity deeply and keep knowledge and techniques on cybersecurity in their minds for long time. We have combined various ways such as computer ethics video clips, logical thinking and rubrics to realize our expectation.

We could not judge the new class in this paper against previous classes, because we do not have quantified data of previous classes. However, we have quantified data of the cyber security class now. We can compare this class with future classes, and this can improve the cyber security of our campus.

6. ACKNOWLEDGEMENT

We thank Mr. Katagiri and Mr. Nakamura who are co-teachers of the class of information processing basics, the group who produced the computer ethics video clips, IPA (Information technology Promotion Agency, Japan) who allows us to use the teaching material of critical thinking. A part of this research was supported by JSPS KAKENHI Grant Number JP16K00197.

7. REFERENCES

[1] Dale, E. 1946. *Audio-Visual Method in Teaching*. The Dryden Press.

[2] Jones, A. 2004. Technology: Illegal, Immoral, or Fattening? In *Proceedings of the 32nd Annual ACM SIGUCCS Conference on User Services* (Baltimore, Maryland, US. 10-13 Oct. 2004). ACM, New York, NY, 305-309. DOI=http://doi.acm.org/10.1145/1027802.1027872

[3] Yamanoue, T., Nakanishi, M., Nakamura, A., Fuse, I., Murata, I., Fukada, S., Tagawa, T., Takeo, T., Okabe, S., and Yamada, T. 2005. Digital Video Clips Covering Computer Ethics in Higher Education. In *Proceedings of the 33nd Annual ACM SIGUCCS Conference on User Services* (Monterey, California, US, 6-9 Nov. 2005). ACM, New York, NY. 456-461. DOI=http://doi.acm.org/10.1145/1099435.1099536

[4] Yamanoue, T., Fuse, I., Okabe, S., Nakamura, A., Nakanishi, M., Fukada, S., Tagawa, T., Tatsumi, T., Murata, I, Uehara, T., Yamada, T., Ueda, H. 2014. Computer Ethics Video Clips for University Students in Japan from 2003 until 2013, In *Proceedings of the 38th Annual International Computer Software & Applications Conference* (COMPSAC2013/ADMNET WS) , (Västerås, Sweden, 21-25 Jul. 2014). IEEE, NJ, 96-101. DOI= 10.1109/COMPSACW.2014.21

[5] Minto, M. 2008. *The Pyramid Principle: Logic in Writing and Thinking* (Financial Times Series). Prentice Hall, NY.

[6] Kawai, H., Takayama, F., Anzai, T., Manome, T. and Yoshida, H. 2003. Objectives and features of e-learning oriented programming courseware for freshmen, *Distributed Computing Systems Workshops, Proceedings. 23rd International Conference on.* IEEE, NJ. 616-621. DOI=10.1109/ICDCSW.2003.1203621

[7] Iwane, N. and Saito, N. 2013. Reuse of mathematical problems and answers with e-learning system, *Humanitarian Technology Conference* (R10-HTC), 2013 IEEE Region 10, (Sendai, Japan, 26-29 Aug. 2013). IEEE, NJ. 227-231. DOI=10.1109/R10-HTC.2013.6669046

[8] Muller, O., and Rubinstein, A., 2011. Work in progress — Courses dedicated to the development of logical and algorithmic thinking, *2011 Frontiers in Education Conference* (FIE), (Rapid City, SD, US. 2011). IEEE, NJ. F3G-1-F3G-3. DOI=10.1109/FIE.2011.6142846

[9] Parham, J. R.. 2003. An assessment and evaluation of computer science education. *Journal of Computing Sciences in Colleges.* Vol. 19, Issue 2. CCSC. 115-127.

[10] Moskal, B., Miller, K., Smith King, L. A. 2002. Grading essays in computer ethics: rubrics considered helpful. In *Proceedings of the 33rd SIGCSE Technical Symposium on Computer Science Education (SIGCSE '02).* (Covington, KY, USA, 26 Feb. – 2 Mar. 2002). ACM, New York, NY. 101-105. DOI=http://doi.acm.org/10.1145/563517.563380

[11] Educational contents for development of personal skill, https://www.jsee.or.jp/?action=common_download_main&upload_id=951 (in Japanese)

New York University's Steinhardt Technology Services: Using Intentional Data Tracking to Achieve Maximum Operational Impact

Lendyll Capitulo
NYU Steinhardt IT Manager
246 Greene St Room 415W
New York, NYU 10003
1-212-998-5377

ABSTRACT

In recent years, the analysis of Big Data has been lauded for its ability to solve complex operational problems, provide meaningful insights, and draw connections across disparate or nuanced sources. Big Data, however, may not be the most effective tool of analysis across all settings. Particularly, within smaller tech operations, the lack of resources required to fully formulate, maintain, and analyze large data sets may limit the benefits of Big Data. Faced with this problem, Steinhardt Technology Services (a small IT Help Desk within New York University) endeavored to develop a data strategy that would allow the team to leverage big data insights without the complications of gathering and analyzing Big Data.

In this paper, the author will discuss the development of Steinhardt Technology Services' data strategy. The paper will first describe Steinhardt Technology Services' data dilemma and how creating and executing an intentional data strategy allowed the group to collect and process meaningful help desk data. Next, the author will describe how the data strategy was leveraged to create and maintain the business practices that maximize Steinhardt Technology Services' ability to execute its mission statement. Finally, the author will discuss future goals and challenges for Steinhardt Technology Services' data strategy.

General Terms
Operation Analysis

Keywords
Data Tracking; Metadata; Ticket Management

SIGUCCS '16, November 06-09, 2016, Denver, CO, USA
© 2016 ACM. ISBN 978-1-4503-4095-3/16/11...$15.00
DOI: http://dx.doi.org/10.1145/2974927.2974943

1. INTRODUCTION
A well-documented and intentional data tracking system can be leveraged to greatly improve helpdesk service. Not only can it provide insight to helpdesk management, it can help small helpdesks remain competitive by quantifying areas of improvement. In this paper, I will first introduce the Steinhardt Technology Services' helpdesk. Then I will discuss the problem of "dirty" data and how it had a detrimental effect on business problems. I will then discuss the Steinhardt Technology Services' solution and how they were able to use the "clean" data to make business decisions. Finally, I'll discuss future challenges that Steinhardt Technology Services will hopefully use data to solve.

2. ORGANIZATION DESCRIPTION
2.1 Demographics
New York University (NYU) is one of the largest private universities in the United States. The university is comprised of 20 schools, colleges, and institutes [1]. In terms of technology support, service models fall into one of two major classifications: either a central technology resource or a distributed (non-central) technology resource. Steinhardt Technology Services is considered a distributed technology resource as it works more closely with the Steinhardt School of Culture, Education and Human Development.

2.2 Steinhardt Technology Services
2.2.1 Organizational Structure
Steinhardt Technology Services (STS) is a technology group that serves the needs of the Steinhardt School of Culture, Education and Human Development. The group is comprised of two sub-teams: the Information Technology Team (SIT) and the Academic Technology Team (SAT). Within the IT Team, there is one manager, two full-time staff members and fewer than 10 student technicians. The student technicians are divided into two categories: core student technicians and non-core student technicians. The group manages the needs of 290 full-time faculty, 5,952 students, and approximately 275 staff [2]. This equates to around 850 unique endpoints (desktops, laptops or other devices), two data centers and 6 production level servers.

2.2.2 Ticket Management Tools
Steinhardt Technology Services uses Zendesk Ticket Management System to manage incident tickets. Zendesk allows for the generation of reports that detail various pieces of meta-data associated with each ticket. [3] This metadata includes ticket tags and certain ticket times (e.g. Time to First Response, Time to First Resolution). The manager of Steinhardt Information Technology

is able to use Zendesk Insights to create custom reports regarding this metadata.

3. STEINHARDT TECHNOLOGY SERVICES DATA PROBLEM

In June 2014, Steinhardt Technology Services had a unique data problem. Data collection and organization was not a priority of the organization. There was no cohesive data strategy or procedures. Without an overall data strategy, the data from Zendesk was unreliable.

It was at this point when STS management team decided to renew investment in the use of data analytics to measure service impact and value within the community. Lendyll Capitulo, who would later become the Manager for Information Technology, was charged with creating an intentional data collection and data management strategy. In order to do so, he would have to overhaul of the entire ticket tagging system.

4. DATA SOLUTION
4.1 Building a Tagging Structure That Works

Due to the historical misuse of the current data tagging system, an overhaul of the structure was required for effective implementation. Instead of focusing on the amendment of past data, the new system would be implemented on all incoming/future ticket data. This decision is what differentiated this effort from previous endeavors. By making a clean break, STS could use their limited personnel to increase productivity moving forward instead of attempting to recoup sunk costs of interpreting messy data.

The easiest data to collect was the time stamp data in Zendesk. Zendesk automatically tracks certain time stamps on tickets such as resolution time, first reply time and client wait time. Since this data is automatically collected, no formal structure would need to be created to capture the data. The hard part was making sense of the most impactful way that timestamp data can be used to give insight on the operation.

Regarding ticket tagging, Lendyll consulted a Steinhardt Professor who is an expert on data coding, Dr. Gigliana Melzi. Dr. Melzi is a Development Psychologist who studies language development of bilingual youth. Much of her work focuses on transcribing videos and coding parent child interactions. In order to accurately assess parent child interaction, Dr. Melzi's research team requires the use of strict transcription coding manual. Lendyll would use Dr. Melzi's coding manual as the basis of creating the first Steinhardt Technology Services Ticket Tagging Manual.

4.2 Ticket Tagging Manual

Version 1 of the Ticket Tagging Manual adopted two important concepts from Dr. Melzi's transcription coding manual: The concept was the use of mutually exclusive tags. The second concept was that the ticket tagging manual would be exhaustive (i.e. that the only tickets that existed are the ones in the manual). By using these two concepts, Lendyll was able to create the underlying framework of STS Ticket Tagging.

For every ticket there are two types of tags. The first type are called Required Tags. Required Tags are used to track certain demographic information and they include "Type of Support", "Building", "Affiliation", and "Academic Department/Administrative Division/Research Group". These required tags were later expanded to include two more categories, "Ticket Complexity" and "Ticket Origin". The tags within each category of Required Tags are mutually exclusive, such that there

will be one tag within each category that can be applied to each ticket. Furthermore, the list of tags within each category is considered to be exhaustive, which means that there are no additional tags within each category outside of the ones listed in this manual.

The second type of tags are Descriptive Tags. Descriptive tags track the types of the problems that we encounter through our helpdesk. Like required tags, the list of the descriptive tags is exhaustive. Unlike required tags, the list of descriptive tags is not mutually exclusive, which means that multiple tags from each category can be applied to the same ticket.

A large part of maintaining the ticket manual is controlling the creation of new tags. Since the ticket manual is exhaustive, a system must be implemented to add tags to the manual (thus allowing the agents to use new tags on tickets). New ticket tags are suggested throughout the month and new versions of the ticket tagging manual are published on the 1st of each month. All changes are documented at the end of the ticket tagging manual in the "Version Control" section.

4.3 Implementing the System

The first ticket tagging manual was published in July 2014 and the new ticket tagging system was implemented July 1, 2014. Now that there was data regarding each ticket with in the tags, Lendyll was able check the total of ticket tags based on Type of Support and compare that data to the number of Solved Tickets reported in Zendesk (see Table 1). By dividing the Total Support Tags by the Number of Tickets Solved and then multiplying by 100, Lendyll was able to derive the Ticket Tag Rate. In August 2014, the initial tag rate was 46%. While this was encouraging for the initial implementation, Steinhardt Technology Services Management had to develop a strategy to increase the Ticket Tag Rate.

As a quick way to encourage ticket tagging, Steinhardt Technology Services Management added an additional checkbox that must be checked off before a ticket can be closed. The "Did you Tag This Ticket?" field improved ticket tagging rates to above 90% within the next couple months. Steinhardt Technology Services finally had a verified data solution that could be used to inform business decisions.

Table 1 Ticket Tag Rate

Month and Year	Tickets Solved	Total Support Tags	Ticket Tag Rate
August 2014 (Pre Checkbox)	289	134	46%
September 2014 (First Month of Checkbox)	528	363	67%
October 2014 (Second Month of Checkbox)	422	348	82%
November 2014 (Third Month of Checkbox)	308	289	94%

4.4 Changes and Controls

Following the addition of the "Did You Tag This Ticket?" field, two subsequent changes that impacted ticket data. The first major change was altering the required ticket tagging field from a text-input separated by commas to 6 separate fields with drop down menus. Text input lead to increased errors as agents would misspell tags or misremember tags. Drop down menus would minimize these changes by standardizing the input for the tags.

The second major change was turning on the Satisfaction Surveys that are sent to users after a ticket has been solved. The user could then report they were either "satisfied with their service" or they were "not satisfied with their service." From these surveys, the Customer Satisfaction rate was by dividing the number of positive reviews with total reviews. While the Customer Satisfaction Rate provided one metric to measure customer interaction, there is limitation when evaluating this data. The Customer Satisfaction Rate tend to look the same each month. 99% of tickets are rated good and around 1% get unsatisfactory ratings. Since the data looks the same month to month, there was no way for STS management to know if the helpdesk had a good month or a bad month. As such, STS needed to find a different more meaningful way to measure helpdesk performance. This lead STS to define the Key Metrics that would become the basis of assessing helpdesk effectiveness.

5. EXAMPLES OF COLLECTED DATA

5.1 Time to First Response

See Chart 1 in Appendix. Steinhardt Technology Services looks at two metrics when looking at First Response time. The first is Average First Response Time. Average First Reply time is influenced by outliers. As a way to control for the influence of outliers, Steinhardt Technology Services also looks at Median First Response Times

5.2 Time to First Resolution

See Chart 2 in Appendix. Chart 2 is a graph of Average First Resolution Time calculated within business hours.

5.3 Ticket Volume

See Chart 3 in Appendix. Chart 3 is an example of the number of Tickets Solved each month.

6. BUILDING BUSSINESS SYSTEMS USING THE NEW DATA SOLUTION

6.1 Determining Key Metrics

With data tracking in place, STS was now able analyze accumulated data to identify and create key metrics. As discussed in Changes and Controls, the Customer Satisfaction Rate does not vary dramatically month to month. A tremendously high proportion (around 97%-99%) of the population is happy with the service with a low proportion (1%-3%) being unhappy with the service. Since these ratings are relatively stable, STS Management had to find another metric to measure quality of service. The two metrics used were Time to First Response (measured in minutes within business hours) and Time to First Resolution (measured in hours).

STS uses Time to First Response to measure the responsiveness of the helpdesk to new tickets. When tickets come into the helpdesk they sit in a general queue while they wait to be routed by the Ticket Router. The Time to First Response measures the time the ticket sits in the queue before the Ticket Router assigns to an agent.

Steinhardt Technology Services uses Time to First Resolution to measure how quickly Steinhardt Technology Services Agents are able to solve problem tickets. Ultimately this metric is a way for management to understand how long our end users aren't able to do their work because of their technology problems.

These two metrics, taken together, give a clear snapshot of the state of the helpdesk. These two metrics allow STS Management to evaluate whether the helpdesk is being responsive to end users' requests and how quickly those requests are being resolved after they are acknowledged. Even though these two metrics appear to be quite simple, Steinhardt Technology Services management were able to create effective business systems that fully leverage personnel and resources.

6.2 Ticket Routing

Once Steinhardt Technology Services has metrics for measuring helpdesk performance, they can start using the data to craft business systems and strategies to fully leverage helpdesk resources. The first problem was finding a way to decrease the First Response Time on a ticket. In August 2014, Average Time to First Response was 337 Business Minutes (see Chart 1 in the Appendix). By implementing a ticket routing system, Steinhardt Technology Services was able to reduce the time to 237 Minutes in September 2014 to 95 Minutes in November 2014. Such a dramatic decrease resulted in better customer interaction and engagement as customers, on average, waited less time to start the troubleshooting process.

While targeting the Average Time to First Response, Steinhardt Technology Services decided to use a two touch system to route tickets. After a ticket has been generated and is sitting in the unassigned ticket queue, the Ticket Router makes the first "touch", that is the first reply on the ticket. After several criteria have been satisfied, the ticket is passed to the technician responsible for resolving the issue. See 6.2.1 for the specifics of the Steinhardt Two Touch System.

6.2.1 Excerpt from the Ticket Routing Manual

At Steinhardt IT, we have a two touch routing system that we use to when we are routing our tickets.

This **First Touch** encompasses the following:

- The ticket has been received and read by the Steinhardt IT Ticket Router
- The ticket router has tagged the ticket with the 5 Required Tags
- The ticket router has assigned the ticket a Ticket Type (See Ticket Type Matrix)
- The ticket has assigned the ticket a Ticket Priority (See Ticket Priority Matrix)
- The ticket router assigns the ticket to the Steinhardt IT Group member who will attempt to resolve the issue.
- The ticket router then comments on the ticket in order to communicate with the community member that their ticket has been received and to let the community member know who will be contacting them regarding the next steps.

After the Ticket Router makes the First Touch, whomever the ticket is assigned to makes the Second Touch.

The **Second Touch** encompasses the following:

- The Steinhardt Agent establishes the location of the end user
- The Steinhardt Agent establishes a time to meet the end user
- The Steinhardt Agent asks for any other details necessary to solve the ticket.

6.3 Ticket Escalation and Assignment

Ticket escalation and assignment is another strategy for creating a competitive advantage using ticket tag data. After the ticket routing system was being used to target certain time stamp metrics, a new problem arose. How should tickets be assigned to technicians? For management, the answer seemed simple. The ticket router should assign a ticket based on the difficulty of the ticket and the ability of the technician to resolve the ticket. In order to make that decision, STS Management had to standardize judgements of ticket difficulty. STS Management developed the Ticket Complexity Matrix along with the Ticket Complexity Required Ticket Tags. Based on the two factors (expected time to completion and probability of complications), the ticket router is able to assign the ticket to the appropriately skilled technicians (see Table 2). New student technicians would handle simple ticket, full time technicians and core student technicians would handle complex tickets, and managers and directors would handle advanced tickets. By standardizing which tickets go to whom, STS was able to focus on reducing First Resolution Time by stopping tickets from being unnecessarily routed to an agent that could not resolve the problem.

Table 2. Ticket Complexity Matrix

	Simple	Complex	Advanced
Expected Time to Completion (direct work)	Less than 1 hour	Between 1 and 8 hours	Greater than 8 hours
Probability of Complications	Low to little	Medium	High
IT Example	Installing a printer locally on a computer	Installing a new printer for a department and installing it on each computer on the floor	Configuring a printer on the print server and pushing out the printer to the entire school

6.4 Staffing Changes

Data from ticket tags has also been essential for predicting staffing levels for Steinhardt Technology Services. Before implementing ticket tagging, most staffing decisions were made anecdotally. After implementing ticket tagging, staffing changes became more of a science. The manager could look at data trends and recommend to the Dean of Operations what staffing changes need to be made.

The first major hire justified by data was the hire of the Information and Systems Administrator. Over the course of the 2015 year, there has been a steady demand for system support tickets when compared to similar months in 2014 (see Chart 4 in the Appendix). While some staff members were knowledgeable in system support, the data showed that there is justification to hire someone who can specialize in system support. When presented with this data, the Dean of Operations pushed to hire a full time systems administrator.

7. Conclusions

The use of data to shape business systems is the future of the helpdesk. While it required much up front work, STS Management is still reaping the dividends from the simple, yet powerful insights that was provided by a new data strategy. Extrapolating from STS example, using a simple, yet intentional, data tracking system allows for a small team to remain competitive in a rapidly changing workplace. In order to fully leverage its power, one has to make sure the data system is intentional and well maintained.

8. Future Challenges

8.1 Service Level Agreements

The new frontier for leveraging this data is to use the data to write and Service Level Agreements. At the moment there is no formal Service Level Agreement between the community and Steinhardt Technology Services. By looking at First Response Times, Steinhardt Technology Services will be able to set a standard of service to make sure the helpdesk is accountable to the needs of the community. From these service standards, a formalized Service Level Agreement will be written so that the Steinhardt Community understand the limits of the service that Steinhardt Technology Services provides.

8.2 Dividing SIT and SAT in Zendesk

Another area of growth using Zendesk data is separating out services from the Information Technology side of Steinhardt Technology Services and the Academic Technology side of Steinhardt Technology Services. By dividing these two services in Zendesk, Steinhardt Technology Services will be able to granularly set service standards within each service that best fits the community needs.

9. ACKNOWLEDGMENTS

I would like to thank our Steinhardt Technology Services Team, Lucas, Kenny, Kevin, Chao, Dave and Marina. Also, I would like to thank Ilana, Manager of the Academic Technology Team, for helping develop some of these ideas.

10. REFERENCES

[1] About NYU. New York University. New York University. Retrieved June 26, 2015. https://www.nyu.edu/about.html

[2] About NYU Steinhardt. NYU Steinhardt. New York University. Retrieved June 26, 2015. http://steinhardt.nyu.edu/about/

[3] Customer Service Analytics. Zendesk. Zendesk. Retrieved May 6, 2016. https://www.zendesk.com/analytic

11. APPENDIX

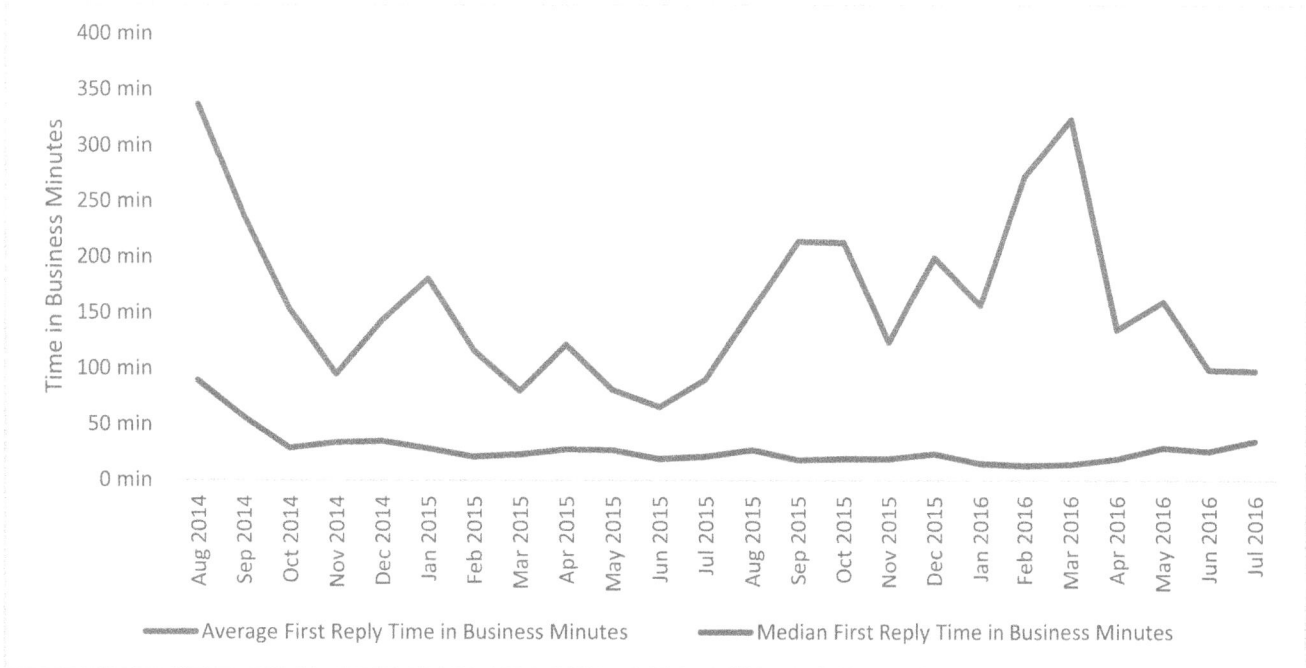

Chart 1 Average and Median First Reply Time

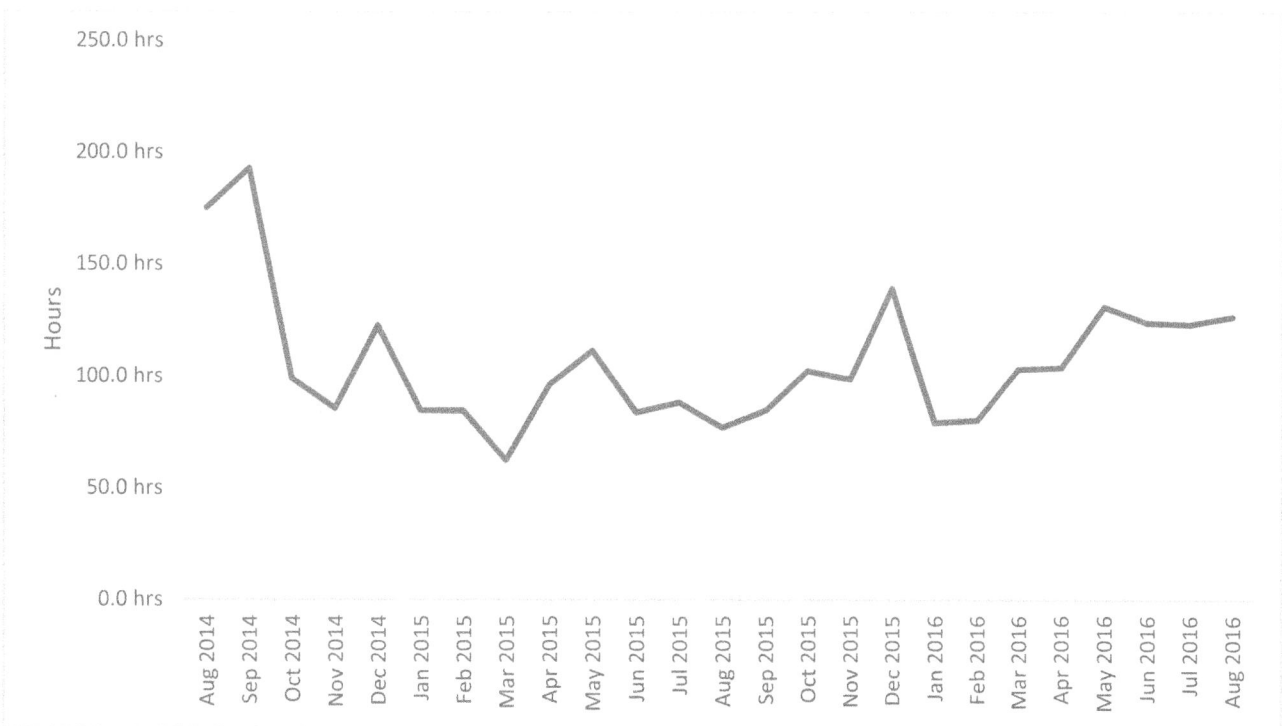

Chart 2 Average Time to First Resolution

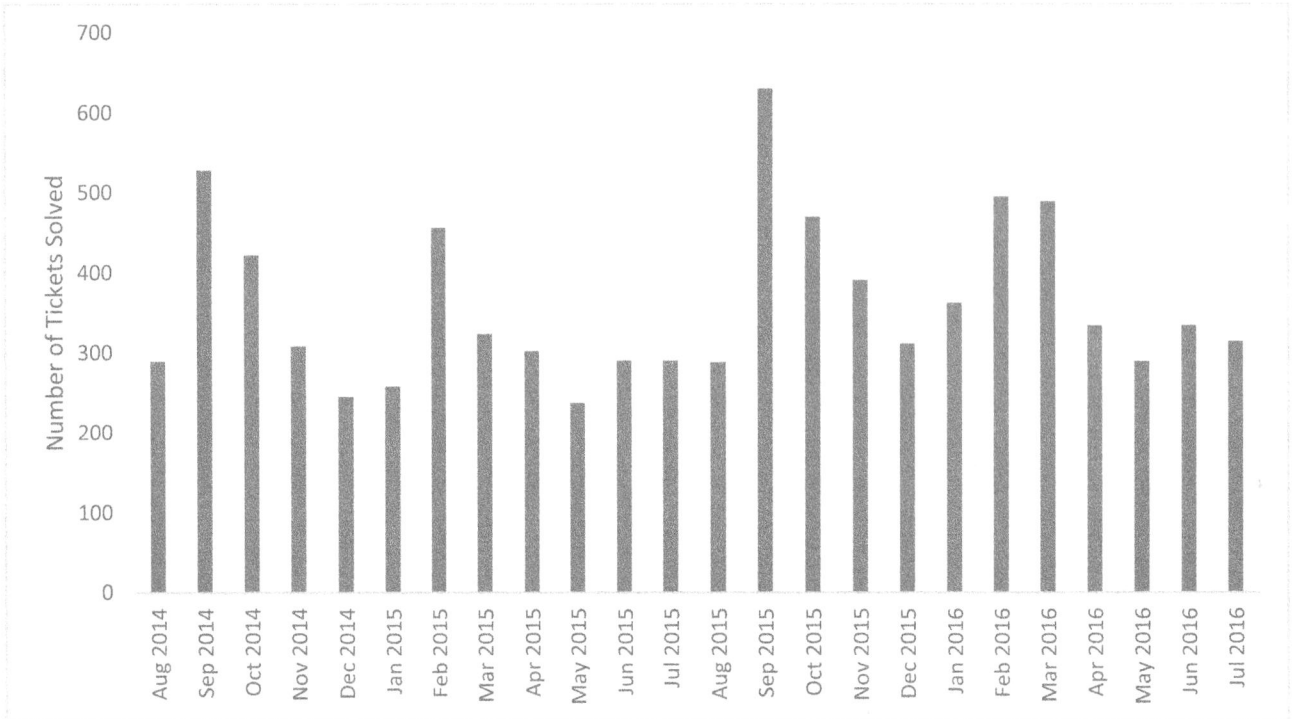

Chart 3 Ticket Volume

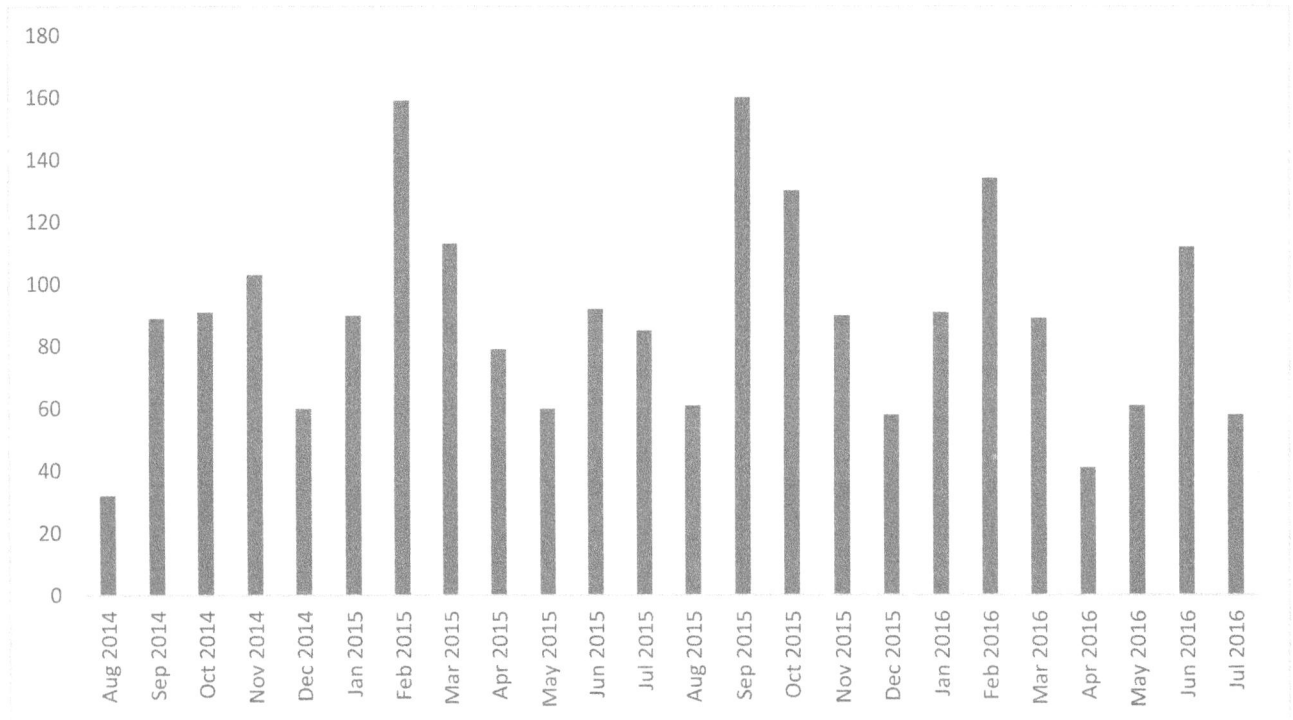

Chart 4 Number of Solved Tickets with System Support Tag

Puppet: Introduction, Implementation, & the Inevitable Refactoring

Shawn Plummer
SUNY Geneseo
1 College Circle
Geneseo, NY 14454
585-245-5577
plummer@geneseo.edu

David Warden
SUNY Geneseo
1 College Circle
Geneseo, NY 14454
585-245-5577
warden@geneseo.edu

ABSTRACT

Puppet is configuration management software that lets you define the desired state for a computer and enforce that state on scheduled periodic executions of the Puppet agent on that computer. About a year and a half after implementing Puppet on our campus, we had a functional but inflexible and poorly organized Puppet configuration code base. We refactored it multiple times before settling on our current layout based on the roles/profiles strategy and Hiera. We will share a brief introduction to Puppet, how it is useful to us and, most importantly, what we learned over 3 years of implementing it on our campus.

Keywords

Puppet; Configuration Management; Sysadmin; Automation; Configuration as Code.

1. INTRODUCTION

SUNY Geneseo is a small liberal arts college in upstate NY, with ~5,700 students and 1,000 faculty/staff. SUNY Geneseo has used Puppet for configuration management since 2012. In that time we have learned a great deal about using Puppet to manage our complex Linux infrastructure. We will describe what Puppet is, how it is useful to us and what we have learned about using it since 2012, focusing on Hiera and the roles/profiles strategy first laid out by Craig Dunn[1] and expanded upon by Gary Larizza[2].

Puppet is an open source configuration management software (with paid for commercial support) created in 2005 by PuppetLabs that uses a client/server model to apply a declarative configuration language to collections of nodes. At a macro level, a Puppet "run" is roughly comprised of the following steps:

1. The Puppet agent running on a node sends information ("facts") about itself to the central Puppet server ("master").
2. The Puppet master uses the information from the agent to decide which parts ("resources") of your configuration code base should be applied to that node. This process is often called "node classification".
3. The Puppet master sends the determined configuration information ("catalog") to the agent node.

SIGUCCS '16, November 06-09, 2016, Denver, CO, USA
© 2016 ACM. ISBN 978-1-4503-4095-3/16/11 $15.00
DOI: http://dx.doi.org/10.1145/2974927.2974950

4. The Puppet agent implements the changes necessary for the node to match the desired state received from the master.

These high-level design choices of Puppet are responsible for both delight and anguish among Puppet users. Puppet's declarative nature allows resource idempotence , The ability to apply the same configuration multiple times without changing the result after the first application, but prevents multiple declarations of the same resource. A centralized configuration code base is easier to manage than a decentralized one, but requires the master to have all the information necessary to determine the catalog for a node based solely on the facts transmitted to the master. Navigating these (and other) tradeoffs is likely the most significant difficulty spike new Puppet users will face, and we were no exception.

2. PITFALLS AND PROBLEMS WITH PUPPET

We began our Puppet journey in 2012 slowly, only adding it to a few hosts and managing simple configurations we considered to be the foundational base of our servers. These configurations included things like static entries in host files, directory server integration for users and groups, authorized ssh keys, package repositories, installed packages, and local administrator accounts. We implemented Puppet's "node inheritance" strategy by assigning these configurations to the default node, which all Puppet agents receive unless specified otherwise.

The ability to define a "base" state that could applied and enforced across all of our servers was quite an improvement over the previous way we did things, which was through Anaconda build scripts and documentation specifying how a Linux server in our environment should be built. Anaconda's structure and syntax encouraged drift among systems built with different iterations of the same script and functionally dissimilar systems that required an entirely different script. Although we could have reduced configuration drift through aggressive use of the %include directive, doing so would neither remediate systems built with previous iterations of the build script nor prevent post-install configuration drift. Puppet made it easier to define, implement, enforce, and maintain baseline best practices.

As we started to get a feel for how Puppet worked and how it could benefit us we started putting more and more configuration into Puppet. We followed Puppet Labs' best practices as much as we could, creating individual modules to manage specific components. Puppet Labs' guidance is that a Puppet module should only handle the installation and management of one piece of software. Your module might install PostgreSQL but it should not handle the configuration of a web server that uses PostgreSQL as well. We wrote modules for managing VMWare vSphere Perl SDK, Selenium, and several other things. What was less well defined when we started was guidance on how to manage your host-specific configuration that make your hosts receive the configuration necessary to actually perform their roles.

Puppet's default method for deciding which configuration artifacts should be applied to a node is to use a special Puppet configuration file called site.pp. This file is the default location for "node definitions" that assign configuration elements to a specific hostname, hostname pattern, or the "default" node. This file, like most Puppet configuration files, supports inheritance. Our implementation of the "node inheritance" strategy saw our "base" configuration applied to the default node, which all explicitly defined nodes inherited from.

Happy with the success of our "base" config, we attempted add a middle layer of inheritance by creating inheritable nodes between the default and leaf nodes that could install and configure common software stacks in our environment such as a web server with Apache, PHP, and certain 3rd-party PHP modules. This quickly got messy; slight differences in the configuration of those stacks between functional node groups, as well as the limitation that Puppet classes may only be instantiated once caused us to abandon this strategy. Interestingly, this attempt resulted in many of the same problems we had with Anaconda: significant code duplication necessitated by slight differences in desired configurations.

2.1 Class Conflicts

Puppet allows a class to be declared as a resource only once[3], but most people new to Puppet expect the later definition to replace the earlier definition. A common problem we would run into was we would declare a class in one of our base configurations applied to all our servers like:

```
package { 'opsview-agent':
 ensure => 'present',
}
```

This ensures that the package named *opsview-agent* is present on a host. If in another manifest we want to make sure that same package is not present:

```
package { 'opsview-agent':
 ensure => 'absent',
}
```

Puppet would throw an error. Without awareness of alternatives, we handled this by defining certain common resources in each node, which resulted in significant code duplication. Each duplicate block increased the probability of drift between those blocks and thus demanded additional management overhead.

2.2 Ordering is Difficult

Prior to Puppet 3.3.0, the only way to control the order resources were applied in was to strictly define their dependencies. Common ordering strategies were to declare *after* or *before* metaparameters within a resource or by defining class ordering *File['/etc/ntp.conf'] ~> Service['ntpd']*. Puppet 3.3.0 introduced as an option and Puppet 4.0 made default "manifest ordering"[4], which applies resources in the order they are declared in your code. Puppet Labs recommends explicitly defining your resource dependencies, even with manifest ordering.

3. ROLES & PROFILES

When we refactored to the roles and profiles methodology first defined by Craig Dunn[1] It solved all of the problems we had been running into. It made our Puppet code far more manageable, extensible, and readable.

A good Puppet module does one thing and does it well. The Apache module will let you configure nearly anything you can imagine about the Apache web server but it won't let you define what firewall ports should be open for a host that is running Apache. A profile is like a logical extension of a module: it is a Puppet class with artifacts like modules, resources, or even other profiles necessary to set up a complete service. For example, an Apache profile would configure Apache and open the firewall ports necessary for people to access it. We have profiles like gsu::profiles::snmpd which configures the SNMP daemon for our environment, gsu::profiles::oracleusers, which defines users for Oracle software and then more complex ones like gsu::profiles::weblogic – which defines how a weblogic host should be setup using include syntax to bring several profiles together (Include-Like behavior[6] allows multiple declarations without problem) and mount points and firewall rules for a weblogic host.

Roles are usually a collection of profiles, although nothing prevents you from including other artifacts in them. They primarily differ from profiles in that a role should be the only resource assigned to a node. A role should include all the artifacts necessary to configure that node to make its desired services available.

You can then combine your defined roles and profiles to to configure something like an Apache Tomcat server, with the settings necessary to run Ellucian Banner software:

```
class gsu::role::base {
  include gsu::profile::yumrepos
  include gsu::profile::packages
  include gsu::profile::localgroups
  include gsu::profile::systemsusers
  include gsu::profile::hosts
  include gsu::profile::base
  include gsu::profile::auth
  include gsu::profile::ssh
  include gsu::profile::pam
  include gsu::profile::autohome
  include gsu::profile::firewall
  include gsu::profile::gsuvmwaretools
  include gsu::profile::puppetagent
  include gsu::profile::shiplogs
  include
gsu::profile::sudo::nexpose_user
}


class gsu::role::tomcat_banner {
  include gsu::role::base
  include gsu::profile::opsviewagent
  include gsu::profile::snmpd
  include gsu::profile::java
  include gsu::profile::tomcat_banner
  include gsu::profile::access::cit_is
  include
gsu::profile::sudo::cit_is_tomcat
```

```
    include gsu::profile::apache_banner

    include gsu::profile::wildcardcert

}
```

You can see here we have made the gsu::role::tomcat_banner include our base role then all of the profiles necessary to be a Tomcat server. Manifest ordering allowed us to easily control the order of the classes by reordering the include statements, although it is worth noting that Puppet Labs still recommends explicit ordering when you need to be sure things happen in a certain order.

Good profiles become like Lego blocks you can use to build up a given server or service on a host. If you need a bigger or smaller Lego block, it is easy to break apart a profile into smaller components or to write a new similar block that does something slightly different. The ease of this process stands in stark contrast to the difficulty we had working with the proliferation of Anaconda scripts and node inheritance Puppet code.

Roles are your business specific names around sets of technologies on a server i.e. *production webserver, Tomcat server, PostgreSQL Cluster* and so on.

Roles and profiles vastly cleaned up the *sites.pp* file, as now each host defined in the *sites.pp* has one and only one role applied to it.

4. HEIRA IS MAGIC

Hiera is a "key/value lookup tool for configuration data"[7] that can be part of your Puppet master. It is often recommended as a complement to roles and profiles, most commonly to separate site-specific information (such as IP addresses) from your profiles code. Other common examples of Hiera use include applying slightly different resources in a profile if the node reports it is "development" vs "production", or allowing per-hostname tweaks to resource parameters like available heap space for the Tomcat Java application.

Puppet 3.x and later have Automatic Parameter Lookup[8]. This helps in that you can use any variable in Heira such as $java_version and if it finds it anywhere in scope it will use it. However, this can make it seem like magic where a variable's definition comes from. With Automatic Parameter Lookup, variables in classes could be getting defined you can't even see in the profile you are looking at.

To combat some of this "magic," we have a coding standard, we took from a suggestion by Gary Larizza[9]. Heira lookups should all be done at the top of a file, so that it is explicit where they are coming from and what will be used in a manifest. This has the additional benefit of being explicit about where a variable is coming from.

```
## Hiera Lookups

## Do Heira lookups and assign to variable
here to make Heira less "magic"

## e.g. $ssh_keys = hiera_hash('gsu::ssh'),
$user_password = hiera('user_password')

## $ntp_servers = hiera_array('ntp_servers')

## Make = signs line up.

$server = hiera('puppet_server')

$environment = hiera('puppet_environment')

$master_port = hiera('puppet_master_port')

$repository_server            =
hiera('repository_server')
```

By defining all Hiera lookups at the top of the file, it becomes far more readable and documented where a given parameter comes from.

5. CUSTOM FACTS

One thing we have found to be easy and extremely useful is that you can easily define your own custom facts to be added to Facter. Facter is the program that runs on all Puppet hosts to gather information about the host to be used for node classification or in your manifests. Default facts include things like OS version, installed RAM, and whether a host is virtual or not. By creating your own files in *module/lib/facter* you can define facts that will be added to the Facter database on all your hosts. For example, we used the following custom fact from https://gist.github.com/mkrakowitzer/10276574 when Heartbleed was a big concern to tell us the version of openssl on all our hosts.

```
Facter.add(:openssl_version) do

  confine :kernel => 'Linux'

  setcode do

    family = Facter.value(:osfamily)

    case family

    when 'RedHat'

      Facter::Core::Execution.exec('/bin/rpm
-q                        --queryformat
"%{VERSION}-%{RELEASE}-%{ARCH}\n"
openssl|paste -d "," -s -')

    when 'Debian'

      Facter::Core::Execution.exec('/usr/bin/
dpkg-query -W -f=\'${Version}\' openssl')

    else

      nil

    end

  end

end


Facter.add(:openssl_built_on) do

  confine :kernel => 'Linux'

  setcode do

    version                              =
Facter::Core::Execution.exec('openssl
version -b')

    if version

      version.to_s.gsub("built on: ", "")

    else

      nil

    end

  end

end
```

Combining this with our Foreman server that collects all Facter output it made it very easy to identify servers with unpatched openssl versions and remediate them.

```
    facter -p openssl_version

0.9.8e-39.0.1.el5_11-i686
```

6. CONCLUSION

Overall, Puppet has been a fantastic tool for our Systems team in managing our growing number of servers and services. While we had many pitfalls and challenges along the way in implementing Puppet and handling all of our services, getting started is the key to success. Due to Puppet's modular nature, getting started small is easy and you can grow and build your configuration like Lego pieces as you grow.

Also, since our initial implementation a great deal of knowledge has been generated in the greater Puppet community both from Puppetlabs and in the open source community. Two resources we would recommend for anyone getting started are:

Puppetlab's self-paced training:

- https://learn.puppet.com/category/self-paced-training

And the control repo from Puppetlabs on github:

- https://github.com/puppetlabs/control-repo

7. REFERENCES

[1] Dunn, C. (2012, May 23). Designing Puppet – Roles and Profiles. Retrieved May 11, 2016, from http://www.craigdunn.org/2012/05/239/

[2] Larizza, G. (2014, February 12). Building a Functional Puppet Workflow Part 2: Roles and Profiles. Retrieved May 11, 2016, from http://garylarizza.com/blog/2014/02/17/puppet-workflow-part-2/

[3] Language: Classes. (n.d.). Retrieved May 11, 2016, from https://docs.puppet.com/puppet/latest/reference/lang_classes.html#resource-like-behavior

[4] Sorenson, E. (2013, December 30). Introducing Manifest-Ordered Resources. Retrieved May 11, 2016, from https://puppet.com/blog/introducing-manifest-ordered-resources

[5] Language: Run Stages. (n.d.). Retrieved May 11, 2016, from https://docs.puppet.com/puppet/latest/reference/lang_run_stages.html

[6] Language: Classes. (n.d.). Retrieved May 13, 2016, from https://docs.puppet.com/puppet/latest/reference/lang_classes.html#include-like-behavior

[7] Hiera 3.1: Overview. (n.d.). Retrieved May 13, 2016, from https://docs.puppet.com/hiera/3.1/index.html

[8] Hiera 1: Using Hiera With Puppet. (n.d.). Retrieved May 13, 2016, from http://docs.puppetlabs.com/hiera/1/puppet.html#automatic-parameter-lookup

[9] Larizza, G. (2014, October 24). Puppet Workflows 4: Using Hiera in Anger. Retrieved May 13, 2016, from http://garylarizza.com/blog/2014/10/24/puppet-workflows-4-using-hiera-in-anger/

Secure Data Management in an English Speaking Test Implemented in General-Purpose PC Classrooms

Hideo Masuda
Kyoto Institute of Technology
Matsugasaki, Sakyo
Kyoto, JAPAN 606-8585
+81 75 724 7956
h-masuda@kit.ac.jp

Masayuki Mori
Kyoto Institute of Technology
Matsugasaki, Sakyo
Kyoto, JAPAN 606-8585
morim@kit.ac.jp

Katsunori Kanzawa
Kyoto Institute of Technology
Matsugasaki, Sakyo
Kyoto, JAPAN 606-8585
kanzawa@kit.ac.jp

Yasushi Tsubota
Kyoto Institute of Technology
Matsugasaki, Sakyo
Kyoto, JAPAN 606-8585
tsubota-yasushi@kit.ac.jp

Yumi Hato
Kyoto Institute of Technology
Matsugasaki, Sakyo
Kyoto, JAPAN 606-8585
hato@kit.ac.jp

Yasuaki Kuroe
Kyoto Institute of Technology
Matsugasaki, Sakyo
Kyoto, JAPAN 606-8585
kuroe@kit.ac.jp

ABSTRACT

The Kyoto Institute of Technology Speaking Test, "English for the 21st Century" is being developed to assess the English speaking ability of undergraduate students learning English as a lingua franca. The ultimate goal of this project is to introduce the computer-based English speaking test as part of entrance examinations to graduate programs. Despite the high-stakes nature of the test, it needs to be implemented in general-purpose PC classrooms mainly due to financial constraints. A secure data sharing system needs to be established between the PCs used for the test and the servers to preserve confidentiality, integrity, accessibility for the audio data. External graders will need access to carry out online evaluation of the collected data.

Also, the computer rooms must resume normal operation soon after the test administration. We administered the first two large-scale feasibility tests (approximately 700 examinees each) in January and December 2015. In this paper we will demonstrate the Windows custom image and secure data sharing tools we have developed for the tests and also report on how they were operated in the actual administration of the tests.

Keywords: PC classroom, computer-based test, online evaluation.

1. INTRODUCTION

In October 2012, Kyoto Institute of Technology (KIT) established a project team to introduce English speaking tests into the entrance examination to graduate programs [1]. Since the onset of the project, the academic and technical staff of the Center for Information Science at KIT have been working collaboratively with the academic staff teaching English at the institute in developing and implementing the computer-based speaking test, and

Copyright is held by the owner/author(s).
SIGUCCS '16, November 06-09, 2016, Denver, CO, USA
ACM 978-1-4503-4095-3/16/11.
http://dx.doi.org/10.1145/2974927.2974957

examining its feasibility and practicability as a high-stakes examination.

The project team decided to develop the computer-based test (CBT) for practical reasons. The difficulty with face-to-face interview tests, which are the prevailing option for English speaking tests, is that it would require employing and training a significant number of experienced English interview graders to assess the ability of some 700 applicants in under a week. Both budget limitations and concerns about the consistency of applying the English language interview grading rubric among so many temporary employees have made a computer-based test an attractive option.

While the amounts of data transmitted in ordinary CBTs are quite limited, far larger amounts of data need to be transmitted in English speaking tests because the sound quality of recorded questions and examinees' responses must be high enough to ensure the fairness required of a high-stakes examination.

Further, highly secure data transmission must be established between the on-campus server used for the test administration and the off-campus server prepared for the external raters to mark the examinees' oral responses. However, given the low frequency of administering the entrance examinations (less than 3 times a year), a large budget cannot be allocated for the installment of equipment used exclusively for the speaking test, not to mention the PC rooms designed for the test. The project team therefore decided to use some general-purpose PC rooms ("PC Labs" in Figure 1) that are used by students mainly for programming exercises [4].

In this paper, we will demonstrate how the computer system in these PC rooms were customized so that the institute could implement the speaking test, ensuring the high level of confidentiality, integrity, and availability required for quality data transmission for the entrance examination. We will also examine the results of the first two large-scale feasibility tests administered in 2015, and discuss further challenges to address to achieve the goal.

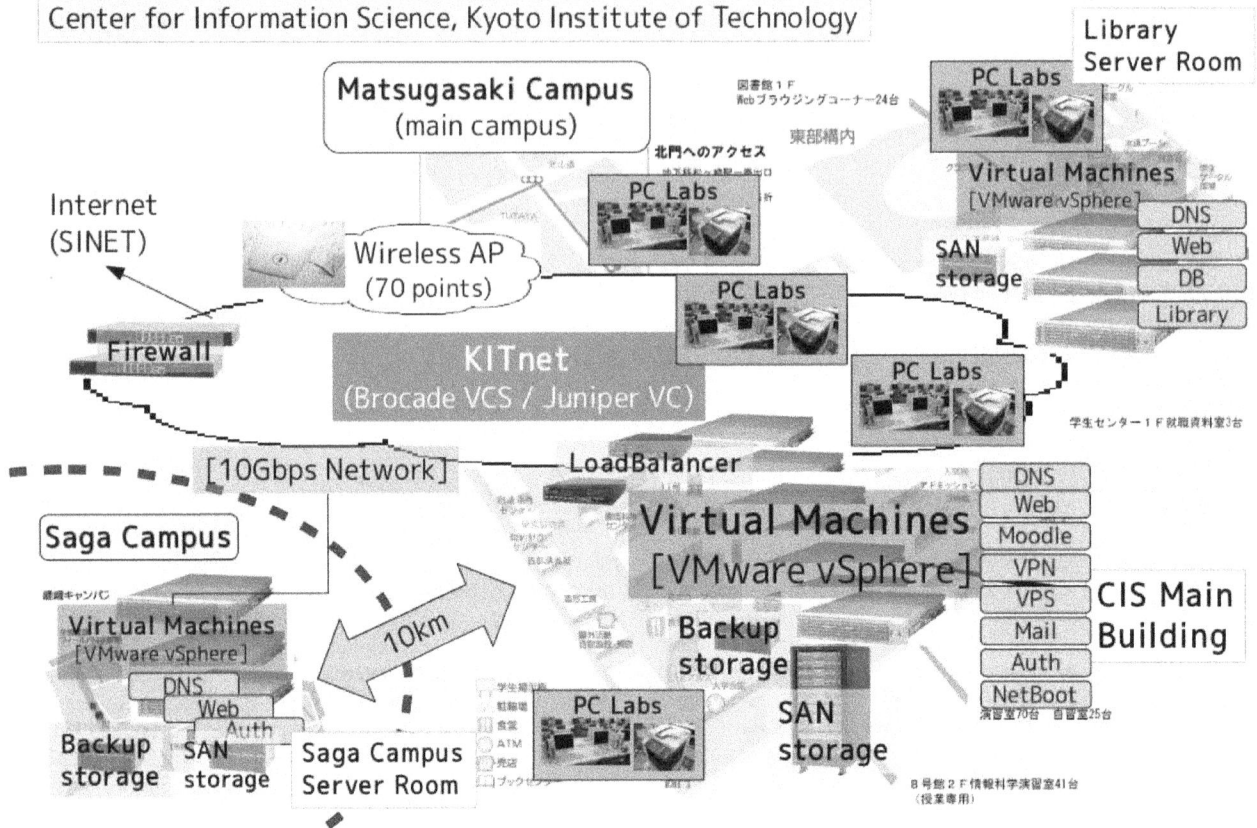

Computer Infrastructure (System9)
Center for Information Science, Kyoto Institute of Technology

March 2014.

Figure 1 Overview of Our Computer System (System9)

2. PREREQUISITES

KIT updates its computer system every four years [2,3,4]. The newest system named "System 9"[4] provides virtual server services, file sharing services, Web services for off-campus users, e-mail services, LMS services, user authentication services, terminal services for computer exercises, printing services and so on (figure 1). In this section, we will explain some of the important services used for the speaking test.

2.1 Network Boot for PC Labs

The terminal system for programming exercises at KIT consists of about 300 PC terminals, and students and faculty staff have free access to the system for self-study and programming exercises. Windows 7 and Linux (CentOS 6) are installed on the PC terminals and users can select either of them depending on their purpose of use. Although the OS in each PC terminal needs to be kept up-to-date for security reasons, it is difficult to treat some 300 terminals separately. Our system therefore utilizes a network boot method to realize updating work in an integrated way. For Windows 7, we have adopted Citrix PVS plus CO-CONV Readcache method, and for Linux, we use NFS root plus unionfs. This enables us to change OS without accessing each client PC's hard drive as long as we prepare necessary OS images and keep them updated on the server. CO-CONV Readcache is a mechanism to cache data blocks in local hard drives and reduces the data traffic at the time of the network boot. This alleviates the

traffic concentration in the case of simultaneous executions of the same application, which often occurs when computer exercise classes are in session.

2.2 File Sharing Server for Individual Users

System 9 uses a moving profile so that clients can use the same settings and access their files at every terminal. As a result, each user's file is not saved on local hard drives, but in the shared file server. The shared file server gives access only to the appropriate files for which the authenticated user has read and write permissions. We also set up a one gigabyte quota restriction to prevent users from creating files without a size limit and consequently suppress file space available for other users. The access protocols to the shared file server are CIFS for Windows and NFS for Linux. The Disk space accessible from Windows 7 is limited to $Home/windows, which is a part of $HOME that is accessible from Linux. This enables users to refer to their files, regarless of the OS they use.

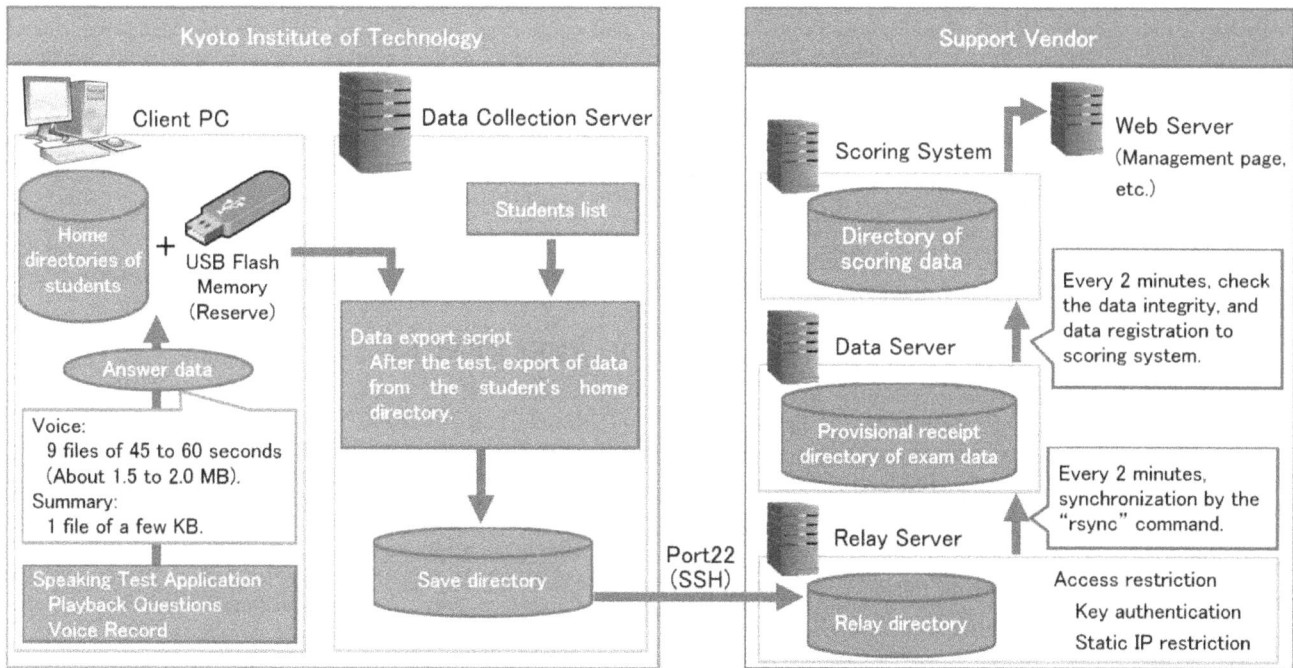

Figure 2 Overview of the Speaking Test backend

2.3 User Management

System 9 has a master authentication database which has the account information of all the students and staff members at KIT. The database is updated automatically during the night. With the help of the master authentication database, the common authentication method can be used and the permission process can be executed only with specific user groups for each service. For the terminals used for programming exercises, there is an active directory server that has the information of students and academic staff only, and the use for administrative purposes is prohibited.

3. REQUIREMENTS

The followings are required for administering the English speaking test in the entrance examination.

[R0] In taking the test, the same conditions are ensured for all the examinees.

[R1] Test items are kept confidential until the commencement of the test.

[R2] No one but those specified in advance can take the test.

[R3] The test is not interrupted or suspended due to network or PC troubles.

[R4] Examinees' oral responses are securely recorded and saved on the server.

[R5] Examinees' oral responses are securely delivered to each external rater.

4. IMPLEMENTATION

Approximately 220 terminals installed for programming exercises in three separate PC rooms are used for the English speaking test. Using these terminals addresses [R0].

In order to prevent access by non-test-taking users, the test administration system is called after each examinee logs on to the Windows system using his or her own account. By registering the examinees' accounts in advance, access by those who are not registered is denied on the test day. Preventing access to the test by users not registered to take the examination addresses [R2].

If access to the external link were required for obtaining the test questions, there would be a greater possibility of network or PC troubles that inevitably lead to the suspension of the test. Our system utilizes a network boot method, and when a PC cannot access the Netboot server, the PC does not work. As a result, the situation where the PC is working but the test questions cannot not be loaded is more likely to be avoided. Disabling terminals with network difficulties addresses [R3].

The test application is embedded in the Windows custom image, and therefore, access to the test application is ensured once the OS image loads. Having the test application integrated into the Windows images addresses [R3].

However, there arises a concern for the leakage of the test questions when the test application is installed on the OS image in advance. To prevent this, the OS image is changed/modified from a general-purpose image to a test image on the test administration day, utilizing the Network boot function. Swapping out the image on the testing day helps address [R1].

In most cases, three or more candidates take the speaking test, using the same PC terminals on the same day. By ensuring that the PC is shut down when each candidate finishes taking the test, his/her data files in the temporary file stage are deleted and cannot be manipulated.

137

Each candidate's oral responses are saved on the file sharing server. The backup is also stored on USB flash memory connected to each PC terminal before the test to be retrieved after the test. The storage area could be prepared on the local hard drive for the same purpose, but higher security can be ensured by saving the backup in USB flash memory. This helps address [R4].

All the oral responses of each examinee are saved in one folder prepared for him/her on the file sharing server, and, employing the rsync plus SSH method, a copy is made in the server used for the rating of the test. When the rating is completed the speech responses on the file sharing server are deleted. This addresses [R5].

5. LESSONS LEARNED

With the system described in the previous sections, the computer-based English speaking test was administered in January and December, 2015. 551 first-year students in the undergraduate program at KIT took the first test, together with 37 anchor examinees who took all three versions of the test used on that occasion. Anchor examinees took the test to help equate the versions. The second test was administered to 575 first-year students and 69 anchor examinees in the following academic year.

On both occasions, the test application was supplied by the test developer we work with one day before the test administration. We installed the test into the base image of Windows 7 and changed the setting of the boot server to boot the new image to the terminals on the test day. Just after the test, we transferred sound files and summary files to the vendor server. In addition, we uninstalled the test application and deployed the base image with out the test to the terminals.

Basically, the feasibility tests were successfully completed, but the followings are the problems for us to solve:

1. Since we deployed the new image for the test just before the test administration, at the first boot, ReadCache was not effective. We should be able to avoid this by booting all the terminals before the actual test.

2. There were a few errors related to writing speech responses to the file sharing system. Although this may have been due to the test application, we need to investigate the causes rigorously.

With regard to the first problem, we are planning to develop a slimmer OS image that only has the modules necessary for the test application and thus reduce the time to create the cache data. The second problem may be solved by further sophisticating the measures the test application has for avoiding temporary writing errors.

6. CONCLUSIONS

In this paper, we have demonstrated the system we developed for administering the English speaking component of the entrance examination in the general-purpose PC rooms and also reported on how the system was operated in the actual administration of the test. We have successfully completed the first two large-scale feasibility tests where some 700 first-year students took the speaking test. One challenge we now need to address concerns user authentication. At present, user authentication is operated as an account database of students and staff members of KIT. However, in order to introduce the speaking test into the entrance examination, user ID and passwords need to be issued for each candidate. We should therefore decide on the way of giving user names to each candidate. At KIT, the user name each student gets issued is based on his/her student number, and s/he uses the user name until s/he left the institute. It is therefore necessary to seek a way of giving individual candidates the user names which they can continue to use after they matriculate to the institute.

7. ACKNOWLEDGEMENTS

This work was supported by JPRS KAKENHI Grant Number 16H03448. Special thanks to e-communications, Inc.

8. REFERENCES

[1] Yumi, H., Katsunori, K.: Development and Execution of CBT English Speaking Test: Evaluation of Trial for Entrance Examination, KOUHOU of Center for Information Science, KIT, No.34, 30-48 (2015, In Japanese).

[2] Hideo, M., Seigo, Y., Michio, N. and Akinori, S.: Using coLinux to Provide a Linux Environment on Windows PC in Public Computer Labs, In Proceedings of the 34th annual ACM SIGUCCS fall Conference, 221-224 (2006). DOI= http://dx.doi.org/10.1145/1181216.1181266 .

[3] Hideo, M., Kazuyoshi, M., Yu, S., Kouichiro, W. and Yasuaki, K.: KIT's Campus Computer System by Virtual Machine Technology and Integrated Identity Service, In Proceedings of the 38th annual ACM SIGUCCS fall Conference, 251-256 (2010). DOI= http://dx.doi.org/10.1145/1878335.1878398 .

[4] Hideo, M., Kazuyoshi, M., Yu, S., Kouichiro, W. and Yasuaki, K.:Distributed Campus Computer Infrastructure - Integrate Education, Research, Library and Office Activities, In Proceedings of the 42nd annual ACM SIGUCCS conference on User services, 93-96 (2014). DOI= http://dx.doi.org/10.1145/2661172.2668055 .

[5] Hideo, M., Kazuyoshi, M., Yu, S.: Low TCO and High-Speed Network Infrastructure with Virtual Technology. In *Proceedings of the 37th annual ACM SIGUCCS fall Conference*, 321-324 (2009). DOI= http://dx.doi.org/10.1145/1629501.1629563.

[6] Hideo, M., Kazuyoshi, M., Yu, S. and Yasuaki, K.: High-Speed Network Infrastructure betwwn KIT's Campuses for Computer System Redundancy, In Proceedings of the 40th annual ACM SIGUCCS Service & Support Conference, 109-110 (2013). DOI= http://dx.doi.org/10.1145/2504776.2504818

[7] Hideo, M., Kazuyoshi, M., Yuki, S., Yu, S. and Yasuaki, K.: Moodle Integration of an Automated Account Enabling System and a User Status Collection System, In Proceedings of the 39th annual ACM SIGUCCS fall Conference, 207-210 (2011). . DOI= http://dx.doi.org/10.1145/2070364.2070418

I'll Guard This Printer With My Life: Colorado College's Journey to Managed Print

Chad E. Schonewill
Colorado College
14 E. Cache La Poudre St.
Colorado Springs, CO 80903
719.389.6941
cschonewill@coloradocollege.edu

ABSTRACT

In this paper, I describe our process of switching over to Managed Print at Colorado College including the results and lessons learned along the way. I also describe our PaperCut initiative and how that has gone.

Keywords

Printers; Printing; RFP; Managed Print; Sustainability;

1. INTRODUCTION

Colorado College is a small, private liberal arts college that uses the Block Plan. Students take one class at a time for 3 and a half weeks. There are 8 blocks per academic year and 2 optional summer blocks. Colorado College is mostly an undergraduate institution, but we do have one Master's program for experienced teachers to get an MAT degree which runs over summers.

Colorado College has approximately 2,000 students and approximately 550 employees.

Colorado College's journey to Managed Print started with a confluence of two events:

1) Our lease agreement with Xerox for copiers was about to expire in late 2011.

2) ITS conducted an inventory of all printers on campus and discovered we had 585 printers (more printers than employees.)

Some members of ITS wanted to take the opportunity of the Xerox lease expiring to make significant changes to the way we handle printing.

We approached our Purchasing department and agreed on a goal of creating a more environmentally and fiscally sustainable printing system.

2. PRELIMINARY WORK

2.1 The full picture before managed print

Before embarking on our Managed Print project, there were essentially three types of printers on campus:

- Xerox copiers
- Networked laser printers
- Desktop inkjet printers

Xerox copiers were handled via a lease agreement with Xerox, and that program was overseen by the Purchasing Office. The lease included the copiers themselves, support from Xerox technicians, and a pay per print model.

Copiers were used in departments, who purchased their own paper and toner supplies. They used a code for copies and their department budget would be charged for copies (but not prints.)

Networked laser printers were part of our annual capital equipment request process each year. If a department wanted to purchase a printer (either net new or a replacement), they requested it via a capital equipment request. A committee reviewed all those requests (which competed with things like computers, buses, and new microscopes) and approved or denied them. As with copiers, departments were responsible for purchasing their own paper and toner supplies for those devices.

Technical support for networked laser printers was handled by ITS. We would directly perform tasks like clearing jams or replacing worn rollers, and would call in a subcontractor for deeper hardware repairs. The budget for those repairs resided in ITS and we had an annual contract with a service provider so the cost would be predictable over time and not variable by paying per repair.

Desktop inkjet printers were purchased directly by departments (or faculty with research funds), and were the most numerous and least efficient devices we had on campus. Departments were responsible for purchasing their own paper and ink supplies, and ITS would help if possible with a problem. If we couldn't fix it, we recommended simply buying a replacement inkjet printer since the devices themselves were so cheap – the ink was really the expensive part.

Most departments on campus had all three types of printers. Usually at least one Xerox copier, more than one networked laser printer, and even more desktop inkjets on each person's desk.

2.2 Problems we identified with the system

When the Xerox lease was about to expire (2011) and after we conducted an inventory and found we had more printers than employees, ITS and Purchasing decided to take the opportunity and work together to design a better printing system from the ground up and design an RFP around it. We identified the following problems with our system:

- Since departments all ordered their own supplies, we were missing an opportunity to leverage an economy of scale and take advantage of bulk discounts.

SIGUCCS '16, November 06-09, 2016, Denver, CO, USA.
© 2016 ACM. ISBN 978-1-4503-4095-3/16/11...$15.00.
DOI: http://dx.doi.org/10.1145/2974927.2974928

- Since departments were charged for copies and purchased their own supplies, other people using "the department's" copier or printer was frowned upon.

- When people called the Help Desk about a printer problem, they invariably characterized it as an emergency even though dozens of other printers existed in the same vicinity.

- Printers were often in private, locked offices and thus inaccessible to anyone else.

- Even though we had nearly 600 printers on campus, any one person only reasonably had access to a small handful. In general, students only had access to about 12 of those printers (in the library and dormitory labs.)

- We were using a large number of inkjet printers, which are notoriously inefficient – low device cost but extremely high cost per page.

- Our service contract for networked laser printers cost too much for the usage we got out of it.

- The amount of paper waste was staggering. We even saw cases where students would print a 50-page paper to multiple printers in the library and take it from whichever printer printed it out the fastest. People also frequently printed to the wrong printer, often several times, or there would be a jam and they'd print somewhere else, then the original job would print after the job was cleared, and other problems.

- The administrative overhead of keeping track of copier codes and charging back departments was a burden and also an annoyance for people wanting to use the copier that they had to input a code each time.

2.3 Goals for the Managed Print system

The IT and purchasing departments created the following goals for the program:

- Design the system in such a way that sharing devices would be natural and encouraged.

- Centralize supplies and maintenance, removing those burdens from department budgets and saving money due to bulk purchasing.

- Eliminate as many inkjets from campus as possible.

- Reduce overall printer inventory and focus on fewer, more efficient printers.

- Make printers much more available to students, including copying and scanning functions as well as color printing.

2.4 Challenges to overcome

In order to accomplish our goals, we knew there would be some difficult cultural challenges to overcome and we underestimated just how big of roadblocks these would be.

- Less convenient printing for employees – anything less than a printer on every person's desk would mean less convenience.

- Need for confidential printing.

- Taking away printers in good working order.

- Loss of control over which printers go where for departments.

- Switching to printers as shared community devices rather than devices owned for private use.

- General resistance to change.

3. THE RFP Process

We proceeded with a typical campus committee and RFP, including several interested parties from around the college.

The committee narrowed it from approximately eight submissions to two finalists: Xerox and OfficeMax.

In addition to the usual sales pitches and meetings, we asked each vendor to visit one of our larger buildings (the same building for both vendors), speak with the employees, and then give us a full sample recommendation of what devices to place where based on those conversations.

The results of this activity were far more useful than any other part of the RFP process in choosing a winner. Comparing concrete details and peoples' experiences in speaking with the representatives gave us more actual data to discuss.

Even so, the committee was nearly split in half between what was seen as the safe choice (Xerox) and what seemed the better offering but was more risky (OfficeMax). OfficeMax was seen as more risky since they hadn't been in the managed print business for nearly as long and weren't as focused on it as Xerox. However, we also thought they would be more vendor agnostic than Xerox. In the end, only one vote tipped the balance between the two, and we chose OfficeMax.

3.1 Lessons learned

If we were to do this RFP again, we would put less emphasis on reviewing the proposals and listening to the sales pitches and more emphasis on specific examples that are directly comparable. In fact, we'd put a blueprint for a building into the initial RFP and ask each company to give a recommended solution of devices and placement for that building given a set of criteria. This would greatly help in directly comparing the solutions.

4. IMPLEMENTATION

We began implementation in late Fall of 2011. We designed the implementation to be gradual in order to spread some of the initial investment and in order for the change to be slower and, we hoped, more palatable to the community. All told, it took us from Fall of 2011 to Fall of 2014 to complete the entire implementation.

We targeted areas with old or problematic devices first, starting with small buildings and houses with only a few employees and devices in order to get the process down and iron out any kinks. Once we felt good about that, we planned the next phase for big administrative buildings during the academic year, and academic buildings over the summer.

4.1 Selling it to campus

Before embarking on our implementation plan, we knew we had to sell the concept to campus. We decided that the best way to approach that was to emphasize the environmental sustainability goal of the program, since it aligned with a strategic goal of the institution and was something that most people on campus professed to care about, and to show the campus a specific example of the program working at our institution.

We started out by quietly conducting the process in our Facilities Services building. OfficeMax flew out a representative, who walked around with one of us from ITS to talk to each person about the goals of the program and what sort of features they needed from printing. The OfficeMax representative inventoried all existing devices and marked them on a blueprint we provided.

After the walkthroughs, OfficeMax sent their recommendation for how it should look. We modified it only slightly by changing one of the models, and then went back to the building to show anyone who was interested the plan. There wasn't much feedback at that time, so we proceeded with the plan and installed the new devices while simultaneously removing the old devices.

It was only after we had done this that we heard some negative feedback about the speed of the change and about wasting remaining toner and ink cartridges and getting rid of working printers. We assured people that the gains would more than make up for that loss, but they were not convinced and we knew we had to do better when we launched the Managed Print Services (MPS) program to the rest of campus.

We let it run for a couple of months and then went back and interviewed people. For the most part they were quite happy with the new system, realizing they didn't miss their small printers as much as they thought they would and enjoying the new devices which were more functional and faster than before. See the before and after blueprints for this sample building in Figures 1 and 2 at the end of this paper. We took some quotes from these customers, and then set about our plan for selling it to the campus.

After completing our pilot in Facilities, we presented the program to our sustainability council and asked them to write a letter of support. They did so, but seemed surprisingly uninvolved.

We created a website to emphasize the goals of the program, track progress toward those goals with a small section on energy savings for each building, and make sure that people had plenty of information to peruse and forewarning about the program rolling out across campus.

Finally, we decided at the last minute to not reclaim any budget dollars from departments, even though we were creating a new centralized budget for all printer device purchases, supplies, and maintenance. Our thought was that this extra incentive would be needed to help campus accept the program, and it's a good thing we decided that.

4.2 Common objections and how to respond

As we proceeded through the implementation, we heard many objections repeatedly, and became better at responding to them. At first we were a little flabbergasted at some of the things we heard, and it took us some time to realize that in many cases people did not raise their actual objections because it would have made them look bad to do so. Instead, they raised what seemed like more reasonable objections that they thought would stop the program instead of saying something more honest like "I really don't want to lose the convenience of printing right at my desk."

We learned that the best way to combat this tendency was to have a direct answer for all those objections and to actually give departments a choice about whether to participate in the program (with a lot of encouragement). It was a tough balance to strike, but we knew we had to use good negotiation skills in order to succeed and that if we came across as forcing the program it would fail regardless of its merits.

Here are the most common objections we heard and how we responded:

1. "I have to print confidential documents daily."

This was the most frequent of all and, though certainly legitimate in some cases, we knew very well that most people did not have multiple confidential documents to print daily.

Thankfully we had a ready answer, which was that all the new devices would support "secure print" – a feature which allows printers to set a password at the time of printing. The document is then held in the printer queue until the person goes physically to the printer to type in the password and release the job.

Even with this feature, some people considered it for a moment and then said they didn't think that was confidential enough. In every case, when asked to explain why, they could not do so beyond saying it was just their feeling.

2. "We can't move the printer to the hallway, anybody could come in off the street and make a copy, steal the paper, or destroy the printer with a crowbar or bat."

To this we responded that even if random people entered our buildings to make copies, steal paper, or even destroy the occasional printer, we would still come out ahead of where we are now so it's a risk we're willing to take. Since we were paying for everything out of a central budget, we were able to back that statement up.

We're now four years into the program and not a single printer has been destroyed with a crowbar or bat, and we're not aware of any paper theft. In some cases, this objection was so strong that we relented and put more devices behind closed doors than intended. Our thinking was to get through the implementation and then revisit moving the devices later on after people were more used to the program.

3. "Isn't getting rid of all these printers and not using their toner up a big waste?"

Our response touched on the efficiency of the new devices and how a quick transition would be beneficial, however, the waste of current resources should not be overlooked. Therefore, a plan to keep both set of devices was put into place. This not only allowed for the depletion of current inventory but a chance for the group to adjust to the new devices.

4. "Hordes of students will descend upon the printers and there will always be a line of 30 people trying to print when faculty need to use them in the morning."

We emphasized that everyone would now have access to many more printers and so could move to a different one if there were a line. We also said that we expected students to mostly use printers in hallways and public areas, so the devices we put in office areas would be used less frequently by students. Finally, we said that we'd definitely keep an eye on that and would adjust, including by adding more devices, if necessary.

5. "I bought this with department / grant money and you're not taking it away!"

We assured them that we aren't the printer brute squad and won't force them to give up the printer, then circled back to the environmental impact of those devices as well as the impact on their budget. If they use the MPS devices instead, they won't have to pay for supplies out of their budget any longer.

6. "I need a printer on my desk to do my job and I can't ever be in the position of waiting for someone else to print."

We reminded folks that they can also use other printers in the building if the one nearest them is in use. Sure, that's less convenient, but at least they'd have the option.

For some people we also tried to use restrooms as an analogy. Restrooms are something important to us all on a daily basis and something that we'd like to have as much privacy as possible for. However, none of us have our own private restroom in our office – we use shared facilities and it isn't so bad.

In addition to this Q&A, we also made sure to emphasize certain things to people as we discussed with them (we learned to do this as we went):

- Our goal is to make printing as efficient as we can without making it a burden.
- We'll watch how it's going and will make adjustments as needed, including adding devices if necessary.
- Think about those times when their printer is not working for some reason and how frustrating that is. In the new system, they just use a different printer nearby to get their immediate need met.
- This initiative aligns with our strategic goal of environmental sustainability; look at how much electricity these printers use.
- We let them keep all their current printers and use up the ink and toner – they let us know when to take them away.
- Departments can still buy more printers than this, but they'll have to pay for the supplies and maintenance. We recommend trying it out on just the managed print devices for a while – if it works, their department could save a lot of money for other things.

4.3 Lessons learned and recommendations
Here are some things we learned from the process and would recommend to anyone else embarking upon it:

- Get the sustainability council involved as early as possible so they are a driver of the process and more invested in it; this will help sell it to a community who will be skeptical.
- Do not underestimate how much resistance there will be to a change like this. For some reason, "on their desk" convenient printing is very important to people and they will surprise you with their vehemence in wanting to keep it.
- Let the change be gradual and allow people to use up the ink and toner in their current devices. This also allows them a safety blanket in the transition which is a big help in them agreeing to it. You will need to follow up periodically and ask if they have any printers ready to go away – be prepared for this to take several years, but you'll get there. People will be much more willing to let go after they see the new stuff isn't so bad and get used to it.
- If possible, do not reclaim the unused budget dollars from departments. The financial incentive was a big practical benefit, and you're going to need that.
- Make participating in the program a choice, rather than forced. We approached it this way and only one

department decided not to participate. A year later they changed their minds.

- Emphasize physically talking with as many people as possible rather than using email blasts, website information, and other impersonal communication methods. You need the opportunity to address those questions and concerns, and your demeanor can be calming to the worriers.
- On a similar note, make sure you talk to individual professors as much as possible, particularly about placement. We made the mistake of thinking that talking to staff assistants would be enough and ended up having to move a couple of printers from their originally planned locations (including performing slight renovation work). Even though we acted fast to fix those, they were political black eyes that we could have done without.
- Do not underestimate how difficult it is to enact culture change. Even now, four years into a successful implementation, we haven't been entirely successful in that regard. People still consider the nearest printer "theirs" and don't think to use another printer if that one is unavailable.
- A few people will fall on their sword for their desktop printer. When this happens, let it go – it shouldn't be too frequent and you want to focus on the overall implementation rather than convincing one stubborn person.

5. PAPERCUT IMPLEMENTATION
After we finished installing the last devices in summer of 2014, we heard feedback from students that printing was still a major pain point for them. Even though they technically had access to many more printers now, they still needed to know the names of each one and how to map it in order to print.

We'd been thinking about buying some form of print queueing and release software to save paper, so we looked for one that would also make it easier for students and employees to use the printer resources on campus.

We didn't do an official RFP this time, but we did look at 3 different options and ended up choosing PaperCut quickly based on the notion that we could have one printing queue on campus that could release to all our different printers provided that we install magnetic card readers.

We fast tracked the purchase and implementation as much as possible so we could have it ready for the beginning of the next academic year – it turned out to be one month late, but once we had it up and running in October of 2014 it worked rather well. We provided instructions for mapping to the one printer queue, and after doing that on their devices students could print anywhere they wanted without having to install additional printers. Furthermore, if they printed something and went to their nearest dorm printer to release it and it was jammed or out of order, they just had to walk to a different printer to release the job.

5.1 Paper saved, but volume increased
Now in its second year, PaperCut saves us about 300,000 sheets of paper per year (roughly 6.7% of our volume). It tracks this by print jobs that were sent to the queue but never released at a printer (since normally those would have printed out.)

However, we noticed a disturbing trend this year in that our overall volume for 2015-16 is almost 28% higher than it was in

2014-15. This is clearly not the direction we want to go, and although we're not actually sure about the reason for this large increase, we expect a big part of it is that PaperCut has made it easier to use printing resources on campus than ever before.

5.2 Lessons learned

PaperCut was a relatively smooth implementation, but one sticking point for us was the single queue system. In order to accomplish that you need to use a universal print driver which will work correctly with multiple different makes and models. In our case, we have mostly Xerox and HP devices.

PaperCut's recommendation was to have one queue for each type of device, but we thought that really diluted the value of what we were going for, so we put a lot of time into finding the right universal driver that would work for all our devices. We eventually found one, and while it's not completely perfect, it does the job well enough.

The other thing to watch out for is PaperCut on Macs – there are a few different ways it can be installed, and we originally chose the method that we thought easiest for end users. However, if people save their username and password to the Mac keychain (which almost all of them will), there are some things to be aware of:

First, if they mistype their password, there is no warning or password error; it will simply not function.

Similarly, when students change their password, PaperCut fails to work because the saved password is no longer valid and the Mac keychain will not recognize that. It's an easy fix (just delete the keychain item), but it's hard for people to know how to do that.

The Mac keychain has been and continues to be the biggest issue with our implementation, though it's actually more of a Mac issue than a PaperCut issue.

6. AWARENESS CAMPAIGN

Now that both Managed Print and PaperCut have been implemented – and we have more than a full year of good statistics – we're hoping to tackle print volume next and see if we can find ways to drive it down.

We approached the sustainability council again, and together decided to start an awareness campaign – the first step in reducing print volume is to make people aware of how much they are printing.

Starting in 2015-16 we pulled data and merged that into an email to every person on campus at the end of each semester. That email detailed how much the specific person printed compared to the average student and the average employee, and also how much we printed overall compared to the previous semester (see figure 3 for an example of this message.)

Names and data weren't shared; it was just a private notification for awareness purposes. Feedback about the campaign has been very positive, though we don't yet know if it will have any actual effect.

7. RESULTS SUMMARY

The Managed Print program has been very successful. In fact, much more successful than we originally predicted.

Goals (from 2.3):

- Design the system in such a way that sharing devices would be natural and encouraged.
    - o We succeeded in this design, but are still working on the culture change.

- Centralize supplies and maintenance, removing those burdens from department budgets and saving money due to bulk purchasing.
    - o Definite success here. All the supply orders are centralized, as is service / maintenance through OfficeMax, and it saves a lot of money.

- Eliminate as many inkjets from campus as possible.
    - o We eliminated over 90% of the inkjet printers on campus.

- Reduce overall printer inventory and focus on fewer, more efficient printers.
    - o Success (see table below.)

- Make printers much more available to students, including copying and scanning functions as well as color printing.
    - o Very successful, though we believe this has resulted in a large print volume increase.

Before	After
$471,000 / year on printing	$161,000 / year on printing
585 total printers	145 total printers
507,000 KWH / year of electricity on printing	256,000 KWH / year of electricity on printing

In its first full year, PaperCut saved 302,000 sheets of paper (6.7% of our total volume.)

2015-16 is our second year with PaperCut, and we're seeing an overall increase in the total volume printed of almost 28%.

8. CONCLUSION

It has been a long and difficult road, but despite everything the program was well worth doing and I would recommend it to other institutions. Depending on your "before" state, the savings can be staggering. We save $310,000 per year or 66% compared to before managed print, and nearly $20,000 per year less in electricity on top of that.

Despite all our efforts to change the culture, it remains quite stubborn. Printer emergencies are still printer emergencies, even with several other printers nearby – employees still only think of using the nearest printer to them and will panic when it stops working. As you might expect, students are adapting to the system much more quickly (especially students who had PaperCut available when they started as freshmen.)

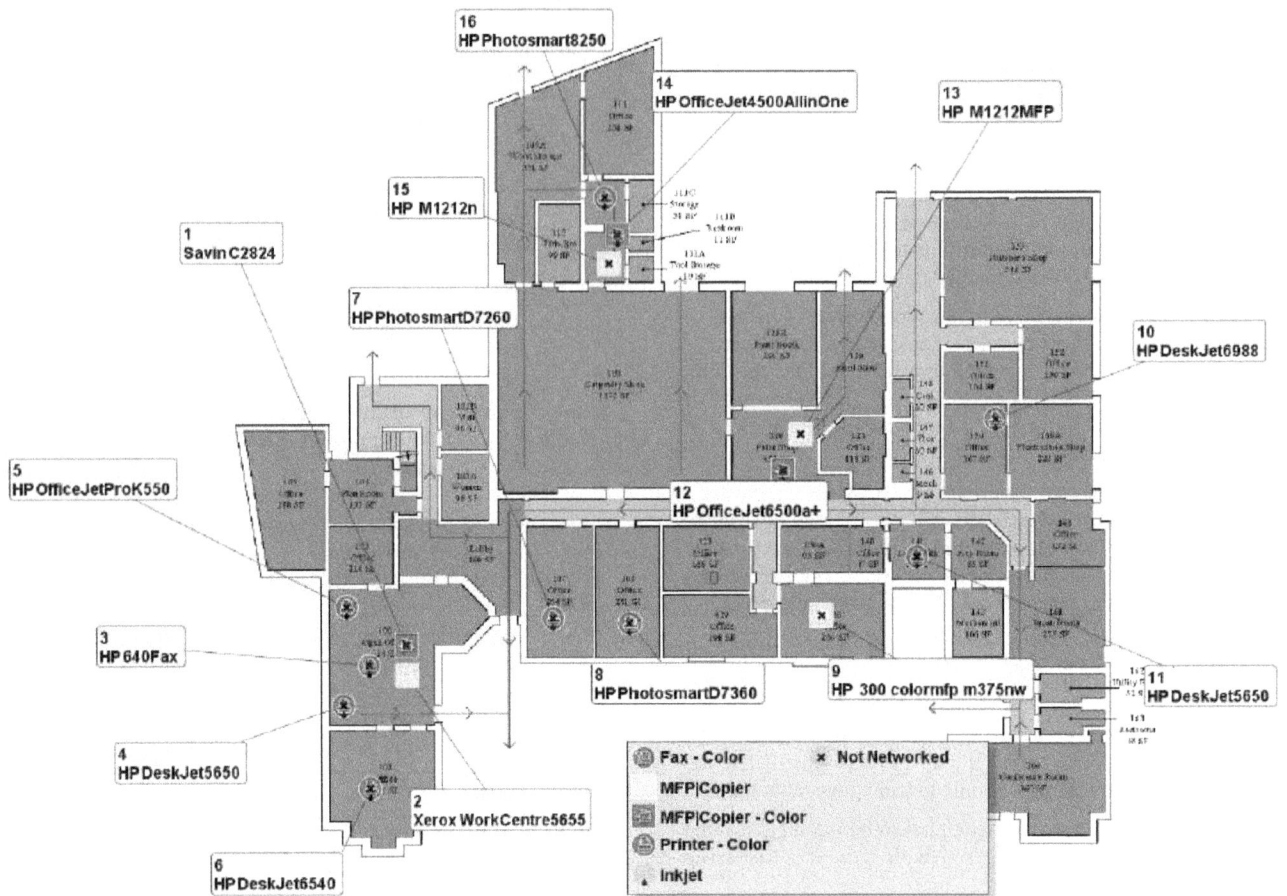

Figure 1. Building BEFORE managed print (16 devices)

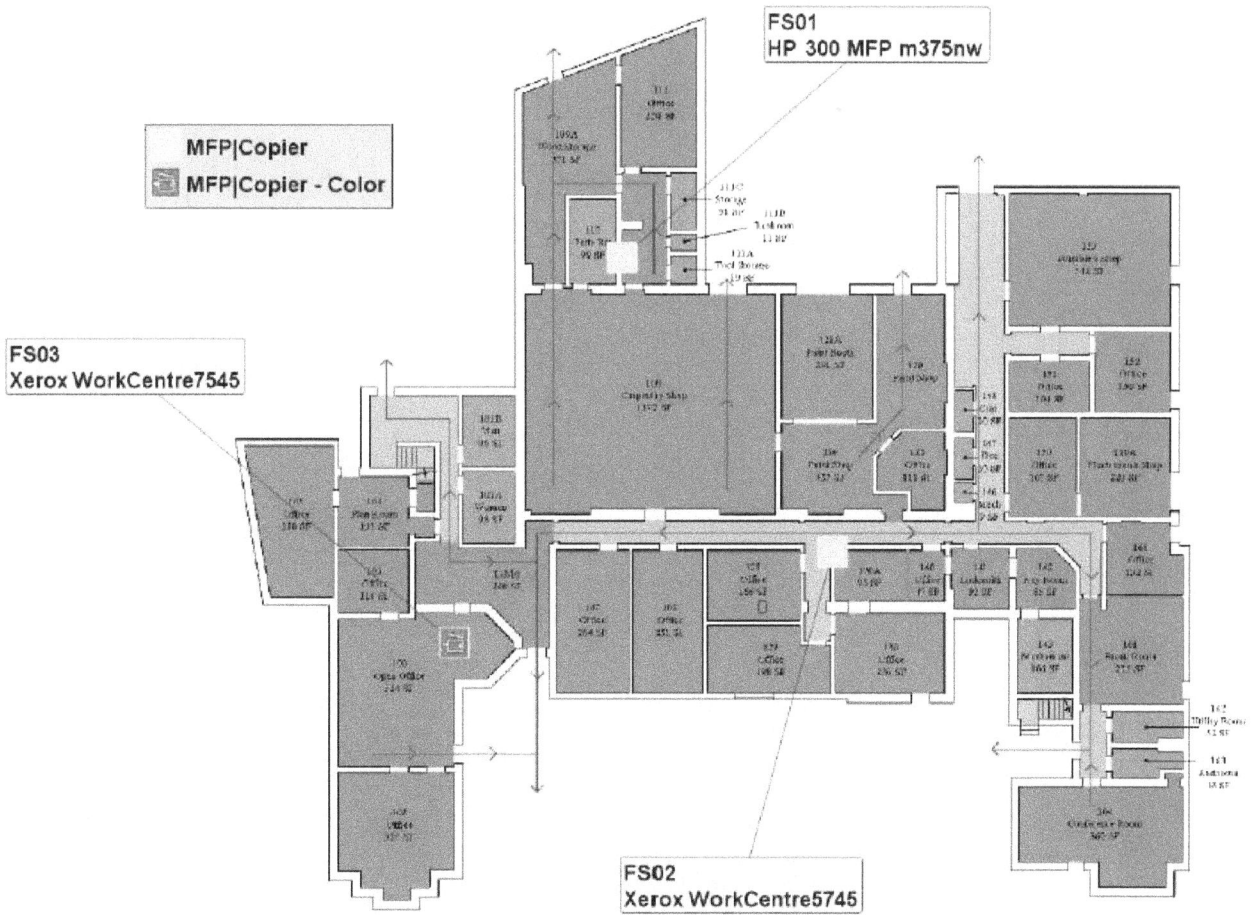

Figure 2. Same building AFTER managed print (3 devices)

The Sustainability Council is writing to let you know how much you have printed on networked printers at CC compared to the average **during Spring Semester 2016** (January through May). *Note: in most cases this number includes copies and faxes in the total.*

You printed: 1,**982** pages
The average CC employee printed: **3,243** pages (a 9% **increase** from last semester)
The average CC student printed: **1,184** pages (a 3% **decrease** from last semester)

Employees are responsible for **51%** of all pages printed; students for **49%**

Altogether, CC printed: **2,539,870** pages in Spring Semester 2016 (5,080 reams of paper, a stack 847 feet tall)! That's a 6% overall **increase** from last semester.

Thanks for helping CC with our commitment to sustainability by minimizing printing as much as possible!

Figure 3. Sample awareness campaign message

Monitoring and Analyzing Wi-Fi Availability and Performance on a University Campus Using Recycled Cell Phones to Aid Students in Selecting Study Areas

Shamar Ward
University Of The West-Indies Cave Hill Campus
Department Of Computer Science Mathematics and Physics
Cave Hill, Barbados
shamar.ward@mycavehill.uwi.edu

Mechelle Gittens
University Of The West-Indies Cave Hill Campus
Department Of Computer Science Mathematics and Physics
Cave Hill, Barbados
mechelle.gittens@cavehill.uwi.edu

ABSTRACT

Wi-Fi availability on university campuses has become increasingly important since services such as email and assignment submission portals for students require them to have internet access on and off campus. This is the case at the University of the West Indies - Cave Hill Campus (UWICHC) where students are required to conduct several online activities including submitting assignments, checking grades and registering for classes online. A survey of opinions of 115 UWICHC students indicated that 96% of the respondents use Wi-Fi to access student services offered by the campus. Ninety-four (94%) also indicated they would like to have access to Wi-Fi information on active hotspots and signal strength in various study areas. In this paper, we present a green system that uses recycled cell phones to collect information about the Wi-Fi status in study areas. The information includes Wi-Fi signal strength, connection speed, download speed and internet availability and is shown to students and staff using a web application. The web/mobile application also displays information on access points in various study areas on a geographical map of the campus. Additionally, the application analyzes the data collected and gives students and IT staff peak times when students encounter difficulty such as poor connectivity or no connection to the internet suggesting that an access point is damaged or needs to be reset. Such information is also beneficial to the IT Department and can increase their response time at the low costs gained from using recycled cell phones sensors.

Categories and Subject Descriptors

H.4.1[**INFORMATION SYSTEMS APPLICATIONS**]: Time management (e.g., calendars, schedules).

General Terms

Management, Monitoring, Student Notifications

Keywords

Wi-Fi Access; Wi-Fi Availability; University Campus; Web application.

1. INTRODUCTION

Many universities offer online services to their students and staff members. This has increased the need for reliable Wireless Fidelity (Wi-Fi) access on campus. Cost associated with the installation of Wi-Fi access points as mentioned by Wang et al. [1] can be high therefore not all areas used by students can be adequately covered. Therefore, students need easily accessible information about Wi-Fi status.

At the University of the West Indies – Cave Hill Campus (UWICHC), students can study both indoors and outdoors. Indoor locations such as classrooms and other reserved rooms are only available for use when they are not booked. As a result, students often have to relocate if a booked activity requires the room. In this case, if a student requires Wi-Fi access they will need to relocate to a Wi-Fi available area. Additionally, based on the students' needs (i.e.to download documents, access software or just browse), the student may need to find an area which not only has Wi-Fi available but has adequate signal and download speed for their intended activity.

One hundred and fifteen (115) UWICHC students were surveyed and ninety-four (94%) indicated that the availability of Wi-Fi access information would assist them in finding Wi-Fi access on-the-go. This could lead to a reduction of the time taken by a student to find a suitable study area allowing them more time to study.

2. SYSTEM REQUIREMENTS

From our survey we determined the functionality necessary to help students find study areas with Wi-Fi connectivity. Our survey of UWICHC students revealed that ninety-five (95%) of the participants use Wi-Fi on campus as shown in Figure 1.

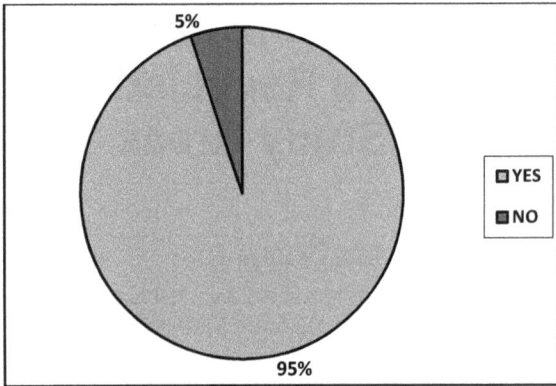

Figure 1 Responses to: Do you use Wi-Fi on campus?

It was also necessary to identify students' current experiences with the Wi-Fi availability on campus. We therefore asked: **How often can you find areas on campus with good Wi-Fi signal?**

Figure 2 shows that 58% of the respondents indicated they sometimes find good Wi-Fi signals on campus whereas 28% of students said they frequently find good Wi-Fi signals on campus. Additionally, 12% mentioned they find good Wi-Fi signal on campus infrequently and 2% said they never find good Wi-Fi signals.

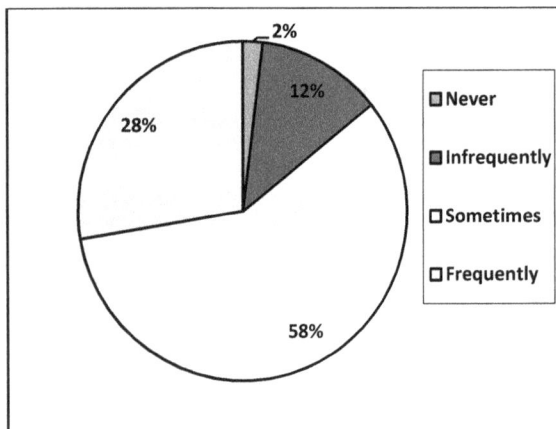

Figure 2 Responses to: How often can you find areas on campus with good Wi-Fi signal?

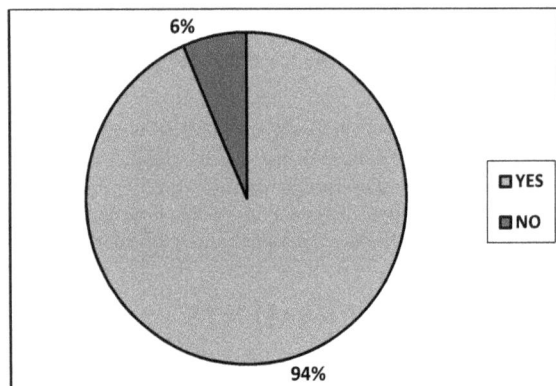

Figure 3 Responses to: Would having information on the active and good signal Wi-Fi areas be helpful.

In Figure 3 94% of students said that having information on good and active Wi-Fi signals would be helpful whilst 6% of students said having such information would not help them.

From this survey we gathered students would benefit from having information on Wi-Fi hotspots around the campus. We can get the following information from Wi-Fi routers:

- Mac Address
- IP Addresses
- Default Gateway
- Signal Strength
- Download Speed

However, only the signal strength and download speed would assist students in selecting their study area. We therefore designed our system to provide students with this information.

3. RELATED WORK

This section explores related work where geographical information is displayed on mobile devices. We also look at works where such Wi-Fi data and geographical data is stored and we examine how the databases are designed and structured. We also examine how other applications monitor and present Wi-Fi information.

3.1 Displaying Geographical Information

We performed a search for applications that deliver geographical information to students. Kestranek et al. developed a system to monitor the sound levels and the number of Wi-Fi connections in various areas to assist students with finding quiet areas to study[2]. This information was represented using the Google ® maps API, and students were able to query this system using short message service (SMS). We believe we can apply the use of the Google ® maps API since we will display similar information to students. In work by Salber et al. the authors developed a system capable of allowing students to track their colleagues and also see information on other resources such as print queues and vending machines[3]. In their work they displayed this information in a three panel view. As shown in Figure 4 the left panel shows the selected resources, the middle panel shows the query results and the right panel shows a geographical map displaying the resource.

Figure 4 Screenshot of Salber et al. application developed for students.

This work uses a map in conjunction with panels so that users can select their required results. This is a useful approach; however, users who have cell phones with small screens may find it difficult to use the multi-panel functionality. In work by Aloul et al. [4]. The authors developed a system capable of tracking persons via the use of their smartphones and attributes such as the following:

- International Mobile Equipment Identity (IMEI) number,
- International Mobile Subscriber Identity (IMSI) number
- Wi-Fi access point they are connected to

Aloul et al. also mentioned that GPS-based tracking systems have been widely implemented and used. However in indoor situations they fail to perform. Aloul et al. stated that others have suggested the use of Bluetooth and 3G technology as well as ultrasound as replacements. Since all of these wireless methods can be used, Wi-Fi would be more practical since Wi-Fi is widely deployed in most buildings[4]. By doing this it may reduce the cost of implementation. In this Wi-Fi supported system by Aloui et al. the only requirement was a Wi-Fi enabled mobile phone equipped with GSM functionality. The mobile application was developed using Java 2 Micro edition (J2ME) which runs on Sybian OS. They used a MySQL database which stored the location of the individual. With the application all the access points within range of the user's device are sent to the server along with the users' International Mobile Equipment Identity number (IMEI) and International Mobile Subscriber Identity number (IMSI) which is used as their identity. SMS requests can be used to check a person's location. The MAC address of the stored access point is returned which is stored in the database is displayed on the map. From this work we see that it is possible to show data stored in a database on a geographical map.

3.2 Database Design and Structure

We then examined how similar systems designed databases to hold the relevant geographical, and Wi-Fi information. Work by Kestranek et al.[2]revealed a system that monitors the sound levels in various areas to assist students with finding quiet areas to study. In this work Kestranek et al. used a MySQL database on an Apache server to store the noise levels and how many persons are currently logged into a given Wi-Fi access point[2]. However, in this work Kestranek et al. did not consider Wi-Fi to be an indicator for students. Therefore, the area might be noiseless and no persons are logged onto the Wi-Fi router because there is no connection available. Our survey indicates students would benefit from having information on Wi-Fi in study areas this could also have an impact on whether students use an area or not. Also in work by Aloul et al.[4] they used a MySQL database to store the location of the person that could then be displayed on a geographical map. We observed it is possible to store similar data to our Wi-Fi information in a MySQL database and represent it on a geographical map. We can use such an approach in our system to display the Wi-Fi status information to students.

3.2 Data Gathering

We also needed to review research done using systems that gathered Wi-Fi data for related activities such as helping with personal efficiencies. Research by Wang et al. uses cell phones connected to a Wi-Fi access point to determine the queue time of persons in a checkout line in a store[1]. They installed a Wi-Fi monitor close to the service desk and ignored signals with a dBm (decibel-milliwatts) greater than a threshold of -45. The MAC addresses were used to uniquely identify each cell phone carried by a person. Additionally, they stored the arrival time of each new customer and their length of time in the queue. Wang et al. also recognized long queues resulted in persons using their cell phones more and it would be much more difficult to use Bluetooth for such a study because more Bluetooth devices are automatically configured to be undiscoverable. However, Bluetooth is another option[1].The RSS trace showed a pattern in RSS for persons based on their distance from the service desk. It was observed the RSS slowly increased for a person who was in the queue and approaching the service point. While at the service point the RSS remained constant and when the person leaves the area the RSS dropped quickly. Wang et al. developed a mobile application and installed it on an Android mobile phone to send packets at a rate

of 10pkt (TCP data packets) per second. By using the power estimator by L. Zhang and et .al[5] that sending 10pkts every 5 min resulted in the consumption of power 54.3 Joule or 180mW.This work shows that it is possible to measure signal strength between devices. We can therefore measure signal strength from access points. Additionally, the work shows that cell phone battery data can be collected. This is important in our work to assess the status of a phone in operation.

3.2.1 Other WI-FI monitoring Applications
In their work Patro et al. measured the wireless experience in a home environment[6]. Previous wireless measurement work used passive sniffers however, Patro et al. gave 30 home users OpenWRT Wi-Fi access points (APs) equipped with network measurement and analysis software. By having software installed on an AP it can monitor traffic coming and out and into the network easily. This work does not take into consideration the user experience with a device external to the router. With our system we can monitor connection time since our devices are external to the router. Additionally, Patro et al. system does not provide this information to end users. Whereas in our application, the primary goal is to display information to users in real-time to assist them in decision making.

4. SYSTEM DESIGN

We were able to define the requirements of a system to satisfy student needs to identify spaces with Wi-Fi availability based on our survey of the students themselves and our survey of the literature. The system is therefore divided into four modules which are as follows:

1. Database structure
2. Collection of data
3. Device monitoring
4. Information delivery

These modules are defined in the sections that follow.

4.1 Database Structure

Our database was hosted on a Linux machine running the Ubuntu operating system. We used a MySQL database similar to the instance mentioned in Kestranek et al. [2] and the work by Aloul et al. [4]. Our database consisted of ten tables. Eight of these tables stored the signal data and download speeds from the four locations as shown below in Figure 4 and 5.

		Id	time	db	bars	response_code
Edit Copy Delete	63621	2016-05-02 11:43:55	-57	3	0
Edit Copy Delete	63622	2016-05-02 11:44:09	-60	3	0
Edit Copy Delete	63623	2016-05-02 11:44:24	-66	3	0
Edit Copy Delete	63624	2016-05-02 11:44:38	-66	3	0
Edit Copy Delete	63625	2016-05-02 11:44:53	-63	3	0
Edit Copy Delete	63626	2016-05-02 11:45:07	-62	3	0
Edit Copy Delete	63627	2016-05-02 11:45:21	-61	3	0
Edit Copy Delete	63628	2016-05-02 11:45:36	-63	3	0
Edit Copy Delete	63629	2016-05-02 11:45:50	-62	3	0

Figure 4: The table that stores the signal strength in decibels-milliwatts (dBm), the Wi-Fi bars and the response code at the given location.

id	date	load_time	download_speedb	download_speedkb	download_speedmb
48784	2016-04-05 06:17:38	34	82000.0	640.625	0.6256103515625
48785	2016-04-05 06:18:11	26	108000.0	843.75	0.823974609375
48786	2016-04-05 06:18:41	17	165000.0	1289.0625	1.25885009765625
48787	2016-04-05 06:21:48	29	97000.0	757.8125	0.74005126953125
48788	2016-04-05 06:22:18	26	108000.0	843.75	0.823974609375
48789	2016-04-05 06:22:48	25	112000.0	875.0	0.8544921875
48790	2016-04-05 06:22:52	31	91000.0	710.9375	0.69427490234375

Figure 5: The table that stores the load time of the UWICHC page in milliseconds and the download speeds in bytes, kilobytes and megabytes.

Our other two tables stored battery information recorded and location of the cell phone. The location of the cell phone is stored so map can be dynamically populated in the event a new location is added the map would not need to be altered.

4.2 Collecting the Data

In previous work [7] we repurposed an out-of-service, damaged cell phone as a door indicator. The cell phone was mounted outside of a computer lab and displayed the status (Available/Not Available) of the lab to students. We used repurposed cell phones here as well to collect data since this approach proved effective in the previous work and was also a low cost solution.

4.2.1. Device preparation

We performed a cell phone donation drive for one week to acquire cell phones for this project. We successfully acquired ten cell phones. However, we then evaluated each cell phone to see if it met our criteria for this system. Each cell phone we accepted had to meet the following preconditions:

1. The cell phone must turn on or boot up.
2. The cell phone must have functioning Wi-Fi capabilities.
3. The cell phone must be able to be recharged.

All cell phones which failed one or more of the criteria were stored to be repurposed in another application. The successfully cell phones were then categorized into operating system types i.e. (Android, Blackberry). An Android application was written and installed on the Android devices to test how long these devices would be able to stay "alive" and submit data to our server without human intervention. The mobile application sent a message to a server every minute. Most devices lasted six to seven days without needing to be reset or restarted. After this process was completed we then designed a mobile application to get the signal strength and to calculate the average download speed. We then deployed the devices in three areas as described in the following section.

4.2.2. Installation of device

Four (4) study areas where selected to have cell phones installed to perform Wi-Fi monitoring these are:

- Tree of Life (Outdoors)
- Sand Pit (Outdoors)
- Shuttle Stop (enclosed)
- Deck (enclosed)

Some study areas are outdoors as mentioned previously, therefore we needed to choose a weather proof housing for the cell phones. We selected 6 inch by 6 inch PVC electrical boxes (as seen in Figure 5) to house the devices since a 6 inch by 6 inch PVC box would easily house the largest cell phones received from our phone drive.

Figure 5: 6 inch by 6 inch PVC box used in study areas to house the cell phones.

The PVC boxes were then outfitted with a 110 volt electrical socket where the charger could be plugged in to maintain phone charge. A complete installation is shown in Figure 5.

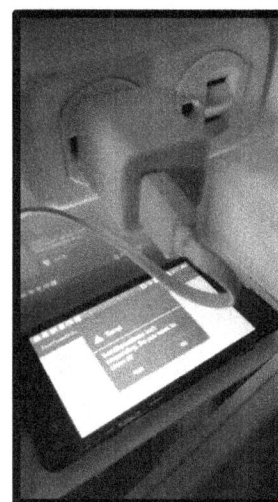

Figure 6: Full installation using a 6 inch by 6 inch PVC box with a 110volt electrical outlet and cell phone charger.

4.2.3. Data collection Application

Four (4) of the ten (10) cell phones passed these criteria and all used the Android operating system. We therefore designed an application to get the Wi-Fi signal strength and calculate the download speed. Our application had three versions which are explained in further detail below:

Version 1

This version of the application used the Android function `getRSSi()` to get the Wi-Fi signal which is measured using the measurement of received signal strength indicator (RSSI). We then used the Android function `calulatesignallevel()` to convert the RSSI value into approximated bars which could be better understood by the user. The application would run in a loop. After it got the Wi-Fi signal strength and submitted it to the database it would then download an Adobe Acrobat ® PDF file of approximately 1.5 megabytes. Before the download commenced a timer was set, after the download was completed the timer was stopped. This time was used to calculate the download speed. With this version we encountered one main issue. The cell phone CPU would go to sleep after 30 minutes. This is issue was resolved in version 2 as discussed below.

Version 2

In this subsequent version we addressed the CPU time out issue by using an Android background service which continues to run as long as the service is sending and receiving requests. However, we recognized the Android operating system can terminate a process which is too intensive and uses too much memory. We therefore needed to resolve this issue for the application to be fully functional and work continuously.

Version 3

In this final version we addressed the issue of the Android operating system killing the application by dividing the functions required into two applications, each calling the other when it was finished performing its task. Each application contained an Android function `Wakelock()` to keep the CPU alive. By restarting the application this would release the memory and therefore the Android operating system would not kill it for memory over use.

4.3 Device Monitoring

Throughout our testing and review of the applications performance we needed to be able to discern if the phone was on and functioning without physically entering the box. Additionally, we also needed to know the phone's battery status remotely to know if it is charging. We therefore designed three mechanisms to monitor each device and its status. These mechanisms are shown below.

4.3.1 Battery Status Indicator

The battery status indicator is used to monitor the battery status of the phone. Our custom application creates a battery level receiver to send the battery level of the phones to our server as a log. During our test there was a power outage at the UWICHC and the battery recorder logs recorded this outage.

4.3.2 Bluetooth Indicator

The Bluetooth indicator is used to identify if the device is still on but is not transmitting data to the server. Our application enables the cell phone to be discoverable indefinitely. Therefore to identify if the device is on, we simple go to that area and check for its Bluetooth signal before entering the box. If the Bluetooth signal exists we know the device is still on and is functioning. However, if it is not we would need to enter the box to identify the cause of the missing signal.

4.4 Information Delivery

From our previous work [7] we noted that students at the UWICHC use various mobile operating systems. Additionally, persons may want to use this application on a laptop and other devices which may not be catered to in a native mobile application. We therefore decided to use a web/mobile interface to deliver the information to students which are discussed below.

4.4.1 Web/Mobile Interface

We developed an application using Google ® maps API 3 to display the information to students. The Google ® map contained the four sample Wi-Fi points represented with red markers as shown in Figure 7.

Figure 7: Google map containing the four sample points as markers.

When one of the markers is clicked, the Wi-Fi signal and download speed at that point is displayed to the student as seen in Figure 8.

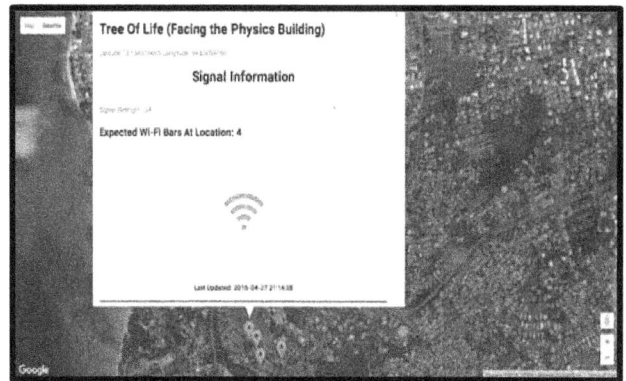

Figure 8: Google map containing the four sample points as markers and the Wi-Fi signal information at that point.

This popup not only contains the signal information, but on scrolling, indicates estimated download information (Figure 9).

We used a graphical depiction and textual data to help users gain a better understanding of download and signals. Based on the available Wi-Fi bars the graphic would change to indicate the number of bars available shown in Figure 10. Additionally a download speed above 500 kilobytes per second shows a green download arrow, whereas a download speed below 500 kilobytes shows a red download button as seen in Figure 9.

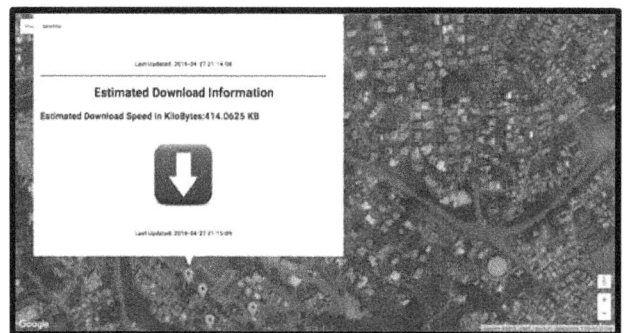

Figure 9: Google map containing the four sample points as markers and the estimated download information at that point.

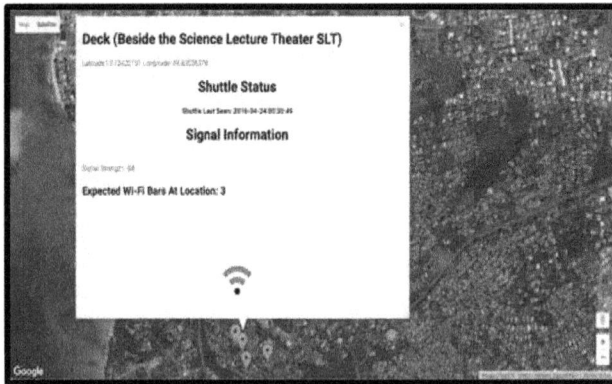

Figure 10: Google map containing the four sample points as markers and the Wi-Fi signal information at that point.

5. RESULTS

Five (5) UWICHC students from the Department of Computer Science, Mathematics, and Physics were selected to go to the study areas at random times to test the performance of the system. They used various devices such as a Motorola Xoom ® tablet, both Windows and MAC operating system devices and five smartphones with the Android operating system. All testers mentioned the Wi-Fi signal indicator worked well and matched their experience when they visited the location. One tester mentioned the system indicated there were no bars at the Tree of Life location and when they visited it there was no connection at all. However, one tester mentioned the last updated time is sometimes not as frequent as it should be and then there is uncertainty about the actual experience.

6. CONCLUSIONS AND FUTURE WORK

In our work we determined that it is possible to use damaged retired cell phones to monitor the Wi-Fi signal strength in a study area as well as the download speed. We also showed that it was possible to display the results on a geographical map in real-time. We asked the five (5) UWICHC student testers who used the application their opinions. All testers were satisfied with our systems' performance and said it would be useful in finding study areas with good Wi-Fi signal, and an active internet connection. By using a web mobile application this reduced the cost of acquiring access to developer testing platform. In the future we will expand the number of sample points from four, giving students more information. Additionally, we will investigate other methods of detecting Wi-Fi signals in various areas other than using a fixed device.

7. LIMITATIONS OF THE STUDY

Our primary limitation in this work was the number of cell phones we had available . We received ten cell phones however, only four were usable for the requirements. This limited how many areas we were able to monitor and advise students about.

8. ACKNOWLEDGMENTS

We would like to acknowledge all the participants of the survey and the Director of Security at UWICHC Mr Oral Reid for his guidance in securing aspects of the project on the campus. Additionally we would like to thank Mr. Ian Estwick from the Campus Maintenance Department for assisting us with the installation of the PVC boxes and the 110v electrical outlets.

9. REFERENCES

[1]   Wang, Y., Yang, J., Chen, Y., Liu, H., Gruteser, M. and Martin, R. P. Tracking human queues using single-point signal monitoring. In *Proceedings of the Proceedings of the 12th annual international conference on Mobile systems, applications, and services* (Bretton Woods, New Hampshire, USA, 2014). ACM,.

[2]   Kestranek, D., Clark, R. J., Sanders, M., Poole, E. S., Marquardt, P., Rabun, J. and Rhodes, J. Spaces Without Faces. In *Proceedings of the Proceedings of the 13th International Conference on Human Computer Interaction with Mobile Devices and Services* (Stockholm, Sweden, 2011). ACM.

[3]   SALBER Daniel, S. D., SMAILAGIC Asim *Supporting Mobile Workgroups on a Wireless Campus.* IBM T.J. Watson Research Center City, 2001.

[4]   Aloul, F., Sagahyroon, A., Al-Shami, A., Al-Midfa, I. and Moutassem, R. Using mobiles for on campus location tracking. In *Proceedings of the Proceedings of the 7th International Conference on Advances in Mobile Computing and Multimedia* (Kuala Lumpur, Malaysia, 2009). ACM.

[5]   Zhang, L., Tiwana, B., Qian, Z., Wang, Z., Dick, R. P., Mao, Z. M. and Yang, L. Accurate online power estimation and automatic battery behavior based power model generation for smartphones. In *Proceedings of the Proceedings of the eighth IEEE/ACM/IFIP international conference on Hardware/software codesign and system synthesis* (Scottsdale, Arizona, USA, 2010). ACM.

[6]   Patro, A., Govindan, S. and Banerjee, S. Observing home wireless experience through WiFi APs. In *Proceedings of the Proceedings of the 19th annual international conference on Mobile computing & networking* (Miami, Florida, USA, 2013). ACM.

[7]   Ward, S. A. and Gittens, M. A Real-time Application to Predict and Notify Students about the Present and Future Availability of Workspaces on a University Campus. In *Proceedings of the Proceedings of the 2015 ACM Annual Conference on SIGUCCS* (St. Petersburg, Florida, USA, 2015). ACM.

An Analysis of Relationship between Storage Usage Distribution and Per-User Quota Value

Yoshiaki Kasahara
Kyushu University
6-10-1 Hakozaki, Higashi-ku
Fukuoka 812-8581, Japan
+81 92 642 2297
kasahara.yoshiaki.820@m.kyushu-u.ac.jp

Takuya Kawatani
Kyosan Electric Manufacturing Co, Ltd.
2-29-1 Heiancho, Tsurumi-ku
Yokohama 230-0031, Japan
t-kawatani@kyudai.jp

Eisuke Ito
Kyushu University
6-10-1 Hakozaki, Higashi-ku
Fukuoka 812-8581, Japan
+81 92 642 4037
ito.eisuke.523@m.kyushu-u.ac.jp

Koichi Shimozono
Kagoshima University
1-21-24 Korimoto
Kagoshima 890-8580, Japan
+81 99 285 7477
simozono@cc.kagoshima-u.ac.jp

ABSTRACT

To prevent resource (especially storage) shortage, information systems such as storage services and email services usually impose an upper bound of resource consumption (quota) per user. In a conservative way, an administrator tends to set a quota value such as the storage capacity divided by the expected maximum number of users for safety and fairness, but it tends to leave large unused storage space, because the users' storage usage pattern shows a long-tailed distribution. In this paper, we analyzed storage usage distribution of some email services to approximate the distribution using a power-law distribution, and proposed a method to calculate an optimal quota value from a target size of storage consumption to increase storage utilization. We applied an optimal quota value we calculated to a real email service and analyzed the effect of quota change. Then, we analyzed actual distributions further to find a better model to approximate the distribution, and found that a log-normal distribution explained the distribution better than power-law. We also analyzed two other universities' email service to find similar distribution in these systems.

Keywords

Email System; Storage Quota Management; Long-Tail Distribution

1. INTRODUCTION

It is always important to distribute available resources efficiently and effectively. Computer systems are no exception. Computational power and storage become cheaper every year, but still it is important to utilize resources efficiently. In this paper, we

focus on storage capacity and utilization of multiuser system. From users' perspectives, it is convenient if they can use as much capacity as possible, but the actual storage capacity of a system is usually limited. To prevent shortage of storage space in a service system, the administrator of the service system usually sets user quota as an upper limit of usable space for each user.

Especially for an on-premise system, the total available storage capacity is decided at the initial system installation, and usually it cannot be expanded on-demand. To avoid service failure caused by resource exhaustion, the administrator tends to set a conservative quota value such as the total storage capacity divided by the expected maximum number of users. But it is not common that all the user equally uses up to their quota value. In many information systems, users' storage utilization patterns exhibit a long-tailed distribution. Only a fraction of users (heavy users) use up their quota, and most of remaining users do not use the system much. In consequence of such a long-tailed usage pattern, applying a conservative quota value causes low utilization of the overall storage resource. On the other hand, it is hard to increase the quota value properly without a guideline.

In this research, we analyzed users' storage consumption of our email services in order to estimate the optimal quota value, which improves the utilization of the storage capacity. Specifically, we analyzed the storage usage history of a university-wide email system (called "Primary Mail Service") in Kyushu University [1][2]. In our previous work [3], we also analyzed our file sharing service (a kind of file storage service), but this time we focus on email systems. After that, we discussed how to estimate the optimal quota value setting which improve the utilization efficiency of storage resource based on per-user storage consumption distribution. By modeling the distribution, we could estimate the optimal quota value from the number of users and the whole storage capacity.

The rest of this paper is organized as follows. In section 2, we introduce our email services in Kyushu University, which are the target of our analysis. In section 3 we analyze the distribution of per-user storage usage in these systems, and how we estimate storage usage using a power-law distribution. In section 4, we analyze storage usage distribution of the current email service further. In section 5, we present two other examples from other universities. In section 6, we describe some related studies. Finally, we present our conclusion and future works in section 7.

2. TARGET SYSTEMS
In this research, we analyzed the university-wide email system at Kyushu University. In this section, first we briefly introduce the number of staff members and students in Kyushu University, which is the number of users for these systems. Next, we describe the details of our (previous and current) mail services.

2.1 Number of users in Kyushu University
Table 1 shows the approximate number of IDs issued by the university-wide authentication service [4] in Kyushu University as of January 2015. The number also represents the number of users of the mail system.

Table 1. The number of IDs in Kyushu Univ. (Jan. 2015)

Role	Total No. of IDs (approx.)
Curricular students	19,000
Non-curricular students	500
Faculty and staff members	9,000
Non-employee workers	1,000
Total	30,500

2.2 Kyushu University Primary Mail Service
Similar to other universities, Kyushu University provides a campus-wide email service as a basis of communication infrastructure. In this paper, we analyzed two services. One is the previous email service operated from July 2009 and March 2014. The other is the current email service operated from March 2014 until now. The details of both services and migration were presented in the previous SIGUCCS [2].

2.2.1 The previous email service
The previous email service was constructed based on Mirapoint appliance servers. The users of this system were staff members (including faculty) only. There was another email service for students, but due to lack of usage history, we could not analyze the storage usage of students in the previous service.

Table 2 shows some numbers related to the resource and limitation of the system from July 2009 to March 2014. The column of "Date" denotes when the values of the row had become in effect. The system provided SMTP, POP, and webmail for free. From January 2011, a premium service class for paid users was started. The service included 10GB quota without message expiration, and IMAP support. In April 2013, the quota value was expanded to 20GB due to requests from paid users.

Furthermore, the quota value was actually a "soft" limit, which meant that a user could store messages even after the using storage size exceeded the quota value. The system sent a warning message to the mailbox of such a user, but didn't block further incoming message. It was because there was a retention period for messages of non-paid users, and expired messages were automatically removed from the system.

Table 2. Resources and limitations (previous service)

Date	Jul. 2009~	Dec. 2009~	Feb. 2011~
Total storage	1,200 GB	1,200 GB	2,600 GB
User quota	100 MB	100 MB	300 MB
Expiration	30 days	60 days	60 days
Max. message size	20 MB/message		

2.2.2 The current email service
The current email service was mainly built using open source software such as Postfix, Dovecot, Squirrelmail, and Roundcube on dozens of CentOS Linux servers. This service supports both staff members and students. Internally, staff members and students are handled separately (by using different VMs and separate NAS storage partitions), but both systems share the physical infrastructure.

Table 3 shows some numbers related to the resource and limitation of the current email service. The column of "Date" denotes when the values of the row had become in effect. The different limitation between staff members and students is the maximum size of a message only. The quota value is "hard" limit in this service, so users whose mailbox reached the quota limit cannot receive further email messages until they remove some messages. Similar to the previous email service, there is a premium service class for paid users which expands the quota value to 40GB.

Table 3. Resources and limitations (current service)

Date	Apr. 2014~	Mar. 2015~	Nov. 2015~
Total storage	10 TB (staff members) + 10 TB (students)		
User quota	1 GB	4 GB	8 GB
Expiration	Never		
Max. message size	20 MB(staff members) / 10 MB (students)		

3. STORAGE USAGE ANALYSIS AND ESTIMATION
The previous mail service had recorded storage usage per user from May 2009 to March 2014 (until the end of the service) every day. By using the record, we first analyzed the situation of storage usage in this system. Then, we approximate the distribution using a power-law distribution (for simplicity) and developed a relationship between a user quota value and estimated storage usage under the specified quota value. By using the relationship, we can determine more optimal quota value for a target size of storage.

3.1 Actual storage usage distribution of the previous email service
We sorted each user's amount of storage usage in descending order and plotted a log-log scale graph with the vertical axis of usage amount and the horizontal axis of the user rank. For example, Figure 1 shows the distribution on January 27th, 2014.

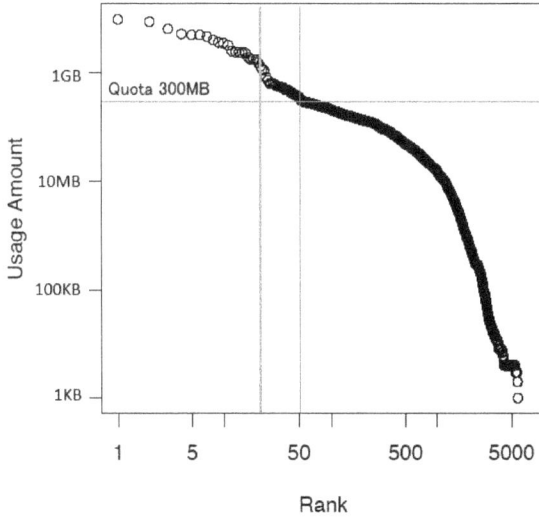

Figure 1. Previous mail service: rank-usage (log-log) (Jan. 27th, 2014).

The red horizontal line in Figure 1 indicates the quota value (300MB) of non-paid (ordinary) users. The blue vertical line indicates the rank (54th) where the user's storage usage exceeded the quota value. The rank 1st to 54th consisted of two user groups. All the users from 1st to 24th (the green vertical line) were paid users whose quota value was 10GB, and actually used more than 300MB. Users from 25th to 54th were non-paid (ordinary) users except one paid user, but they exceeded their quota value of 300MB. As described before, it was because the quota value was a "soft" limit. The system sent a warning message to the mailbox of such a user, but didn't block further incoming message or delete old messages automatically. To simplify the discussion, we will exclude users using more than 300MB and inactive users who didn't use storage space.

3.2 Storage usage estimation

In this section, we discuss the relationship between storage usage and quota value. The actual storage consumption among users wasn't homogeneous as shown in section 3.1. It was like a long-tail distribution such that only a fraction of users used up to their quota limit and most of users only used little space. Based on the distribution, we tried to estimate a quota value to increase the storage utilization.

3.2.1 Symbols for modeling
We use the following symbols for modeling.

S: Target size of storage usage

u_i: Storage usage amount for user i ($i = 1 \dots n$)

U: Actual total usage ($U = \sum u_i$)

q: Quota value for users

S denotes the target storage space decided by an administrator, and it is not the total amount of storage in the system. For example, there is storage of capacity 1TB in a mail system, and the administrator thinks users may use up to 75% of the total capacity, then S is set to 750GB.

3.2.2 Approximation by Power-Law Distribution
First, we approximated the distribution as a power-law distribution. Figure 1 doesn't seem like a linear graph as a whole, but the partial graph with higher ranked users (~500) seems almost linear, and these are dominant users to use most of storage space. In addition, we could simplify calculation using a power-law distribution, because we can represent the distribution by two values (intercept and slope).

Figure 2 shows a concept of storage usage estimation. It shows the relationship between the real distribution and approximation in a log-log plot. The vertical axis is the usage amount of each user and the horizontal axis is the rank of the user by the usage amount. The line P denotes approximated usage values by a power-law distribution. We suppose the intercept of the line P as q (quota value), and calculate the slope (a scaling exponent a) by using the real distribution observed.

A power-law distribution is represented by (1).

$$y = f(x) = qx^a, \qquad (1)$$

where a is a scaling exponent. To take logarithm of both side of (1), it is transformed as follows:

$$\log y = \log qx^a = a \log x + \log q. \qquad (2)$$

Let $Y = \log y$, $X = \log x$, $Q = \log q$, then we obtain

$$Y = aX + Q. \qquad (3)$$

Equation (3) is a linear function with gradient a and intercept Q, so we could simplify the estimation.

The sum of all bars equals to U, and the area under the line P is an estimated usage amount U'. The difference between each bar and the line P is the error of estimation. We could make sure that the line P was always above all the bar, then the error became an extra capacity margin. Also please note that the graph is in log-log scale, so the error is relatively small because most of error part is in the lower right part of the graph.

By using an estimation by a power-law distribution (1), the total estimated usage amount U' is as follows:

$$U' = \sum_{x=1}^{n} f(x) = q \sum_{x=1}^{n} x^a \qquad (4)$$

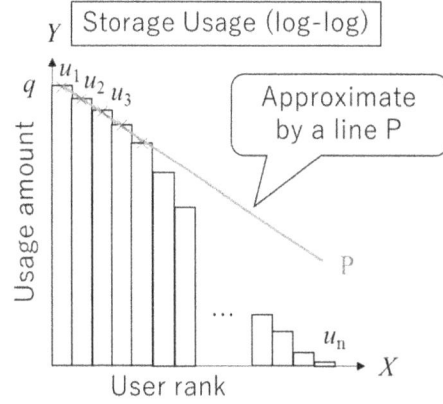

Figure 2. Concept of storage usage estimation

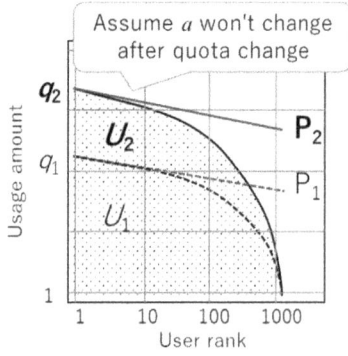

Figure 3. Distribution change after increasing the quota

3.2.3 Estimation of the optimal quota value

Consider changing the quota value from q_1 to q_2 ($q_1 < q_2$) in order to increase the storage utilization. Let U_2 as the storage usage when the quota value was changed to q_2. We need to select q_2 where U_2 won't exceed the target capacity S while increasing storage utilization.

Let us discuss how the usage distribution would change after changing the quota value using Figure 3. After changing the quota value from q_1 to q_2, users' usage distribution would form new distribution. P_1 denotes an approximated distribution under the quota value q_1. If new distribution retains a similar gradient under the quota value q_2, the distribution will be similar to P_2. There is another possibility that it will become a distribution with a steeper gradient, but a steeper gradient means less storage consumption. To change the quota value in order to increase storage utilization, it is better to use an estimation which over-estimates users' consumption. So we assume the gradient won't change after quota change.

By using (4), we can estimate new quota value q_2 with the target size of storage usage S as follows:

$$q_2 = \frac{S}{\sum_{x=1}^{n} x^a} \qquad (5)$$

3.2.4 Example using the previous email service

In this section, we use an actual distribution from our previous email service to calculate the scaling exponent a. We used the usage distribution as of January 27th, 2014. To simplify, we excluded paid users, users whose usage was exceeded their quota value, and inactive users who stored nothing in the system. The number of remaining ordinary users was 4,139.

We used R [5] for nonlinear regression analyses to estimate the gradient of the power-law distribution. We used only the top 400 users for the estimation, because adding lower rank users will make the gradient unnecessarily steeper. At the result, we got the gradient (scaling exponent) as $a = -0.404485$.

On January 27th, 2014, the actual storage usage of ordinary users we took into consideration was 70GB. We calculated the value of U' by (4) with the gradient -0.40 and we got $U' = 71.91$GB.

If we want to set the target size of storage usage S as 2,000GB, we could estimate the optimal quota value as about 8.1GB by (5).

3.3 Applying to an actual service

When we had the result in section 3.2.4, our mail system had already been replaced to the current email service. So we decided to change the quota value of the current service in March 2015 (1GB at that time) to 4GB at first. The current service had 10TB storage, so even 8GB quota (~2TB target) seemed fine, but we thought we should be cautious because it is harder to reduce the expanded quota value later. Before the quota change, the entire storage consumption (sum of all the users) was increased 700MB/day in the email service for staff members. After the change, it was increased to 2GB/day. It was because top 100 heavy users had already hit 1GB quota, and they started to accumulate more messages after the quota change. Such increase rate was not a big issue, so we concluded that it should be safe to expand the quota again, and we changed the quota value to 8GB in Nov. 2015.

3.3.1 Comparison of distributions before and after quota change

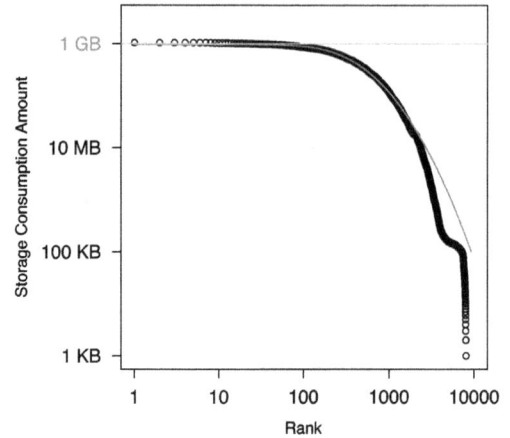

Figure 4. Distribution before quota change (Mar. 2015)

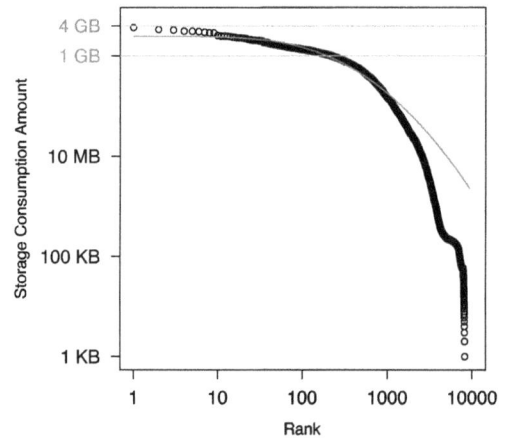

Figure 5. Distribution after quota change (Aug. 2015)

Figure 4 and Figure 5 shows distributions before and after the quota change (please disregard a curved red line for now). As mentioned before, in Figure 4 the top 100 users had already hit the quota value (1GB). That means an approximation by a power-law distribution might not be appropriate because the estimated scaling exponent becomes too shallow, which causes too much over-estimation. On the other hand, in Figure 5 most users don't hit their quota yet, and power-law estimation seems reasonable. We are still collecting data after changing the quota (twice) for our future work.

4. BETTER THAN POWER-LAW

In this section, we analyze storage usage distribution of the current email service further. In previous sections, we used a power-law distribution to approximate the actual storage usage distribution, but it is too simplified. In addition to a power-law, we selected other long-tail distributions including log-normal and exponential distributions, and performed nonlinear regression analyses to find the best fit distribution among them. Again we used R [5] for nonlinear regression analyses, and also calculated the value of AIC (Akaike's Information Criterion) to evaluate the fitness. Among candidates, the model with the smallest AIC value is the optimal model.

Table 4. AIC values of the email service for staff members

Date	Log-normal	Exponential	Power-law
2014-12	190567	181296	240136
2015-03	189127	175907	241305
2015-04	220443	213468	262697
2015-07	223660	225381	247474
2015-10	225128	228030	253537

Table 5. AIC values of the email service for students

Date	Log-normal	Exponential	Power-law
2014-12	403469	442402	485569
2015-03	399326	438545	480637
2015-04	473582	521261	571332
2015-07	405774	451361	479651
2015-10	429753	473030	499305

Table 4 and Table 5 shows AIC values calculated for each distribution with parameters obtained by nonlinear regression analyses. The double line between Mar. 2015 and Apr. 2015 denotes the quota change from 1GB to 4GB, and colored cells are considered the optimal. For the email service for staff members, both exponential and log-normal were close and better than power-law, and for students, log-normal was always the best. By these results, we considered that approximation by a log-normal distribution was generally the best. Possibly the change between log-normal and exponential was caused by hitting quota (because most students were not affected by the quota value), but we don't have a good explanation yet. Red curves in Figure 4 and Figure 5 show estimated log-normal distributions.

5. SYSTEMS IN OTHER UNIVERSITIES

In section 4, we showed that a log-normal distribution fit with the actual storage usage distribution of the email system in Kyushu University. In this section, we analyzed other universities' data to see if this feature is not local to our university. Two universities (Kagoshima Univ. and Shizuoka Univ.) provided their data.

5.1 Kagoshima University

Kagoshima University provides mail service to staff members using "DEEPMail". The total amount of storage capacity is 2TB, and the user quota is 1GB. A quota alert message will be sent to a user when the user's storage usage exceeds 800MB. We received

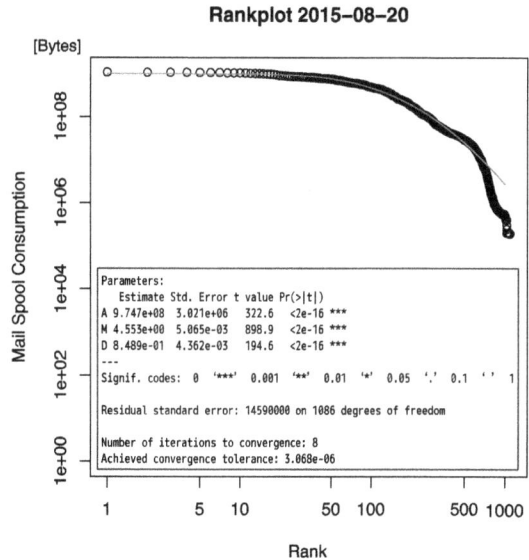

Figure 6. Kagoshima Univ.: rank-usage (log-log) (Aug. 20th, 2015).

storage usage data from Mar. 2015 to Aug. 2015. Similar to section 4, we estimated the distribution of storage usage by a nonlinear regression analysis. Figure 6 is an example of actual distribution graph. The red line in the graph denotes the estimated log-normal distribution. We concluded that log-normal distribution estimated the actual distribution the best.

5.2 Shizuoka University

We also received one-day sample data of email storage usage from Shizuoka University. The data included 1,643 students of Faculty of Informatics, Shizuoka University. The quota value was 200MB. We estimated the distribution of storage usage by a nonlinear regression analysis. Figure 7 is the actual distribution graph. The red line in the graph denotes the estimated log-normal distribution. We concluded that log-normal distribution estimated the actual distribution the best, too.

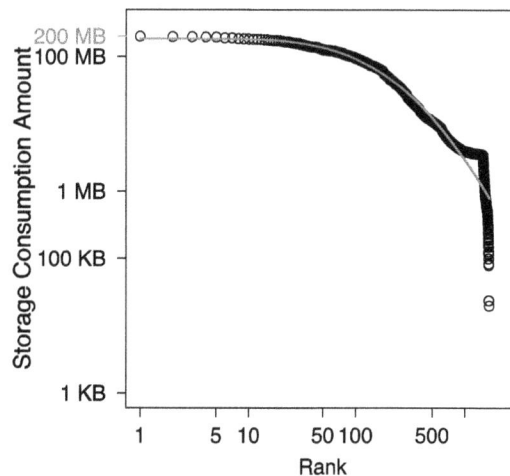

Figure 7. Shizuoka Univ.: rank-usage (log-log)

157

Of course, we cannot conclude only with these result that a log-normal distribution is a universal feature of email storage usage distribution, but at least we can say it is not local to our university, and it might be a good candidate as a hypothesis.

6. RELATED WORK

In article [6], Mitzenmacher mentioned that file size distributions were best modelled by a power-law distribution or a log-normal distribution. He surveyed about log-normal distribution and power-law distribution and reported that these distributions appeared frequently in various phenomena studied in economics and natural science. Also he showed that log-normal distributions had arisen as a possible alternative to power law. In our work, we also confirmed that user's storage usage distribution matched well with log-normal distribution in mail system and file sharing system of Kyushu University. As Mitzenmacher described in [6], we also didn't know an explicit model why the distribution was similar to log-normal distribution. It is our future work to establish a user behavioral model to explain how the distribution is formed.

In article [7], Kuninaka, et al. mentioned that a log-normal distribution appeared in various complex systems. They showed that many phenomena considered to be a normal distribution were actually fit better to a log-normal distribution. For example, people's height distribution was considered to be a normal distribution, but children's height distribution in a growth period fit better to a log-normal distribution. Also they showed that log-normal was more appropriate than power law or Zipf's law for representing population of cities [8]. User's storage usage could be considered to be in a growth period because it grows in time course, and might form a log-normal distribution. We want to study that more closely later.

In article [9], McKnight discussed future planning of storage preparation in information systems. He showed that "(total volume size) = (number of users) * (user quota) * 1.4" is a reasonable starting point for the initial purchase. It was based on his professional experience as a data storage administrator, and the reasoning was not discussed.

7. CONCLUSION

In this research, we analyzed the actual storage usage of email system and proposed a method to estimate overall storage usage from the user quota value by using power-law approximation. We also showed that a log-normal distribution is more suitable to approximate the storage usage distribution of various email system.

As a future work, we want to realize the relationship between three parameters of log-normal distribution (A, μ, and σ) and the quota value. Without the relationship, we cannot use a log-normal approximation to determine the optimal quota value. Actually we should be able to obtain a "bell curve" of a normal distribution using an appropriate log-scale histogram of the actual storage usage distribution if it is a log-normal distribution, and we can observe the change of parameters through the history of usage.

Another problem is the reason why a storage usage distribution exhibits a log-normal distribution. Especially for email system, a user's social network might influence the number and size of messages. Possibly such a network theory will explain the distribution.

8. ACKNOWLEDGMENTS

Our thanks to all the users using our mail services, and staff members of the Primary Mail Service working group to develop and maintain these systems in Information Infrastructure Initiative of Kyushu University. Also we appreciate Kagoshima University and Shizuoka University which kindly provided their usage data of email services.

9. REFERENCES

[1] Fujimura, N., Togawa, T., Kasahara, Y., and Ito, E. 2012. Introduction and experience with the Primary Mail Service based on their names for students. In *Proceedings of the SIGUCCS 2012* (Memphis, TN, October 17 - 19, 2012). ACM, New York, NY, 11-14. DOI= http://dx.doi.org/10.1145/2382456.2382460.

[2] Kasahara, Y., Ito, E., and Fujimura, N. 2014. Introduction of New Kyushu University Primary Mail Service for Staff Members and Students. In *Proceedings of the SIGUCCS 2014* (Salt Lake City, UT, November 2 - 7, 2014). ACM, New York, NY, 103-106. DOI= http://dx.doi.org/10.1145/2661172.2662965.

[3] Kasahara, Y., Kawatani, T., Ito, E., Simozono, K., and Fujimura, N. 2015. Optimization of Storage Quota Based on User's Usage Distribution, In *Proceedings of the 2015 IEEE 39th Annual Computer Software and Applications Conference Workshops (COMPSACW 2015)*, 149-154. DOI=http://dx.doi.org/10.1109/COMPSAC.2015.221

[4] Ito, E., Kasahara, Y., and Fujimura, N. 2013. Implementation and operation of the Kyushu university authentication system. In *Proceedings of the SIGUCCS 2013* (Chicago, IL, November 3 - 8, 2013). ACM, New York, NY, 137-142. DOI=http://dx.doi.org/10.1145/2504776.2504788.

[5] The R project for statistical computing, http://www.r-project.org/.

[6] Mitzenmacher, M. 2004. A brief history of generative models for power law and lognormal distributions. *Internet Mathematics*, 1, 2, 226-251. DOI=http://dx.doi.org/10.1080/15427951.2004.10129088

[7] Kobayashi, N., Kuninaka, H., Wakita, J., and Matsushita, M. 2011. Statistical features of complex systems–toward establishing sociological physics–. *Journal of the Physical Society of Japan*, 80, 7, 072001. DOI=http://dx.doi.org/10.1143/JPSJ.80.072001.

[8] Kuninaka, H. and Matsushita, M. 2008. Why does Zipf's law break down in rank-size distribution of cities?. *Journal of the Physical Society of Japan*, 77, 11, 114801. DOI=http://dx.doi.org/10.1143/JPSJ.77.114801.

[9] McKnight, C. J. 2006. Cost analysis and long term planning over the lifecycle of an enterprise storage solution. *Journal of Technology Management & Innovation*, 1, 5, 87-95.

The Road to Building AV Support in Higher Ed

Raymond Pfaff
Senior Audio Visual Technologist
NYU Steinhardt
26 Washington Place, 5th Floor
New York, NY 10003
212-998-5796
raymond.pfaff@nyu.edu

ABSTRACT

This paper will discuss the formation and continuing evolution of Steinhardt Technology Services' Audio Visual (AV) Support Service. This service was created in response to New York University's technology enhanced education initiative. The Steinhardt School of Culture, Education and Human Development leveraged this initiative in order to grow their Technology Services catalog by offering AV support. This decision was influenced by a large increase of support requests for Steinhardt's learning spaces. Steinhardt Learning Spaces are physical spaces on campus with installed technology that are used by faculty, staff, and researchers. The AV Support Service was formed in April of 2015 and this paper will delve into the successes and challenges of spearheading a new technology-based service within higher education and the various changes that have occurred in the last year (2015-2016). The expansion of the service from a single full-time staff member to the addition of two part-time workers will be addressed, and subsequent changes to internal operating procedures will also be outlined. Analytics pulled from our ticketing system will help to illustrate the growth of the service as well as the diversification of requests including troubleshooting, event support, training, and technology instructional recommendations. We will also discuss what changes need to take place going forward and how the service will need to grow in order to accommodate the increased demand for AV support.

Categories and Subject Descriptors

K.6.2 [**Management of Computing and Information Systems**]: Installation Management – *computing equipment management.*

General Terms

Management, Performance, Human Factors, Standardization.

Keywords

AV Support, System Design, Instructional Design, Dispatch, Onboarding, Metrics, Trends, Zendesk.

1. INTRODUCTION: WHO WE ARE AS A SCHOOL AND AS A TEAM

The Steinhardt School of Culture, Education and Human Development was founded in 1890 at the heart of New York University's campus in Greenwich Village, New York. Formerly known as NYU School of Education, it is the first institution within the United States to be created with the focus of pedagogy as a form of study. NYU Steinhardt is home to eleven academic departments spanning across disciplines like Communicative Science and Disorders, Education, Humanities and the Performing Arts. The university is home to 5,934 students from over eighty different countries.[1] The student body consists of 47.57% master's students and 42.77% undergraduate.[1] The faculty consists of 291 full-time members.[1]

Steinhardt Technology Services' (STS) Audio Visual (AV) Support Team creates, supports and maintains installed technology equipment in all Steinhardt learning spaces as well as provides scheduled and on-demand training and demonstrations. The AV Support team offers troubleshooting support for community members having problems with equipment. Currently, there are 90 learning spaces in 9 buildings throughout Steinhardt's eleven academic departments. There are 591 End Users (291 faculty members and 300 staff) that use these spaces throughout the year for a variety of needs. The function of these spaces ranges from:

- **Presentation** – Having the capability to present media from a room computer or one's own device to either a single or multiple displays.
- **Video Conferencing** – Having the capability to conduct a video conference call through an application-based platform such as BlueJeans or Google Hangouts to a fully integrated codec system such as Polycom.
- **Specialized** – Locations that exist exclusively for the needs of a department.

2. DATA GATHERING TO UNDERSTAND THE CULTURE AND COMMUNITY

Before we could improve and grow the AV support service we needed to understand existing trends. To start, our biggest interest was determining how many tickets STS was receiving a month for AV support and which departments were requesting the support. We pulled all AV tickets from Zendesk, our ticketing sysem and categorized closed tickets based on building, departments, and learning spaces.

We also needed to collect an inventory of Steinhardt Learning Spaces. This process resulted in a significant spreadsheet, which by the time it was completed, thoroughly documented over 90 learning spaces, all organized by location, room number and department. We would later use this document to map out the scale of our service as well as the diversity of our required knowledge of this technology. With our inventory spreadsheet the team could now search for a space and pull information on the associated department, contact information for the overseer of the space from that department, full hardware list of technology within the space, supported software, whether or not it was under a service contract with an AV vendor, and the start and end date of those contracts.

In order to provide the best service we needed to meet with each department and to discuss their needs and concerns for their learning spaces. To make the most of these conversations we pulled reports from Zendesk, which focused on the time frame of Fall 2014 to Spring 2015, which helped cultivate an understanding. While this was a small sample size, it helped us gain perspective on the amount of tickets received throughout the year.

We wanted to create a data visualization from 2014/2015 to 2015/2016. [Table 1]

Fall 2014 saw a total number of tickets very close to the number received during the Spring of 2015. Prior to the Spring 2015 semester our IT group, in addition to their standard workload, handled these tickets. Our tags up until that point were simply tracking whether or not requests for AV support were being received. As a result, we were not able to see who was actually requesting the support.

Table 1. Solved AV Support Tickets 2014 – 2016 [2]

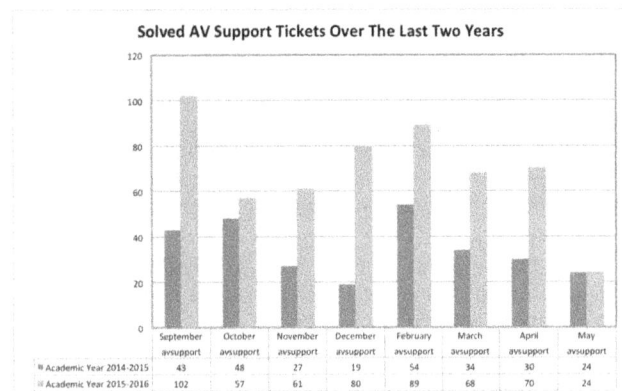

In the Fall of 2015, there was a total of 102 AV tickets resolved in September alone (doubled from a year ago). This rise in ticket volume presented a unique opportunity to begin analyzing data to identify trends. The first piece of data we needed to identify was who was requesting the help. Once that information was gathered, we could dive into what they needed in order to feel more empowered and technologically independent and capable.

By generating reports within Zendesk we were able to see where our tickets were coming from and who was sending them. As the graph below shows, of the 102 tickets in the month of September 82 came from three buildings.

Table 2. Solved AV Support Tickets by Location in September 2015 [2]

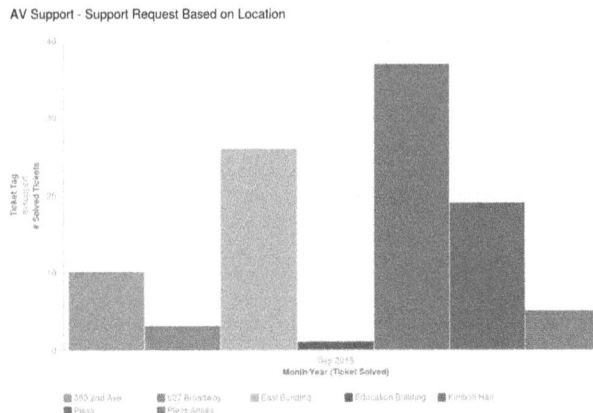

Of those 82 tickets, four departments were accounting for 86.5% of the total. One department in particular immediately caught my attention, Applied Psychology.

Table 3. Solved AV Support Tickets By Department in September 2015 [2]

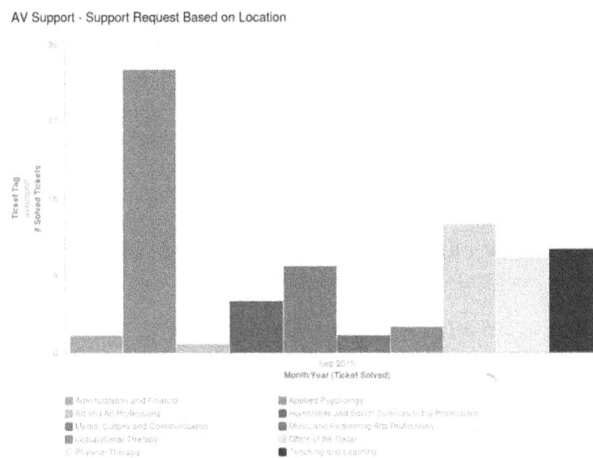

With 33 tickets from the Applied Psychology department, we decided the best course of action was to schedule meetings with the department to discuss this trend. We wanted to spend time getting to know their administrative team, the issues they face, and articulate regarding support. Those initial conversations grew into a series of scheduled discussions between our team and other Steinhardt departments throughout the Fall 2015.

What I quickly learned was that we needed to change the perspective the departments held regarding what kind of support they can receive and when they could request it. Throughout the months of October and November 2015, we continued to conduct one-on-one meetings and focus groups with different faculty members and administrative teams. From the discussion transcripts we were able to pull the following anecdotal information:

- For many faculty members the departmental administrators are their first line of tech support.

- Many faculty members will depend on admins to submit tickets on their behalf.

- Most administrators are too busy to aid immediately or not properly trained to resolve the issue.

- Most administrators would like to be better trained but want to break the cycle of being viewed as support technicians.

- Both administrators and faculty feel this pattern causes heavy stress during the start of a class or event.

- Administrators did not look to place blame but simply viewed the current situation as the way things are

Through these conversations, I realized the majority of the departments that did report issues had little confidence that an issue requiring immediate attention would be resolved within a timely matter. The departments that did not report their issues were unaware that Steinhardt Technology Services offered support for learning spaces. It was at this time that I realized that in order to be successful at developing an AV support group, I would need a strong relationship with the administrators to not only bring them into the fold of reporting issues appropriately but to also gain their confidence in instituting change.

A noted point of frustration for administrators was the number of issues their faculty members had with using the rooms. They would only reach out to our AV support group in the moment they were experiencing technical issues or confusion in handling the technology in the rooms. This created a heavy, time-sensitive strain on courses and meetings in session. This approach was restricting their use of our learning space's capabilities as well as their perception of what AV support could do for them.

These realizations led to an effort to change the culture of communication regarding learning space issues. We conducted follow-up discussions to urge the departments to reach out regardless if they had dealt with a similar issue in the past. The importance of each individual reporting his or her own needs via email or placing a call to our 2HELP number was stressed. Most importantly, we encouraged staff and faculty to contact us in advance of their class or meeting. If the community contacted us outside of their moment of crisis we could change their experience and grow our services.

3. USING DATA TO IMPROVE SERVICES

As each month passed, our requests for support continued to grow and, in most cases, more than doubled that of the previous year (See Table.1). During this time, proactive measures began to help remove the notion of AV support existing only for troubleshooting. In Spring 2015 we generated our first set of required tags for AV Support. Required tags such as building location and requester's associated department allowed us to begin to collect information that would show us where our tickets were coming from.

Starting in December, we began to refine the categorization of AV Support tags by specifying the type of support needed. While this did not result in a complete categorization, it did reveal that AV Support was shifting to a proactive service. We began to provide pre and post semester preventative maintenance, troubleshooting and multiple forms of training. At the time of this publication, the following chart highlights the full list of support services for AV Support at Steinhardt.

Table 4. AV Support Type Tags

Tag	Description
preventative maintenance	Maintenance regarding morning tech checks or pre semester full Preventative Maintenance initiatives. The ticket type should always be listed as a "Task"
troubleshooting	Troubleshooting should be considered any assessment based work done within a space to diagnosis a reported issue (post)
dispatch	Dispatch should be considered any instance in which a technician needs to be on site, on the phone, virtually through Teamviewer
indvidualtraining	All AV tickets that are facilitated via a one on one training
grouptraining	All AV tickets that are facilitated via a group training
standby	Standby would be considered any in advance request for technical assistance. An issue is not necessarily present.
consultation	Any instance where an agent meets with a member of a department to discuss support
backupequipment	Any equipment brought into a room because of a failure ie, backup projector
documentation	Creation of any documentation for a learning space (instructions, room overview guide, etc)
install	When technology is being installed into a learning space
servicecalls	AV Vendor has to come to service room

In February, we began tagging according to specific issues. This resulted in more accurate totals for analysis. Out of the 91 AV Support tickets solved during the month of February, our biggest recurring issues that were related to hardware were in the form of Crestron, projectors and room computers. This data allowed for us to plan the phasing out of the current component and began researching optimal replacements.

Table 5. Solved AV Support Tickets By Specific Issue in February 2016 [2]

AV Support - Specific Issue Breakdown

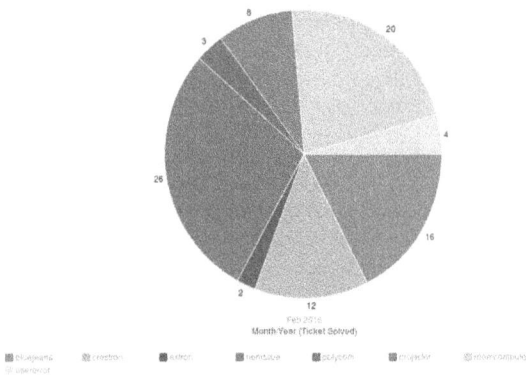

Data from the month of February revealed that the majority of requests were NonIssue, which is defined as a request for AV evaluation, training or other future events. These requests were not related to troubleshooting or user error.

4. WHICH SERVICES WERE ADDED AND WHAT OPERATIONAL PROCEDURES CHANGED?

In the Fall of 2015, two student workers and I made our way through all 90 learning spaces. We ran needed system updates, replaced damaged cables and conducted exhaust system checks. It also marked the first phase of our Learning Space onboarding and branding.

During the process, we created a form of documentation called Room Overview Guides. These documents cover the data we collected during our inventorying during the summer to provide a visual representation of a room to our end-users. These guides cover information such as the department contact, the functionality of the space, the room capacity and key features. At this time we also branded the rooms by placing STS backgrounds on all room computers as well as help stickers by the room controls with our contact information. [3]

The data we collected for February 2016 showed that our community was receptive to change. Communication through room overview guides and proper space branding helped bridge the gap and allowed for us to communicate with more people. In the end, both the end-users and our team are winners thanks to our efforts in January. This triumph, however, did not remove the work still to be done.

Our goal has always been to support teaching and learning with technology. Spring 2016 semester revealed major strides in responding to issues, proactively providing support to our community before an issue occurred, and preparedness for the future. After conducting training sessions with each department prior to the start of the semester, we began to break new ground in redefining our AV support culture. By sharing our data with each department as it relates to their requests, we were able to target their most pressing needs and help them plan for the future. We also created internal documents to improve knowledge transfer and communication. These covered specific topics, frequently asked questions, room functionality, etc.

For example, in the case of Applied Psychology, they needed additional support for video conferencing in the Spring. We worked with the administrators to map out all of the known dates video conference calls would be occurring so that we could schedule an AV technician to be onsite. We also conducted additional one-on-one training for those faculty members who would be facilitating the calls. This involved:

- Creating Bluejeans accounts for the faculty
- Showing them how to use the video conference interface
- Reviewing the setup of the room they would be using
- Most importantly, how to help their colleagues who would be joining them on the other end of the call should they experience any issues.

This approach resulted in more faculty members not only adopting our standard software platforms (such as Bluejeans over Skype) but also allowed for faculty to become more independent knowing they have easy access to support through every phase of the process.

Furthermore, in Spring 2016 we designed the first easy-to-use videoconference room based off of the data we had gathered from all of our video conferencing support tickets. [4]

5. CONCLUSION & LOOKING TO THE FUTURE

Now that we have covered the first full year of Steinhardt's AV Support service and explored the obstacles we have overcome, we approach the question of "Where do you go from here?" In order to answer that question, I think it is important to acknowledge the success we have had thus far. Our success in growing a service from a secondary task to a dedicated full-time position offering multiple forms of support (and still growing) is illustrative of the success of our efforts. The key factors in the success of this service were communication and time spent creating strong community ties. Without buy-in from Steinhardt's core departments on both an administrative level and faculty level, the needed cultural shift would not have occurred to allow all of this to be possible. Their trust in our team allowed us to focus on creating new standards of service and redefining daily practice to better train our staff and ultimately better serve them.

Overall, we have been able to improve the community's perspective of AV Support solely being a dispatch-based service. By having both administrators and faculty involved in our consultation options, training, and scheduled standby services, we have been able to reduce our dispatch call totals throughout the spring semester. In February, dispatch accounted for 50% of all appropriately tagged tickets. This exceeds the number of dispatch tickets in May and June (which were around 30%). There is a direct correlation between this decrease and the rise of other service trends. With preventative maintenance and standby accounting for over 35% of April's tickets, we see a sharp drop in May's total dispatch calls during the busy month of finals. At this time we see standby solidify itself at 30% of total tickets for two months, making it just as prevalent as dispatch. At this point, we see that our efforts to grow our service are yielding positive results. There is still more work to be done to ensure more accurate data, improved performance and eventually set standards to ensure minimal emergency dispatch calls. Our future can now be dictated by only the limits of our efforts and creativity.

162

As our unique skill sets continue to grow and we continue to foster our key cultural values, we are able to gain a new perspective and address current trends more holistically and most importantly, keep pace with the ever-changing tech landscape of higher education. In short, where do we go from here? We go forward and with each step we become better equipped to proactively, rather than reactively solve AV support issues at NYU Steinhardt.

6. ACKNOWLEDGMENTS

Thanks to Jeffrey Lane, Ben Vien and Ilana Levinson for their guidance and trust. Also, thank you to the past and current members of Steinhardt Technology Services IT and AT group for all their hard work year round.

7. REFERENCES

[1] Web Site: http://steinhardt.nyu.edu/about/at_a_glance July 22, 2016

[2] Web Site: https://steinhardt.zendesk.com July 22, 2016

[3] Web Site: http://steinhardt.nyu.edu/technology/learning_spaces

September 14, 2016

[4] Web Site: https://steinhardt.zendesk.com/hc/en-us/articles/214255143 September 14, 2016

2016: A Site Odyssey

Sara May

University of Rochester

44 Celebration Drive, Suite 3.100

Rochester, NY 14620

sara.may@rochester.edu

ABSTRACT

What started as the creation of a service catalog turned into a full-scale website redesign in a new web content management system. Join the University of Rochester on a three-year journey to map information technology services in a decentralized, multi-campus environment. Along the way, we will excavate the remains of bygone websites, wade through political waters, conquer mountains of content, explore information architecture, and navigate the bumpy roads of change.

CCS Concepts

• Information systems~Web searching and information discovery • Information systems~Service discovery and interfaces • Human-centered computing~User interface design • General and reference~General conference proceedings • *Social and professional topics~Project and people management* • *General and reference~Evaluation* • Human-centered computing~Usability testing • Social and professional topics~Centralization / decentralization

Keywords

service catalog; website; website redesign; information architecture; content; communication; usability; web writing; change management

1. INTRODUCTION

The University of Rochester (UR) is a private research university comprising seven schools, a regional medical center, and a civic art museum on seven campuses in western New York. Information technology (IT) support for the University's 11,000 students and 23,000 faculty and staff is decentralized. There are two main IT organizations: University IT, which is the central IT department, and Information Systems Division, which supports the Medical Center and its affiliates. There are a number of smaller IT groups that support the specific needs of certain divisions and a center that provides supercomputing services for researchers throughout UR.

Given the complexity of the institution and its IT support model, clearly communicating the unique set of IT services available to each user is a significant challenge. As the EDUCAUSE Center

SIGUCCS '16, November 06-09, 2016, Denver, CO, USA

© 2016 ACM. ISBN 978-1-4503-4095-3/16/11...$15.00

DOI: http://dx.doi.org/10.1145/2974927.2974941

for Analysis and Research IT Service Catalog (ECAR-SC) Working Group considered, how do you present IT services "to a wide variety of users across multiple schools, campuses, and departments, each with access to a distinct set of services delivered by a variety of service providers?" [1]

2. BUILDING A SERVICE CATALOG

In 2013, University IT decided to create an IT service catalog to better represent IT services to users in this decentralized environment. "The IT service catalog is in many ways the front door of IT," the ECAR-SC Working Group notes. "It is a vehicle used to communicate and provide clarity to constituents about the IT services available to them [and] to help improve customer relations by sharing information and setting expectations." [1]

2.1 Research and Analysis

While compiling a list of IT services and their providers, the Help Desk invited distributed IT staff and users who frequently contact the Help Desk to discuss what they look for from the University IT website and what they would ideally like to see in a service catalog. Users identified an icon/category-based search and an index-based search as the two methods of organization they would prefer to navigate IT services. A usability practitioner then conducted a heuristic assessment [5] to suggest service categories, organization, and primary and secondary details that should be provided about each service.

2.2 Design and Development

Based on this research, the Help Desk developed their first service catalog prototype [6] with three design goals: helping users learn about a service, request/stop a service, and find and compare the cost of similar services. The team initially focused on just centrally provided services to accelerate the prototyping phase and prove the service catalog's value; then they would seek buy-in from distributed IT service providers.

The first prototype included 12 service categories, each containing several sub-categories. There were also options to navigate by alphabetical list (index) or service provider. Each catalog listing included the following service attributes:

(1) Service name
(2) Service description
(3) Service provider
(4) Cost
(5) Contact information for service owner
(6) Link for more information

The team then conducted usability testing where they asked faculty, staff, and student users to interact with the prototype. In individual sessions, users were presented with scenarios [7] to see if they understood the service categories. For instance, when presenting a user with the scenario of getting a NetID for a new employee, would the user go the Accounts service category?

Then, users were asked to complete specific tasks to see if the web interface design met the goals. For example, faculty test users were asked, "You have a DVD player delivered to your room for every class, but you changed your curriculum and no longer need it. How can you cancel the delivery for the rest of the semester?"

Results of the first round of usability testing showed users were struggling with how services were organized and with the association between some of the icons and categories. It often took several attempts before users could find the correct service when navigating by category, which users most preferred. Users also did not find value in browsing services by service provider; they just wanted to find the service that was available to them, regardless of who supported it.

So the team conducted a card sort exercise [3] to better understand how faculty, staff, and students would organize and navigate IT services. In concurrent group sessions, each user was given about 25 cards with one service written on each card. Users were asked to group the services in any way that was meaningful to them, then label the groups using blank cards.

The team developed a second prototype using the naming and grouping patterns that emerged from the card sort and incorporating the other feedback from the scenario sessions. Then they repeated the process of usability testing and prototyping again.

2.3 Results

Service catalog navigation improved with each iteration. Users were able to find what they were looking for faster with fewer attempts. However, while users found the idea of a service catalog helpful in navigating IT services, they quickly became confused when they clicked for more information about a service, which took them out of the service catalog and into the University IT website. Users also remained unsure which services were available to them in their specific roles.

Ultimately, we determined we were not thinking big enough. Over the years, as University IT reorganized and its service portfolio grew, its website lagged behind with no clear owner or vision. By the beginning of 2015, the University IT website was in many different templates at once—every iteration of the site's design over the past 15 years—creating a fractured image of the department and a confusing experience for users. Dozens of web editors maintained sections of the website in three content management systems, which caused numerous inefficiencies and inconsistencies. Duplicative and at times contradictory content was strewn throughout the site. Search results were clogged with years' worth of irrelevant and/or outdated information.

Creating a stand-alone service catalog without touching the website that contains all the service details was like putting a fresh coat of paint on a house with a crumbling foundation. The service catalog was only addressing the surface of the problem while leaving the larger issues of usability, information architecture, and the accuracy and sustainability of service information to worsen.

3. BUILDING A SERVICE CATALOG... TAKE 2

A new team, composed of IT communications staff and a web developer, worked alongside the Help Desk manager to develop a new approach that would address both the need for a service catalog and the entrenched issues with the website.

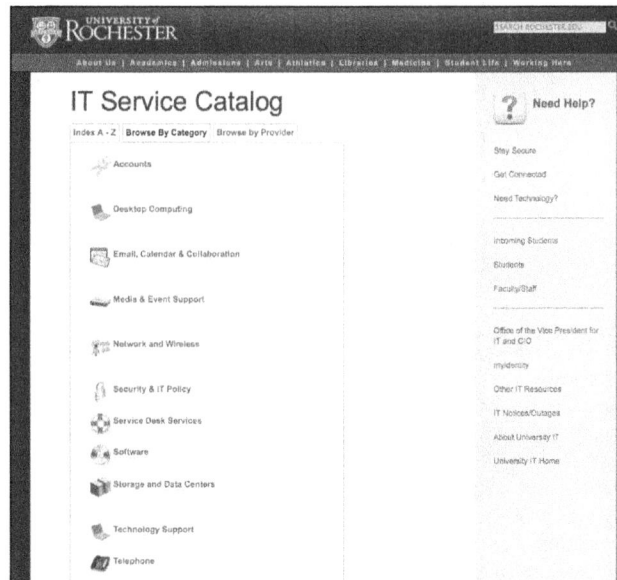

Figure 1. First service catalog prototype: homepage on category view

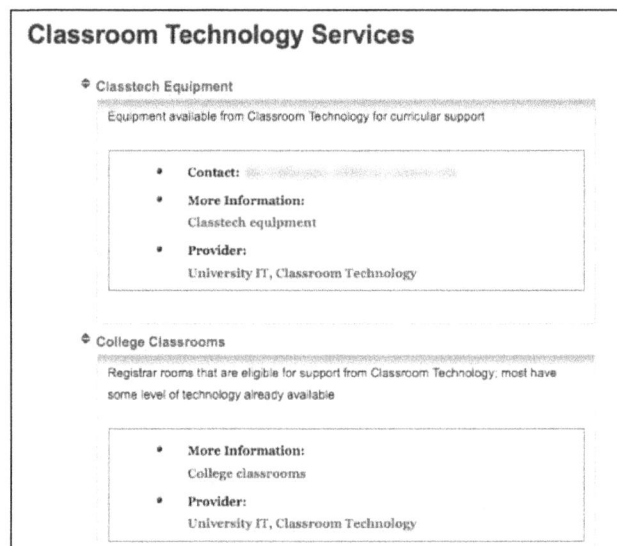

Figure 2. First service catalog prototype: services in classroom technology sub-category

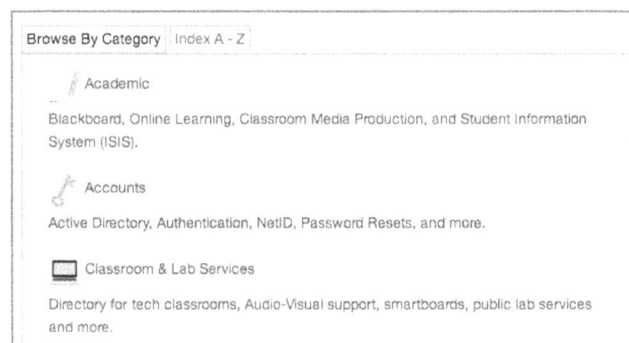

Figure 3. Second service catalog prototype: homepage on category view

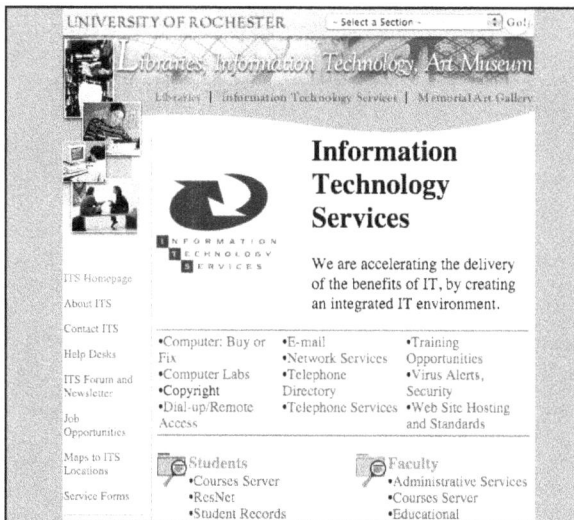

Figure 4. Webpage design circa 2000 that was active in the old University IT website in 2015

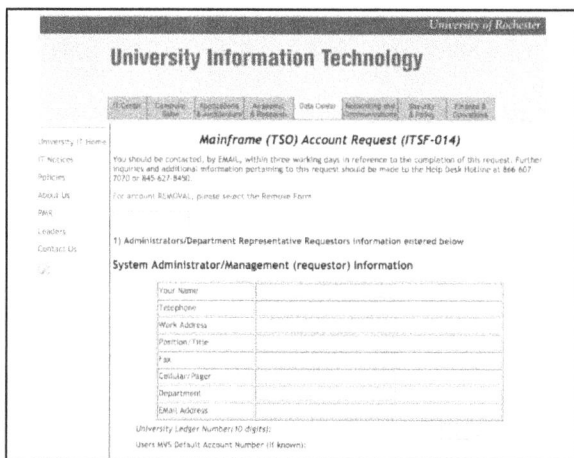

Figure 5. Webpage design circa 2007 that was active in the old University IT website in 2015

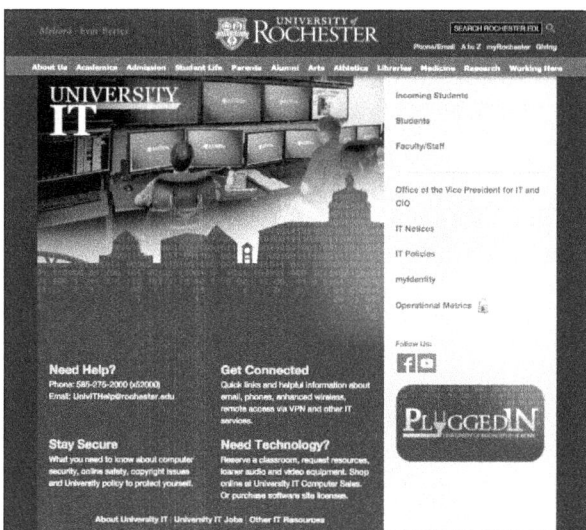

Figure 6. Webpage design circa 2012 that was active in the old University IT website in 2015

3.1 Research and Analysis

Before beginning any new design work, we spent about two months compiling an inventory of more than 1,500 University IT webpages, forms, assets, and redirects, noting their URLs, where they were managed, and by whom. [4] We audited all of the webpages' content, evaluated page analytics, and cross-referenced the inventory with the list of services created during the original service catalog project. Using this information, we determined what content was still needed, what could be decommissioned, and what was missing.

3.2 Design and Development

3.2.1 Conception

Based on our research, lessons learned during previous iterations of the service catalog, and usability testing results, we proposed a new design: integrating the concept of the service catalog into a new University IT website as the primary method of navigation.

Rather than adding to the patchwork of University IT websites, we decided to completely redesign and consolidate them (where possible) into a single, cohesive website. Our ultimate goal was to create a "one-stop shop" for how the entire UR community could request, access, and use IT services. Instead of organizing the new website by how the department itself was organized (as the website was at that time), we would organize it by service categories—a more meaningful, user-centric approach.

Considering our many audiences with myriad needs and preferences, we proposed keeping the index of all services as an alternative navigation option and providing additional alternatives with service lists by user group and a site-specific search.

To ensure consistency and cohesiveness, we would develop a template for a service landing page. This would be the equivalent of a listing in the previous service catalogs and include the following service attributes:

(1) Service name
(2) Description
(3) Users (whom the service is available to)
(4) How to request/access the service
(5) Documentation (e.g., tutorials, FAQs, etc.)
(6) Support contact
(7) Status (e.g., outage, maintenance, pilot program)
(8) Cost
(9) Related services
(10) Related policies

3.2.2 Challenges

While the project team agreed this was the best approach, there were many challenges to bringing the concept to fruition.

History: With three failed attempts to build a service catalog, staff at all levels of the organization were disillusioned and resistant to trying a fourth time. The lack of adoption of the previous service catalogs created the perception it was wasted effort and there would never be agreement on a path forward or a tangible final product.

Scope: The original scope of the service catalog project exploded with the addition of a complete website redesign. The service catalog was already two years in the making, and many wondered how much longer it would drag on.

Priorities: In the midst of budget cuts, operational needs, and numerous projects—including two major system replacements—many questioned why and how to prioritize the service

167

catalog/website redesign. Without consensus, a clear vision, and an understanding of the benefits that could be achieved, it seemed like an extra instead of a necessity. The website has been like this for years; why change it now?

Politics: Leadership all had different opinions and expectations of a potential new website and how it would present their services. How could we garner agreement among so many perspectives? And with the service catalog no longer a freestanding website but essentially the central IT department's website, how would we address the issue of decentralized service provision? How could we help users find all the information they want in one authoritative place, but not step on the toes of the distributed IT support groups?

3.2.3 Approach

We first debated the optimum number of service categories for usability as a navigation menu. Earlier service catalog prototypes had anywhere between 8 and 17 top-level categories and between 3 and 16 subcategories. Based on the usability testing results, we eliminated all subcategories and decided 8 to 12 categories would be ideal. Then we created wireframes [9] of the new homepage and service pages.

In early 2015, we pitched the new concept and design mockups to the Vice President for IT and leaders of each unit of the central IT department, UR's largest school, and the research computing center. We presented revised wireframes and mockups over the course of two months until all parties agreed on the scope, design, and ten service categories.

3.2.4 Project Plan

With just two partially allocated staff and an intern developing the new site, the group agreed to a phased approach. Although it was not ideal, it would have been difficult to build a large website over the course of a year and ensure the integrity of its content while the existing website was still being updated frequently.

We sought to minimize the time that the current website and new website would be concurrently active. Using the content inventory, we created a thorough project plan and prioritized the order in which content would be migrated and created. The team committed to architect, design, and populate the new site with at least one service per category by the end of the summer. To coincide with the beginning of the fall semester and prevent incoming students from having to learn two IT websites, we initially focused on the most widely used student and faculty services (e.g., learning management system, email, wireless network). The remaining three months of 2015 would be spent completing the migration of the existing web content to the new site. As each service migrated to the new site, the old pages would be decommissioned and redirected so the information would not exist in two places at the same time. The services we identified as not having any existing web content would be added during the first three months of 2016.

3.2.5 Communication

To gain buy-in and cooperation from central IT staff with yet another iteration of the service catalog, we presented the new approach and mockups in a series of meetings with the management team, Staff Leadership Group, and web editors. Communicating with each of these groups early in the process was essential to rallying the staff behind a shared vision for our digital presence and completing the project in an accelerated time frame.

3.2.6 Information Architecture

It is vital for the longevity of the new site that its structure allow for growth. Building from the ground up, rather than retrofitting the existing site, enabled us to architect it accordingly.

We used taxonomies extensively to classify and organize information in the new site. Each service, for instance, is tagged with one or more service categories and user groups. The navigation menus and filtering options are then built on these taxonomies, enabling users to navigate according to their needs and affiliations. As we add or remove services or update their user groups, the navigation options update automatically. This taxonomy structure helps ensure the site is sustainable as the department and its service portfolio evolve in the coming years.

Taxonomies also allow us to cross-list services with multiple names in the index. For example, we use tagging to list UR's learning management system under 'L' for its function and under 'B' for its system name, Blackboard. Cross-listing helps users locate services in the catalog no matter how they refer to it.

3.2.7 Design

Our focus in the design of the new website was to provide actionable, contextual information in a consistent manner, no matter what the user's role, which device the site is accessed from, who manages the webpage, or who provides the service.

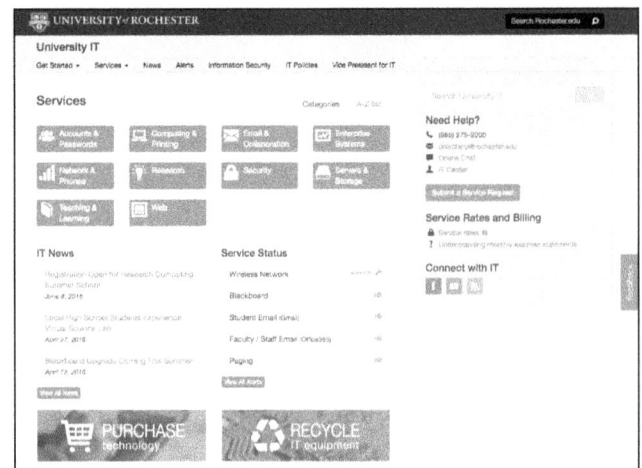

Figure 7. New University IT homepage: category view

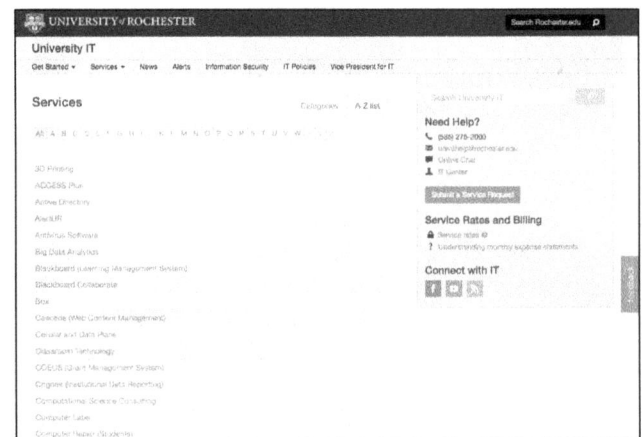

Figure 8. New University IT homepage: index view

168

First, we developed mobile-responsive templates for common content types, such as services, tutorials, frequently asked questions, and alerts. We used Bootstrap [2], an open-source front-end framework, to ensure consistency in visual elements such as tables, icons, and call-out boxes. Throughout the templates, we used call-to-action buttons—instead of embedded links like the previous site—to clearly indicate to users where they can take a desired action, such as logging in to a system or submitting a help ticket. All of these elements help us create and maintain a cohesive user experience throughout the site, even with multiple web editors.

The service template acts as a "one-stop shop" by integrating all information about each service in one place. The service provider and cost are listed in the sidebar, while the service description, documentation, whom the service is available to, related services, and policies (where applicable) are provided in the body of the page. How to access or request a service is clearly indicated with a prominent call-to-action button. Any news stories or alerts about maintenance or outages appear in color-coded pop-ups at the top of the relevant service pages.

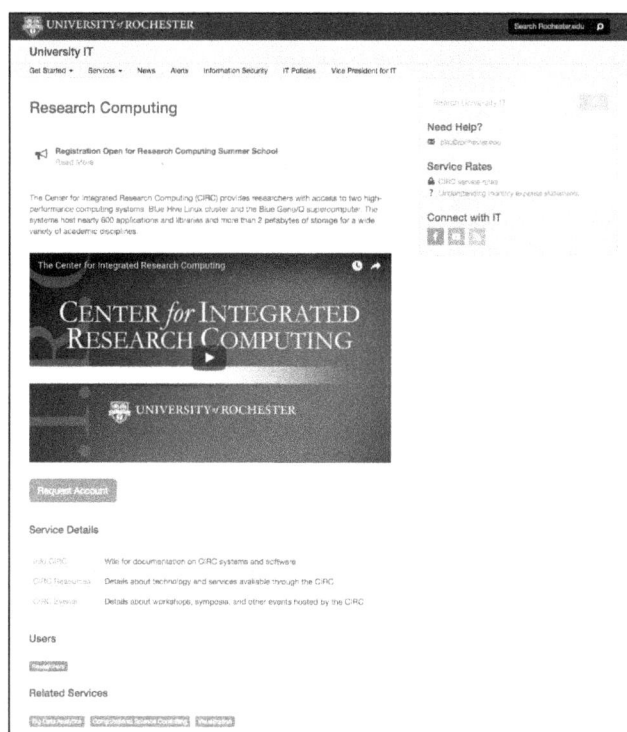

Figure 9. Service landing page with contextual news pop-up

To address decentralized service provision yet maintain a comprehensive catalog of IT services, we strived to balance usability and not duplicating content maintained on distributed IT groups' websites. Every service, regardless of provider, has a service page in the catalog for findability. The provider/help contact is listed in the sidebar, consistent with every template type in the new site. This help information is contextual to the service a user is viewing, but is provided in a consistent way and a consistent location so users always know what to expect and where to go for help. For services provided by any group besides the central IT department, additional information links from the service page out to the provider's website.

3.2.8 Content

On average, website visitors read only 20% of the words on a webpage. [8] Most users are scanning, rather than reading text word for word. Therefore, we optimized our web content following these guidelines:

- Be concise
- Use common language (e.g., avoid jargon, acronyms)
- Make text scannable (e.g., use headers, lists, call-outs)
- Embed valuable links in web copy that is contextually relevant, rather than using "click here"
- Make clear calls to action

Using sufficient white space in the site design further enhanced users' ability to scan the content.

The department's communications strategy has evolved in recent years to use more multimedia in explaining IT services, documenting tutorials, and delivering on-demand training. We featured multimedia content more prominently on the new website to engage visitors and help them learn more about the IT services available to them.

To support our vision for a cohesive department identity in the copy as well as the design, we eliminated references to individual teams within the department and instead used "University IT." Most users were not familiar with the department's internal organization, and using internal team names created the impression that they were separate service providers, rather than all being part of a single department/service provider. Using just the department name was clearer and more evergreen.

To help maintain consistency once web editors resumed content updates, the IT Communications Team developed a Web Style Guide. It details the content strategy and provides guidelines for common text, formatting, and image issues.

3.2.9 Analytics

Google Analytics was an important part of our strategy for analyzing the effectiveness of our architecture, design, and content decisions and ensuring the long-term success of the new website. In addition to the traditional page analytics, we used Google Tag Manager to configure event tracking on all call-to-action buttons, help links, downloads, and embedded videos. Click tracking provides a more granular and holistic view of how users interact with the site.

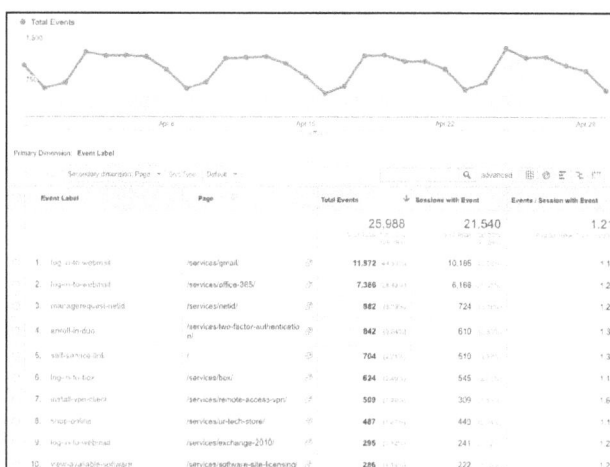

Figure 10. Event tracking in Google Analytics

3.3 Implementation/Results

Over the course of the project, we decommissioned more than 1,000 webpages that were outdated or no longer needed, migrated more than 500 webpages into a single content management system (CMS), and developed about 300 new webpages to fill gaps in content.

Launching the redesigned website in phases was difficult, as expected. Despite our efforts to broadly communicate the website redesign to the community, many users were caught unaware. Longtime users, such as department administrators, had the hardest time with the change. The Help Desk was prepared to field inquiries about the website, and they guided users through the transition. We also collaborated with distributed IT staff to deliver more targeted communications to their customers. However, once the redesign was completed, the new website's consistency and functionality were well received.

Search results improved significantly after decommissioning and redirecting the old webpages, optimizing content in the new website, and working with other departments to update their websites' links to our website. There was a misconception among many IT staff and users that search results would clear out automatically as the websites switched over. In reality, it took a few months as Google crawled our website on a monthly basis. The new pages climbed in the search results as we fostered their authority over time and as old pages were removed, decreasing competition for those keywords. Now, most service landing pages are among the top results for their selected keywords.

Consolidation into a single CMS had many benefits. On the front end, tight integration among alerts, news, and service pages provides more contextual, up-to-date information for users in one place. On the back end, there is decreased web maintenance for IT staff with only having to support one system. Web editors also find the new CMS easier to use than the old ones, which has resulted in faster turnaround time on web updates.

With a single, authoritative source of information online, service owners have been more proactive in ensuring their webpages are updated anytime there is a change. Internal project management processes surrounding website documentation and end user communication are clearer as well.

4. INTERNAL PROCESS CHANGES

After such a long process to correct years of web disorganization and neglect, we instituted two major changes within the central IT department to prevent it from happening again.

4.1 Website Ownership

The IT Communications Team has assumed ownership of the website as a key marketing and communications tool for the department. They oversee the strategic planning for the site, consult with service owners on how to best represent their services online, serve as a resource for web editors, and maintain the website's style guide and documentation.

4.2 Website Management

We significantly reduced the number of web editors from 25 to 5 (excluding the Help Desk, which publishes alerts about service outages and maintenance). Having fewer web editors ensures that they update webpages more frequently, so they require less re-training and remain familiar with the overall site strategy, organization, and style. The web editors back each other up so we are more efficient across the department, rather than insular within teams.

5. PLANNING FOR THE FUTURE

We regularly review Google Analytics reports and user feedback to assess the website's effectiveness, refining the site as needed. Click tracking will also help shape departmental strategy beyond the website. For instance, analyzing how many users viewed videos embedded on the website, and how much of the videos they viewed, can inform our use of multimedia in our communications strategy. When combined with help ticket metrics, tracking how many website visitors contact the Help Desk, which method they choose, and from which service pages they initiate requests for help can highlight areas of our website, service documentation, or support strategy that could be improved. Ultimately, we will use analytics as a tool for better data-based decision making in the future.

6. REFERENCES

[1] Adižes, T., Chavira, R., Venezia, L. D., et.al. The Higher Education IT Service Catalog: A Working Model for Comparison and Collaboration. EDUCAUSE: ECAR Working Group Paper (Apr. 10, 2015).

[2] Bootstrap. http://getbootstrap.com

[3] Card Sorting. https://www.usability.gov/how-to-and-tools/methods/card-sorting.html

[4] Content Inventory. https://www.usability.gov/how-to-and-tools/methods/content-inventory.html

[5] Heuristic Evaluations and Expert Reviews. https://www.usability.gov/how-to-and-tools/methods/heuristic-evaluation.html

[6] Prototyping. https://www.usability.gov/how-to-and-tools/methods/prototyping.html

[7] Scenarios. https://www.usability.gov/how-to-and-tools/methods/scenarios.html

[8] Weinreich, H., Obendorf, H., Herder, E., Mayer, M. Not Quite the Average: An Empirical Study of Web Use. *ACM Trans. Web* 2, 1 (Feb. 2008), Article 5. DOI=http://dx.doi.org/10.1145/1326561.1326566

[9] Wireframing. https://www.usability.gov/how-to-and-tools/methods/wireframing.html

Author Index